The Social History of Agriculture

The Social History of Agriculture

From the Origins to the Current Crisis

Christopher Isett and Stephen Miller

ROWMAN & LITTLEFIELD
Lanham • Boulder • New York • London

Published by Rowman & Littlefield
A wholly owned subsidiary of
The Rowman & Littlefield Publishing Group, Inc.
4501 Forbes Boulevard, Suite 200, Lanham, Maryland 20706
https://rowman.com

Unit A, Whitacre Mews, 26-34 Stannary Street, London SE11 4AB,
United Kingdom

British Library Cataloguing in Publication Information Available

Library of Congress Cataloging-in-Publication Data
Names: Isett, Christopher Mills, author. | Miller, Stephen, 1968– author.
Title: The social history of agriculture : from the origins to the current crisis / Christopher
    Isett and Stephen Miller.
Description: Lanham, Maryland : Rowman & Littlefield, 2016. | Includes bibliographical
    references and index.
Identifiers: LCCN 2016031934 (print) | LCCN 2016034390 (ebook) | ISBN
    9781442209664 (cloth : alk. paper) | ISBN 9781442209671 (pbk. : alk. paper) | ISBN
    9781442209688 (electronic)
Subjects: LCSH: Agriculture—History—Case studies. | Agriculture—Social aspects—
    History—Case studies.
Classification: LCC S419 .I78 2016 (print) | LCC S419 (ebook) | DDC 630—dc23
LC record available at https://lccn.loc.gov/2016031934

Printed in the United States of America

For our children: Joaquim, Sebastian, and Isabella

Contents

Maps

Africa

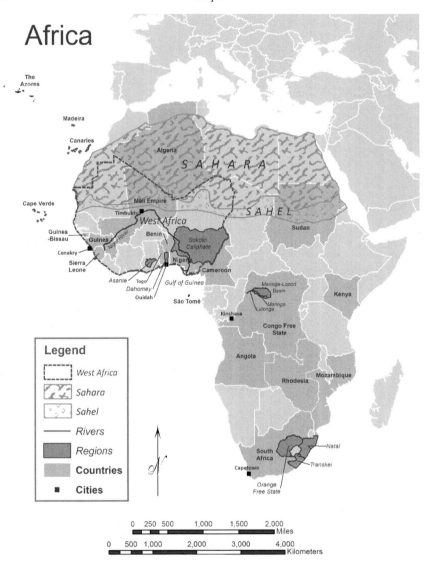

Africa

Eurasia

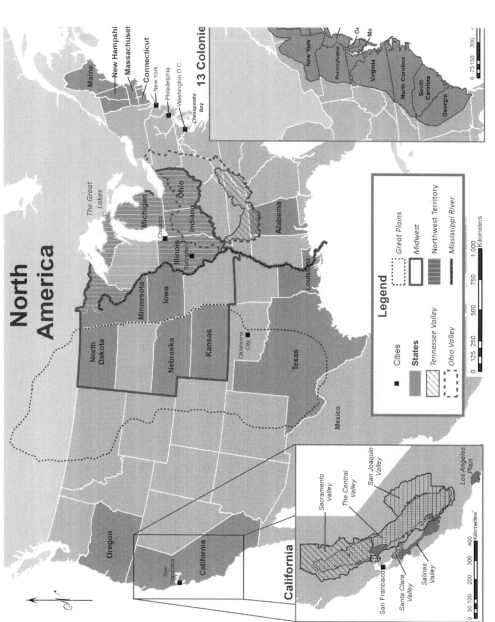

North America

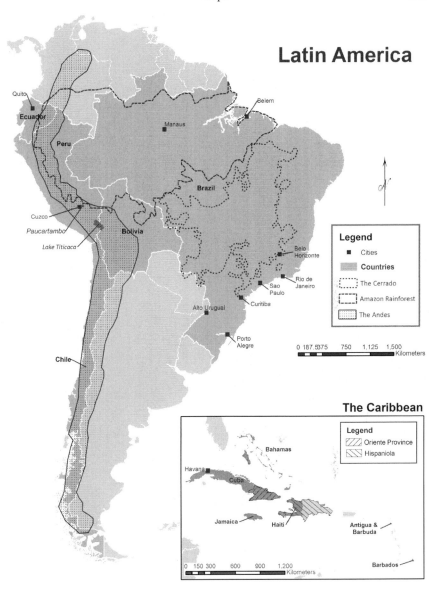

Latin America and the Caribbean

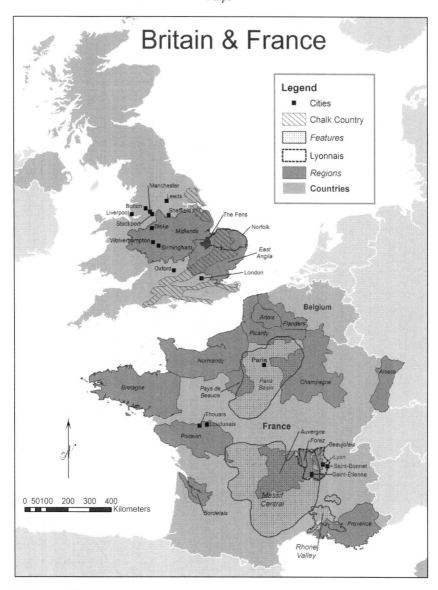

Britain and France

Acknowledgments

We have accumulated many debts along the way and are gratified to acknowledge those here. We begin by thanking and recognizing the importance of Robert Brenner and his work. We both took his graduate seminar at UCLA in the 1990s and our historical understanding has been shaped by his theoretical interventions ever since. Numerous experts have read and provided helpful comments. We thank the three anonymous reviewers for Rowman & Littlefield, each of whom made the book better. In addition, David Roediger read and provided feedback on early drafts of chapters 5 and 6 and Katharine Gerbner did the same for chapter 5. Spencer Dimmock gave crucial advice on chapters 1 and 3. Matthew Sommer read and discussed chapter 4. Charles Post provided excellent advice on many aspects of the book and did an expert critical reading of chapter 6.

Colleagues at the University of Alabama at Birmingham, the University of Minnesota, and other universities and colleges pointed us in the direction of texts in translation and scholarly works outside our own expertise, and some met to discuss elements of the book. These include Ellen Amster, Venus Bivar, Sarah Chambers, Michael Vann, Vinayak Chaturvedi, Vivek Chibber, Mark Overton, Adam Guerin, Eva von Dassow, Preston Perluss, Brian Steele, Adam Hochschild, Andrew Keitt, John Van Sant, George Liber, Douglas Frey, Chris Kyle, Robert Jefferson, Zephyr Frank, Bruce Campbell, Andrew Gallia, David Miller, and Rus Menard.

We would like to thank Paul Cheney for providing the opportunity to present ideas for central parts of the book to faculty and graduate students at the Modern France and Social History Workshop of the University of Chicago and Patrick O'Brien and Kent Deng for the chance to present the discussion of Tokugawa Japan in the Department of History at the London School of Economics.

Students in graduate seminars at the University of Minnesota and the University of Alabama at Birmingham read and discussed with us crucial books and articles that shaped our interpretations of agricultural societies in different regions and epochs. The staff at Sterne Library of the University of Alabama at Birmingham provided expert assistance in locating contemporary accounts (primary sources) of farming. We would also like to thank our students Tyler Boesch and Samuel Jane-Akson, who read and gave us invaluable feedback on the clarity of our argument.

Finally, we would like to express our appreciation for Susan McEachern, Alden Perkins, and Rebeccah Shumaker. Rebeccah and Alden guided the manuscript to print with great patience and even greater speed. Susan, as a longtime champion of the book, provided advice and sound criticism that markedly improved its quality. Of course, all errors of fact or omission remain our own.

Introduction

The association of civilization with settled agriculture is old. It exists in our history books but also in our language. Our word "culture" comes to us from the Latin *colere*, meaning "to tend," "to cultivate," or "to husband." The agricultural sense is materialized in the cognate "coulter," which is the blade of a plowshare. As the literary critic Terry Eagleton notes, "We derive our word for the finest human activities from labour and agriculture."[1] We believe that the etymological link between culture—and the society that produces it—and farming is apposite.

We have titled this book *The Social History of Agriculture* because of our conviction that farming—indeed, all economically productive activity—is a reflection of the society in which it is conducted, not the other way around. To put it another way, we argue that people's choices of what to grow, the technologies to use, and the labor regime to employ are shaped by their societies.

Going further, we maintain that some social arrangements are more important than others in shaping economic means and goals. We emphasize the political and legal arrangements that emerge from the negotiations and conflicts between those who toil and those who receive the surplus, profit, or interest. These arrangements are necessarily the outcome of the history of a place and people and of the antagonisms between the major classes.

In this regard, we maintain that people are born into a world of already formed class relationships and that their capacity to achieve the social solidarities needed to reshape those relationships is continuously undermined insofar as they continue to live and work as disaggregated individuals, families, or communities. It follows that rather than change these relationships people on the whole make their way in the world as it is given to them,

1

pursuing avenues that best allow them to get ahead within limits imposed by their society's class arrangements.

That said, ruptures in these arrangements, though rare (in the long history of humanity), do occur. How else can we explain the demise of peasant societies and the appearance of capitalist farming? At certain times and places we see that a set of class relationships appeared that required people to cut costs systematically and with regularity relative to the value of what they produced. In other words, they had to maximize their earnings by cheapening their costs. Consequently, people had to specialize in the goods that gave them the best return in the market for their labor and allowed them to buy more with a given amount of effort and investment.

These social relationships should be familiar to us. They are the ones in which we find ourselves today and we call the system that they produce "capitalism." They constitute a world that requires those with land, factories, and capital to seek incessantly a higher rate of profit, to bring goods to market at a lower cost than before, to build up cash reserves, and to cut costs by investing in ways to get more output (value) from a given level of input (labor). The result has been a constant though unsteady rise in the relative value of goods and services.

But we wish to reiterate that this is a world that exists only under peculiar, historically specific social conditions: when people have no option other than to sell a specialized "good" in the market, which for most simply means labor power, *and* when people are free to move from one line of work to another. The first condition is a constraint, whereas the second is a kind of liberty. Capitalism is present only when *both* conditions prevail.

As implied, people have not always lived in these circumstances. For thousands of years humans were not required to specialize (to move from line to line in search of higher returns), their labor and capital were not always free to move, and most importantly they had before them alternative social and cultural possibilities and goals. We contend that agriculturalists' direct access to land, often supported in law and everywhere in custom, protected them from the otherwise precarious act of specializing. We call these peasant societies.

It is worth noting that even where markets existed, as they certainly did in the ancient, medieval, and early modern worlds, choosing to plant all or most of one's land in a cash crop was neither always rational nor possible. Indeed, this probably did not even occur to people whose primary concern was securing enough grain to carry their family to the next season. Before the modern era, crop failures were frequent. Growers of cash crops found themselves caught in "price scissors" whenever grains failed to mature: as food prices moved rapidly upward, the price of their inedible crops tumbled. The social and economic fallout from subsistence crises lingered for years.

These circumstances were treacherous to specializers and subsistence farmers alike. But by drawing on experience and by diversifying their effort—spreading their time over different crops and different types of land—in order to provision directly as many of their needs as possible, agriculturalists had a greater chance of surviving these shocks. If communities came together to share some of their labor, land, tools, and livestock, then their ability to survive was further improved.

Premodern agriculturalists were aided in this effort by their social connection to the land. Diversification was possible, and specialization avoidable, because premodern agriculturalists enjoyed strong rights and claims to their land, or part of it, as well as some control over their labor and implements. In other words, they were able to begin production each year without having to go to the market to acquire their most fundamental inputs and so avoided having to make production decisions on the otherwise risky basis of prices. Time and again, we shall see, agriculturalists chose on the basis of their possession of the land, and in the face of ineffective markets, to diversify production and minimize their reliance on the market *to the greatest extent possible*.

This understanding begs the question: How do we account for the appearance of modern, capitalist agriculture in the face of the longstanding peasant propensity to avoid specialization and to focus the family's effort instead on the self-provisioning of everything from food to fiber? The standard answer—and the one we commonly see today in history and economic texts— is that change comes in increments and through experimentation. A population sufficiently large to support the appearance of towns, it is argued, encourages peasants to sell their surpluses for profit. Just as they gain by bringing goods to the market at the lowest possible cost to themselves, so these market-oriented producers benefit from purchasing their needs from others similarly dedicated to finding ways to lower their costs.

In other words, it is commonplace today to argue that in the past rural folk chose out of self interest to commit to producing for the market. This formulation is not without its value. The transition to capitalist agriculture certainly entailed of farmers that they devote ever more of their resources (land, labor, and savings) to raising products for the market and that they dedicate themselves to ever-greater degrees of specialization in the process. It is also true that capitalist agriculture requires of farmers that they incessantly search out product lines that deliver the greatest returns to their work while expending capital on tools and improvements that reduce their overall costs. It is no coincidence, given the persistence of this view, that it was the father of modern economics, Adam Smith, who offered the earliest complete formulation of this account in the *Wealth of Nations*. Smith believed that economic growth in the first instance was the natural outcome of the human "propensity to truck, barter, and exchange" and in the second of the "invisible hand's" requirement that farmers and manufacturers in competition secure the highest price for their effort by bringing down their costs.

Given evidence to the contrary, we argue that it cannot be assumed that in the presence of markets individuals will freely choose to specialize. Nor can it be presupposed that market conditions will permit the accumulation of capital or encourage its investment along the lines that meet the requirements of modern economic growth. To do so is to assume that people in the past behaved more or less as we do today. Yet, despite its fundamentally ahistorical premise, the ease with which historians and others slip into this false analogy should be readily apparent. We hear it stated all the time in different ways. It has become commonplace in the media and in scholarly work not only to conflate growth and markets but also to see the market as a zone of liberation.

We might say that current thinking about political economy and rural history offer little more than a return to nineteenth-century liberalism. The comfortable and rather self-satisfied bourgeoisie of the 1850s (found mostly in western Europe, but also in North and South America and in cities from Cape Town to Hong Kong) had concluded that the free market was the best cure for "feudal" privilege and religious obscurantism. They liked to remind the working classes and rural poor, at home and in the colonies, that science and democracy—the two pillars of bourgeois culture—paved the way to individual realization. We have returned to this view insofar as mainstream accounts of the origins of the modern world search for indications that people in the past were as inclined to exploit market opportunities for personal advancement as we are today. And, as they did so, they freed themselves (and the rest of us) bit by bit from the limitations of monopolistic landlords, oligarchic patricians, and monopsonistic merchants.

We argue that modern economic behavior is contingent on historically produced social relations. We hold that it is in the interest of individuals to strengthen their position within the existing social relations. It follows therefore that social relations must be rewritten before economic behavior is recast. We do not mean by this that our economic choices—the ways we work and our working goals— are determined by tradition or culture. This is far too nebulous a view of things. Rather, we mean that the social relationships that determine how people gained access to land, and what control they had over their own labor et cetera, shaped the way they farmed and what they farmed. Culture—our view of the world—is a reflection (sometimes imprecise) of these material conditions, not its cause. Because we can just as easily expect willy-nilly actions to reproduce rather than transform a social order, much as our everyday behavior today reproduces capitalism, substantive change of the sort that inaugurated our modern world must have occurred at the societal rather than individual level and, implicitly, it was political in nature insofar as it was generalized. Thus, we contend that the social conditions for capitalism arose in the first instance from large-scale political conflicts between those who toiled and those who took a surplus.

As we shall see in chapter 3, in the attempt to put society back together in the wake of major social crises, those who controlled the land and those who worked it found themselves having to survive in the market under unprecedented conditions. Once entangled with the market, economic actors found that in order to continue to profit they had no choice but to specialize further, to switch from line to line in search of the highest returns to their time, and incessantly to seek out new ways to manage their costs in response to the prices their goods receive. As each producer adjusted their methods others had to follow.

Another question remains: How do we account for the very different ways people have farmed in the past, from the natives of the pre-Columbian Andes, to the former sharecroppers of socialist Cuba, to the peasants of contemporary Brazil?

This book is structured around roughly drawn periods, beginning with the Neolithic and ending with the contemporary epoch. Each chapter examines the social world and habits that shaped agriculture in a particular place and a moment in time, with attention paid to both those who ruled and the biblical "hewers of wood and drawers of waters." Consequently, the book will describe how serfs, slaves, freeholding peasants, tenants, sharecroppers, and members of the communes and collectives prepared and cultivated their fields. And we will examine how lords and aristocrats, monarchs, colonists, bureaucrats, landlords, land barons, patricians, speculators, and latifundistas, as well as merchants and industrialists, sought to bend rural labor to their needs. As this range of descriptive terms for laborers and members of the ruling class suggests, the struggles over the agricultural surplus produced a great variety of legal and customary obligations and rights, and thus we will have to pay close attention to these relationships and struggles.

In their struggle to reproduce themselves, agriculturalists and ruling elites must confront not only each other but also nature. Humans have of course an inordinate capacity to convert their environment, and farming is, at its root, the shaping of the landscape to make it grow edible plants and support exploitable livestock. Seasonal monsoons, rain forests, temperate pastures, arid coastlines, and mountains are therefore crucial to understanding the choice of crops and rotations, the kinds of improvements, the necessary tools, the availability of livestock. But, even as we pay attention to the effects of nature on farming, we want to emphasize that environment is not history. People can and have shaped and reshaped the landscape to meet their needs, and they are ingenious in their ability to find alternatives for such basic needs as clothing, fuel, implements, and housing. Even in the Andes—certainly one of the most extreme environments—humans not only found means to eke out a living on the land but did so in ways that supported a sophisticated society and a far-reaching state.

Finally, for ease of reading, we have chosen to provide footnotes for the original quotes used to illustrate our subject, but not for other details. An extended bibliography appears at the end of this book, where readers can discover the sources for our account, as well as a list of references.

NOTE

1. Terry Eagleton, *The Idea of Culture* (Oxford: Blackwell, 2000), 1.

Chapter One

Settled Agriculture

The Ancient Origins of Community, State, and Empire

In this chapter we examine two questions. First, how—and in what ways—did the earliest dominant classes organize themselves to make and enforce claims on the produce of those who put in the back-breaking hours needed to bring in crops and raise livestock? Because the laboring classes lived in their own communities, which they established a priori to promote security in food and defend against outsiders, early ruling elites who had separated themselves from work had no choice but to build up the organizational means to force the payment of taxes and rents. While ruling elites, as a group, may have had an interest in promoting agriculture, it seems that their ability (and perhaps willingness) to coordinate and limit their mutual predations for the "greater good" of their class was undermined by their need to build up private wealth and power in political competition with fellow elites. Thus, premodern states were less coordinating bodies for organizing society than taxing instruments over which elites competed for control in their efforts to enhance personal income and status.   *funds are to pay for upkeep of armies*

Our second question (and one to which we return in each chapter of this book) is how the struggle for control over rural production shaped farming. Pre-capitalist agriculture was for the most part organized on small holdings within peasant communities, whose members worked with varying degrees of cooperation to provision their households with food, clothing, and shelter. They grew their provisions, exchanged little except by barter, and thus felt no pressure to reduce costs and improve systematically in the ways capitalist farmers are compelled to do. The societies in which they lived were therefore relatively simple by contemporary standards.

Peasant communities nevertheless exhibited great diversity partially on account of the distinct strategies pursued by the elites. In this and subsequent chapters we will see how political struggles over the surplus could press peasants into penury, trap them in debt, subject them to forced labor, reduce them to sharecropping and tenancy, bind them to the land, and even enslave them. Combinations of all or some of these regimes are found in all pre-capitalist societies and whichever one predominated depended upon the outcomes of political struggles. In other words, by leveraging political power pre-capitalist rulers captured various shares of the harvest and so helped to shape the labor regimes. In this chapter, we take up the political conflicts that emerged at the dawn of settled farming before exploring them at length in three case studies: Mesopotamia, ancient Rome, and Han China.

THE FOUNDING OF AGRICULTURAL SOCIETIES

The Fall of Man in Genesis elicits impressions of human finiteness and vulnerability, an estrangement from the "divine," suddenly inaccessible. The Fall causes the plentiful food of the Garden of Eden to disappear and precipitates labor "by the sweat of the brow." The Greek story of Prometheus, a hero who brings fire, farming, and technology to humans, portrays him as the perpetrator of a crime warranting merciless repeated punishment. It attests, like the Fall of Man, to a sense of guilt, as if humans took control over nature without the right to do so. The Fall of Man and the myth of Prometheus were composed by the same dispersed peoples, originally belonging to the first agriculturalists of the Near East about nine or ten thousand years earlier.

For the previous 190,000 years of their existence, humans had subsisted on wild, non-domesticated, resources. The reports of travelers of the early modern period, and the research of modern archaeologists, anthropologists, and ethnographers, suggest that hunter-gatherers lived in small cooperative groups with fluctuating membership and enforced their specific practices and customs through consensus without rulers or hierarchies. If they had one or two prominent women or men, they usually had practical reasons for doing so.

Anthropologists of a range of political stripes have been led by their research on societies in different times and continents to conclude that hunter-gatherers lived cooperatively amid equality. They acquired their subsistence and consumed with members of the group, who as a whole scorned boasting and other self-aggrandizing behaviors. They teased, ignored, banned, or, in extreme cases, killed the offenders. Humility, humor, and strict protocols about distributing meat helped keep people on an even footing. Inequality militates against cooperation, whereas groups accustomed to sharing stood at an evolutionary advantage over disparate individuals. People all had the strength for hunting and fighting, and could be of service to one another in the quest for survival. Sharing the spoils reinforced the egalitarian behavior.

Hunter-gatherers regularly made eight to twelve changes of abode a year within a large foraging area. It was impossible, in these circumstances, to hold other human beings captive. People did not find it worthwhile to accumulate anything beyond a spare bow and arrow or a carrying bag of possessions. Homicides and violent feuds existed, but warfare was rare. To small social groups, the risk of death of the most vital members was too great to justify war. Quick punitive raids were the preferred mode of combat. On occasion, opposing parties settled their dispute through protest and displays of displeasure, throwing missiles at too far a range to do harm, until one of them departed. Groups hardly ever fought to capture women, plunder, or territory, and generally expended little time and energy in training for combat.

Humans domesticated plants and animals sometime prior to 10,000 BC and began to rely on farming in the Near East about nine thousand years ago. The dependence on agriculture entailed work, health hazards, and social complexity. Hunter-gatherers expended less time and energy obtaining food than did agriculturalists. They lived longer and grew taller. Farmers had a diet of root and cereal crops inferior to the nutritional balance enjoyed by hunter-gatherers. The first farmers were also subject to crop failure and new pathogens carried by livestock. Looked at in this way, the Israelite and Greek myths capture psychologically the irreversible boundary and loss that accompanied the dependence on agriculture.

The question is why humans started to depend on domesticated crops and livestock. Hunter-gatherers maintained a low population density through infanticide and prolonged lactation, which causes widely spaced births. In the late Ice Age, the environment could only support the sparsest population of humans. But about thirteen thousand years ago, rising temperatures made the climate less severe, caused evergreens and birches to spread across formerly grassy plains, and deprived great herds of grazing land. These conditions, combined with the toll taken by human predation, made some large animals go extinct and reduced the numbers of others.

Humans had to search for more stable food supplies to compensate for shortages. They began to adapt to fish runs, animal migrations, and nut harvests by gathering quantities in a short time, and by processing and storing them for later use. These trends made people more sedentary, required additional labor, and led to population growth. The finiteness of local resources eventually compelled emigration, death, or cultural innovation: better fishing boats, planting, farming, herding or domesticating animals.

One must keep in mind, however, that archaeological findings from the Natufian culture of the Levant in the Eastern Mediterranean prior to the introduction of agriculture show an increase in sedentism in fewer and larger settlements rather than a general demographic expansion across the region. The evidence from the sites does not show that a growing human population exhausted the supply of wild resources and then invented agriculture to survive. Rather, it shows that as the first agricultural communities appear in the record, one also observes a sudden related occurrence of housing, tools, and patterns of religious practice. The development of an agricultural economy and this outpouring of culture went hand in hand rather than the first causing the second.

Similarly, the excavations show diverse animal remains and then a sudden concentration of them. The pattern rules out the sequence of specialized hunting gradually leading to greater control over the animals and then domestication of this food source. It suggests that the origins of herding must not be confused with the economy founded upon it. One might more accurately imagine the origins of herding as a modification of the cultural interface between people and animals—that is, the human desire to dominate living things and exercise power over them.

Overall, the archaeological record suggests that there was a certain kind and level of social complexity prerequisite for the emergence of agriculture. The difficulty at the time was not domesticating animals, planting, and raising food. Humans had been familiar with these arts for some time. The difficulty, rather, was arranging a society and rules for producers and consumers to subtract from their stock of alimentation the seeds and animals necessary for the coming agricultural season. People required complex relationships to establish recognized rights, and to protect their fields and animals from other browsing animals and other groups of humans. Above all, they had to develop rules for distributing the fruits of their work in a sustainable manner.

One of the themes of this book is that different societies have reacted differently to population growth, technology, and markets. Their reactions have been conditioned by the particular relationships between the groups and classes and by the choices people make within their social context. These relationships, we argue, constitute the source of demographic change, new technologies, and markets. In the case of the Neolithic Near East, none of the complex relationships intrinsic to agriculture could have emerged in any simple or direct way from the stress of a growing population on its plant and animal resources. These people hedged against food shortages by making use of seasonal harvests of wild plants. A more sedentary life led them to allow less time between births and generate a larger population. The inhabitants of the Near East came to rely on the domestication of wild grains and did not foresee the consequences of doing so. But it stands to reason that for them to depend on agriculture, they first had to change their attitudes and relationships to one another, or else they would have suffered mass mortality or reverted to the familiar practices of dispersal to new areas for hunting and gathering.

While the human population expanded after the end of the Ice Age, it did so intensively only where agricultural economies took hold. Recent discoveries in northern China, one of seven confirmed sites of independent agricultural origins, show advanced farming systems as early as 8,500 years before the present. Humans lived sedentary lives in northern Peru for at least a millennium without agriculture, and in villages on the northwest coast of North America without ever depending on farming. Inhabitants of the Tehuacán Valley of Mexico began to depend on agriculture several millennia before they settled in villages or developed dense populations. In short, while the transition to our era of warm climate led people to search for more reliable food sources such as cereals, each group of hunter-gatherers did so in different ways in accordance with their particular societies. They responded to the threats and opportunities of profound landscape change by developing unique unforeseeable strategies.

One consequence of this dependence on farming was the transformation of the landscape. Agricultural economies have always shaped the natural environment far more than they have been shaped by it. Sheep did not originally bear wool. Cows and goats did not generate excess milk, and chickens did not lay surplus eggs. Humans separated the wild populations for selective breeding and, via experimentation, tailor-made the animals for cheese, butter, clothes, tent coverings, and materials for leather shields and armor. Domesticated animals stripped pasture of grass cover, and then rainfall denuded the hills of soil to the point that the landscape never looked the same again. When people gathered wild grains, they selected against the abnormal gene causing the ripe seeds to stick to the plant head, for such grains appeared as prizes for the gatherer. But once humans started to sow these seeds, the selection worked in the opposite direction, in favor of the non-shattering heads and for the survival of the abnormal genes. Evidence of grain farming includes a larger seed, a lighter and smaller glume, and a tough rachis that holds the grains securely to the plant.

The oldest and most basic form of farming, slash-and-burn or swidden agriculture, created fields where forests grew naturally. Farmers familiar with the natural habitat cut the vegetation, spread it over the area to be planted, and then burn it. The procedure adds nutrients to the soil and kills pests and weeds. The farmers then plant the land for one to three years until the soil loses nutrients. They then abandon the area, clear more land, and prepare new plots. The original plot requires about ten years for bushes and trees to grow and make it suitable for agriculture again. Swidden agriculture, which persists to this day, requires no more than an axe, a hoe or digging stick, and rainfall.

THE SUMERIANS

A radically new type of agriculture characterized by irrigation and plowing took shape around 5,800 BC along the Euphrates river channels. Mesopotamia has slight erratic rainfall, extremely hot summers, and harsh, cold winters. It would be desert if not for the rivers. But with natural and man-made irrigation, the alluvial soils of the lower plain sustain intensive farming. The land then provides high yields that, in the final centuries of the fourth millennium, began to support cities in the delta from Urum in the north through Kish, Nippur, and Ur in the south. The inhabitants grouped tracts of farmland outside the walls of cities along the channels of the Euphrates. The city of Uruk grew remarkably from 3000 to 2700 BC, as tens of thousands migrated from the countryside to take up residence. About forty dense cities, each independent of the others, grew up in the Babylonian plain of Sumer and Akkad in the peak period of the third millennium. Lagash and Uruk, the largest, may have had thirty-six thousand adult males.

Gilgamesh, the part-god part-human hero of the Sumerian epic bearing his name, provided an admiring third-millennium survey of the urban setting: "One square mile is city, one gardens, and one clay pits, as well as the open ground of Ishtar's temple. Three square miles and the open ground comprise Uruk."[1] The gardens referred to plantations of date palms. These provided fruit, fiber for rope, wood for furniture, doorframes and roof beams, and fronds for making houses, mats, and baskets. Date palms overhung large portions of the cities and provided partial cover from the intense sunlight for legumes, vegetables, and fruit trees to grow at different levels below them.

Another change associated with irrigated agriculture, even more momentous than urban life, was the first phase of male dominance. Prior to agricultural economies, men generally hunted and women gathered. Pregnant and breastfeeding women would have endangered reproduction if they had taken part in the hunt. Women participated equally in decisions on where and with whom to live. Gender equality fostered wider-ranging social networks, helped hunter-gatherers to share and learn innovations, and thus constituted a human evolutionary advantage. In societies characterized by slash-and-burn farming, the men cleared the land, and the women burned and farmed it. These divisions of labor did not entail gendered dominance. But irrigation and plowing facilitated a new sexual division of labor in which men concentrated on agriculture and women faced a greater workload including domestic tasks. The technological turn favored larger families. If women had plowed and herded, they would not have spent much time bearing and rearing children, and reproduction would have been at risk.

Above all, the men took note of the civilization, erected upon their irrigation and plowing, and began to feel some sort of transcendence. They perceived their ability to overcome the natural setting. Humans no longer represented themselves as a generalized supernatural force concentrated in objects or persons. They ceased to revere objects, animals, or other natural phenomena as symbols of the clan. Humans no longer pictured themselves adrift in their surroundings, threatened by obscure forces and safe only amidst the group of families related through a common ancestor or marriage. Farming led to a separation from, and distrust of, nature and led its practitioners to imagine ancestor cults and sky gods. The divine command to "be fruitful and multiply," found in Genesis, is typical of an agricultural and pastoral ethic. Agricultural societies developed the concept that human destiny lay in the laps of the gods, that sexuality constituted a threatening force liable to upset the stability of male dominance, and that land had to be controlled, like an ancestor made generous when lavished with favors. In this cultural context, males began to represent themselves in their accomplishments. They usurped a superior status and the right to make decisions regarding the household and lineage.

Men also began to represent their accomplishments through the accumulation of power and resources relative to subordinate social classes. Much of the labor that went into the irrigated farming of the sixth millennium BC involved a high level of cooperation. People had to work together to gather and treat sand, clay, palm trees, and reeds, and perform all the other tasks necessary to build houses between the rivers. Some people oversaw all of this work, especially since grain storage, essential to hedging against the vagaries of the harvests, required an administration. Inhabitants stockpiled the grain in great buildings whose supervisors laid claim to the prestige of guarding the community's sustenance. These officials had enormous responsibility and justifiable grounds for demanding obedience and praise. Their supervision of the food stock gave them reason to consign the majority to lives of work and deprivation. The rulers received the surplus, controlled the means to reproduce their status, and reflected all that society had created through its visible ability and extraordinary effort. They thus came to associate their control over resources with the good of the city as a whole.

The rest of the inhabitants regarded the rulers, on some level, as the embodiment of their highest values. In contrast to the semi-migratory practitioners of slash-and-burn agriculture, the inhabitants of Mesopotamia actually took possession of a delimited land and made it their own. Whereas villages previously had materialized as appendages, so to speak, of the soil, Sumerian cities consisted of their peoples and offered them the protection of the lands. Mesopotamian agriculturalists faced the claims of other societies to their farms and protected their livelihood through their membership in the city. The collective protection of the farmland entered into the moral character and personality of the people. The inhabitants gained dignity, not through the accumulation of private wealth, but through participation in social labor and the consequent ability to sustain themselves. Population growth, of course, made it difficult for residents to sustain their kin, and wars enhanced the power and resources of the rulers. Increasing the productivity of the land required new methods of farming, combinations of labor, and intensified work regimes for the majority of inhabitants.

In spite of these disaggregating forces Sumerians together gained a sense of accomplishment through participation in the rites of the city. They came to regard their rulers as vital intermediaries between themselves and the erratic uncontrollable forces that determined the success of farming and the fate of the inhabitants dependent on it. The rulers stood at the apex of the social order, oversaw its labors, led the religious celebrations of the inhabitants' achievements, and commanded the armies that protected the fields and granaries.

The rulers used the central building of Uruk, known as the ziggurat, to supervise the political and religious order. The ziggurat was a terraced-step pyramid of successively receding levels towering over the lowlands. It formed part of a temple complex with buildings for worship, storage, artisan work, and government. The temple hierarchy and councils of citizens shared power with, and ratified the decisions of, the rulers. The councils had administrative and judicial powers in several towns and villages by the end of the third millennium BC.

Differences in wealth and status appear in the burials and grave architecture of southern Mesopotamia. An inscription on a statuette in Lagash circa 2100–2000 BC numbered a small elite of temple personnel, a larger group of high officials, many farming experts and managers, and a mass of sheep and cattle workers, as well as miscellaneous people taking care of oil, handling boats and forestry, and laboring. The texts about agriculture, available from sites such as this one, came from large estates with hundreds and thousands of acres under cultivation. Slaves appear in these texts as a negligible portion of the labor force. Rather, the people in the various ranks of the labor process received different rations as remuneration. The temple stewards, for instance, received twice as much as high officials. The authorities around the temple also made grants of land to officials for their upkeep. The rations of the lowest grade of personnel attained only 20 percent of those of the temple stewards.

The temples' rations offered the lowest grade of laborers an inadequate supply of food. Many laborers thus survived thanks to household plots of land. Evidence of these plots exists in the middle Euphrates in northwest Syria, about one hundred kilometers east of Aleppo. The plots usually did not even amount to one-third of a hectare, or less than half of what a household needed to survive. The mass of urban dwellers most likely had these sorts of plots. They owned spades, hoes, and flint sickles but had to rent draft animals, and on occasion plows, from the public institutions. These peasants also rented lands from the temples and made annual payments in kind with a portion of the harvests, though these lands represented small shares of the temples' holdings.

The Farmer's Instructions: A Sumerian Agricultural Manual offers a wealth of detail about the cultivation of the land. This 111-line text consists of advice addressed by a farmer to his son. It does not promote innovation, for farming in general, when practiced for the sustenance of a community, is oriented toward the avoidance of novelty and of the corresponding risk of crop failure and famine. The text simply notes the tried and proven practices.

The *Instructions* open with forty lines on the renewed cropping of fallow land. They make reference to the common practice of leaving arable fields unseeded after plowing for a period of time in order to recover natural fertility on alternate years. They also indicate the preoccupation of the entire society with the levels of salt in the soil caused by irrigation. From Baghdad to the Gulf, the land has hardly any natural incline for drainage. The salt in the water remained after evaporation. According to the *Instructions*, "When you are about to take hold of your field [for cultivation], keep a sharp eye on the opening of the dikes, ditches and mounds [so that] when you flood the field the water will not rise too high in it. When you have emptied the field of water, watch its water-soaked ground and assure that it stay 'virile' for you."[2] The text thus provides an illustration of the manner in which agriculturalists softened the soil in July and August for plowing after a year of fallow. The lines offer a classic description of leaching, which was essential to removing the salt from the soil and preparing it for farming.

The *Instructions* recognize the link between irrigation and increased cereal production, thus directing the grower to make four irrigation flows or applications of water to the fields, the last shortly before the harvest to fatten up the food grains. The *Instructions* date from the end of the Ur III period, also known as the Sumerian Renaissance, a period characterized by increases in settlements and a large number of new canals to support them. The authorities drafted laborers, including the army and prisoners of war, for the great efforts and resources invested in road projects, the digging of canals, and the back-breaking work of removing silt from them. Royal inscriptions attest to the social value placed on the irrigation channels.

The *Instructions* allude to plowing with draft animals. Plowing enhanced the productivity of the land by 400 percent relative to manual tilling. Farmers used the ard or sliding plow, the French *araire*. The true plow, the French *charrue*, would have damaged the arid soil of Mesopotamia. The ard, by contrast, did not turn the soil over. It loosened the upper crust of the ground without breaking the capillary network through which moisture would have been lost. The ard was light, portable, simply made, and reasonably priced for even the poorest farmers.

The Sumerians combined the ard with seeders to make them remarkably productive. The seeder plow, used even before the third millennium BC, was the most advanced agricultural technology of ancient Mesopotamia. The *Instructions* describe the way it was used:

> Draw eight furrows; closely ranged furrows strangle their barley plants. When you apply the seeder plow to the fields keep an eye on your man who drops the seed, let him drop the barley-goddess each two "fingers." Have him drop 1/60 liter to each 6 meters. If the seed does not penetrate the womb [of the furrow] replace the peg of the tongue of your plow [i.e., adjust it to go deeper].[3]

In this way, the farmer had to make sure the person feeding the hopper of the plow took care to drop the seed properly. The seeder plow was a labor-intensive instrument requiring two or three persons on each team to drive, sow, and turn the oxen.

The evidence of the seed expended per area of arable land indicates that farmers attained yields as high as thirty times what they sowed. These extraordinarily high yields resulted from the seeder plow, which made it possible to set crops out in rows and hand hoe weeds between them. Efficient weeding permitted the crops to grow more vigorously and abundantly, while the seeder plow allowed the Sumerians to sow very little relative to their harvests. When it was introduced in Britain, it is estimated to have halved the number of seeds expended relative to broadcast sowing by hand over a plowed field. The farmers using the seeder plow around 2100–2000 BC expended far fewer grains than do modern Iraqis sowing barley broadcast.

The rations paid by the temples for this labor consisted above all of barley, which yielded more calories per hectare than did wheat, did better on marginal land with high salinity and limited water, and ripened weeks earlier. Barley figured prominently in northern Mesopotamia, where farmers did not have the benefit of irrigation, especially when they augmented output by cultivating marginal lands and required a reliable crop.

It is commonly believed that the temples organized military-like brigades of semi-free and coerced subordinates to perform the large-scale labor required to build and maintain the irrigation networks, till the fields, and bring in the harvests. Yet given the low levels of productivity obtained through coerced farming and extractive landlordism in other periods and regions, it is unlikely that people working under duress could have put in the careful work building the elaborate complex of canals and achieving the high yields on the arable lands.

Scholars have made much of the Sumerians' civic-solidarity and devotion to municipal gods. The long and bloody resistance mounted by certain cities to Sargon in the twenty-third and twenty-second centuries BC, and again to Hammurabi in the eighteenth century BC, offers indirect evidence of this municipal loyalty. Consider the pride of the early generations of Sumerians who lived through the miracle of urban civilization. The higher social strata, which participated in the municipal councils, no doubt saw the cities as their own accomplishments. Yet this pride can only serve as a conjectural explanation of the motivation behind the skilled labor manifest in the irrigation systems and productive farming. Like those of the skilled Egyptian builders of the pyramids, the motivations for Sumerian agriculture will probably remain rather obscure.

ANCIENT ROME

High politics and culture in the ancient Greco-Roman world were distinctly urban, apparent in monumental architecture and expressed in the richness of civic life and the general patrician disinterest for what went on beyond the city walls. Yet the achievements of these civilizations rested on farming. The patrician class that administered, governed, and partook in civic affairs did so because incomes from their estates afforded leisure, the taxes levied on the rural population paid for public projects, and villages sent their young men off to wars of conquest and expansion. Xenophon captured this truth when he wrote, "While agriculture prospers all other arts are vigorous and strong, but where the land is forced to remain desert, the spring that feeds the other arts is dried up."[4] Yet, the work of farming was widely denigrated. When Cicero wrote, "Of all means of acquiring wealth there's nothing better, nothing more profitable, nothing sweeter, nothing more worthy of a free man, than *agricultura*," he was criticizing his fellow patricians for their lack of interest in the subject.[5] Thus, *rusticus* is not only the Latin term for an inhabitant of the countryside but also, like our derivative "rustic," an oaf and a person both uncouth and uncivilized.

The disdain for farming was undoubtedly associated with the widespread use of slaves, the scale and intensity of which was so great that we can say it was an innovation of both the Romans and Greeks. While the slave was a feature of earlier neighboring societies in Mesopotamia and Egypt, there the status of bonded men and women was shaded by gradations of dependence and freedom that were absent in the Greco-Roman world. These civilizations were thus built upon a broad mix of agrarian workers: bonded and penal labor were more common than outright slavery, while significant numbers of free peasants were scattered across the countryside in small, partially autonomous communities. By contrast, the degree of Greco-Roman dependence on slavery was unprecedented. In Periclean Athens, there were three slaves for every two free persons. In Sparta, servile Helots outnumbered citizens. The institution of slavery was so accepted by the Greeks that Aristotle remarked without reflection, "The people who cultivate the land should be slaves."[6] In the time of the Roman Republic, in 200 BC, slaves in Italy numbered six hundred thousand in a total population of five million and, by Julius Caesar's death in 44 BC, there were three million slaves in a total population of 7.5 million. Some were domestics, others were employed in workshops, on galleys, and in mines. But most Roman slaves farmed their masters' estates.

Ancient Italian farming was not always dependent on slaves. The city of Rome emerged from small autonomous communities of freeholding peasants. Revolt against the monarchy in 509 BC established a republic dominated by aristocratic patricians who managed popular democracy. While republican institutions served to suppress the popular will, non-patricians or plebians who entered government quickly adopted the norms, behaviors, and interests of their superiors. Magistrates were elected by assemblies weighted to ensure a majority of the propertied classes. Elected tribunes, with the power to veto the acts of consuls and the senate, typically furthered their personal goals and ambitions by channeling the discontent of the poorer classes toward patronage, and thus prevented the institution from becoming a truly democratic organ. Meanwhile, few Roman peasants could aspire to the rich peasant status of their earlier Greek counterparts, who by contrast constituted an effective democratic check on elite power. Consequently, Rome's stunted democracy ensured that peasants disproportionately bore the land and head taxes and the brunt of imperial adventures.

The early republic tapped for military service a pool of citizen-peasants or *assidui*, with the means to arm themselves. The institution proved very effective in filling the ranks of Rome's early legions. As each round of conquered territory was divided and allotted to land-hungry peasants, the numbers of *assidui* swelled, thus making way for the next wave of conquest. But starting with Hannibal's traumatic invasion of Italy in the third century, *assidui* ranks were thinned faster than they were replenished. Their property qualifications were twice reduced, eventually falling below what was necessary to sustain a family, until finally the republic resorted to drafting landless Romans or *proletarii*.

Prolonged military absences left many farms poorly tended, and as peasants defaulted the wealthy acquired their land and built up their holdings into ever-larger estates or *latifundia*. They brazenly seized *ager publicus*, or public lands, that peasants had used to round out their diet by pasturing animals and foraging. Men like the patrician Lucius Somitius Ahennobarbus (born in 49 BC) owned two hundred thousand acres, while among the younger Pliny's (61–113 AD) many holdings was a single Tuscan estate of three thousand acres. Populist efforts to offer relief failed in the face of patrician opposition. As early as the second century BC the plebeian tribune Tiberius Gracchus warned that an impoverished peasantry threatened the republic's stability and advocated the redistribution of land from the wealthy to the poor. His *Lex Sempronia Agraria* stipulated the enforcement of a long-ignored regulation that prohibited personal holdings greater than 500 *iugera* (125 hectares), though in concession to the wealthy he allowed for each son in a household to hold an additional 250. Land held in excess, Gracchus recommended, would be bought by the state and redistributed in small holdings of thirty *iugera* (7.5 hectares). But patricians were hostile to any redistributive programs and for his efforts Gracchus was murdered on the senate floor. The depth of elite fury was captured by Plutarch, who remarked on the "cruelty and unnatural insults with which they abused his dead body."[7]

Slavery went hand in hand with the growing size and number of patrician estates and the decline in the condition of the peasantry. "Then the poor, who had been ejected from their land," wrote Plutarch, "no longer showed themselves eager for military service, and neglected the bringing up of children, so that soon all Italy was conscious of a dearth of freemen, and was filled with gangs of foreign slaves, by whose aid the rich cultivated their estates, from which they had driven away the free citizens."[8] In other words, the incessant wars that weighed down on the free peasantry yielded both land and slaves, for which the elites developed a rapacious appetite. The suppression of revolt on Sardinia in 177 BC produced so many slaves that it begot the phrase "as cheap as a Sardinian."[9]

Whereas slavery in Greece strengthened an already robust peasantry, which could afford to acquire them to work, it was an expression of peasant duress in Italy, where it was associated with indebtedness and the rise of the *latifundia*. These patrician-owned estates, worked by slave gangs and producing cereals, oil, and wine, were an innovation of the Roman Republic and their value rested on urban demand. The Roman town was first and foremost a political site. It housed the administrators and garrisons that governed and taxed the surrounding countryside and was the primary residence of the patrician class. Vast outlays of cash by the emperor, senate, and patricians on public works, military triumphs, vote buying, and conspicuous consumption supported urban artisans, plebs, and hangers-on.

Though the *proletarii* or landless urbanites never exceeded one-tenth of the population, they nonetheless constituted a significant enough market in basic food, wine, salt, and oil to underwrite the profitability of the *latifundia*. By the time of Julius Caesar, Rome was home to three-quarters of a million urban plebs who consumed 150,000 tons of grain, seventy-five million liters of wine, and thirty million liters of olive oil every year. By orienting estate production toward this market, the patrician landowners benefited greatly from the reinforcing cycle of territorial expansion, the capture of slaves, and the growth of Rome.

Yet profiting from this demand for food was not a simple feat. The slow pace of technological change was a constant drag on farm productivity, and so remained a great limitation on the size of the non-farming population. First, simple tools and methods were the norm. In Italy and across the Mediterranean, land was prepared for centuries with only the simple sole-ard or sliding plow, a tool better suited to tilling and weeding than plowing. Though the shallow-plowing ard helped retain soil moisture, this did not compensate for the reduction in the release of nutrients that otherwise comes from deeper plowing. Yet the contemporaneous and heavier Gaulish wheeled plow remained narrowly confined to the heavy soils of northern Europe. Labor-saving scythes that were a common sight during haymaking did not replace the cheaper and less efficient sickle at harvest time, despite the time-sensitive and labor-intensive nature of this back-bending work. Second, only latifundia afforded large animals such as oxen, which were prized for their drafting power and prolific manuring. Third, beyond the farm gate, overland methods of transportation were slow and expensive, allowing only those in close proximity to a town or the sea to benefit from urban demand. Finally, the thin Mediterranean soils required peasants and estate owners alike to give over a significant portion of their land to fallow, while the region's unpredictable rainfall produced great variation in harvests. The sum effect made the risks of crop failure acute. Bad harvests averaged three in four years for legumes and one in four years for wheat. Remarking on the latter, Columella wrote that "summer and winter do not come every year with the same countenance; the spring is not always rainy or the autumn moist."[10]

Using simple tools, working weak soils, and threatened by inadequate rain, not to mention locusts and harmful molds, the first goal of peasants and estate managers alike was to grow a generous surplus of grain. Though the well-to-do preferred the taste of naked or non-hulled wheat such as *vulgare*, estates and peasants preferred to plant a hardy hulled wheat called emmer, as well as equally hardy barley, millet, panic, and rye. Peasants planted these low-priced grains to feed their families. Estate owners fed emmer to their slaves and sold it to the urban poor, who lived on simple flatbread and porridge. In contrast to *vulgare*, which fetched a higher price, emmer tolerates thin soils, poorer topography, and colder temperatures and brooks both wet and dry years better. Its thicker husk protects it from insects and disease and prolongs storage as well. Pliny tells us that peasants planted emmer on the poor soils of the Italian mountains and, despite a growing season cut short by cold temperatures, yielded enough grain to fill their bellies. But emmer was favored also by those working the warmer plains below because it did well in fields turned with the sole-ard. The preponderance of emmer in the Roman diet was an expression of the fragility of the farming system and a general inclination toward caution and away from experimentation.

Had they wished to maximize their earnings, agriculturalists would have focused their efforts in wheat, but they instead raised a wide array of crops and livestock. To round out their diet, peasants and slaves planted turnips, beans, lentils, and chickpeas in addition to grains. These might be inter-cropped, especially on small holdings, to ensure at least one good harvest, even though the practice depleted soil nutrients more swiftly. Lupines were fed to livestock, a vegetable garden was kept, and fruit trees were tended when marginal hill land was available. In fat years, they built up their livestock for hides and meat. Rather than build up contiguous farms, peasants dispersed their fields across topographies and soil types, and they varied sowing rates and the spacing of plants as needed, so that a natural disaster striking one field might leave another untouched.

Understanding the risks associated with farming in Italy, agronomists writing for the owners of the latifundia advocated against monoculture, no matter how invested in commercial farming. Rather than advocate the regularization of fields by leveling, irrigating, or draining, they advised dividing the latifundia according to local topography and soil and selecting crops suited to each micro-environment. To avoid disease, infestations, and soil depletion, they urged rotating fields between grains, legumes, and lupines, and recommended the pasturing of animals on fallow fields for their manure. Finally, they recommended exploiting marginal land by planting fruit-bearing vines and trees. In short, agronomists advocated farming practices that best met the food and clothing needs of the slave workforce, supplied materials for the estate's basic maintenance, met the consumption needs of the owner's household, and brought income from the sale of cash crops while avoiding excessive risks.

The other great concern of agronomists was finding work to keep field hands busy throughout the year. For the smallholder, using household labor to the fullest could mean the difference between good and lean years. A farm of ten *iugera* (2.5 hectares)—the size given by Caesar to his veterans—planted entirely in wheat needed no more than 105 days of work; probably fewer given that some land was left fallow every year. Yet, it would not produce enough food to feed a family. Under these conditions, peasants were hard-pressed to make ends meet, and yet they had few opportunities to round out incomes. We know from Columella that growers of grapes hired workers, but he also described effective means by which small-holding peasants might greatly reduce their need to spend precious cash on hired help. With the exception of cheap textiles, manufacturing for the market was dominated by the great estates, which had readily exploitable slave labor on hand to make tiles, amphora, and other low-quality but necessary items.

With few opportunities off farm, most peasants had to find outlets for their excess labor in their own fields. Making the most of their condition, they turned to intensive husbandry, intercropping, weeding, and gathering and preparing compost. They planted and tended vines and fruit trees. They herded cattle, goats, and sheep on mountainsides, and they kept busy during the winter delivering fodder to the fields. If they had access to a market town, they added cash crops such as flax, grapes, and oil, which required more labor than did grain and yielded a good price. But, as Gregory of Nazianzus wrote in the fourth century, "those of us who dwell far from the sea derive no advantage from those things in which we abound nor can we obtain what we lack, as we can neither export what we have nor import what we need."[11] Despite their best efforts, most peasants remained trapped, burdened by underemployment, taxed by the state or paying rent, and unable to save capital. Describing the precariousness of rural life, the second-century physician Galen wrote:

> For those who live in the cities, in accordance with their habit of procuring sufficient grain at the beginning of summer to last for the entire coming year, took from the fields all the wheat, barley, beans and lentils, leaving the other legumes (which they call "pulses") to the rustici, although they even carted off no small portion of these to the city as well. Consequently the peasantry of these districts, having consumed during the winter whatever was left, were literally compelled for the rest of the year to feed on noxious plants, eating the shoots and tendrils of trees and shrubs, the bulbs and roots of unwholesome plants.[12]

On the great estates there was also the twin tendency to augment the workload while squeezing consumption, though it came from a very different source. The commercial orientation of most estates encouraged the extension of the workday, in an effort to increase the saleable surplus, and the suppression of the slaves' consumption, as a means to lower costs. The social condition of slavery determined the manner in which this was done. Faced with the fixed cost of his workforce (the price of purchasing and maintaining the slaves), and its obvious reluctance to work for no wages, the managers of *latifundia* had little choice but to force effort from their slaves under the threat of violence and to fill their year with as many productive chores as possible. Thus, slaves were not only put to work in the fields, where they planted, tilled, weeded, manured, and harvested crops, they were charged with pasturing and tending livestock on marginal hillsides throughout the year, and commended to produce manufactured items over the slower autumn and winter months. In addition, slaves were often required to spend their downtime growing food and making up clothing for personal consumption. By filling the slave's work year with productive chores, overseers hedged against price spikes for basic commodities that threatened profits from the sale of oil, wine, and manufactures.

Thus, Columella writes that the large estates were most profitable when they were self-sufficient. Estate owners had, of course, no qualms about provisioning their slaves the bare minimum and, when slaves were plentiful and very cheap, working them to death might prove more commercially viable than feeding them. But typically they were fed on the crops they grew and, when essentials were unavailable, estate managers arranged to move grain, oil, and even wine among their master's *latifundia* or bartered with neighboring estates. In any case, the work of commercial farming began only once the basic food needs of slaves were met by the slaves themselves. In other words, labor on the most commercial estates spent many hours meeting basic subsistence.

Roman observers such as Cato, Columella, and Varro underlined the importance of arboriculture (fruit and nut trees) and viticulture (grapes) on both *latifundia* and the peasant farm. Cato commented that olive trees yielded steady and reliable income despite the comparatively low prices of olives and oil. Not only does the olive tree tolerates acidic, alkaline, and other marginal soils typical of the poor peasant farm, it requires little fertilizer and resists drought, disease, and fire, and a new tree can grow from the roots of a dead one. Peasants can plant food crops underneath or graze livestock under their boughs. Finally, olive trees do not compete with field crops for family labor, while providing employment in tasks such as pruning during the winter lull. It is little wonder that Roman agronomists universally recommended olive trees despite the lower prices fetched by the fruit, which Cato ranked fourth in value of nine cash crops.

Winemaking, by contrast, proved highly profitable. Profitable viticulture entailed careful, labor-intensive tending, which lent the crop to both underemployed small-holding peasants and *latifundia* with slaves to work. A single hectare of vines might need upward of 825 hours of labor each year, versus 74 for olives and 367 for grain. Obviously the labor supply placed limits on how big a vineyard could get. On the *latifundia*, any expansion had to be met by the addition of slaves. There were also significant capital outlays involved in the purchase of young vines, the building of lattice trellises, and the construction of winemaking equipment. But the greatest limitation on winemaking was the market. Because overland transportation was prohibitively expensive, and moving bulky goods across long distances was economical only along the shipping lanes of the Mediterranean, winemaking was profitable only in the environs of the major cities or close to the ports. Whether small farmers under the best of conditions could profit from viticulture or olive trees is less clear. By the first century, the small-holding peasants of Italy were typically relegated to marginal lands, lived far from the towns, and often lacked the skills to nurture vines and trees and the capital to purchase the specialized tools and improve the land.

In sum, the lives of ancient agriculturalists were rendered precarious by both social and environmental conditions. Yields were low, crop failures common, and by the republican era most peasant holdings were too small to support a household. Families survived so long as they had access to other resources, particularly uncultivated land on which to procure wild berries, greens, acorns, and small game. Yet the availability of such land and its products turned on the peasants' capacity to prevent elites from enclosing it. Under these conditions, the peasants banked on a low-risk strategy that combined a broad mix of crops and livestock with the building up of social ties to neighbors and superiors.

Located too far to take advantage of urban demand, most peasants focused on household and community needs. They devoted the majority of their time and land to grains that did well under trying conditions (emmer, barley, millet, panic, rye). Peasants added enough pulses and vegetables to fill out their diet, as well as flax and small animals to provision fiber, leather, skins, and meat. Their simple diet is seen in Symilus, the peasant described in Virgil's *Moretum*, who ate no meat and prepared his own bread. Peasants in proximity to towns rounded out their incomes by selling surplus food and cash crops, just as Symilus sold vegetables. But for these households chasing market demand was the least of their priorities. They instead emphasized maintaining the family and preparing the way for their children to marry.

As for the cities, the task of protecting plebs against hunger was left to members of the elite and the state. Patronage on a massive scale fed the urban hungry with crops expropriated from the lands of defeated enemies in Sicily, Sardinia, Africa, Spain, and Gaul. In fact, by Caesar's time the magnitude of the non-farming population (in towns and the army), not to say the wealth of the elites, far outstripped what the Italian peasant and *latifundia* could support. Rome's state of permanent war and conquest was thus an expression of agriculture's low productiveness, with each fresh conquest furnishing the resources and manpower needed to maintain the urban classes and prepare for the next wave of expansion.

As peasants struggled to provision their households and meet their obligations to the state, elites drew incomes on their offices and leveraged political power to enforce debts, acquire land, and capture slave labor. Yet the *latifundia* they cobbled together were, as we have seen, remarkable for the proportion of land and labor devoted to provisioning the workforce and the masters' homes. Whereas the mass of self-provisioning peasants felt no compulsion to cut costs, and certainly lacked the wherewithal to do so, the *latifundia* owners invested energy into squeezing more work from their slaves rather than making them more productive with additions of tools and capital. When all is said and done, the total agricultural output of the empire grew through labor intensification and territorial expansion.

In contrast to the leisurely pace of innovation in tools and methods, the social makeup of agricultural production underwent significant changes between the early and late empire. The prosperity of the *latifundia* economy rested on a steady stream of cheap slaves to replace those dying in the fields. Thus, when the empire approached its territorial limits and new sources of slaves dried up, owners of estates were forced to secure labor through new means. They increasingly broke up their estates and rented them out in small units. While these new arrangements were not without challenges, they benefited from the tenant's willingness to exploit his family's labor to the fullest both to meet the rent and to feed his family. Cato noted this phenomenon much earlier, when he observed that intensive cultivation was only viable among the peasantry, who "works with his children or with people he has to support in any case."[13]

With these changes, the *latifundia* adopted a strikingly new character from the fourth century AD on, and the laws pertaining to leaseholds changed to recognize these developments. These came first to estates belonging to the emperor and the Roman state. In the first half of the second century, two laws gave tenants or *coloni* on these lands permanent tenure. Under *lex Manciana* and *lex Hadriana*, tenants could not be removed so long as they fulfilled their basic obligations. The government intended these generous terms to encourage the careful tilling of its land and the safeguarding of food security. Whether influenced by these laws or not, tenants on private estates secured similar rights. To strengthen their hand, they turned to communal institutions and appealed to customary rights when petitioning local courts. Local administrators often accepted these appeals, fixing rents, granting permanent tenure, and even offering rights of inheritance.

The extent of these measures naturally met with resistance among the elites. Emperors Severus, Diocletian, and Valentinian each tried to legislate against them. But in the first decades of the fourth century, matters were settled in the tenants' favor when Constantine forbade rent increases, ostensibly to encourage better farming. The vigorousness of the law's implementation depended upon the local balance of power between landlords and communities as well as the outlook and power of the local officials who adjudicated disputes. Where tenants improved their standing, however, the gains were significant. On one fifth-century estate in North Africa, they held permanent rights and could freely sell their land or pass it on to children.

Nevertheless, the state was willing to allow tenant advances to go only so far. It had an interest in seeing that rents were paid so that landlords could meet their tax obligations. Adjusting to changes in land tenure, therefore, the emperor Diocletian reformed the tax system. He assessed and then fixed the levy on the crop grown, not on the amount or quality of land, in the hope that greater uniformity would yield higher receipts. But these changes required that landlords pay taxes on all the assessed land, even if there were no tenants. In an effort to assure landlords the labor they needed, the state also required cultivators to remain in their village of origin. Under a fourth-century law, *coloni* "are not to abandon those lands by whose harvest they are maintained or whose cultivation they have undertaken, and they cannot move about freely but are bound to the owner of the estate. A landowner who takes them in is subject to punishment, while the owner of their estate of origin has the right to recall them."[14] As the state turned increasingly to landed magnates to collect both the land and head taxes, it conferred greater authority to them over the *coloni*. Magnates used this authority to bind still more peasants to the land. Under Constantine II, these developments reached their logical conclusion when *coloni* were required to remain with the land when it was sold.

Thus emerged the *coloni*, a type of tenant restricted in mobility but secure in land tenure, and the precursor to the European medieval demesne, or manorial land that feudal lords kept for their own private use. Under the new social order landlords were guaranteed a workforce, but they could not remove tenants, raise rents, or restructure their estates. These protections were granted initially to prevent large landowners from monopolizing local resources, threatening the rural economy, and undermining the fiscal stability of the empire. But the need to stand behind the landlord's rights to gather rent also led the state to enforce immobility. The outcome for farming was a reduced incentive for landowners who, unable to levy market rents, had no reason to invest in farms but every reason to acquire more land. Left to their own devices, the *coloni* continued the peasant practice of self-provisioning, building up farms through hard work, and securing their children's marriages. This tendency left a legacy to the subsequent generations of medieval farmers.

HAN CHINA

In the turmoil of China's Warring States period (475–221 BC), the philosopher Mencius (372–289 BC) argued that productive agriculture was the "root" of political order and state legitimacy. The virtuous ruler, he contended, safeguarded the realm by promoting the well-being of the peasantry. In Chinese political discourse since the time of Mencius, peasants ranked second only to the "gentleman-scholar," who served the monarch, and stood above the artisan and merchant in their importance to the state and society. The gentleman, who pursued "self-cultivation," was not expected to farm. Yet farm labor was not so denigrated as to banish the peasants from the political realm. The differences with Greco-Roman writings are worth pondering: while Greco-Roman writers idealized rural life, it was understood only to be a panacea for urban corruption; when Cicero writes of the sweetness of farm work, he does not expect his sort of people to pick up a hoe. Farm work for Cicero was the responsibility of slaves and the slave stood outside politics. Consequently, Greek and Roman elites were existentially incapable of exalting the labor of slaves and by extension peasants. In ancient China, where slavery played no significant role in the economy, there was no political need for such clearly marked distinctions between the laboring and leisured classes. Chinese elites could thus praise the work of their tenants, without calling into question their own status or position. In annual ritual practices of the ancient Chinese state, which presented the emperor and empress as an idealized peasant couple, the elevated vision of the peasant is clear. Thus,

> the emperor himself plows to supply millet for the sacrificial vessels; the empress herself tends the silkworms to supply robes for the sacrificial rites. This does not mean that the realm lacks good farmers and women workers, but rather that it is not as desirable to serve your ancestors with what others have produced as it is to serve them with what you have produced yourself.[15]

This concern for agrarian matters grew out of specific circumstances. In *earlier* the fifth century BC, the long-standing house of Zhou lost political control of its territories and internecine war ensued. Rivals carved out fiefdoms, bailiwicks, and kingdoms, which they defended with armies and taxes levied from their peasants. The longevity and intensity of subsequent military operations wrought profound changes to the political, social, and physical landscape. While battlefield luck made for sudden shifts in the fortunes of kings and their states, rulers survived longer when they were able to innovate and to develop more effective institutions and arrangements for extracting and mobilizing their resources. The state of Qin was especially successful in this regard, eventually beating out contenders to establish China's first empire in 221 BC.

The Qin road to power was long and arduous. Under threat from aggressive neighbors, poor in resources, and situated on the western periphery of Chinese civilization, its early kings embarked on a series of reforms that aggregated power to the throne, weakened aristocratic followers, and brought lands and peasants more firmly under the king's authority. In the early third century BC, the countryside was divided into new administrative units that cleared the way for the implementation of a single legal code and tax system. Within the new counties and districts, land was divided among farmers and, to encourage early marriage and childbearing, all adult males were endowed with enough land to support a family and required to divide property equally among their sons. Through these efforts, the ruling house hoped to lay the foundations for a viable and growing peasantry subject to taxation and conscription. By strengthening peasant rights to the land, the ruling house hoped simultaneously to inhibit the emergence of local magnates, who might otherwise hamstring its control over the rural surplus and labor, and to render elites reliant upon office and service for their income.

The Qin empire was short-lived. By his death in 210 BC, the founding emperor had failed to transform a highly effective and predatory war-making state into a vehicle for stable, peacetime rule. His harsh and exploitative reign sparked rebellion, and in 202 BC the peasant and rebel leader Liu Bang defeated his main rivals and proclaimed the founding of the Han dynasty. Posthumously known as Gaozu, or the High Ancestor, he set in motion reforms that built on the successes and precedents of the Qin yet anchored imperial rule more securely. A peasant himself, Gaozu had a personal understanding of the penury of his class and concluded, like Mencius, that royal authority ultimately rested on a directly taxable, self-sufficient, and stable peasantry. He was therefore deeply apprehensive of petty tyrants and local headmen who forced peasants into debt, compelled labor from them, acquired their lands, and removed households from the royal tax rolls.

To head off such developments, the early Han emperors recruited commoners to serve the throne, a practice that would reach its apogee in the imperial civil service exam regularly given from the Song dynasty onward. These so-called men of talent possessed personal characteristics and skills suited to loyal service. They often came from families that had succeeded over generations in accumulating modest landholdings, but had not risen to even the lowest noble rank. They were natural opponents of hereditary rank and wealth, and typically supported the emperor in his goal of protecting the smallholder and diminishing grandee power.

Their concern for the small-holding peasant became increasingly discernible in imperial ideology. The early Han emperors, their counselors, and statecraft thinkers—like Mencius before them—maintained that farming was the source of all wealth. Taxes levied on peasants supported their projects and financed costly frontier defenses. Rents received by landholders, by contrast, supported their lives of leisure and, through their expenditures, also paid the wasteful incomes of merchants and artisans. For ancient Chinese thinkers, like the much later French physiocrats, economic value outside of agriculture was so inconceivable that the Han emperor Wen decreed agriculture the foundation of his empire in 176 BC. Reverence for the hardworking peasant was of course self-serving insofar as imperial authority rested on political stability, which rested on yearly grain surpluses. But precisely for this reason, officials and emperors took practical measures to improve farming and to protect rural communities through the promotion of farming and the construction of granaries.

Yet, ultimately, the imperial impulse for expansion ran up against the desire for rural stability. As in Rome, the cost of expanding and defending the empire fell squarely on the shoulders of the peasantry. In a population of fifty-four million, one million served in the army, another thirteen million performed a month of corvée labor every year, and every adult male paid the annual poll tax. Freeholders paid an additional fixed land tax, which was not especially onerous, taking about one-fifteenth of the harvest, but they were also subject to a slew of levies and fines that added to their burden. Tenants paid half their harvest in rent, while scraping together enough to meet labor obligations and levies from what remained. Thus despite efforts to protect the peasantry from predatory landlords and the like, the total burden of obligations pushed many over the edge, compelling families to take on debt, sell

land, and bind themselves as servile laborers and sharecroppers to the households of rich and powerful men in return for protection and debt forgiveness.
Against the wishes of the monarchy, grandee landlords accumulated extensive landholdings, built up armies of dependent households, extended their
influence over rural communities, and, while taking up residence in the provinces, carved out personal bailiwicks.

By the second half of the first century AD the level of land concentration,
and the influence of magnates over local society, were destabilizing. To stem
the tide, successive emperors put out calls to free dependent and servile
households and to redistribute land to the poor. It was recommended that in
every community land be divided into nine equal parts in the shape of the
Chinese character for "well," written as 井. In what was known as the well-
field system, responsibility for the center zone was shared and used to meet
fiscal obligations to the state, while the outer fields went to support individual households. These reforms threatened the wealth of powerful men and,
much like those recommended by Gracchus, they were quashed. More dramatically, the official Wang Mang seized the throne in a coup d'état in 9 AD
and embarked on a grand enterprise to rectify government and society by
declaring all land to be state property. His reign ended abruptly when landed
magnates rose up, restored the Han, and put one of their own on the throne.
Predictably, the power of grandee landlords grew faster thereafter.

In the face of increasing exploitation, the overall population grew on the
basis of migration, colonization, and the steady turn to more intensive farming. By the second century AD, the population approached sixty million,
extending north to Manchuria and south to the Yangzi Delta and Sichuan
Basin. Whereas the population of the frontiers remained sparse, that of the
long-settled areas grew faster than did the additions of new farmland. The
average size of holdings shrank to five hectares or less by the second century.
Those peasants who did not migrate had no choice but to look for ways to
raise yields. Fallow farming disappeared, while ancient texts promoted assid-
uous tilling, weeding, and field preparation. Tools were honed to these specialized tasks. A variety of spades, hoes, sickles, planting sticks, and light
plows appeared to support more intensive tasks. By contrast, large tools were
in short supply. While a few implements such as axes were already fashioned
in iron, the iron plowshare was never widely used because its cost was well
beyond the means of all but large landowners and its capabilities made little
sense on a holding of a few hectares.

Irrigation systems and water-control projects were built on a larger scale
often funded by the state to expand the tax base. Though many of these
developments were visible in the earlier Warring States period, not until the
first and second centuries do we see their full elaboration. By that time,
peasants were more attentive to plowing and preparing their fields. They
tilled the soil more thoroughly, weeded more frequently and carefully, and

expended more effort all year long gathering, preparing, and spreading fertilizers. Describing the litany of things to be done, the emperor's counsel Chao
Cuo wrote that "peasants plow in spring, weed in the summer, and store in
the winter. They cut undergrowth and wood for fuel and render labor services
to the government. . . . Thus all year they cannot afford to take even a day's
rest."[16]

A particular feature of Chinese farming since at least the Han dynasty,
and a signal of the already great pressure of population on the land, was the
diminution of animal husbandry. The earliest treatises on farming recognized
this, focusing the bulk of attention on the discussion of grains and vegetables
while treating the care of livestock as an afterthought, if at all. Land was too
scarce a resource to put under pasture. Nomads, to be sure, raised herds of
cattle, sheep, goats, and horses but did so on the sparsely populated grasslands of the steppe. Chinese peasants, by contrast, kept a few easy-to-tend
scavengers such as chickens, goats, and pigs, but few animals of greater size.
The premodern Chinese diet consequently consisted in the main of cultivated
or wild vegetables served over boiled grains.

The principal grains of ancient China were millet (both paniculated and
spiked) and wheat. (The growing of paddy rice surpassed millet and wheat
only after the twelfth century.) Millet, which is indigenous to China, requires
a long growing period but was valued for its tolerance of poor soils, high
winds, and dry weather. The spiked foxtail millet was preferred for its taste,
but because it drops seeds easily peasants must weed thoroughly or have
plants grow haphazardly across their fields. Wheat came to China from West
Asia, along with barley, and was quickly established as a preferred food of
the well-to-do. The physiognomy of wheat and barley favored their rotation
with millet, as the root systems of each draw nutrients from different depths
of the soil. When rotated with millet and fast-ripening beans, winter wheat
had the benefit of yielding a third crop over two years.

As Han peasants strove to raise yields, they devised and slowly adopted
new methods of field management. Under the "alternating field" or *dai tian*
system, land was lightly plowed with low ridges and shallow furrows, into
which seeds were dropped and then lightly covered. As the plants grew, more
soil was pushed from the ridges to the furrow to support the elongating stems
and keep the roots from exposure. By the end of the growing season the field
had been made level. The *daitian* field system had the advantage of requiring
only simple lightweight tools. The furrows and ridges could be laid out with
a hook plow that required no iron and could be pulled by people or with a
hand-wielded hoe. The earth could be shifted from the ridges to the furrows
by hoe or hand. A seed drill improved germination rates, but it was not at all
necessary.

Compared to peasants who sowed broadcast on raked or lightly plowed
fields, the neatly spaced rows of the alternative field system facilitated weed-

ing, channeled water to the germinating seeds and young plants, and im
proved ventilation which reduced mold. Because the whole system needed
nothing more than simple mattocks, rakes, spades, and hoes, peasants got
higher yields for little capital investment. Thus, in the face of mounting
pressure brought on by population expansion and the burden of state levies,
peasant families found they could survive by exerting greater effort. They
eliminated the fallow by gathering and spreading more fertilizer and intro-
ducing new rotations; they planted their fields to achieve three harvests over
two years; and they found ways to raise yields through better tillage and
improved field systems.

These developments were not without their difficulties. The elimination
of fallow coupled with the more frequent and denser planting of crops inevitably depleted soils faster than before. More frequent weeding reduced competition for nutrients, but only helped so much. Accordingly, peasants devoted ever more labor to gathering pig manure, chicken droppings, and night
soil, to which they added composted waste. Owing to their small farms, and
the early abandonment of pasturing large animals, the supply of manure,
compost, and night soil was limited. To make up for shortfalls, peasants
rotated nitrogen-fixing legumes, which the early agronomist Fan Sheng reported gave good yields on poor soils, made for excellent catch crops, and
restored tired fields. It appears that by attentive weeding, gathering and
spreading compost-fertilizers, taking up the "alternative field" system, and
planting legumes, peasants were able to forgo fallowing without significant
reductions in yields. This was undoubtedly a remarkable achievement, since
peasants in Europe continued to fallow fields well into the Middle Ages. The
more intensive use of land in China raised the land's carrying capacity to
new world-historical levels while allowing households to survive on much
smaller holdings.

By the end of the Han dynasty, the basic elements were in place of the
labor-intensive agriculture that characterized the Chinese countryside into
the nineteenth century. Peasants had abandoned fallow farming for annual
cropping and sustained very few oxen and water buffalo for plowing and
carting. The accompanying strain on the soil was balanced by greater attention to rotations and more time spent tilling, dressing, and weeding. An
increase in the variety of tools available for these tasks suggests the greater
attention and care. But these tools did not signify a breakthrough to sustained
growth of the sort that occurred in England in the sixteenth century. These
tools were accompanied by (and facilitated) ever greater work, while yields
showed only modest gains. The heavy wrought-iron plow and the seed drill,
which might have facilitated more advanced husbandry, were not widely
used and saw few improvements over the next millennium and a half.

Until the arrival of capitalist industry in the eighteenth century, the extraction of rural surplus via the control of land and labor remained at the center of all economies and their political systems. In this chapter we have noted the efforts made by ancient elites to build up states, support and control local administrators, and manage the countryside, all with the aim of appropriating the agricultural surplus. But unlike capitalism, in which agricultural profits derive chiefly from market-determined rents, in premodern societies elites took surplus in the form of politically fixed and customary rent as well as various forms of captured labor. The political nature of the legally derived right to compel work from slaves, and other types of dependent labor, is self-evident. We have pointed to its repercussions for elite interests and behavior, the organization of production, and technological change, and we will revisit these issues in our discussion of slavery in the New World. Unlike slaves, however, premodern peasants largely controlled their land and labor. This state of affairs obliged the elites to compel the transfer of surplus by one means or another. Through their control and building up of the state and local courts, elites imposed fines, levies, and taxes and in return received payments in service typically of a monarch. They also levied rents on lands over which they held customary claims, sometimes legally negotiated with peasant communities. Under these conditions, however, elites were kept apart from and had little control over the day-to-day running of the farms, which left peasants to pursue their own priorities. The most important of these was the provisioning of their households and communities with as much food and clothing as possible. As a consequence, most of what peasants grew never made it to the market. They remained immune from the systematic pressure, imposed under capitalist conditions, to cut costs through saving, investing, and improving.

NOTES

1. *Myths from Mesopotamia: Creation, The Flood, Gilgamesh and Others*, trans. with introduction and notes by Stephanie Dalley (Oxford: Oxford University Press, 1989), 51.

2. D. T. Potts, *Mesopotamian Civilization: The Material Foundations* (London: Athlone Press, 1997), 71.

3. Ibid., 79.

4. Xenophon, *The Economist*, accessed May 5, 2014, http://www.gutenberg.org/files/1173/1173-h/1173-h.htm.

5. G. E. M. de Ste. Croix, *The Class Struggle in the Ancient Greek World: From the Archaic Age to the Arab Conquest* (Ithaca, N.Y.: Cornell University Press, 1981), 122.

6. Thomas E. Wiedemann, *Greek and Roman Slavery* (New York: Routledge Press, 1981), 127.

7. Plutarch, *Caius Gracchus*, trans. John Dryden, accessed April 23, 2014, http://classics.mit.edu/Plutarch/gracchus.html.

8. Plutarch, *Parallel Lives*, trans. Bernadotte Perrin, Loeb Classical Library, vol. 10 (Cambridge: Harvard University Press, 1921), 161.

9. Jerzy Kolendo, "The Peasant," in *The Romans*, ed. Andrea Giardina (Chicago: Chicago University Press, 1993), 207.

10. Columella, *De Re Rustica*, trans. Harrison Boyd Ash, Loeb Classical Library, vol. 1 (Cambridge, Mass.: Harvard University Press, 1941), 20.

11. John K. Evans, "Wheat Production and Its Social Consequences in the Roman World," *Classical Quarterly, New Series* 31.2 (1981), 429ff.

12. Ibid., 441–42.

13. P. W. de Neeve, *Peasants in Peril: Location and Economy in Italy in the Second Century B.C.* (Amsterdam: J.C. Gieben, 1984), 28.

14. Dennis Kehoe, *Law and Rural Economy in the Roman Empire* (Ann Arbor: University of Michigan Press, 2007), 168.

15. Susan Mann, *Precious Records: Women in China's Long Eighteenth Century* (Palo Alto: Stanford University Press, 1997), 152–53.

16. Mark Lewis, *The Early Chinese Empires: Qin and Han* (Cambridge: Harvard University Press, 2007), 110–11.

Chapter Two

From Antiquity to the Eve of Agrarian Capitalism

Peasants and Dynastic States

Too slight a coverage for so long a period?

This chapter takes up the long period between the ancient world and the early modern divergence of capitalist regions from the general tendency elsewhere for farming to continue along traditional lines. These traditions were colored by the character of peasant communities, the availability of common lands, the practice of diversified crop mixes, and the habit of barter between people familiar to one another. These forms of rural life, we have noted, amounted to rational strategies developed over centuries to mitigate the effects of the all-too-common crop failures, brought on by inclement weather, disease, and pests, as well as state and ruling-class expropriations. Peasants demonstrated remarkable resilience in resisting, sometimes with much success, the efforts of landlords and states to control their labor and appropriate its fruits as well as imagination as they strove to meet their basic consumption needs.

In this chapter's examination of agriculture in western Europe, the Andes mountains, and West Africa, the peasants, we will see, adapted their families, communities, territories, tools, and techniques to assure their livelihood. The key questions concern the dynamics of these rural communities. How did peasants organize themselves and their farming in order to assure their existence amid the vagaries of war and weather? What sorts of practices did they develop to regulate and ensure access to farmland? And how did the ways in which they defended their harvests from the demands of overlords and empires shape the evolution of agriculture?

In the millennium following antiquity, we will see, people led remarkably similar lives across the globe despite the particular elaborations of their communities, states, and families. The poverty of techniques, tools, and machinery, and the paucity of domestic animals, brought all human activity back to the strength of human labor. People everywhere, to paraphrase Thomas Hobbes, had a nasty, brutish, and short life.

FEUDAL EUROPE

> William, abbot of St Denis in France and the convent of the said place . . .
> having taken counsel of good men we . . . liberate . . . our bondsmen of . . .
> Villeneuve, Gennevilliers, Asnières, Colombes, Courbevoie and Puteaux, laborers in these villages at the time of the grant of this liberty, with their wives and . . . heirs . . . to issue in the future from their bodies. We have delivered them in perpetuity from the burdens of servitude by which they were formerly held to us. [1]

This document—issued in 1248 as part of a wave of enfranchisements liberating the peasantry of western continental Europe in the twelfth and thirteenth centuries—speaks to one of the basic features of feudalism. The dominant classes had to use force to deprive the peasants of personal rights and take the products of their labor, either in the form of compulsory work on manorial land that a feudal lord kept for his own private use, known as the demesne, or in the form of rent in kind or in money. Rural households, made up of laborers, wives, and heirs, became the basic units of the economy over the course of the tenth century. The households possessed land for their subsistence and had no need to work for the benefit of others.

Another feature of feudalism was the communal organization of agriculture. No one spent time alone at the beginning of the twelfth century. People lived amid the social groups with whom they shared an economic existence and protection against abuses. The communities arose partly out of the fact that the households divided their holdings among the different zones of the villages' arable land. The peasants had allotments of the various qualities of the village fields, a share of the risk of crop failures, and less overall vulnerability to misfortune. The absence of roads between allotments suggests that tillage was carried out in a common plan at the same time for all. The peasants also made common plans for the use of pastures and fisheries, quarries for stone, and woods for lumber and fuel. The peasants' outlook on the world took shape within their communities and against the lords who claimed these resources and sought to charge for their use. At times, the strength of communities gave the peasants the wherewithal to challenge the bonds of servitude and led lords, such as the abbot of St Denis, to free them from feudal constraints.

Collective farming made possible unprecedented levels of output. Agriculturalists had long planted wheat or rye in the fall for their bread and soup.

But around the year 1000, with the advent of the social and political relations described above, the relations we define as feudal, communities began to sow spring courses of barley and oats, for brewing and bread, and of peas and lentils, amenable to long-term storage. Peasants rotated these spring crops with the basic cereals in such a way that if bad weather ruined the harvest of the winter wheat, the peasants still survived on the oats. The rotations lessened soil exhaustion and helped the peasants spread their labor over the agricultural year, avoiding overextension at planting and harvest time, while making it more productive by avoiding long periods of idleness.

An even greater improvement was the diffusion of the plow. This instrument, unlike the ard (the French *araire*, the scratch or swing plow), had iron at its head to split the earth and a tailpiece (coulter) to shape the fields in furrows and facilitate drainage. At the end of August, after a year and a half of fallow, the peasants plowed the land to break and aerate it, and bring nutrients up to the crop roots. A few weeks later, the peasants plowed a second time to further break down the soil and push grasses and roots into it. They seeded the land after waiting another fifteen days. Peasants added a third plowing prior to the seeding between 1150 and 1250, and a fourth one on the best farms toward 1300. Plowing entailed heavy costs in animal power, and the villagers had to pool resources and work together. They also had to shape their allotments into long strips, because the plow teams, unlike the ard, did not turn around easily and worked more efficiently when pulling together in one direction.

The plow permitted a closer combination of cultivation and animal breeding. In the ninth century, to make plowing practicable, peasants developed collar harnesses and began to shoe horses and cattle to prevent the hooves from wearing out. Peasants used draft animals to cart hay, and after 1000, on the best soils of the Île-de-France, they started to use draft animals to pull the harrow, after the last plowing of the fallow, to level the land, break up clods, and uproot weeds. In the 1200s, peasants began to feed oxen better and select them for a better breed. Livestock spent the winter in newly built sheepfolds, cowsheds, stables, and barns equipped with haylofts. Their excrement was collected day and night, and mixed with other organic matter taken from forests and uncultivated lands, to create compost. The peasants thereby conveyed the fertility of the pastures, where the animals grazed, to the arable fields, where their crops grew.

The abundance of rural ironworks attests to the development of agricultural technology. Scythes, knives, shovels, sickles, and wheeled carts appeared in the records of the duties collected by lords on the goods passing through their jurisdictions. Axes and stone saws made land clearances easier. Billhooks, hoes, picks, spades, pitchforks, and rakes appeared in inventories at the end of the 1200s. Together these inputs amounted to a capital value ten times what had existed in the tenth century.

Advances in farming paved the way for demographic growth. The population of England grew from two million in 1086, when the *Domesday Book* was written in the wake of Duke William II of Normandy's conquest of the country, to 5.5 million in 1300. French families had about four to six children in the eleventh and twelfth centuries, and the population grew slowly and steadily as a result. Extensive land clearances further indicate the increase of population and production.

All things considered, the collective farming of the peasant villages of feudal Europe facilitated growth. Yet one must bear in mind that it did not have an inherent tendency to constant improvement. The peasants possessed land and the means to sustain themselves, and saw the expense of plows, horses, and iron tools as income wasted if they could manage without the new inputs. Horses, for instance, move one and a half times more rapidly than do oxen, and can work for two more hours a day, but contract diseases more readily and cost three or four times more to buy and feed. Peasants therefore continued to rely on oxen and donkeys even in the rich wheat fields of the Paris Basin. In the fifteenth century, many peasants still made use of wood implements. They continued to use the ard as late as the eighteenth century in the south of France, bereft of rich silt soils. Some medieval communities still used the ard in the north because of the high costs of the plow and of the teams of animals required to use it. Moreover, although plowing improved soils and yields, it also caused some of the liberated organic matter to erode in drainage, depleted the nitrogen content, and diminished fertility over the long term through accelerated mineralization of the humus. The peasants struggled to build up their livestock and, through them, replenish the soils of the arable fields, but struggled even more determinedly, under the pressure of population growth, to bring more land under cultivation, often at the expense of the meadows for grazing.

The feudal lords, for their part, invested in political accumulation rather than in agricultural improvements. Their constant warfare to seize one another's lands and dependent peasants made it more logical for them to invest in building up their political communities than in their agricultural domains. Otherwise, their fiefs might be seized by other lords. For this reason, the monetary wealth from farming had much less value in the 1100s than did the power derived from loyal knights. The dominant classes of feudal Europe were warriors, not farmers.

The generous giving of gifts, money, or favors, a quality known as largesse, set the lords apart and nourished their nobility. They spent on military equipment and luxury goods to attract and maintain vassals. These expressed affection, not for fathers and relatives, but for the lords from whom they received a noble lifestyle. Lords gave everything away in order to gain renown and surround themselves with friendships, for these constituted the essential elements of their power and the safest means of assuring wealth.

They found nothing better to do with the surplus food taken from their serfs than to feed young men in training to become knights. Many years and resources went into preparing young nobles to take up the sword. This weapon, in the feudal rulers' self-image, represented the divinely ordained vocation for combat and distinguished the nobles from the mass of the population given over to farm labor.

All of the time and resources expended in military capacity served above all to impose levies on the peasantry. As castles went up across the countryside around the year 1000, political authority consolidated in autonomous manors, and the lords began to enjoy feudal rights to extract labor services, justice fees, produce, and money. The distinctive feature of feudalism was the appropriation of judicial authority over the territory of the manor. It assured that the benefits of the growth, generated by peasant agriculture, went to the men of war, violence, and rapine. The knightly armaments and the militarization of the authorities, which appeared stunningly at the end of the twelfth and the beginning of the thirteenth centuries, comprised the most visible signs of the economic progress.

The lords' feudal rights, like the peasant communities, partially facilitated this progress. One of the most lucrative rights was the lordly monopoly over the mills for grinding grain, and their accessories for brewing beer and pressing oils. To recover the expenditure on hydraulic energy, the lords forced the peasants to do their milling exclusively at their facilities. Developed in the ninth and tenth centuries, this expenditure propelled the rest of the economy, especially the development of artisan work on textiles, as well as the spread of iron mills after 1116 and windmills in many parts of France after 1150. The hydraulic instruments on view in the *Encyclopédie* of the eighteenth century were the same ones developed in feudal Europe. The hand mill for grinding corn became a traditional device favored by the peasants and artisans as a means of evading the seigneurial monopoly. The Benedictine abbot of St Albans near London chose to symbolize his victory over his tenants by confiscating their stone hand mills and using them to pave his parlor floor. In another symbolic act, in the rebellion of 1381, the peasants invaded the monastery and tore up their ancestors' hand mills from the pavement.

Yet on the whole, feudal rights diverted capital away from agriculture. According to the introductory document, the abbot of St Denis "delivered [his peasant communities] . . . from all the burdens of servitude . . . from formariage, chevage, [and] mortmain,"[2] feudal exactions foisted on the peasantry in the late tenth and early eleventh centuries. Formariage, also known as merchet, referred to the lords' right, enforced in their courts, to approve, and collect a tax on, marriages. Chevage referred to ground rent per unit of land, paid in kind or money, as a reminder that the peasants could not quit the manor without permission and that the lord might call them back. Chevage was determined primarily by political relationships, not free bargaining. It was not altogether different from tallage or aid, known as *taille* in France, collected irregularly and arbitrarily by the lords when they asserted the need to collect revenue for protection. Mortmain, the distinctive right of the feudal manor, permitted the lord to inherit a serf's lands. The lords customarily invoked mortmain to collect a death duty, known as heriot in England, consisting of the heir's best beast and an entry fine, amounting sometimes to two years' rent, from the new farmer of the fields. Lords also collected protection tolls from merchants and pilgrims passing through their jurisdictions.

The tithes collected from peasants by the Church constituted an integral component of feudalism. The exploitative function of the manor was so palpable that it could not have existed for as long as it did without the mystification and concealment of the penitential system and sermons of the church. The ideology of the three estates—clergymen devoted to spiritual duties, lords to defense, and commoners to the provision of material needs—could not be credibly taught by the lords. These used force to reduce the peasants to serfdom and dictate their place of residence. The lords fined, beat, and humiliated the peasantry. Feudal society was violent at its very basis. For this reason, only the clerics could hope to win acceptance of the holy obligation to accept servility and the levies in money rents, manorial rights, labor services, jurisdictional profits, and the like.

Commerce, like the clergy, held the feudal manor together. It developed out of the feudal relations, rather than as an external force corrosive of them. Many inhabitants, from poor wage earners to well-to-do clergymen, did not produce all, or even some, of their subsistence needs. Most of the peasants' resources went to money rent, jurisdictional fines, and state taxes. Peasants used markets to get the cash needed to make these payments and to buy indispensable goods such as salt. The feudal lords needed cash to buy weapons and luxuries for their political communities and states. It is for these reasons that the bulk of the markets were founded by barons, monastic seigneurs, local lay lords, and a few bishops. The markets grew rapidly in scope at the end of the 1200s, as merchants conducted international and long-distance trade in luxury wines, spices, silks, armaments, armor, and mercenaries purchased by the dominant classes.

The artisans producing the goods for the markets kept prices up by creating guilds to enforce standards, restrict output, and limit entry into their economic lines. They made some innovations but did not face competitive pressure to specialize, build up cash reserves, or introduce new devices for, and ways of, manufacturing. The commodity dealers did not apply their capital to agriculture or industry in innovative ways. Merchants bought cheap and sold dear and required the regulation of trade to prevent competition from forcing purchase prices up and sale prices down. Merchants relied for this regulation on the political communities of the feudal landowners. Bankers served as creditors to princely, aristocratic, and ecclesiastical spenders.

The profits of the merchants and bankers depended on the ability of monarchs and nobles to take income from peasant agriculture, purchase commodities, and service loans. In short, the circulation of goods and money supported noble power and perpetuated the feudal economy.

Feudalism was thus based on political regulations and coercive exactions from the peasants. The lords appropriated more resources over the course of the twelfth and thirteenth centuries, as the peasants labored more intensively to plow, improve the soils, and raise output. Yet as we will see, intensive farming reduced the quantity and quality of the cattle relative to the sown acreage, and diminished the fertility of the soil over the long term. Thus, feudal farming could only continue to increase lordly income and accommodate population growth by dint of outward expansion. The lords acquired territory eastward across the Elbe and attracted laborers to their new manors by offering seed, livestock, equipment, secure landholdings, and larger shares of the harvests. Peasants followed to flee the bonds of serfdom, abuses of power, and land scarcity. Saxons moved across central Europe to set up German villages, interspersed with Slavic ones, in places such as Transylvania. Norman adventurers carved out feudal principalities in southern Italy, which later formed the Kingdom of Sicily. The Crusaders spread feudalism to Syria from 1099 onward. Feudalism conquered the Iberian Peninsula in the twelfth and thirteenth centuries and later reached out from Portugal and Spain across the Atlantic to the Americas.

In addition to the outward advance of the feudal world, surviving charters show assarting, the clearing of lands for use in agriculture, in much of western Europe as early as the tenth century. Assarting extended farming at the expense of woods, wetlands, and other common areas used as pastures and fisheries, and as sources of timber and fuel. In England, the acreage sowed in cereals nearly doubled between 1086 and 1300. No greater area would be sown in grain until the beginning of the 1800s.

In France, around the year 1100, the lords began to grant enfranchisements consisting of fixed payments, in lieu of the arbitrary levies of tallage, so as to encourage the peasantry to bring new lands under cultivation. Even the king of France, according to the Statutes of Lorris issued in the twelfth century, granted favorable terms to attract peasants to new settlements on royal lands. As these enfranchisements and charters multiplied, peasants were tempted to flee to places of liberty, and the lords had to improve the terms on their manors to retain laborers. Peasants played lords off of one another, because the lords needed them to valorize newly cleared land. The peasants came to regard the feudal bonds as intolerable, and the lords, such as the abbot of St Denis, had to relinquish formariage, chevage, mortmain, and other servile levies. By the end of the 1200s, the remaining fixed payment, known as the *cens*, amounted to a mere recognition of lordship, a modest portion of the peasants' resources and of lordly incomes.

The one feudal burden rarely mentioned in these enfranchisements was labor services. It is absent from the document liberating the communities under the abbot of St Denis. The reason for this absence is that forced labor had never constituted a major component of French feudalism. When lords foisted feudal rights on the peasantry around the year 1000, these rights consisted of pecuniary privileges. The lords who did enjoy rights to labor services could demand no more than the carting of wood, repairing or renovating their chateaus, mowing what remained of the demesne meadows, or cultivating the domain vineyards.

English lords benefited to a much greater extent from labor services. In the wake of the Norman conquest of 1066, one notices a sudden increase in the documentation of English society. Lords built up a baronial state by compiling surveys, court rolls, rental documents, and manorial accounts. The Norman conquerors set up a national system of common law granting all freemen access to the king's courts and consigning all unfree peasants to seigneurial jurisdictions. As prices increased in the 1200s, the lords used this feudal state to have the tribunals define the peasants as their unfree dependents. The lands of the peasants, a third of the country, had to hand over 50 percent of their output to the lords in the thirteenth century. French peasants, at this time, gave up only about 10 percent. English demesne land covered one-third of the cultivated surface, much more than did the demesne land of France. English lords added to the labor services of their peasants in the regions, such as the Thames Valley in the shadow of London, where the growing urban market provided an incentive to augment output.

French lords, by contrast, had difficulty taking advantage of the inflation of the late twelfth century, because their demesnes only covered about 5–10 percent of the cultivated surface. The nobles had hardly any land on the plateau of the Lyonnais. At the beginning of the 1300s, most of the lordly lands in Bar-sur-Seine had revenue inferior to ten *livres prisis*, a small sum on which to live. Many nobles had a lifestyle hardly distinguishable from the peasants. The lords of the Paris region sought to reimpose the arbitrary levy of tallage but were thwarted by peasant resistance. The peasants consolidated their freedom during the reign of Saint-Louis from 1226 to 1270 when the taxes they owed the lords became unvarying. As the price of land and grain rose with the population, the fixity of feudal dues led to a decline in their real value.

Many French nobles coped with this drop in estate incomes through positions in the service of grand seigneurs who retained large domains and benefited from seigneurial rights still in existence in various parts of the country. The abbot of St Denis, in the document of 1248 liberating his peasant communities, stipulated that "we do not hold them free of the respect and other duties which by reason of patronage the law demands of the liberated towards the authors of that liberation."[3] As the customary dues, which were invariable and collected in money, lost value, the lords garnered more wealth from shares taken directly out of rural production through mills and ovens. Grand seigneurs asserted rights to portions of more plenteous herds and of the output of lands newly cleared and cultivated.

The abbot of St Denis maintained "the other river tolls (*tonlieux*) and customs . . . reserved and due by . . . [the previously mentioned villages] as the other freed men in our other villages pay us." The enfranchisements specified "that in the said villages . . . we shall be paid dues on the retailing of wine by tavern keepers."[4] Peasants planted more and more vines, and these remaining feudal rights permitted the great lords to impose lucrative regulations on the wine trade. The more eminent noble families forced the peasantry to pay for the use of their wine presses and often had a price advantage thanks to their right, known as bavin, to set the date for the peasantry to sell its wine. These monopolies, like the levies on herds, newly cleared land, mills, and ovens, were taken in kind and increased in value as prices rose. Lords collected rents in kind in the mountainous parts of the Beaujolais at the end of the 1200s. Most of the properties of the Bordelais had to cede portions of their harvests to the lords. Tithes, moreover, were not converted to fixed money payments and still amounted to about 10 percent of a farm's animals in the 1200s. They generally benefited the upper clergy, bishops, abbots, and cathedral chapters who also owned feudal domains. Peasants had to pay *lods et ventes* ranging from about 8 percent of the price of land sales in Île-de-France to over 25 percent in the Lyonnais.

These remnants of the feudal manor all depended on the continued existence of the lords' tribunals. Since the end of the tenth century, seigneurial judges had collected fixed fees for legal cases, seized the property of those put to death or banished, and imposed fines for brawls, disputes, and other minor offenses. The abbot of St Denis made it plain that "we preserve . . . over the individuals of both sexes the justice of every kind that we have over our other freed men."[5] Seigneurial justice remained one of the pillars of noble privilege down to 1789.

Lordly tribunals would have disappeared along with the other manorial rights were it not for the monarchy. From the thirteenth century onward, large domains and seigneurial rights belonged above all to the wealthiest, most influential nobles, who began to rely on the king's administration and tax system. These high nobles and barons in the service of the king capitalized on population growth by approving new towns, roads, navigable rivers, and markets on which they levied tolls. The king farmed out his domains to purchasers of offices interested in his fiscal rights. Royal *prévôts* leased their offices to financial managers interested in the spoils.

The old military aristocrats and princes followed the example of the king in leasing out their reserves and perquisites to clergymen, merchants, and well-off peasants who often collected dues in ways more tyrannical than the

Chapter 2

countryside had formerly known. In the Île-de-France, the leaseholders retained a portion of the output for their own coffers, and with the rest made deliveries in kind to the towns for the lords to have well-provisioned tables and lucrative surpluses to sell on the market. The lords inserted instructions into the leases regarding the crop rotations so as to prevent intensive farming, soil exhaustion, and variations in their income. They usually retained the management of their woods so as to have a stream of cash from timber sales.

As customary dues and estate incomes fell, knights of noble birth began to seek patrons among these great families, who still received considerable income from peasant agriculture and who offered payments or fiefs in order to build up followings. In this way, the erosion of demesnes and rents in the late twelfth century served to tighten the bonds of formerly autonomous lords. The aristocrats thus received the homage and service of relatively poor knights, of the clerks needed to compose their titles, and of the sergeants and marshals needed to carry out patrols and quell unrest. The French monarchy established greater interior peace in the thirteenth century by holding more rigidly all of the warriors who had lived more tumultuous lives and caused internecine warfare one hundred years earlier. Under the aegis of the king and high nobility, the formerly independent nobles saw to the functions of government and collected the peasant surpluses through taxation and seigneurial levies.

This trend toward feudal centralization under the monarchy gained impetus in the crisis of the fourteenth century. The 1200s saw a gradual process of overpopulation and mounting poverty of ever-widening strata of the peasantry. The burst of productivity of previous centuries, as new lands came under the plow, ran its course. The lands of lesser quality became infertile after a few years of farming and had to be abandoned for good. The first contraction of the arable area took place on the fringes of the village lands as the year 1300 approached.

On the main fields of western Europe and England, productivity began to decline, as the growth of the arable surface diminished the area for animals and, in turn, adversely affected open-field plowing and transportation. The delicate but necessary balance between stock-raising and agriculture gave way by the end of the 1200s, as pasture lost out to arable, and peasants began to lack manure and winter fodder. Overstocking of remaining pasture with animals degraded its quality. Archaeological evidence of carcasses suggests that animal weights in the fourteenth century fell below what they had been in times of more abundant pasturage.

Crop yields diminished to around three grains for each seeding in the late thirteenth and early fourteenth centuries. Poor harvests then meant hunger in short order and a prolonged subsistence crisis if the peasants had to eat their seeds rather than retain them for the next season. The same circumstances depleted stocks of sheep on English estates during harsh winters. The death rate mounted from 1290 onward among the mass of the undernourished laborers at the mercy of variable harvests and climatic hazards.

Summer rains of the first decades of the fourteenth century muddied roads, inundated streams, and ruined output on the village lands of northern Europe. Cold winters simultaneously froze over parts of the North and Baltic Seas. Hunger and illness eliminated about 5–10 percent of the population. The land could no longer support so many inhabitants and did not allow for population growth even after the famine came to an end. Children who survived the famine may have had stunted development and greater suscepti-bility to disease. The crisis deepened when the plague epidemic, which began in the Middle East in 1346, swept across Europe and killed about a third of the population.

The decrease of output and population diminished seigneurial revenue in the first half of the 1300s, and English lords sought compensation by pillag-ing other elites at home and abroad. The state raised taxes on the peasantry to fund military adventures. The first phase of the Hundred Years' War wit-nessed a bloody, expensive struggle between England and the Valois dynasty under Philip VI of France. By 1376, English lords even began to fight one another. Their factional struggle reached a climax in 1399 with the ousting of Richard II.

The crisis also provoked popular revolts against the lords. Toward the end of the thirteenth century, as the population pressed on the available farmland, grandees such as Philippe le Bel, holder of the comté de Champagne, began to close off certain woods to collective usage and increase the periods during which others were off-limits. Some farm animals were deemed destructive and barred from pastures. The first great popular uprising took place in 1323–1328 in maritime Flanders, where the peasants' use rights had been restricted and the remaining ones seemed menaced. The areas with the most unrest were those with the fewest moors and forests, and where the lords protected them from densely populated settlements. The lords' attempts to enforce government taxation and servile obligations, such as exclusive hunt-ing rights, provoked the Jacquerie of 1358 in northern France. Peasants de-stroyed castles, and tortured and murdered hundreds of nobles and their families before succumbing to the armies of the king and nobility, and suffer-ing brutal reprisals.

In England, agricultural prices fell intermittently, together with the popu-lation, for nearly two hundred years after 1300. Salaries, in contrast, mounted relative to cereal prices in the first decades of the fourteenth century. English lords, however, had organized themselves more effectively than had their counterparts on continental Europe, and in 1351, they imposed a law requir-ing peasants to remain on the manor and provide the rent and services preva-lent prior to the plague. The Statute of Laborers obliged smallholders, not engaged in an industrial craft, to work under these politically regulated conditions. Judges chosen among the landed classes formed commissions to enforce the rates, fined violators, and prevented wages from rising as rapidly as they did on the Continent.

Conflict over these conditions became frequent in England over the following decades. The key issue was freedom of movement, namely the status of personal serfdom or unfree tenures, and the seigneurial and royal records expressed the conflicts in these terms. Discord climaxed in the rebellion in 1381 when the peasants burned the records of manorial courts in an effort to put an end to the lords' privileged status and their ability to arbitrarily impose rents.

The lords defeated the uprising but could not prevent the peasants from quitting the manors. The lords' efforts to cooperate in keeping wages low gave way to competition for scarce tenants. The peasants won their freedom by the second quarter of the 1400s through resistance and setting lords against one another. They went to the lords offering free tenancies in the legal copy of the manorial roll where the terms were stated. Feudal controls of farming dissolved, and the appropriation of peasant surpluses declined dramatically, over the next hundred years.

During this same period, however, the lords made alliances with better-off members of the peasant community to establish property rights over the land. The English peasantry had always been differentiated. Wealthier serfs accumulated bits of their neighbors' land to have holdings sufficiently large to support a numerous household. They even exploited the labor of fellow peasants, particularly amid the overpopulation, plot fragmentation, and indebtedness in the thirteenth century. This tendency did not break the community apart, because the lords had an interest in keeping it together. The multiplication of households and plots around the demesnes assured the rent and labor needed to fund the lords' political communities. The well-to-do peasants actually rallied their fellow villagers to stand as one against lordship, protect common rights, and resist onerous impositions. These wealthier serfs thus did not turn into capitalist dynasties, as they typically divided up accumulated lands on inheritance. They sought, in essence, to diminish threats to their existence by avoiding dependence on the market and assuring sufficient offspring to maintain them in old age.

But over the course of the fourteenth and early fifteenth centuries, as prices collapsed and direct farming of the land became unprofitable, the lords turned to these yeoman peasants to rent out their demesnes, dues, and court perquisites. From the 1330s through the 1360s, the court rolls, litigation over land licenses, and instructions to seigneurial stewards show a deliberate policy to confiscate plots acquired illegally by the peasantry and to stamp out illicit land transfers that could rob the lords of entry fines. The monarchy and Parliament, the early Tudor state and its courts, granted the lords the right to arbitrarily raise the entry fines or rents on land transfers, including inheritances, of the peasant holdings on their manors.

In the 1500s, the lords relied on the monarchy to quell violent unrest, which set half the counties ablaze, as the peasants sought to vindicate and confirm their customary rights. The rural masses, however, could no longer rely on the leadership of the better-off, most powerful stratum of the peasantry, which had detached itself from the community with the aim of helping the lords undermine titles of inheritance, regulate the costs of using the land, and, in this way, establish de facto private property rights over most of the country. As the lords ceased to rely on feudal constraints they became known as what we now refer to as the gentry. These landowners later restricted the authority of the crown—in contrast to the contrary trend toward royal absolutism in France—whose fiscal independence could have been drawn from the lands they came to administer as their own.

On the Continent, the end of the famine, disease, and armed conflict of the fourteenth century ushered in a golden age for the peasantry. In 1470, when recovery from the fourteenth-century crisis was in full swing, most European villages had only half as many inhabitants as they had had in the early 1300s. The peasants concentrated agriculture in the best fields on silt-laden plains and rich alluvial valleys. The survivors of the high plateaus, hilly zones, and areas of thin, chalky, or sandy soils migrated back to the best lands in an opposite trend from the expansion of the High Middle Ages prior to the crisis. The average size of farms increased to the capacities of a single family to cultivate them with the help of a few servants. This reconfiguration of the fields increased productivity. Whereas pillage and looting had killed off farm animals during the fourteenth century, the simultaneous retreat of the sown area, and the advance of grassland, permitted the number of cattle to increase more than four times over in many parts of France by the end of the 1400s.

The seigneurial classes of France found few rural inhabitants in need of tenancies. Peasants had greater bargaining rights vis-à-vis large landowners. They probably sowed more crops than they needed in order to hedge against bad harvests and to cover the increasing weight of royal taxation. The prices to be gained from surpluses diminished as cereal supplies, between seasonal and periodic scarcities, kept ahead of demand. The lordly classes had less leverage over the peasantry, faced growing pressure on their income, and stood in greater need of the king to build up a state and assure their access to revenue and status.

ANDEAN FARMING IN THE TIME OF THE INCA

The greatest variety of climate is enjoyed by the mountain zone. Its deeper valleys and basins descend to tropical levels; its higher ranges and peaks are snow-covered. Between are the climates of half the world compressed, it may be, between 6,000 and 15,000 feet of elevation and with extremes only a day's journey apart.[6]

While we have suggested that agricultural economies shaped the natural environment far more than they have been shaped by it, the dramatic topography that lies between the Pacific coast of Peru and Chile and the Brazilian rain forests is an obvious exception to this rule. A person traveling east from the Peruvian coast passes quickly from verdant littoral to desert before reaching the Andean foothills. Climbing to 1,500 meters, our traveler encounters dry lower slopes of cactus scrublands that give way to highland tundra at 3,500 meters. From here to the continental divide the journey is punctuated by intermontane valleys and the high plateau plains of the altiplano, covered in herbaceous plants, dwarf perennials, tubers, and grasses. Above the altiplano is a zone of permanent snow and frost that begins at five thousand meters, but having crossed the highest snow-covered peaks, and started on the eastern Andean escarpment, our traveler is welcomed by progressively warmer and moister weather as the descending Pacific winds cool and unload their moisture to create the Amazon rain forest.

The general aridity of the Andes poses challenges to agriculture, as three forces collude to prevent moist air from penetrating. The Humboldt current delivers cold water from Antarctica, cooling temperatures from Argentina to Ecuador and drying the air. The South Pacific anticyclone further reduces air moisture. Finally, cold air rushing down from the Andean peaks toward the Pacific produces a vast rain shadow that stops only at the coast, where a fog belt supports a narrow band of intensive farming. Of the wide area between the coast and the mountains, a sixteenth-century observer noted that "not a twentieth of this large stretch of land is productive."[7]

Although arid conditions pervade the western escarpment and altiplano, sudden changes in altitude and morphology produce micro-ecosystems and local biomes that support farming. Intermontane valleys receive relatively more rain, as moist air rises over the windward slopes and cools, and are also warmer than surrounding plateaus and plains. On the high altiplano the thin atmosphere lets through more of the sun's warming radiation, raising daytime temperatures during the summer to seventeen degrees Celsius, which is enough to grow potatoes and raise camelids. And finally along the coast the moisture-laden fog deposits enough water to support the cultivation of cereals.

Dramatic shifts in terrain and altitude also mean that different microecologies rub against each other: "The frost line," wrote geographer Isaiah Bowman, "was near the line of division between corn and potato cultivation and also near the line separating the steep rough upper lands from the cultivable lower lands. . . . Below us were well-cultivated fields, and the stock was kept in bounds by stone fences and corrals; above, the half-wild burros and mules roamed about everywhere, and only the sheep and llamas were in rude enclosures. *Thus in half an hour we passed the frontier between the agricultural folk below the frost line and the shepherd folk above it.*"[8] The genius of the indigenous peoples was their ability to work across the abutting ecologies in order to provision as full an array of crops and animals as possible.

Alongside coca, cocoa, manioc, and hot peppers, maize was grown on low-altitude intermontane valley floors and hillsides, where villagers built terraces to retain soil and water. At higher altitudes, between 1,500 and 2,000 meters, peasants added quinoa, potatoes, beans, and squash to maize. At 2,500 meters and higher, potatoes displaced maize entirely. (Potatoes were so important to the peoples of the altiplano that they measured time by how long it took to boil them.) To hedge against poor harvests, altiplano peasants grew different cultivars alongside cold-resistant crops such as lysine-rich quinoa, the tuberous oca, beans, and edible lupins for oil and protein. From 3,500 to 4,500 meters arable farming gave way to grazing camelids, which converted the high-sierra grasses into wool, leather, and meat. Finally, hugging the coast, peasants harvested two maize crops a year, along with cotton, yuca, sweet potatoes, potatoes, beans, guavas, avocado, star apple, achira (an edible flowering plant with a starchy rootstock), and squash, while fields were maintained by spreading bird dung. Pedro de Cieza de Leon wrote of this zone, "The natives . . . bring a great quantity of the dung of birds from the rocks, to apply to their crops of maize, and they find it so efficacious that the land, which formerly was sterile, becomes rich and fruitful. If they cease to use this manure they reap little maize."[9]

Bird dung was so important to the growing of maize that the Inca prohibited the harming of coastal birds and had it transported into the mountains. According to the chronicler Garcilaso de la Vega, the son of an Inca noblewoman and a Spanish conquistador,

> In the time of the Inkas, such care was taken to guard these birds in the breeding season, that it was not lawful for anyone to land on the isles on pain of death, that the birds might not be frightened, nor driven from their nests. Neither was it lawful to kill them at any time, whether on the island or elsewhere, also on the pain of death. Each island was, by the Inkas, set apart for the use of a particular province, and the guano was fairly divided, each village receiving a due portion.[10]

As the gathering and spreading of guano suggests, peasants were not idle exploiters of their environment but engineers of the landscape. They pushed farming into inhospitable zones and in the process fashioned regions of tremendous crop diversity. As they spread potato cultivation across the Andes, peasants developed four hundred different cultivars, which they classified by taste, processing, cultivation, and frost resistance, and they planted as many as fifty varieties in a single locale. Similarly, the peasants of the tropical mountainous region of Paucartambo had developed eleven varieties of maize suited to growing alongside quinoa, tuber-bearing oca, ulluco, mashua, achira, avocados, tree tomatoes, beans, squash, and of course potatoes. To broaden their diet, they took lysine-rich quinoa, which grows at mean temperatures as low as six degrees Celsius, uphill and through selective breeding planted it on marginal soil and hillsides. Other examples of adaptation include lupins and amaranths, both high in necessary amino acids, yet suitable to poor soil and able to withstand the bright sunlight of higher elevations. Finally, some nine thousand years ago, the Andean peoples domesticated the llama and alpaca for fiber, meat, fuel, fertilizer, and portage, though they never bred them for milk or plowing.

While peasants often succeeded in both occupying inhospitable ecological niches and growing a variety of crops to meet their needs, the ecological constraints sometimes compelled the abandonment of polyculture. When this was the case, communities dispersed their members across biomes to exploit multiple ecological niches simultaneously. The resulting colonies resembled an island archipelago stretched across different production zones. On occasion, colonies were a day or two's journey apart, exploiting the compression of microclimates and ecologies up the mountainside described by Bowman. On other occasions, they were separated by significant distance, with forests, valleys, and mountains between. To meet the needs of all members of these far-flung households, the community orchestrated the movement of necessities along the archipelago. Wools were moved from the puna to the intermountain valleys, freeze-dried potatoes from the hillsides to the puna, and maize and maize beer from valley floors to upland zones. Thus, the early inhabitants of Quito (Ecuador's high-altitude capital) could feel that a meal without salt and capsicum pepper was incomplete despite the fact that neither was grown locally.

Remarkably, these exchanges were conducted without markets. Instead of merchants responding to differences in supply and demand, bonds of reciprocity and obligation, rooted in village self-governance and strengthened through communitarian identities, were enough to circulate necessities from areas of surplus to areas of deficit. The basis of this cooperation was the social group called the *ayllu*, a combination of families making up part or all of the village who claimed kinship on the basis of real or fictive descent from a common ancestor.

Whereas the household managed day-to-day farm work, the *ayllu* acted as a corporate and self-governing body within the village, managing disputes, protecting rights, and holding and apportioning vital resources. The most important of these was land, which was held in common and divvied up among members in fractions of a *tupu*, a variable amount of land deemed sufficient to support a single adult for one year. Husband and wife each received one *tupu*, for each son they received another, and for daughters they were apportioned half a *tupu*. To protect the community, allotments were returned to the corporate body when a person departed or died and land sales or exchanges were forbidden. In the words of de la Vega, land was "returned to the community because no one could buy or sell it."[11] In communities marked by hierarchies of more and less prestigious households, higher ranks received more land. When possible, their allotments were also scattered across a greater number of production zones, offering these families a fuller basket of goods. High-status males obtained additional land from polygamous marriage and were expected to behave as patrons to those below them, dispersing desirable items like alcohol and textiles as well as assistance in times of hardship. Nevertheless, great care was taken to ensure that all families within the *ayllu* had land sufficient to their basic needs. Sons and daughters received shares, the *tupu* was adjusted by size to account for regional variations in land productivity, and all members had rights to forage, hunt, and fatten animals in common forest and pastures.

The pattern of land tenure suggests that the male head of household directed much of the farm work. Yet kin and neighbors were also known to pool labor and share work at key times of the year so that on occasion, "the work of cultivating . . . [the fields] was done on a communal basis, and the individual who did not work in sowing got no share of the harvest."[12] To strengthen community solidarity, farming was accompanied by ritual and song while harvests were a time for communal ceremony and celebration. Such habits encouraged the better-off to distribute necessities and scarce items to poorer families, and plastered over small but obvious differences in wealth and prestige. But because the *ayllu* also organized the colonization of new ecological zones by its members, the celebration and continuation of shared identity of the larger group eased the reciprocal movement of scarce but needed goods along the archipelago. In sum, Andeans developed social and cultural rather than market means for securing the full range of resources they needed to maintain families.

The adaptation of social forms to the ecological challenges of the Andes no doubt did much to alleviate the difficulty of life at such high altitudes. Nevertheless, dearth was more common than in contemporaneous Eurasia and Africa. But the slim margins above subsistence that characterized Andean farming, and which undoubtedly encouraged mutual support and the sharing of resources, were not simply the upshot of climate and altitude. They resulted too from the very simple tools at hand. Bronze was too brittle to be used in farming, while the Andeans lacked iron-making technology. Tools—whether for clearing, chopping, scraping, drilling, digging, or cutting—were consequently honed from wood and stone, which prevented deep working-over of the soils, while the available camelids were never adapted to drafting.

Throughout the Andes, soils were prepared using the *chaquitaclla* or "foot plow" (also known as a fulcrum shovel), which consisted of a wooden staff and footrest, lashed just above a fire-hardened point (see the third image in the photospread). By stepping down on the footrest, the operator drove the plow point into the soil before rocking it back and forth to loosen and turn the earth. Though the foot plow was suitable to working hillsides, where the animal-drawn plows introduced by Europeans were difficult to operate, it was slow going. Even planting a small field in potatoes required a large number of adult men and women. Describing fieldwork, de la Vega wrote that men

> work in bands of seven or eight, more or less, according to family and neighborhood groups. By lowering their ploughs at once they can raise clods of earth so large that anyone who has not seen it could hardly credit it. It is remarkable to see them perform such a considerable task with such weak implements, and they work with great speed and ease and never lose the rhythm of the song. The women work opposite the men and help to lift the clods with their hands, turning the grass roots upwards so that they dry and die, and the harrowing requires little effort. [13]

The method had not changed by the 1960s, when the geographer Daniel Gade observed that "three men, standing side by side, and working backwards up a slope, each opens a furrow with his foot plow. The man in the center sets the pace for both the man on the left and the man on the right. The clods of earth are broken up by two women who crouch on either side of the central furrow." [14]

The most common tool used by Andeans then and now was the hoe, which peasants used to weed, bank up soil, spread manure, and aid irrigation. The importance of this very simple tool speaks to the attentiveness with which Andeans tended their fields. Gade observed that of all the crops Andeans planted in the 1960s "maize is the most pampered crop . . . and more work goes into its cultivation than into that of any other." [15] Two months after planting, Gade tells us, the peasants used their hoes to weed and prepare fields for irrigation. In the process, furrows were dug, straightened, and deepened to improve water flow, and earth was continually banked around the base of the plant as it grew for support against winds. Ideally, the field was irrigated every ten or fifteen days, the peasants at pains to make sure each plant received water. These steps were repeated with intense bouts of weeding in between. The labor-intensive nature of Andean farming continued through harvesting when, lacking the sickle, peasants uprooted each maize plant by hand.

There were tremendous challenges to maintaining soil fertility. Because the mixed farming of animals and grains was uncommon in the pre-Columbian Andes, a peasant had either to go to great lengths to acquire fertilizer or rest the land. The most common fertilizer was human feces, "which they regarded the best. They go to great trouble to obtain it, and dry it and pulverize it in time for the sowing season."[16] The nearest sources of animal manure were far away, found among the highland camelid herds or gathered from the guano-covered rocks of the Pacific coast. Despite Inca-constructed roads and rope bridges, and levies of transport workers and herds, the movement of bulky goods such as fertilizer was arduous. Consequently, "a great deal of land was left over to lie fallow and uncultivated."[17]

Despite every effort to improve land, simple tools and rudimentary field systems inevitably yielded tiny surpluses and, as noted, communities responded by exploiting as wide a variety of crops and cultivars as possible. Though early accounts shed only partial light on pre-Spanish times, mid-twentieth-century observations of Andean farming are worth considering. The typical 1960s Andean farm of the Inca Cuzco region was a "composite of fields" in which peasants grew the "greatest array of crops" as a "form of crop insurance, such that [i]f one or even two of the crops should fail, several others will ordinarily succeed and thus the specter of famine will be kept away."[18] In the highland tuber-growing zones, peasants planted a wide variety of cultivars, which they intermixed with rows of oca and mashua or añu—a local root vegetable. When possible, they put about two-thirds of their land in this mix and another third or so in maize and quinoa. Some land was always left fallow, the weeds turned under when it came time to plant it. On land suited to maize, one-third was planted in two different maize cultivars so that "during any one harvest, one of the two types succeeds . . . and some crop of maize is thus assured."[19] Remaining land was planted in the root vegetable *arracacha*, or squash, cabbage, and lettuce. Thus, even in the 1960s the impulse to prioritize subsistence was powerful: "The cash crops quite clearly occupy their favorable ecological niches, but those grown mainly for subsistence are cultivated over as wide an area as peasants *can expect to receive some return, even if small.*"[20] Within the *ayllu* formation a precarious equilibrium was thus achieved between population needs and production.

That was how conditions appeared at the moment the first Inca king set out from Cuzco in the late 1430s on a course of imperial conquest that upset the existing balance between land, labor, and food. Everywhere they went, the Inca interlopers imposed taxes, conscripted young men, resettled communities, and diverted labor to state projects. Forced to produce more or suffer reduced earnings at the hands of their new masters, most responded the only way they could: by mobilizing as-of-yet underutilized labor to work longer hours and more days. Communities put people to work irrigating fields, constructing terraces, and gathering more manure. Some had no doubt already come close to exhausting their options before the Inca arrived and imposed unendurable hardships.

Yet the Inca also moved to augment productive capabilities by enhancing coordination across and between communities and ecologies and by extending farming into new zones. They thus made opportunistic use of known technologies and adaptations, such as maize-growing in the intermontane and terracing, and pushed these deeper and more broadly to achieve greater farm output across the empire. They also extended and intensified the archipelago systems by transplanting entire social groups from one end of the empire to the other to open new lands to farm.

At their height the Inca ruled over a patchwork of ethnically and linguistically distinct groups spread across many ecological niches and production zones. The Inca—at once an ethnic group, social elite, and ruling house— appeared first north of Lake Titicaca in the Andean highlands. In the mid-1400s, having concentrated power in the throne and reorganized his administration, the Inca monarch Pachakuti-Cusi Yunpanqui moved from his city-state at Cuzco into the altiplano to the southeast, conquering the entire Titicaca basin, and to the northwest, where the kingdom acquired coastal lands stretching from modern-day Ecuador to northern Chile. His successors pushed out the empire's borders, reaching as far south as the modern city of Santiago and eastward over the Andes into the Amazonian forests. By the 1520s, through conquest and incorporation, the Inca ruled some twenty million subjects spread over two million square kilometers from southern Chile to Ecuador and Bolivia.

Captured populations were taxed to maintain elite consumption and fund state projects. These resources were used to construct the basic accoutrements of civilization: cities, monuments, fortifications, temples, and roads. The Inca added administrative specialists, including priests and provincial administrators, and of course built up the military. As in Rome, each round of imperial expansion secured the resources for the next. In the words of de la Vega,

> the chief boast and purpose of the Inkas was to bring new races into their empire and reduce them to their laws and customs, and as they were already so powerful, they could not desist from engaging in new conquests, which indeed was necessary to keep their vassals occupied in increasing their estates and to use up their revenues, consisting in supplies, arms, clothing, and footwear.[21]

In new imperial territories, local dignitaries, chiefs, and lineage leaders (known collectively as *curacas*) were incorporated as vassals and civil servants. Some achieved noble rank, swelling its number and adding to its ethnic complexity. Tribal groups on the fringes of the empire were required to provide tribute in local specialties and frontier soldiers. Yet, whereas the Inca way of expansion and incorporation mirrors those of other premodern empires, its approach to expropriating agrarian surplus was unusual. In ancient China and Rome the metropole's revenues derived from land taxes, trade monopolies, and labor services (both slave and corvée). The Inca by contrast relied entirely on labor services. Thus Bernabé Cobo, a Jesuit who lived in Peru and the Andes from 1599 to 1630, could remark, "All their wealth consists in the multitude of vassals which they possessed."[22] To put this labor to work, the Inca also laid claim to all land, dividing arable and pasture between the crown, temples, and communities, with harvests allocated accordingly. Describing the Inca-imposed land systems, Cobo wrote:

> When the Inca settled a town, or reduced one to obedience, he set up markers on its boundaries and divided the fields and arable land within its territory into three parts, in the following way: One part he assigned to Religion and the cult of his false gods, another he took for himself, and a third he left for the common use of the people.[23]

Using terms familiar to Europeans, Cobo also noted that all land belonged to the Inca, and communities held only access or "usufruct" rights. In the premodern world, ruling-class demands on farm surplus were always grounded in claims to land, though these typically did not amount to complete and total control over its disposition. Communities opposed such demands, defending their own claims on the basis of tradition, history, and lineage. For its part, the Inca countered such resistance by seizing some land and some labor, but left enough of both for the community. Hence, the sixteenth-century chronicler Polo de Onegardo wrote that the Inca "appropriated everything the Indians had . . . leaving for each . . . only what was necessary to maintain human life." If Polo's claims are true, the rapaciousness of the Inca was indeed highly developed: the peasants, he continues, "were kept in perpetual personal service, without leaving them any fruit beyond subsistence."[24] Yet we can confidently conclude that most communities acquiesced to Inca rule because a sufficient portion of land, however small, remained under their control and in this regard the Inca acted much like the rulers of medieval Europe, who took a share of the land and peasant labor but left enough of both to the community for it to persist.

The Inca's reordering of the countryside demanded sophisticated systems of administration. The most significant figure in this regard was the provincial overseer, who levied the all-important labor tax. At its height, the empire was administered through eighty or so provinces, each headed by a governor typically selected from among the Inca nobility. The population within each province was divided into two or three *saya*, each ten thousand households strong and governed by a member of the indigenous elite. Each *saya* was further subdivided into units of 1,000, 500, 250, 100, and 10 households. The vassal lords of one hundred households or more received land worked by peasant servants and were expected to provide gifts to the population in an act of reciprocity for its labor on behalf of the crown. In this fashion, the entire cost of provincial administration was borne by the local population in a fiscal system that underwrote imperial expansion at reduced cost to the central state. All the more remarkable, the population was managed without the benefit of a written script but through knotted strings called quipui.

To fill state labor requisitions, local officials maintained a count of available men. Under Inca convention, all married men between ages twenty-five and fifty were subject to labor service—some two million men in all—for a period of two to three months every year. In the orderly villages described by Cobo, "overseers and administrators . . . took great care in supervising their [royal and temple lands] cultivation, harvesting the products and putting them in storehouses. The labor of sowing and cultivating these lands and harvesting their products formed a large part of the tribute which the taxpayer paid the king."[25] The highland pastures and herds of llama were similarly managed. The wool from crown and temple llamas was gathered separately from those herders assigned to watch over state and community flocks.

By custom, the king announced the beginning of the farm season by cutting the first furrow, much like imperial China. In the provinces, governors and overseers parroted this ritual performance: they commenced work on royal and temple lands but soon retired to observe from the sidelines and enjoy "banquets and fiestas" while the "common people remained at work," laboring in teams and by task as on their family plots: "these Indians divided the work they had to do by lines, and each task or section of work was called a *suyu*, and, after the division, each man put into his section his children and wives and all the people of his house to help him."[26] Only after a family's tasks on royal and temple land were completed might its members turn to their own fields or herds. Not surprisingly, therefore, male heads of large households were considered fortunate, because they were able to complete their duties early.

Despite these organizational achievements, there were limits to the crown's ability to raise revenue from agriculture. First, increased farm work on crown and temple lands required a commensurate increase in time overseeing and disciplining peasants and took away from peasant subsistence. In the Inca homeland, where governance was most robust, assigning more overseers was perhaps possible. But abroad, Inca rule was more tenuous and compromised by reliance on indigenous and ethnically distinct vassals, many of whom shared more in common with their underlings than with their masters. Second, given the state of farm technology and the tremendous constraints imposed by the Andean environment, there was little that individual households or villages could do to raise yields apart from increasing the time and effort spent gathering and applying the inadequate supplies of manure. In the face of such limitations, the Inca focused their efforts where they had a clear advantage and turned organizational capacities, which they had built up and honed in war, to large-scale infrastructure projects. Irrigation, for example, expanded farming beyond the organizational means of small and dispersed communities.

Describing the ways in which the Inca transformed the provinces through engineering, de la Vega recorded,

> Because the country falls within the torrid zone, irrigation is necessary and great attention is paid to this: not a single grain of maize was planted without irrigation. . . . When the Inca [king] had conquered any kingdom or province . . . he ordered that the agricultural land should be extended. This implies, of course, the area under maize. For this purpose irrigation engineers were brought. . . . These engineers made the necessary irrigation channels, according to the amount of land that could be turned to account. . . . Having dug the channels, they leveled the fields and squared them so that the irrigation water could be adequately distributed. . . . A water channel was commonly brought fifteen or twenty leagues to water a few measures of soil, so that it should not be wasted.[27]

The extension of irrigation into new areas was accompanied by the building of terraces "on the mountains and hillsides, wherever the soil was good." De la Vega continued,

> In order to make these terraces, they would construct three walls of solid masonry, one in front and one at each end. . . . Above the first platform they built another smaller one, and above that another still smaller. In this way the whole hill was gradually brought under cultivation, the platforms being flattened out like stairs in a staircase, and all the cultivable and irrigable land being put to use. If there were rocky places, the rocks were removed and replaced by earth brought from elsewhere to form the terraces, so that the space should not be wasted. The first platforms were large, according to the configuration of the place: they might be one or two or three hundred measures broad and long.[28]

Terracing added acreage, deepened soils for better root growth, reduced erosion, and brought irrigation. Together these improvements reduced the need for fallow and extended maize cultivation into the arid intermontane. The mobilization by the Inca of native labor for these and other tasks suggests that some portion of it was formerly underutilized, whether by choice (i.e., Andean peasants—like many others—preferred leisure over drudgery) or by social impediments to its full exploitation and mobilization. Regardless, Inca organizations proved successful in harnessing underemployed labor to advance more intensive farming systems. The dual objective of maximizing surplus and supporting peasant subsistence was captured in a remark by Cobo: "No one receives more [land] than precisely the amount necessary to subsist." While ramping up as best they could the surplus they took from local communities, the Inca knew to leave enough time and land to local communities to farm in ways best suited to their basic needs.

As significant as these engineering projects were, nothing affected the Andean social fabric more than the Inca policy of colonization and forced resettlement, which touched perhaps a quarter of the population. Known as *mitmakquna*, some colonists were skilled laborers aggregated by the state in communities that made specialty products for elites. Some were security risks—troublesome indigenous groups dispersed to all corners of the empire where they were no threat to the center. Others were farmers resettled, in some cases, to unfamiliar ecologies. The Inca moved highland altiplano herders to the coastal plains to farm, and cultivators from the intermountain valley to the herding puna pastures. Colonists were required to grow highly desired crops like maize, coca, peppers, cotton, and fruits for the crown. Thus in Cochabamba, Bolivia, the entire resident population of one valley was removed and fourteen thousand colonists were brought down from the adjacent altiplano and put to work growing maize for the state. By the turn of the sixteenth century, farm colonies dotted the empire, stretching from Argentina to Ecuador, raising crops and livestock for state use.

In constructing an empire the Inca proved to be successful political borrowers. In the thirteenth century, the people of Cuzco were still pastoral and marginal. The center of Andean cultural and political advances lay to the south among the Tiwanaku who inhabited the Titicaca basin. The Tiwanaku had established means of circulating agricultural goods among the ecological niches that surrounded the lake basin. They benefited from agricultural innovations, such as raised fields and irrigation, which supported their growing population. The state that took shape in this ecology was adept at expropriating surpluses while organizing and assuaging subjects. But it was not aggressively expansionist. The Inca, by contrast, excelled in war making, the mobilization of subjects, and the marshaling of the farm surplus for imperial expansion. By dint of experimentation they developed a remarkable capacity to secure the allegiance of provincial elites and align the elites toward their imperial project.

As the Inca cast their administrative web across new ecological zones they copied the Tiwanahu and linked up existing colonies of farming archipelagoes to weave complex social and economic interconnections. They tapped into existing formations to extract resources and to enhance the circulation of goods, moving large amounts of maize and maize beer into the highlands and textiles from the highlands down to valley floors. Drawing on existing norms of exchange and reciprocity, the Inca rulers painted themselves as divinely benevolent and nurturing providers of goods for their subjects. By replicating and in some cases replacing the functions of the *ayllu*, they became essential to the well-being and survival of the community.

In this context the Inca portrayed labor obligations not as duties but as reciprocity. In return for service, the Inca offered goods delivered from distant biomes. When times were hard, the ruler issued disbursals from his granaries. But the relationship was anything but symmetrical. What the crown took in forced labor far exceeded what was dispensed as "gifts" and what communities once got for free from their relatives they now received at the cost of their labor service.

Ultimately, the Inca polity served the interest of a small clique. The state, including its officers, was an instrument for colonization and expansion, social control, and expropriation. While the Inca raised agricultural production, and perhaps facilitated population growth, the crown and its coterie of priests and nobles were the major beneficiaries, using the state to enhance their prestige and income by diverting peasants to their own ends. The Spanish, who arrived at the end of the fifteenth century, were of course equally skilled imperialists and brought with them better weaponry, effective battlefield methods, and disease. Eliminating the Inca, they substituted themselves at the head of a new empire in order to reorient expropriation in the service of themselves and the Spanish crown.

PRE-COLONIAL WEST AFRICA

When humans first journeyed out of Africa some eighty thousand years ago, they were not yet farmers. It cannot be said with certainty whether farming was brought back from the ancient Fertile Crescent, whether it had indigenous origins, or whether it emerged from interactions between imported and native knowledge. But we do know that before France's William of St Denis was compelled to relinquish his authority over the abbey's serfs in the twelfth century, Africans had built sophisticated states on the basis of agriculture. At their most hierarchical, these were adept at coordinating social classes, controlling labor, extracting agricultural surpluses, organizing long-distance trade, waging war, and assimilating neighbors. Governments of elites ruled over diverse societies of farmers, merchants, metalworkers, carpenters, weavers, and other craftsmen. In the interstices of aggressive kingdoms lived stateless people, who relied almost exclusively upon farming but lived in egalitarian and isolated groups. Among the stateless, there was little differentiation, there were no exploiting classes, and important decisions were made in common.

Across this variegated social and political landscape, two constant features were Africa's low population density and its low-yielding and extensive systems of farming. Environmental features no doubt contributed. On the one hand, the laterite soils of sub-Saharan Africa are low in organic matter and high in iron oxide, often respond poorly to plowing, and both erode and leach easily when cleared of natural vegetation. On the other, the bite of endemic tsetse flies sickens livestock that might otherwise draft plows and provide manure, both of which are associated with high-yielding cultivation in the premodern world. Nonetheless, even where these features are absent, pre-colonial Africans are known not to have taken up labor-intensive and permanent cultivation. While environment is significant, political and social factors are just as salient when explaining Africa's agricultural systems.

Unable to mobilize the level of work and inputs needed to counter soil degradation, which required regular weeding and careful tillage and plowing in addition to constant manuring, the great majority of pre-colonial African peasants maintained the ancient practice of swidden farming. Also known as fire-fallow or slash-and-burn, swidden is the clearing of land by fire to exploit the nutrients in ash to grow crops. Once the ash nutrients are depleted, land is left to revegetate before it is again cleared and planted. The reliance on ash means that the type and density of the natural ground cover set limits on subsequent yields since otherwise swidden fields are not especially well tended. The stumps of large trees are often left in the field, because peasants lack the tools and animal power to remove them, the fields are irregular and unfenced, fertilization and irrigation are rare, and little effort is made to prepare the soil for seeding, which is typically done broadcast.

The main distinction among pre-colonial swidden cultivators was their choice of crops. In the wetter forest zones, they tended plantains, roots such as New World manioc, as well as cocoyams and yams, which were especially favored because they were hardy and matured quickly. They added supplementary plants such as okra, beans, squash, and melons to take advantage of the differences in their root morphology and requirements for sunlight. Polyculture along these lines suited the low nutrient soils typical of West African forests and by piling up soil around plant bases, forest peasants concentrated the valuable organic humus where it was needed most, while developing good tillage for root growth and protection against waterlogging.

Cereal cultivation took over in the more arid zones. It dominated the drier woodlands, the grassy savannahs, the semiarid shrubland, and uplands. Native sorghum and millet (both pearl and fonio varieties), as well as wheat and barley, and later New World maize, were most common. While maize thrives throughout Africa, wheat and barley remained confined to the southern margins of the Sahara. As in Eurasia, millet was well adapted to drier habitats while sorghum was more common in the wetter zones, and consequently a long millet-sorghum belt tracks the border between zones of high and low rainfall across northern West Africa. Everywhere grains were grown, peasants tried to intersperse native and New World groundnuts, cowpeas, pigeon peas, beans, sesame, and manioc to round out their needs.

In the absence of plentiful fertilizer, overplanting and sustained cultivation swiftly degraded soils and caused ecological damage. Even fields planted in carbohydrate-rich root crops, which demanded less of the soil than cereals, and whose leaf canopy provided some protection from erosion, needed to rest at least four years after two consecutive years of planting. Fields planted in cereals required still more time to recover. The need for prolonged fallow kept peasants on the move, as they cleared, planted, and abandoned fields in the manner typical of swidden farmers, while the low yields inhibited population growth.

It might seem that Africans were trapped in a cycle of low yields, sparse population, and extensive farming. Yet there were pockets of intensive farming, characterized by greater numbers of people and such features as terraced hillsides, fruit and oil trees, permanent and bounded fields, irrigation, corralled livestock, weeding, and careful tillage and soil preparation. Over several centuries peasants in eastern Zimbabwe, for example, improved tens of thousands of hectares by constructing terraces and digging irrigation channels, preparing pits for livestock and manure collection, and by attentive tilling. Peasants of southeastern Nigeria built deep humus beds on hillsides, framed by terraced walls for planting. Contemporary farmers of that region continue to till terraced fields, rotating their crops and spreading composted mixes of household waste, grasses, and tree leaves. How and why these systems came together is not entirely clear, but a combination of natural factors, such as the availability of water for irrigation, and social factors such as greater political coordination and in migration were at work. When these conditions fell away so too did these intensive systems. In short, intensive farming was the exception, surviving only as long as the engineered environment held and the population was sufficiently concentrated and politically organized.

As we have said, because peasants everywhere found it difficult to innovate, insomuch as surpluses were precarious and innovation was costly, they developed sustainable and low-cost solutions that drew on tried-and-trusted technologies and methods to make maximum use of family labor. It made sense therefore for peasants to come together in larger groups to protect and regulate access to land in ways that balanced land, labor, and household consumption.

On the eve of colonialism, land in Africa was typically held and administered by villages. Elders, kinship leaders, selected headmen, or a village government distributed land according to custom and on the basis of equity. At times and in places communal land was inheritable, passing from one male to his heir, but village government always prevented the transfer of land to outside persons. Cultivators retained some or complete control of the harvests, which they shared with family members and those neighbors who provided labor assistance during the year. While it appears that land was held outright at some times and in certain places, this practice was so rare that historians conclude there was no pre-colonial African land market. In other words, customary land systems precluded the emergence of a class of rentier landlords and prevented the levying of dues and other obligations.

While African peasants met their basic food and fiber needs without recourse to markets, this is not to say they were "primitive" or "irrational." Quite the opposite: our point is that African peasants found ingenious and practical ways to meet their needs without resorting to sales and purchases. With most or even all of their production unaffected by the requirements of market exchange, and thus not subject to cost-cutting pressures, they developed crop rotations that fulfilled their needs directly. They mixed animal husbandry with crops when possible and always engaged in polyculture. They adopted New World crops, especially maize and manioc, when these appeared and where they proved suitable. Furthermore, communities endeavored to provide the basic social conditions necessary to maintain and regenerate families. They compensated for comparatively simple tools and methods by sharing labor and decisions, while providing all members with farmland and access to surrounding resources.

So long as the majority of peasants spent the bulk of their time growing the same array of crops, there was scant need and opportunity for trade. Indeed, exchange arose only along the borders between adjacent ecological zones, where peasants grew complementary but different crops. The logic of this trade betrayed its limits, however, because in the absence of both proximity and diversity the commercial exchange of goods was minimal. Overall, the low levels of agricultural productivity—and by implication, the small surpluses—depressed peasant demand in general and especially for manufactured goods. Iron makers, who were quite prolific in West Africa, rarely manufactured farm implements, while rural families provisioned their own cloth and household accoutrements rather than acquire them from others. Trade was thus largely limited to high-value items that bore the cost of long-distance transportation yet were beyond the reach of common folk. The vibrant trans-Saharan caravan trade (in gold, salt, ivory, fine cloth, tree nuts, and slaves) connected the elites of coastal West Africa to the inland cities of Jenna and Timbuktu, and beyond to Sudan and the Mediterranean. Yet it hardly touched the rural majority.

While this trade enriched regional merchants and elites, and required the mobilization of labor for extraction and transportation, it stimulated state building rather than agricultural production. Thus, points along key transportation routes acquired strategic value to merchants, kings, chiefs, and warriors who competed for control. In a process dating to the tenth century, and accelerating in the sixteenth, warriors descended upon formerly isolated and autonomous communities in West Africa in search of wealth and power. Some were interlopers, spun off from the Mali Empire, which was itself the product of an earlier warrior migration out of the Sudan. Others were tributaries of the Mali king, paying homage and taxes in return for his recognition of their local authority. Still others were indigenous strongmen who mustered bands of fighters and staked out territory. Regardless, these warriors moved along established trade routes, seeking opportunities to raid and establish camps from which to control the hinterland.

Merchants were also implicated in the process of state building. Already strategically placed, these households looked for monopoly opportunities and they did not shy from using force, sometimes reaching out to influence local chiefs and sometimes to take direct control. Finally, entrepreneurial chiefs sought out warriors and merchants, granting them administrative duties, monopolies, and prestige in return for fealty and service. Gradually territories in western Africa were pieced together to form larger, bounded kingdoms.

Kingships thus emerged among West Africa's Bono, Yoruba, and Akan people, as power brokers attracted clients and brought others to heel. Mande merchants and warriors were especially effective, moving into Guinea and beyond from the south, bringing their distinctive political and religious practices and taking control of towns and transport routes. Mande ironworkers also migrated, parlaying their skills into privileges. Wherever kingship took root, social stratification followed. Society was not only divided between kings and subjects, but separated further into royal and non-royal nobles, freemen, slaves, and occupational castes such as blacksmiths and tanners. As state building accelerated, previously stateless peoples found themselves entangled in new hierarchies. Yet some managed to continue beyond the reach of kings: the peoples of the Guinean forest remained stateless, while the coastal Balanta communities continued to govern themselves through consensus.

The strength of monarchies lay in their military and political organization. These instruments allowed for control of trade, the collection of duties from indigenous populations, and the power to force tribute from weaker and semiautonomous neighbors. But even with their organizational accomplishments West African kings had a very difficult time forcing levies from the rural inhabitants. Insofar as they were unsuccessful in interjecting themselves between land and laborer, they failed to break community control over the surplus. Thus, throughout the pre-colonial period land rent and taxes remained minor sources of royal income and, consequently, the social relations in which peasants were embedded remained little changed despite the political developments whirling overhead. Peasants continued to eke out their living, from season to season, on land held more or less in common, relying on the help of neighbors when labor was stretched, and acquiring most or all of what they needed within the village and its immediate surroundings.

This all changed, however, when the Atlantic trade in African slaves unleashed novel forces in west African societies. Though slavery was of course not new to the region—the relative scarcity of labor was conducive to its practice—it remained the exception to the rule and, more importantly, was conspicuously absent from agricultural production. The violence that attended the export of some eleven million Africans to the New World was more sustained, intense, and widely felt than pre-existing practices. It provided the incentive for more aggressive wars as well as new weapons for waging them. In the wake of English and French slaving ships, better-armed and highly motivated African elites extended their domains and tightened their grip on the countryside as they moved out to capture more slaves. As the slave trade grew, so did the number of coastal and inland garrison towns and slaving posts.

Developments along the coast of Benin illustrate the dramatic changes wrought by the slave trade upon west African polities and societies. Founded in the early sixteenth century, the Ouidah Kingdom drew upon its dominion of the Bight of Benin to seize control of the passage of slaves from the hinterland to the coast. By the early eighteenth century, however, a rival and more militarized kingdom that specialized in slaving raids on stateless peoples was taking hold inland. In 1727, by which time it was successfully selling slaves directly to Europeans, the army of Dahomey moved decisively against the Ouidah and in turn monopolized the regional slave trade. Both kingdoms built up garrisoned urban centers away from the coast from which they managed the seizure, movement, and sale of captives to the Europeans. Surrounding peasants were recruited and cajoled to grow millet and, increasingly, New World crops like sweet potatoes and maize to feed the townsfolk. Their productivity was described by a European observer, who noted that "the natives were so industrious that no place that was thought fertile could escape being planted."[29] As the need for food grew, African slaving states seized land, on which to put some of their captives to work, and laid claim to the surpluses of the free peasantry in the form of rents, levies, and taxes.

As existing patterns of rural life fell apart, peasants were left to adapt as best they could. One of the more interesting developments followed upon the internal displacement of rice-growing communities by their expansionist neighbors. For centuries peoples of west Africa had grown oryza glaberrima or black rice. It had spread north from the Niger River delta to the Ivory Coast and on to Senegambia, where it arrived around the year 1000. From the coasts it was taken inland to the Guinea highlands. By the sixteenth century black rice was cultivated by stateless and stratified societies alike. It was common to the hierarchically organized Mandinka, who lived inland and on the highlands, as well as the stateless Balanta and Baga peoples of Guinea, who lived in decentralized, unstratified social groups along the coast. While the former planted the black rice on unirrigated, dry fields, the latter engineered intertidal zones, where sweet river and ocean water mixed. By harnessing the natural sequences of tides and delta flooding, they exploited black rice's tolerance of acidity, salinity, iron toxicity, and phosphorus deficiency to produce bumper harvests. In the process, the Balanta and Baga extended cultivation into an otherwise inhospitable environment.

The coming of the Atlantic slave trade, and the appearance of highly predatory African states, had two important effects on black rice cultivation. First, bands of the stateless Balanta and Baga, pushed out of their traditional homeland, took refuge in coastal mangrove forests and gathered there in sufficient numbers to afford more intensive as well as permanent paddy farming. Second, through their interactions with Europeans the Balanta and Baga attained the iron needed to fashion tools capable of clearing the mangrove and turning the heavy coastal soil. Recounting the history of black rice cultivation, a Balanta man reported to historian Walter Hawthorne that "before the arrival of the first Portuguese in this land, Balanta did not have an iron kebinde [a fulcrum shovel] since we did not have iron. Thus our kebinde was made completely of wood, the cutting edge being burned with fire to make it more durable. The work of the farmer was very difficult considering how rudimentary the kebinde was. Balanta society only gained knowledge of iron after the arrival of the first Portuguese traders."[30] As in the terraced fields of eastern Zimbabwe and Nigeria, the Balanta and Baga responded to new opportunities and threats by re-engineering their landscape and in the process developed a more productive yet labor-intensive farming system.

In contrast to the river deltas, where black rice thrived in the tidal sweep between ocean and sweet water, it did not take to the brackish water of the mangrove forest. Untreated, the salt content of the soil and water was too high. In response, communities under took major engineering projects to prepare the soil. Groundwork began with the shaping of earthen tidal walls or dikes, built to the height of meter high. Holding back the tides, the dikes deprived the mangrove of water, exposed roots, and eventually killed it off. Fire was used to remove the dead shrubs, while larger and tougher trees were dug up with the iron kebinde. At the same time, holding ponds, canals, and sluicegates were constructed to collect and channel rainwater to the recently cleared land, where it sped up the desalination of the tidal soils. The entire process of desalination required two to three years and nothing could be planted during that time.

As time for planting drew closer, the communities built seedling beds on higher land in which to raise young plants for transplanting. To prepare for transplanting, the new paddies were flooded again with tidal water to ease the heavy work of turning and aerating the soil. This was done by bands of young men, working in unison with the fulcrum shovel. When ready, the tidal wall was closed off for a month and the introduced salt was left to dissipate before planting. Over the course of the growing season, sweet water levels were adjusted using the network of ponds, channels, and sluicegates. The work of keeping the mangrove at bay continued, as did the constant repair of the dikes and channels. At the end of the season, the paddies were drained and the rice was pulled from the ground, bundled, and carried to a dry place for threshing and storage. What livestock the community had was left to graze and manure the fields or seashells were burned and then applied for fertilizer.

Black rice paddy farming required tremendous coordination, engineering know-how, and meticulous soil treatment. The expenditure of time and effort was clear to European observers, whose accounts dwell on the density of cultivation across large numbers of fields interlocked by water channels and dikes. Along the Upper Guinean coast the adventurer La Courbe observed in the 1680s that "the low lands, and those that are watered by ordinary spill-over from the heavy rains at the height of the season, or inundated by springs or currents coming from higher up, are all planted in rice."[31] He continued, "I see lagoons of rice all along the side of the river." He noted too the management of water through catchment ponds, channels, and dikes. "The fields," he wrote,

> are traversed by little causeways, from space to space, to prevent the running off of water; in the first place, after it rains, they sow the rice that grows in the water. . . . They cut up their land by means of small dikes that retain water so that the rice is always bathed; because it likes to be in the water; and it grows as the water rises. . . . The lands that are flat and well irrigated are perfectly cultivated, and they do not use but [fulcrum] shovels of wood provided with a flat piece of iron at one end and a long handle to cultivate.[32]

Adding details, in 1793 Samuel Gamble wrote,

> The Bagos are very expert in cultivating rice. . . . The rice they first sew [*sic*] on their dunghills and rising spots about their towns; when 8 or 10 inches high [they] transplant it into Lugars made for the purpose which are flat low swamps, at one side. . . they have a reservoir that they can let in what water they please. . . . The instrument they use much resembles a Turf spade with which they turn the grass under in ridges before the water which by being confined Stagnates and nourishes the root of the plant. Women & Girls transplant the rice and are so dextrous as to plant fifty roots singly in one minute.[33]

Speaking to the long days and years of work, Olfert Dapper wrote in the 1640s,

> Those who are hard-working can cultivate three rice-fields in one summer; they sow the first rice on the low ground, the second a little higher and the third . . . on the high ground, each a month after the previous one, in order not to have all the rice ripe at the same time; this would bring them into difficulty with regard to cutting the rice, since it is cut ear by ear or stalk by stalk—a very wearisome task.[34]

The complexity of this new mode of rice cultivation required novel social organizations to mobilize and maintain the necessary intensity of work. Among the Balanta, village councils determined the area to develop and then guided the community's labor to construct the tidal walls, clear the mangroves, and leach the soil. Fields were allocated by the eldest male of the founding village house, though each was responsible for cultivating its own paddy field. Households may have held on to their fields, with sons inheriting from fathers, but the sale of paddy fields was taboo. The ban reflected both the communal effort to bring it into and maintain production and certainly the villagers' desire to ensure the subsistence of the community whose entire labor was needed.

The household was not always the basic unit of production and consumption, however. Along the Gambia River, village headmen directed the effort of communal work on the paddy. The harvest was shared among villagers. On occasion women performed some or all field work, while men always did the heavy lifting needed to build and maintain the system. Whatever the organization of work in the different communities, the cultivation of black rice was an example of the ways in which Africans adapted their environment, drew upon and created novel social organizations to facilitate work and solve problems, and, when conditions were ripe, engaged in intensive, sedentary farming systems.

It appears, however, that while slavery propelled the expansion of black rice cultivation at first, its toll on the population may have eventually been too great. As young men and women were hauled off in chains, paddy acreage shrank and, while more and more field work was given over to women, this was not enough to make up for the total loss of farmhands. Rice systems with less infrastructure, requiring less labor, weathered better. But the total extent of black rice growing probably shrank and cultivation moved away from the labor-intensive mangroves to the easier-to-work tidal zones and highlands. In this way, the Baga system shrank to less accessible estuaries of Guinea-Bissau and Guinea-Conarky, and the so-called Rice Coast was reduced to Sierra Leone. But greater changes still were on the horizon, after the slave trade ended and when full colonization began in the nineteenth century.

In sum, it seems that in Africa the building up of sophisticated states was associated with the appearance of labor-intensive farming. Conversely, in the absence of organized expropriating elites, peasants appear to have been inclined to rely upon ash to the near exclusion of other fertilizers, to leave land fallow for years and sometimes decades, and to employ simple wooden hand tools. The absence of the heavy plow and draft oxen (even among the Balanta) has been explained by ecology—the poverty of laterite soil and the tsetse fly—yet neither was adopted in those areas of West Africa where soils were more suited and the tsetse fly was absent. Certainly, peasants knew hungry months and even years, which could have been relieved by more intensive farming. Yet this sort of farming only appeared in the wake of well-organized and predatory states. Undoubtedly, the relative success of communities and the intensity of farming varied greatly with the outcomes of local and regional power struggles over land, labor, and surplus.

This brief survey of agriculture in the period between the Neolithic age and the year 1500 points to the extraordinary variety and difference, which continue to the present, in the ways humans manipulated their environment to grow food plants and raise meat, hide, and fiber. With important exceptions, such as slavery under the ancient Greeks and Romans, this remarkable variation was the upshot of millions of peasant households seeking their subsistence. In places as contrasting as tenth-century Japan, China, India, France, Guinea, and Peru, households relied on the labor of their members and neighbors to meet simple needs on land held by communities or families. Where they existed, ruling elites generally recognized such customary claims to land and labor, because they found it difficult to terminate them. They instead focused their attentions on building states to levy fines, dues, and fees, which they distributed among themselves. The important point is that taxes, rents, and labor dues were fixed politically and had little to do with market prices.

Yet, as this chapter shows, state formations took distinct forms in different parts of the world. Europe consisted of innumerable autonomous lordships possessed by dignitaries with profound roots in the rural communities. Princes had to respect the authority, honor, and property of these seigneurial elites. Kings sometimes conquered neighboring states by gaining the support of foreign barons and dukes but then had difficulty holding them if they could not maintain the loyalty of the lordly classes. If they extinguished some of these aristocrats, new ones always emerged to either oppose or support the kings depending on the particular circumstances.

In America, by contrast, the Inca sent out officials to manage the provinces and absorbed local elites into the state structures. The Inca successfully defended the borders against hostile neighbors unable to play factions inside of the empire off of one another. In Africa, peasants were managed from a social distance, often too great for elites to exert much control. Unable to disrupt the peasants' control over land or labor, the elites concentrated on controlling trade with only a cursory interest in the peasant surpluses. The Atlantic slave trade altered the balance by encouraging kings to raid villages, pushing peasants onto more easily defended but otherwise marginal lands along the coast, and prompting in turn the development of intensive rice cultivation there.

These basic political differences may have influenced the progress of the respective agricultural economies in the first centuries of the second millennium. The three continents undoubtedly had much in common. Peasants oversaw the farming on both sides of the Atlantic. They diversified their crops, bartered within their communities for the things they needed, and held property in common in order to assure the annual supply of their needs at a time when natural disasters and wars could swiftly and easily wipe out one's livelihood. Common property, communities, and crop diversity ensured that bare necessities were attainable even in the worst of times.

But the political differences, rather than any innate or cultural superiority, may account for the relative advances of feudal agriculture relative to the farming in America and Africa. The farmers of America and Africa showed much creativity in their arrangements for community bartering over wide areas and their capacity to make inhospitable ecologies productive of domestic animals and grains. Europe, however, had more productive arable fields with draft animals, plows, sickles, and carts. These fields may have arisen out of the deeply rooted feudal political arrangements. Feudal agriculture provided the resources for European rulers to eventually project their power over the Atlantic in the fifteenth and sixteenth centuries.

Table 2.1. Chief Differences among Pre-capitalist Farmers

	Hunter-gatherers	Sumerians	Ancient Romans	Ancient Chinese	Peasants in Feudal Europe	Pre-Columbian Andean Peasants	Pre-colon Peasants
Communities	Small nomadic cooperative groups	Relatively urban	Relatively urban	Rural	Rural	Extensive across ecological zones	Autonomo
Labor intensity	Lower than all settled farmers	High	Relatively high; much fallow land	Most intensive; little to no fallow land	Tending upward/ receding fallow until early fourteenth century	Low though tending higher under Inca in fifteenth century/ much fallow land	Low with ε fallow
Means of farming	Non-dependence on farming	Seeder plows	Simple tools; ard rather than plow	Spades, hoes, sickles, planting sticks, light plows	Heavy plows, draft animals	Wood fulcrum shovel	Slash-anc swidden f:
Labor productivity	None	High	Low	High, but little to no growth	Relatively high	Low	Low
Main crop	Wild grains and other natural food-bearing plants	Barley	Hardy hulled wheat called emmer	Millet and wheat	Wheat/rye/ oats/barley	Potatoes, maize, quinoa	Manioc, c yam in for sorghum, more arid
Slavery	Complete liberty	Absent from farming	Common	None	None	None	Fueled gro kingdoms in farming
Basis of elite power	Egalitarian	Granaries from	Patrician plantations	Dynastic empire	Self-ruling lordships	Kingdom incorporates local	Kingdoms innumera

		temple estates				chiefs	communit[y] independ[ent] rulers
Means of taking wealth	None	Hierarchy of rations from granaries to temple workers	Slave labor	Taxation of peasants; landlords compete with state taxation	Labor and dues from serfs bound to land	Chiefly labor conscription and some taxation	Control ov[er] distance l[ong] trade; little exploitati[c] farmers
Warfare	Rare	Relatively uncommon	Constant: to obtain slaves and resources	Warfare, but less than Rome and feudal Europe	Cult of warrior/ constant combat	Conquests created Inca empire	Relatively uncommo[n]

NOTES

1. Georges Duby, *Rural Economy and Country Life in the Medieval West* (Columbia: University of South Carolina Press, 1968), 513–14.

2. Ibid.

3. Ibid.

4. Ibid.

5. Ibid.

6. Isaiah Bowman, *The Andes of Southern Peru* (New York: Henry Holt, 1916), 122.

7. Bernabé Cobo, *History of the Inca Empire: An Account of the Indians' Customs and Their Origin, Together with a Treatise on Inca Legends, History, and Social Institutions* (Austin: University of Texas Press, 1979), 4.

8. Bowman, *The Andes*, 56. Italics added.

9. Pedro de Cieza de Leon, *The Travels of Pedro de Cieza de Leon, A.D. 1532–50, Contained in the First Part of His Chronicle of Peru*, trans. and ed. with notes and introduction by Clements B. Markham (London: Hakluyt Society, 1864), 361.

10. Garcilaso de la Vega, *Royal Commentaries on the Incas and General History of Peru*, 9 vols. (Austin: University of Texas Press, 1989), 1: 246.

11. Ibid., 246.

12. Cobo, *History of the Inca Empire*, 214.

13. De la Vega, *Royal Commentaries on the Incas*, 1: 244–45.

14. Daniel Gade, *Plants, Man and the Land in the Vilcanota Valley of Peru* (The Hague: Dr. W. Junk B.V., Publishers, 1975), 38.

15. Ibid., 121.

16. De la Vega, *Royal Commentaries on the Incas*, 1: 246.

17. Cobo, *History of the Inca Empire*, 213.

18. Gade, *Plants, Man and the Land in the Vilcanota Valley*, 94.

19. Ibid., 95.

20. Ibid., 96. Italics added.

21. De la Vega, *Royal Commentaries on the Incas*, 2: 280.

22. Quoted in John V. Murra, *The Economic Organization of the Inka State* (Greenwich, Conn.: JAI Press, 1980), 100.

23. Cobo, *History of the Inca Empire*, 211.

24. Quoted in Murra, *The Economic Organization of the Inka State*, 94, 97. Bernabé Cobo notes that no household "was granted more [land] than just enough to support himself" in his *History of the Inca Empire*, 213. More sympathetic to the Inca than Polo or Cobo, Garcilaso de la Vega suggests otherwise: that peasants received "rather too much than too little" for personal use. See *Royal Commentaries on the Incas*, 1: 242. However, most contemporary historians are of the opinion that the Inca were very effective exploiters of their subjects.

25. Cobo, *History of the Inca Empire*, 211.

26. Ibid., 211–12.

27. De la Vega, *Royal Commentaries on the Incas*, 1: 241–42. A "measure" was enough land to produce 1.6 bushels of maize.

28. Ibid., 242.

29. Robert Harms, *The Diligent: A Voyage through the Worlds of the Slave Trade* (New York: Basic Books, 2002), 159.

30. Walter Hawthorne, *Planting Rice and Harvesting Slaves: Transformations along the Guinea-Bissau Coast, 1400–1900* (Portsmouth, N.H.: Heinemann, 2003), 45.

31. Olga F. Linares, "African Rice (Oryza Glaberrima): History and Future Potential," *Proceedings of the National Academy of Sciences of the United States of America* 99 (2002), 16361.

32. Ibid.

33. Judith Carney, *Black Rice: The African Origins of Rice of Cultivation in the Americas* (Cambridge, Mass.: Harvard University Press, 2001), 19.

34. Ibid., 21.

Chapter Three

Agrarian Capitalism in the Early Modern World

Divergence in Eurasia

For the first twelve thousand years of human dependence on agriculture, farmers focused their attentions on securing their basic needs in food and fiber. They did so primarily on family or communal land using household and village labor. Religious leaders, urban patricians, state office holders, and feudal lords leaned on the authority of states to compel fines, levies, and taxes on agricultural labor, or they relied on the peasants' insufficient land-holdings, and their need for wages and tenancies, to wring resources out of them. Under these social conditions, change and innovation came very slowly.

In this chapter we explore the origins of modern economic or capitalist growth in agriculture, as producers no longer farmed for their needs but rather to accumulate wealth through market exchange. Under these novel circumstances, the pace of innovation in farming picked up remarkably, underwrote the reorganization and expansion of manufacturing, and injected new dynamism into the age-old relationship between town and country. The question taken up in this chapter is what prompted the earliest shift to capitalist agriculture, and more specifically what particular social conditions underpin modern economic growth. We argue that political struggles unique to fifteenth-century England and seventeenth-century Japan transformed the social relationships of both nations and thereby unintentionally established the conditions for capitalist expansion and modernity.

ENGLAND

John Worlidge, a resident of Chalk Country, wrote about agriculture in the second half of the seventeenth century at a time when the volume of publications on the subject was growing in England. He synthesized the extant knowledge into *A Compleat System of Husbandry and Gardening* . . . , in which he wrote,

> Inclosed Parcels of Land that have been formerly taken out of the Field-Land or Commons . . . excel the other in every respect, though of the same Soil, and only a Hedge between, and what yearly value they bear above the other. And also by the great quantities of Land that have within our memories laid open, and in common, and of little value, yet when inclosed, tilled, and well ordered, have proved excellent good Land, and suddenly repayed the present and greatest expense incident to Inclosure. [1]

Worlidge makes clear that time and investment produced monetary worth rather than any tangible use for the farmer. The popularity and broad acceptance of his work suggests that the reading public assumed as natural and obvious that humans strive to amass the money needed to control commodities. They did not imagine that this assumption was unique in history or that it would lead England down a separate developmental path from the other states of Europe.

As we have shown, this assumption cannot be attributed to the stimulus given by the economic demand and market opportunities of the towns and the actions of self-interested actors in response. Around 1500, England had a small proportion of urban residents relative to nearby Belgium, Germany, France, Italy, and Spain. France had fourteen towns of more than twenty thousand inhabitants and twenty-one of ten thousand to twenty thousand. England had two towns of ten thousand to twenty thousand, and only London had over twenty thousand, though it was smaller than Paris and Lyon. Clearly, if the market opportunities of the towns provided the spur to rural development, one would not expect to find England at the forefront of the agricultural revolution.

But England did undergo such a revolution, and to explain it, one cannot focus solely on economic incentives. What distinguished England from other countries, besides the inconsequentiality of its towns, was its political and social relations. In particular, the lords' intra-class bonds, forged through the monarchy and Parliament, the early Tudor state, and its courts, made it possible for them to consolidate and conserve relatively large landed estates by western European standards all through the medieval period. More importantly, the lords availed themselves of their political cohesion to lay legal claim to the rest of the land. They imposed the right to arbitrarily raise fines or rents on transfers of peasant plots. The peasants of the 1300s and 1400s could go to the king's courts to enforce the conditions of their customary farms, but these were not necessarily favorable, because the lords maintained the right to levy variable fines on inheritances and other exchanges of the holdings.

In the early 1400s, the low levels of population in England, consequent upon the famines and plagues of the fourteenth century, made the lords anxious about securing peasants to work under their authority. The peasants took advantage of the circumstances to get the lords to compete for their services. In this way, the peasants succeeded in eradicating the bonds of serfdom that had up to that point restricted their freedom of movement. Though they did not gain outright possession of their copyholds (plots within the lord's former feudal jurisdiction), they had ended serfdom in the sense that they were no longer bound to the lord's manor.

By the sixteenth century, the English peasants' unique status, of legal freedom yet tenuous rights to the land, permitted the lords to modify the levies on tenures. A smallholder might pay a low annual fixed sum, in lieu of the forced labor formerly required on the feudal estate, but pay a much higher and changeable entry fine when starting to farm the land. This payment should not be confused with rent, because it may not have borne any relation to farm earnings or land values. Such payments resulted from a long evolution of custom. But when custom enabled it, the lords could match the payments to economic rents through the manipulation of entry fines.

Revolts broke out in the early 1500s over this very issue, as peasants fought to defend their customary holdings. The authorities quelled the revolts and prevented the peasants from establishing the conditions prevalent across the Channel in France of unvarying payments for the use of the land and right to pass it on to descendants. English farmers thus had to take up leases and, to fulfill the terms, had to produce commodities and obtain money. They had to compete with one another on commodity markets, and amass gains by cutting their costs. They had to narrow their choice of crops and livestock to those in demand, reinvest their gains at the end of the year, adopt improvements developed by competitors, and constantly shift their farm inputs between economic lines in response to changes in commodity prices. Once the economic leases existed, even the tenants who enjoyed customary tenures and more security, but who might also have to sell some produce to make ends meet, faced the prospect of going under, because the sale prices were set by farmers pressed by competitive standards of productivity. A universal drive thereby took hold to transform production through growing efficiency and squeezing costs.

Peasants on the European continent, concerned first and foremost with growing food for their households, had large families to ensure that at least one male would reach adulthood and support elders no longer able to work. In England, by contrast, farmers in competition with one another had to maximize their price-cost ratio and found it prejudicial to have and support many children. Whereas peasants subdivided landholdings to permit their children to establish households, English farmers could not put themselves at a competitive disadvantage by diminishing the value of their property. Their children therefore had to secure their own income to form a family. Accruing this income took time, and marriage ages, and rates of celibacy, increased. For this reason, the English population hardly grew relative to its past and to the French in the fifteenth and sixteenth centuries.

These trends led to the consolidation of relatively large farms compared both to the subdivision and fragmentation of landholdings in England during the 1200s and to contemporaneous developments in continental Europe. Small farms insufficient for a family's livelihood became uncommon in the Forest of Arden and Midlands by the end of the fourteenth century and grew rarer still over the subsequent century, as commercial estates increasingly dominated the agrarian landscape. In the Chalk Country, in 1560, many landholdings consisted of reconstructed demesnes—that is, the manorial land that the former feudal lord had kept for his own private use. These landholdings were run by the tenant farmers of the former lords, whom historians refer to as the gentry once they no longer imposed feudal constraints on the peasantry. The landholdings were worked for wages by servants and laborers under the management of the tenants. While these landholdings made up an overall minority, they subsequently became the normal type and accounted for the greater part of the agricultural production by the end of the seventeenth century. Family farmers had virtually disappeared by the end of the 1700s. Small-holding peasants no longer had their own plows and lived solely by day labor across this part of eastern and southern England.

Since farm workers did not have plots of land, and since tenants had to sell their output to pay for leases, the inhabitants of England, unlike peasant farmers elsewhere, who saw to household needs on the farm, had to buy virtually all of the basic goods on the market. They thus constituted a mass of consumers capable of sustaining a flow of invention and experimentation. By the 1540s, economic ventures such as woad growing, starch making, stocking knitting, and tobacco growing began to attract investment. The homes of rural inhabitants had aprons, petticoats, shirts, sheets, napkins, tea cloths, and all sorts of thread by the seventeenth century. New occupations and by-employments diversified industry and turned peasants and laborers into consumers of brass pots for the kitchen shelf, colorful stockings, knitted caps, and other goods of this sort. The dyeing industry had success in smooth, closely woven woolen cloth without a nap, made from tightly twisted yarn. It did well in linen and canvas, in coarse wool for blankets and stockings, and in other lines for domestic consumers. The cheapness of these goods later won them a place in foreign markets.

Price increases of imports such as oil, and woad in the 1540s and 1570s, spurred energetic efforts to produce coleseed and rape domestically. These crops achieved success by the end of the century, when the schemes for draining the fens went forward, and coleseed proved ideally suited to the new soils. Farmers in Oxfordshire and other regions began to cultivate grasslands and meadows of fodder, and thus facilitated a dramatic increase in the productivity of the cattle business by the early 1600s. The number of draft animals relative to sown acres more than doubled. Draft animals increased the working capital of arable farms and enhanced labor productivity. Consequently, English agriculture was already highly productive in 1700, even relative to most European countries in the late nineteenth century.

During these early beginnings of the agricultural revolution, the relative prices of farm rents and products moved upward from the early 1500s to the second half of the 1600s, and the farmers and landowners did not face much pressure to make major investments in cost-cutting methods. But then, over the period from 1660–1669 to the 1730s and 1740s, wheat prices fell by 25 to 33 percent. As some farmers succeeded in bringing down the rent of their tenancies, landowners in the early 1700s had little choice but to compete with one another to attract the best tenants by improving their farms. Landlords offered larger farms suited to the adoption of labor-saving technologies and specialization. Investment in agricultural methods, which presupposed preliminary expenses, amounted to the sole means for landowners to maintain their level of income. Farmers improved production in an attempt to cut costs and sustain their standard of living in the face of falling prices. Their competition with one another prevented them from holding down output and stabilizing prices. From 1650 to 1750, English farmers produced a surplus beyond their domestic needs and exported part of their harvests. One should thus note that the chronology of gains in productivity did not follow the incentives of high prices. To the contrary, English farmers enhanced output relative to the expenditure of labor on account of their unique situation of having to compete with one another to maintain their market shares at a time of low prices. The consequence was relatively cheap bread, a declining cost of living, and mounting per capita real income.

The farmers produced these surpluses, first and foremost, through convertible husbandry, namely the growing of clover, sainfoin, and ryegrass. Worlidge wrote,

Meadow and Pasture Lands are of so considerable . . . advantage to the Husbandman, that they are by some preferred above Arable, in respect of the Advantage they bring annually into his Coffers, with so little Toil, Expense and Hazard, far exceeding in value the Corn Lands [NB, in Britain at that time "corn" referred to "wheat" and not, as in America, to what the British called "maize"]; and of principal use for the Increase and Maintenance of his Cat-

tle, . . . the chiefest strength he hath for Tilling and Improving his other
Lands.[2]

The meadows and pasture, consisting of fodder crops, that is to say hay,
straw, or similar food for livestock, prevented drainage and nitrogen loss by
hosting fertile bacteria and absorbed rich minerals and atmospheric nitrogen.
They nourished and augmented the stock of farm animals and then materialized as additional fertilizing manure for the arable fields. The growth and
recycling of biomass accumulated organic matter in the soil over the long
term. From Worlidge's perspective, which for centuries was common only to
English commentators, meadow and pasture augmented income relative to
expenses.

By improving the soil, tenant farmers facilitated the introduction of crops
requiring extra fertility, but bringing higher returns, such as turnips, cabbage,
potato, corn, flax, hemp, and sugar beet. In Norfolk, farmers planted a season
of turnips between the winter and spring grains and, to break this three-year
succession of demanding crops, planted an enriching fodder legume such as
clover in a quadrennial rotation. Variations of this rotation with turnips,
legumes, and grains spread to other counties in the seventeenth century.

To make these cropping patterns effective, farmers acted to recover manure lost when cattle were penned on fields and fallow lands. They employed
labor to build stables for cattle so that they could collect all the manure.
Worlidge wrote that "Horse-Dung is the most common of any Dung whatsoever, by reason that Horses are most kept in Stables, and their Soil preserved, yielding a considerable price in most places; the higher the Horses
are fed, the better the Dung is by far."[3] To nourish the horses, the farmers
enlarged the arable surface of grasses at the expense of cereals. Temporary
grasses covered in manure and rotated after a few years of tillage generated
better animal feed, which in turn facilitated breeding, improved the quality of
the livestock, and enhanced the yield of milk. English bovines yielded four to
five times as much milk, and three to four times as much meat, in 1850 as
they had in 1300. The augmentation of animal products and draft power
added to the capital stock of farming.

The agricultural surpluses came secondarily from the floating of water
meadows. According to Worlidge,

> In the watering of Meadows, you may observe that the superficial gliding
> watering thereof, doth infinitely advance its Fertility, and accelerates its
> growth or vegetation; not so much from the fruitfulness of the Water, (al-
> though that be a very great help, and some Waters abound very much with that
> *Universal Subject*) but by its condensation and preservation of the *Subject*, as
> appears by the warmth and early springing of such Meadows, where the Water
> thinly and superficially moves over it.[4]

Flowing a sheet of water over meadows permitted a second crop of hay in summer and, even better, fertilized the meadow with rich sediment in winter and kept it free from frost so that grass grew better and earlier. The floating of water meadows enabled farmers to feed and maintain more horses and livestock. It was made possible by investments in trenches, dams, and sluices to divert the stream water through gutters. The practice had become the norm on the farms of gentry landowners by 1657.

A third aspect of the agricultural revolution consisted of the expansion of the agricultural surface. Landowners made major investments to drain progressively more of the fen molds in the early seventeenth century. The draining was accomplished through strait cuts or new rivers to carry superfluous water from the peat fens through the enlarged outfalls to the sea. Investors made the Bedford Level into good winter ground by the middle of the 1650s. The fen soils turned out to be highly productive for the farmers. Likewise, soil improvements throughout the country made it possible to reduce the amount of fallow from about 35.9 percent of the arable surface in 1300, at the demographic peak of the Middle Ages, to only about 16 percent of it in 1800. Crop acreage mounted from about 6.73 million in 1300 to 9.66 million in 1800.

Driven by the compulsory laws of competition, landowners had to engross their farms to attract viable tenants. They inevitably came to regard unimproved land, which did not bring forth monetary value, as waste and assumed that it should be confiscated. Worlidge argued that the advocates for common land, on which rural inhabitants could graze their livestock, were "so brutish to persist in so injurious and unthrifty a method of Husbandry, both to themselves, to their Neighbours, to the Poor, and the Common wealth in general." He wrote that "if such Objectors would but rightly examine . . . they would soon find, that such Privileges of the Poor do very much injure them . . . For . . . by spending a great part of their time in seeking and attendance after their Cattle; They neglect those parts of Husbandry and Labour, that otherwise would maintain them well. . . . These open . . . Counties," Worlidge continued, "by reason of the multitude of these Cottagers, are Producers . . . of the vast Numbers of . . . Idle Persons . . . not so usual in places where every man hath his proper Lands Inclosed, where every Tenant knows where to find his Cattel, and every Labourer knows where to have his day's work."[5]

Bills passed in acts of Parliament enclosed growing acreage of common pasture and waste over the course of the eighteenth century. But even before this time, landowners grouped their fields together through common agreement. Worlidge complained that "although (by many) the greater part of the Interested Persons are willing to divide and inclose it, yet if but one or more envious or ignorant Person concerned oppose the Design . . . the whole must unavoidably cease."[6] It was only these "injurious" cases (from Worlidge's perspective) that landowners had to resolve, in the eighteenth century, through the costly acts of Parliament.

The consolidation and growing scale of farms, made possible by enclosures, led to rising land rents, because they allowed tenant farmers to achieve economies of scale and reduce expenditures on labor. To be sure, the new husbandry—the labor-intensive root breaks, the reclamation of barren land, enclosures, hedging, in-fencing, building farms, and laying accommodation roads—required more work, not less. Yet apart from threshing machines, labor-saving equipment did not appear before 1850. People could not have performed all of the required labor, because much less than half of the male workforce was engaged in farming—slightly fewer laborers, that is to say, in 1800 than in 1300, the demographic peak of the Middle Ages, despite the big expansion of the arable surface.

The extra labor for the new husbandry came from the growing number of horses. Worlidge wrote that "the *Horse*" was the "strongest, swiftest, and most necessary of all Beasts . . . for the *Plow* and *Cart*, and for the *Pack*."[7] Growers augmented their horsepower about sixfold from 1300 to 1800. At the end of the eighteenth century, farm workers had at their disposal about 3.5 man-hours of horse labor for each hour of their own exertion, whereas French farm workers had only 2.1. In southeastern England, labor productivity rose 4.4 times from 1300 to 1850 in grain farming. By contrast, whereas output per worker in agriculture grew after the Black Death in Italy, it then persistently declined as the population increased over subsequent centuries. If the productivity of agricultural labor stood at an index of one hundred in England, it stood in France at only fifty-two in 1750 and forty-four in 1850.

In this way, in the seventeenth and eighteenth centuries, the number of agricultural laborers per acre declined, whereas the output per acre doubled. Nominal wages still managed to keep up with the cost of living despite continuous large-scale warfare between the 1780s and 1815. The wages then increased by about 30 percent from 1815 to the mid-1850s. The country imported hardly any wheat up until the early 1820s, despite the doubling of the population since 1750 and despite the growth of the non-agrarian population from 55 percent to around 65 percent of the total. These facts are attributable to the continuing rise in agricultural labor productivity. Between 1750 and 1850, output per worker in agriculture grew by about 60 percent, while crop yields rose, at minimum, by 40–50 percent. The exceptional productivity of English farming owed nothing to the country's colonies, coal, or industry.

The economies achieved in labor costs altered the ecological geography of the country by forcing uncompetitive farmers in areas of heavier soil to move into cattle rearing. In the Middle Ages, winter corn dominated in southern and western Norfolk, whereas spring crops, particularly barley, occupied most of the acreage of the fertile soils of the eastern part of the county. But by the late 1500s, the pattern was reversed, as winter corn, at this point exclusively wheat, dominated the acreage of the east, while spring barley expanded at the expense of winter rye in southwestern Norfolk. A switch to pastoral husbandry on the heavy clay soils of the center and southern part of Norfolk paralleled the specialization in wheat in the east. The farmers of southern Norfolk converted arable to pasture prior to 1580, and the fall in prices after 1660 accentuated the trend by constraining many of them to abandon arable farming altogether.

The light soils of the chalk, limestone, loams, and sands of the south had for centuries been left to sheep pasture because of their inadequate fertility for permanent cropping. But after 1650 these lands were found to hold advantages for fodder cropping and began to maintain cereals in the system of convertible husbandry. They drained freely, and had a long working season and low traction costs. According to Worlidge,

> The greatest advantage to the Husbandman, is what annually yields its increase without a renovation of expence in Ploughing and Sowing; as we find in the *Clover-grass . . . St. Foyn . . . La Lucern, Ray-grass . . .* in the Southern parts of *England*, where have been the most of these Grasses propagated; and was the occasion of the many endeavors that were used by some Northern Grasiers to obtain a Law to suppress the Improvement in the Southern parts. [8]

The ill-drained vales and heavy soils of clay in western and northern England had long been one of the country's main granaries but could not sustain the new crops. The landowners of these areas, in spite of improvements to Midlands river navigation, could not match the low cost of the excess grain and fatstock produced in the southern parts, and attempted to use political means to suppress the improvements there. Worlidge referred specifically to

> that fatal Winter 1673, that it preserved almost all of the Cattle in those Countries, or places where these Grasses were most sown; and Hay at no great price, when in the Western and Northern parts of *England*, through the defect of Hay, and scarcity of Pasture, the greatest part of their Cattle perished, and were forced to seek a supply from those parts, whose Markets they used to furnish. [9]

Accordingly, the stimulus given to mixed farming by the meadow grasses for the livestock on the light lands of the south and east separated the zones of the highest profit. The Midlands were edged into dairying and rearing store beasts (leaving fattening to farmers with the forage crops in the south and east). In the 1600s, some of the pastoral regions ceased to grow cereals for their own support.

Pasture farming, however, is far more economical in labor than is cereal growing. Taking up domestic industries was a remedy for the loss of work among those dispossessed by the enclosure of parishes laid down to pasture. The late seventeenth and early eighteenth centuries saw the growth in domestic manufacturing in these parts of the country that had once been one of the country's chief agricultural producers. Leatherwork and the making of cloth, hosiery, lace, and nails thickened in northern and Midlands areas. Where mechanization took hold, manufacturing congregated far from towns along the rivers from which it drew power. It was later that the fortuitous presence of coal beneath many of these areas brought heavy manufactures based on the steam engine and coke-smelted iron and allowed light manufacturing to concentrate next to its markets.

In this way, English agriculture laid the basis for industry, first and foremost, by compelling rural inhabitants reliant on the market to abandon uncompetitive farming in certain regions. As they focused on manufacturing, new towns sprung up out of rural areas in the seventeenth century to take advantage of the underemployment and low wages. A number of smaller urban centers grew at a rate more than four times that of England as a whole and more than doubled in population. Birmingham, Manchester, and later Liverpool emerged as towns toward the end of the seventeenth century and by 1800 had between seventy thousand and ninety thousand inhabitants, the second, third, and fourth largest cities in the country, having grown fiftyfold or more in the previous century. Other industrial towns such as Leeds, Sheffield, Wolverhampton, Stoke, Bolton, and Stockport grew faster than did London. In continental Europe, quite the reverse, urban growth occurred in the capital cities with administrative, military, and legal employment and large ports with long-distance trade. The population of small towns on the Continent stagnated or declined between 1600 and 1750, as they lost their autonomy, and industry spread across the countryside.

Agricultural improvements also developed the consumer market. As mentioned previously, tenant farmers specialized their output for the market, and like agricultural laborers had to purchase clothing, shirts, skirts, breeches, coats, doublets, and shoes. Gains in agricultural productivity resulted in relatively cheap bread and yielded disposable income for the purchase of stockings, gloves, shoestrings, buckles, hats, caps, bands, cravats, neckerchiefs, and tuckers. The number of kilns making stoneware grew tenfold from 1700 to 1750, and the output of pottery and glassware went mostly to the domestic market. The conclusion must be that the period saw cheap living and the social depth of demand. The export market for industry actually diminished relative to sales within England during the seventeenth century and by 1700, domestic outlets consumed the bulk of the textile output in volume and at least half in value.

Agriculture, finally, supplied ample energy sources and raw materials to limit the upward movement of input costs for industry and transport. Farmers reared so many horses that the overall power available to the economy outside of agriculture swelled about twentyfold from 1300 to 1800. In 1841, manufactures of gloves, shoes, saddles, tanned animal skins, and other goods, dependent on the leather of domestic farm animals, employed more adult male laborers than did the iron, steel, and engineering industries. The woolen industry, supplied almost entirely from English sheep, employed nearly a hundred thousand men in 1841, while an even greater number worked as tailors and stockingers, as well as in knitwear and in the manufacture of headwear. Perhaps 10 percent of the adult male workforce labored in wool-related employment in 1841.

All in all, it is clear that the development of the English economy did not result in the first instance from the market opportunities offered by urban consumers, or from any favorable endowment of waterways or raw materials such as coal, but rather from an agrarian structure that compelled farmers to compete and cut costs. Farmers had to specialize in different classes and subdivisions of employment and invent better methods. They increased the capital stock and thereby augmented the demand and the price for labor. Yet this stock also increased the productivity of work, and the number of commodities produced at a constant rate of manual effort, such that the rise in the price of labor was offset by the even greater value created by it. The commodities were purchased for the most part by domestic consumers—first in the countryside, then in the new towns—who obtained necessities on the market rather than on the farm, and who had disposable income thanks to the falling relative price of bread, itself a result of the gains in agricultural productivity.

In the seventeenth century, many rural inhabitants had a balanced diet of wheat instead of rye, a little bacon, some salt, fruit, and cheese, whereas French peasants ate bread and soup. The English population grew more rapidly than did the French owing to lower mortality rates tied to a higher standard of living. The French produced more children, as more died, and parents must have been attuned to this condition in their reproductive strategies. Whereas urban growth, rising productivity in agriculture, and improving real incomes went hand in hand in eighteenth-century England, the evidence points to a different pattern indicative of growing strain on the land in France.

TOKUGAWA JAPAN

In 1856, the daimyo or lord of one of Japan's two hundred or so domains approached three village headmen for a loan to cover the cost of running his household. In response, the headmen threatened to resign and offered to procure the loan only if their lord agreed to rein in his budget, fire servants, and expel his idle brother. Two centuries earlier, when the Tokugawa house brought peace to Japan, such outspokenness by commoners against their masters was unimaginable. At that time, Japan's ruling elite expected and received obedience. However, by the early nineteenth century Japan's ruling order was moribund and such disrespect for authority was increasingly commonplace.

Lords had fallen heavily into debt as the cost of maintaining their families, castles, and a large and growing number of hereditary followers outstripped their incomes. Their condition worsened as they failed in the face of successful village resistance to raise their primary source of income—the land tax. The ruling Tokugawa house, headed by the shogun, was better off than those of its vassals. Not only did its domains include one-quarter of all farm land, but the shogun took income from monopolies in foreign trade, through the imposition of extraordinary levies and forced donations, and by manipulating the national currency. Nonetheless, the failure of the Tokugawa house to reverse the financial straits of domainal lords tested their support, while the widening gap between the feudal character and agenda of the ruling order and the dynamism and mobility of Japan's rural economy, posed intractable political problems. These came to a head in the 1860s, leading swiftly to the end of Japanese feudalism and the appearance of the modern Meiji state in 1868.

The village headmen who refused to give loans to their lords, or acquiesce to increase the land tax on their own villagers, were responding to new social forces below them. The fact that villagers so openly resisted new taxes, and that headmen were more inclined to heed these demands and refuse new levies, was an expression of how far circumstances had changed since the early seventeenth century, when the Tokugawa house took power and set about restoring order. In 1620, just two decades after Japan's reunification under the Tokugawa house, an English trader observed: "This government of Japan may well be accounted the greatest and powerfulest tyranny that ever was heard of in the world for all the rest are as slaves to the Shogun."[10] The question is how this tyranny came undone and was replaced by a highly dynamic agrarian economy capable of delivering growing wages and driving rural industrialization before the Meiji.

The institutional arrangements devised to enforce Tokugawa power unleashed unforeseen forces that hollowed out the feudal state and left it unable to respond to the changes at home and abroad. In 1600, Tokugawa Ieyasu (1543–1616) took the title of shogun and set about building the institutions of rule. He continued proven strategies and added new ones in his effort to check the power of the daimyo, even as these men retained private authority over their hereditary bands of warriors known as samurai. The most important of these strategies was the so-called *kokudaka* system, through which Ieyasu reorganized the 270-odd domains into taxpaying *han* that were rated by their total rice output (the *kokudaka*) and distributed among daimyo according to their loyalty. Wherever possible, trusted and related daimyo were placed on prime domains and in strategic locations close to the shogun's residence in Edo, while untrusted daimyo were placed in poorer domains, far from Edo, and often in difficult-to-defend areas.

To weaken military capacity, daimyo were forbidden to build new castles and compelled to forsake firearms. To encourage loyalty, they were required to house their heirs near the shogun's palace in Edo and take residence there triennially. To preclude the creation of threatening alliances among daimyo, Ieyasu asserted the right to veto marriages. Finally, he took for himself the authority to transfer daimyo between domains. To enforce these arrangements, Ieyasu built up a new bureaucracy at Edo that he manned with a professional staff drawn from the ranks of his samurai.

To ensure greater control over the countryside, the shogun backed efforts to pacify the rural population. New laws and refurnished daimyo house rules enhanced punishments for disloyalty and samurai were removed from villages, where they had resided for centuries, and forced to live on a stipend in their lord's castle town. The removal of the samurai from the village through the law of *hei-no-bunri* fundamentally reshaped relations within the broader ruling class and between the ruling class and the peasantry.

Because daimyo in the sixteenth century were often prohibited from entering the lands of their samurai retainers, they were unable to survey their fiefs thoroughly and, as local justice was often the prerogative of retainers, abuse of peasants was rampant. These interferences in daimyo authority not only cut into their income but often caused costly rebellions. But *hei-no-bunri* removed armed men to the castle towns and severed retainers from their traditional sources of income and power. Though the financial burden on the daimyo of the new stipend was great, the initial benefits were significant. Those retainers who refused to move to the castle towns were disarmed, lost their status, and were reduced to peasants. Those who moved to the castle towns were dependent on their lord's largesse. Thus deprived of their personal fiefs, samurai lost the ability to maneuver independently or in opposition to their lords.

In sum, the institutional arrangements that made possible the *kokudaka* system rested upon the shogun's subsequent move to pin the peasantry to their villages, to continue the subordination of the daimyo by weakening their defenses, and to emasculate the armed retainers. In short, the *kokudaka* required the top-to-bottom reorganization of society. In return for compliance, Ieyasu offered the ruling class both political stability and enhanced seigneurial incomes. But, to make good on this offer, Ieyasu had to move in

concert with the daimyo against village elites who stood between the state
and the general body of peasants.

Over the course of the sixteenth century, rural society had become militarized. Peasants took up arms—becoming *jizamurai* or warrior-farmers—in
defense of their communities. In his efforts to open the village to greater
taxation, Ieyasu unleashed the so-called Sword Hunt first on his lands and
later on those of his vassals. Village by village, weapons were confiscated,
the peasantry made compliant, and land productivity measured and registered. Simultaneously, the power of village elites was attacked. Known collectively as the *oyakata*, the most powerful households of the village had
across the sixteenth and seventeenth centuries oriented village institutions
and associations to aggrandize land and compel labor services from the poorer households around them. They indentured some villagers as hereditary
servants (*fudai genin* and *genin*) and then appended them to their households.
Others were set up as branch (*bunke*) households with full village membership, but held to the main family by corporate bonds. Others lived as separate
and unrelated households (*nago*), but were required to provision labor services or pay rent.

Because these arrangements prevented the ruling elite from taking a
greater share of rural income, Ieyasu set himself to break *oyakata* control
over the village. As his men disarmed villages and registered land, they also
freed the various types of dependent and branch households and set them up
as self-supporting farmers. Land was taken from the *oyakata* estate and given
over to former dependents, or *kobyakushu*. These households were also encouraged to occupy property abandoned by samurai who left for the castle
towns as well as any nearby scrap of waste or deserted land.

This bundle of reforms was intended to set up hundreds of thousands of
smallholders across the country, each with land sufficient to meet their tax
obligations and feed their families. However, the mechanics of tax collection
had the unintended effect of opening the way for old and new village elites to
regain some lost ground. Though the total take of the Tokugawa land tax was
determined by the land's productivity, the daimyo's agents collected the tax
not from individual households but as a lump sum. Yet there were no clear or
enforced procedures for choosing the village headmen assigned to press taxes
from individual villagers, or for the collection of individual tax receipts. The
headman's only obligation was to meet the total levy. How he did so was
largely up to him. Beginning in the early seventeenth century a motley crew
of former oyakata, rusticated samurai, village bullies, and upstart peasants
rose to village head and proceeded to leverage their newfound authority over
tax collection to build up personal landholdings, while protecting themselves
against schemes emanating from the castle towns to reduce their influence.

They purposely set up detached branch families and servants on holdings
too small to be viable and disenfranchised the poor and weak by excluding

them from the official registries of village members. They shifted a relatively greater burden of the land taxes onto weaker households and they took advantage of the fact that property rights remained poorly defined to recoup land. As these assaults on their holdings and assets unfolded, smallholders also witnessed the slow but steady degrading of their farms through subdivision. With the reestablishment of social order, and the taking away of land from estate holders and its distribution to their formerly dependent households, peasants had once again started to marry early, have children, and set up their sons on their own farms. Consequently, between 1600 and 1700, Japan's population grew by at least 30 percent, and perhaps as much as 50 percent. Desperate, many peasants sold, commended, or pawned their farms. In a reversal of earlier trends, the period between 1670 and 1730 witnessed a dramatic increase in tenancy and land concentration.

The Tokugawa state tried to prevent the collapse of the small-holding sector by banning land sales and land forfeitures. It even promulgated implausible bans on land sales (1643) and on subdivision (1673). Yet, even as the Tokugawa sought to protect smallholders, it undermined their solvency by raising taxes: an increase in the effective tax rate on land from 29 to 36 percent in 1722 instigated an upsurge in land forfeitures and sales. Peasants responded by commending their land to powerful households in exchange for debt relief, patronage, and protection. But landlords, seeing the possibility of higher rents, had no desire to burden their lands with such claims. They pushed for and got outright transfers of land from poorer villagers. These developments went against the interests of the state but, having pulled the samurai out of the village, the domain lords and central government were unable to intervene to prevent the dissolution of Ieyasu's project and soon sided with landlords in an effort to stabilize their own tax stream. In 1723, the central government recognized the forfeiture of debtor land.

The number of landless and near-landless households thereafter rose even as Japan's population stopped growing. These processes were first felt in the peripheries (Shimano, Aizu, Yamanashi, Fukushima, Matsumoto), where holdings were more fragmented to begin with; labor patronage was more likely to persist; taxes were higher because domains tended to be more contiguous and therefore more easily managed; and peasants were burdened with the cost of converting dry-land grains such as buckwheat or cotton to rice for tax payment. Moreover, peripheral landlords were more likely to be former samurai, who remained behind to manage their holdings, and who therefore started off with far greater prestige and authority within the village. Consequently, their estates tended to be quite large, spread over many villages, and easier to protect against Ieyasu's reforms. Nevertheless, land concentration and dispossession of the smallholder was felt near the centers of power too. In some hamlets as many as two-thirds of households living between 1685 and 1870 were tenants. In the villages of the agriculturally rich Kinai plain near Kyoto and Osaka, 50–70 percent of households were landless by the nineteenth century. By the time of the Meiji Restoration, 70 percent of all land was worked by tenants. In sum, while Ieyasu's reforms raised initial tax receipts and pacified the country, they failed to create political structures that might protect the small-holding tax base. As that was undercut, so too were state revenues.

Circumstances did not seem especially conducive to economic growth circa 1700. Landlords appeared set to levy rents regardless of productivity, while the heavily indebted peasantry was probably too poor to accumulate and improve even if they had wanted. However, as village landlords and the rural poor competed over the latter's labor new possibilities opened up. Finding it impossible to re-create the prior labor regimes, which were built upon various forms of captured and bonded labor as well as fixed dues and rents, the new landlords had little choice but to turn to leasing or hiring laborers. At the same time, they improved their ability to raise their income by insisting on the right to replace tenants at will and willy nilly they tied rents to land productivity. In the face of such pressure, tenants had little choice but to compete for leaseholds by demonstrating an ability and willingness to experiment and innovate in pursuit of higher productivity.

Given the sequence of developments, it is clear that new forms of tenancy in land did not appear in response to markets; rather, the establishment of capitalist property relations in the countryside ignited commercialization, pushing market forces deeper and further than ever before, and in turn unleashed growth. A multitude of agricultural innovations followed, picked up by the most commercial agriculturalists first. Commercial growers improved irrigation, an essential component of paddy farming. They adopted new and better rice seeds as well as new tools such as the *senba-koki* (which separated the grain from stalks), *sengoku-toshi* and *mangoku-toshi* (which threshed the rice and separated rice from chaff), *karausu* (which separated the grain from the husk), and *bitchu-guwa* (weeding tools and plows). Japanese peasants also adopted more effective crop rotations and improved their management of the soil by increasing their use of traditional fertilizers as well as experimenting with superior ones, using fish, oil, and bean cakes, for example. The prices of these commercially available fertilizers remained stable even as demand for them grew, pointing to a highly responsive manufacturing sector that scaled up production in ways that kept costs low. Many of these improvements were known on the Continent and appeared in agricultural treatises, but given the very different social relations on the land, and the continued emphasis on subsistence, they went largely unused in China. Whereas the productivity of labor in China stagnated, Japanese labor grew more productive and all-important rice yields grew from the middle of the eighteenth century on.

That land productivity grew at a time of general labor shortages was all the more impressive. Beginning in the 1720s, the number of births fell and the population stopped growing. For the next 130 years it remained roughly at twenty-six million. The exact causes are unclear, but a combination of factors seems to have been at work. First, the age of marriage rose. The growing pool of poor men were compelled to put off marriage until they had acquired sufficient skills or capital, or not marry at all. Second, and more importantly, as women's wages rose, especially in domestic textile manufacturing, parents put off finding husbands for their daughters in order to capture their wages. Daughters' earnings helped to build up the family holding or offset the cost of setting sons up. Consequently, most women from poor households married after their twentieth birthday and one-third married after their twenty-fifth. As women and men put off marriage the birth rate fell and its effect on the labor market was clear. As population growth stopped, competition for labor drove wages up 75 percent between the 1720s and 1820s.

Parallel and related developments in manufacturing reinforced these trends. Like much of the early modern world, cities in Japan were primarily sites of consumption. When Ieyasu forced samurai into the castle towns, required daimyo to embark on triennial visits to Edo, and placed trade in key commodities such as rice and silk in the hands of urban guilds, he created vast consumption cities. The network of roads he built to facilitate the swift movement of troops doubled as trade routes. Consequently, Japan was one of the most urbanized countries of the seventeenth century, with one-fifth of its population in towns and cities. At half a million people each, Edo (Tokyo) and Osaka were the world's largest premodern cities. Though economically constrained by feudal political arrangements, castle towns were nonetheless sources of early markets for tenant farmers.

By the 1750s, however, the center of commercial dynamism had left the castle towns for the countryside. The relative cheapening of grain, made possible by rising output and labor productivity, meant more cash in the hands of villagers and their demand for manufactured goods rose. Manufacturing became an increasingly profitable outlet for labor and capital. The relative value of cotton manufactures to rice rose from 18 percent to 105 percent in the century after 1714, an indication of the improving terms of trade for manufacturers.

Initially taken up by tenant families and smallholders who were eager to supplement farming income and utilize underemployed family labor, manufacturing became the most important source of earnings for many. Weaving specialists known as *oriya* abandoned farming altogether and congregated to create industrial districts where they managed small workshops with many workers and looms. In 1842 in one Izumi village there were eighteen weaving specialists and fifty family workers, along with five indentured servants and eighty-two hired pieceworkers: the largest employer in this village had twenty-one workers, of which only six were family members. Ten of the eighteen households in the village had entirely abandoned farming and only 14 percent still farmed. In parts of Owari in 1845, only one in five households farmed, whereas just under one-third worked entirely in weaving. In another district, 322 weaving specialists in forty-two villages employed 1,435 looms and the eight largest producers owned 15–29 looms each. Again the contrast to China is stark, where only the poorest families devoted themselves entirely to weaving, they did not hire assistants, and they were confronted by worsening terms of trade as the price of grain rose faster than cloth. Sidelines were not the dead end in Japan that they were in China.

Rising real wages in weaving meant that as Japanese households sloughed off farming and spent more time in manufacturing they saw a rise in income and standards of living. Unable to locate in the guild-controlled cities, manufacturers congregated in rural towns, along water and roadways. Following cheap labor and rural market trends, they made swift inroads and soon cut into the profits of the established urban producers who for two centuries had benefited from monopoly protections granted by the state. In 1744, Kyoto guild weavers already complained of competition from rural weavers and demanded that the state put an end to these illicit producers. However, growing rural demand for manufactured goods, the spread of industrial crops, and the fact that the countryside offered few restrictions combined to create a space in which this new breed of merchant only grew stronger. Recognizing their growing importance the otherwise conservative 1840 Tempo Reforms finally abolished the guild system and, by 1859, 90 percent of silk textiles were produced under the supervision of rural producers and marketed by small-town merchants.

By the middle of the nineteenth century a novel class of commercial landlords-cum-merchant-manufacturers known as *gōnō* dominated social and economic life. Because political institutions remained closed to the *gōnō* on account of their commoner status, these men had no choice but to reinvest their capital in productive enterprises, thus benefiting and driving the dynamic rural economy. They did not fully abandon their interest in farming, in part because of the inability of lords to raise the land tax to match productivity gains. The *gōnō* led the way in greater use of fertilizers, draft animals, and new rice strains, as well as better farm management methods. But they also took a portion of their profits and invested in trade and manufacturing. By virtue of their prominence in the rural economy they emerged as powerful advocates for village interests against feudal authority. Like the village headmen who refused to give their lord a loan without setting conditions, *gōnō* wished to protect themselves and villagers from feudal fines, levies, and forced loans. But as landlords, merchants, and workshop owners, politically invested in maintaining the commercial property and labor markets that secured their profits, they were also targets of rural discontent.

In the nineteenth century, the *gōnō* looked for a new political constitution that would end feudal impositions from above, liquidate trade monopolies, and protect them from the growing tide of popular demands from below. The Meiji Restoration of 1869 provided that solution. Though the success of the subsequent transformation was not guaranteed by the presence of the *gōnō*, or by the dynamism of the rural economy, it is inconceivable without them. After a period characterized by political activism, liberal reform, and conservative counterattack, the 1889 constitution gave the *gōnō* a voice in politics, recognized their property rights, provided them with security against civil unrest, and disenfranchised the rural masses. The commercialization of agriculture deepened, now reaching those secluded areas where peasants and cottagers had held out. Industrialization accelerated, with the emergence of large business conglomerates or zaibatsu that combined trading groups, industry, and manufacturing banks in conjunction with state support. The full transition to capitalism was swift. By 1900, Japan competed internationally as both an imperial and industrial power.

The transformation of English and Japanese farming was not inevitable. It did not flow from the steady evolution of markets, the removal of barriers to growth by progressive sections of the elites, or by a human propensity to truck and barter, as argued by Adam Smith and his current followers. In fact, the generalized farming for the accumulation of money, rather than for the useful purpose of obtaining food and fiber for the household and community, was isolated to a few corners of the early modern world and only then on account of the outcomes of prior political struggles over land, labor, and surpluses.

In early modern England and Japan, the ruling elites and peasants came into conflict over the customary questions of personal liberty and rights. The outcome was in these two cases anomalous because the subsequent political settlements gave rise to novel economic modus operandi. In Tokugawa Japan and Tudor England, governmental reforms to consolidate the feudal order ended the subordination of villagers to lords and village grandees and, while new arrangements endowed villagers with the means to see to their own livelihood, these also required that peasants take up leaseholds or hire themselves out as laborers. In fairly short order, English and Japanese landholders gained the ability to change rents regularly in accord with the land's productive value. Drawn into competition, lease-holding farmers had no option but to abandon the age-old practice of self-provisioning and instead specialize for the market place. They methodically built up cash reserves, delayed marriage, recruited labor among their landless neighbors, and plowed earnings into agricultural projects likely to garner higher returns relative to the expenditure of their time and effort.

The more successful farmers gradually compelled the less competitive ones to leave agriculture for alternative pursuits. At first, they worked up manufactured goods in concert with farming, hoping to hold onto their land, but sloughed it off as their earnings from manufacturing superseded those from agriculture. Manufacturing towns, supplied with cheaper and cheaper food and raw materials from the increasingly productive rural economy, sprung up in a spurt of new urbanization and introduced a new dynamism to the town-country divide. These developments stood in marked contrast to the evolution of agricultural practices in contemporaneous France and China, to which we turn in the next chapter.

Before we turn our attention to those countries, however, it is worth pausing to consider how capitalism spread. Whereas we contend that the English and Japanese transitions to capitalism are best understood as the unintended outcome of the struggle between (and among) elites and peasants to take a greater share of the rural surplus, this is not to say that capitalism's subsequent spread need adhere to the same mechanisms. Once capitalism matured and operated on a more global scale, others were able to copy it and in so doing initiate their own capitalist development. In other words, it did not take hold outside of England and Japan in the same manner that it first appeared. As we shall see, in twentieth-century France, Taiwan, and Brazil, creating capitalism was an intentional policy of elites and states. But just as we have seen in England and Japan, these later transitions were not straightforward—they did not flow from the existing global division of labor and the peasants' desire to benefit from trade, which they could hardly have done given their lack of global competitiveness—but required significant state effort, intervention, and often coercion.

NOTES

1. John Worlidge, *A Compleat System of Husbandry and Gardening; or, The Gentleman's Companion, in the Business and Pleasures of a Country Life . . . The Whole Collected from, and Containing What Is Most Valuable in All the Books Hitherto Written upon this Subject; . . .* (n.p.: J. Pickard, A. Bettesworth, and E. Curll, 1716), 21.

2. Ibid., 27.

3. Ibid., 113.

4. Ibid., 13.

5. Ibid., 21–22.

6. Ibid., 22.

7. Ibid., 263.

8. Ibid., 43.

9. Ibid.

10. Michael Cooper, *They Came to Japan: An Anthology of Reports on Japan, 1543–1640* (Berkeley: University of California Press, 1965).

Chapter Four

Malthusian Limits in the Early Modern World

Peasants and Markets

In the conflicts of their respective feudal eras, the rural populations of England and Japan not only gained freedom from legal restraints but also found themselves bereft of land with which to support themselves. They therefore had to compete against one another for tenancies and sell their farm output on the market for the money to obtain and maintain the leases. English and Japanese farmers had to accumulate surpluses, make their time monetarily valuable, and eke out more value with every added input of labor and capital. Early modern France and China did not follow this path of economic development (see table 4.1).

The inhabitants of France and China not only secured legal freedom but also the landholdings with which to support themselves. Consequently, they did not have to maximize the monetary returns of every moment of labor. In many cases, when faced with the opportunities of markets and pressures on resources, the peasants of France and China actually found it rational to put in extra time working rather than spend household income on labor-saving implements. This path of labor-intensive expansion has been called involution, a term describing the addition of greater and greater quantities of labor—whether in field work or household manufacturing—at stagnating or falling hourly returns. The rising labor inputs allowed peasants to subsist on smaller and smaller holdings, but provided no avenue to save and invest. In the best cases, earnings at the end of the year were greater than they otherwise would have been, but hourly productivity and wages did not grow and savings were minuscule. The peasant custom of setting up children by subdi-

viding the family holdings, tools, and capital among them encouraged involutionary behavior insofar as subdivision yielded smaller and more fragmented farms. Subsequent generations thereby found themselves having to devote
more household labor per acre to generating additional income from their
now smaller farms. In this way, the peasants' possession of the land did not
ultimately work to their advantage.

Moreover, since the spare household labor, relative to the inadequate size
of their plots, made the peasants of France and China intently seek remunerative employment, they succumbed more readily to landlords interested in
appropriating the benefits of their work. Unlike England and Japan, the managers of larger farms in France and China found that they could profit by
substituting the toil of the growing pool of land-hungry peasants for relatively expensive and labor-saving tools. Consequently, the peasants' tenacious
grip on the land, coupled with the desire to establish sons on holdings of their
own, strengthened the hand of employers, who had added incentive to exploit
the cheapness of their neighbors' labor as land grew relatively dearer. In this
way, village differentiation—the process whereby some managed to build up
larger farms while others sank into poverty and even landlessness—offered
opportunities for profit yet relieved the better-off peasants of the requirement
to cut costs by improving tools and reducing labor inputs.

Finally, it should be noted that well-to-do villagers of France and China
sought at every opportunity to leave farming and join the state, where greater
incomes and status were to be found. They invested capital in the pursuit of
degrees and the purchase of office.

In short, in both France and China one observes growth of output without
transformative development, or Malthusian involutionary growth. Thomas
Malthus famously argued in his 1798 essay on population that there was a
natural and unstoppable tendency for population to outstrip resources.
Though this "iron law" has long been discredited, the tendency among peasant societies for output to grow at the expense of labor productivity has long
been observed. To flesh out the manner in which this occurred, and its
underlying causes, we will take up two questions in this chapter. How did the
growth of the population and markets affect agricultural techniques? How
did the peasants contend with the demands of landlords, state officials, and
their households' consumption? In answering these questions, we will show
that the peasants of France and China developed inventive and original forms
of labor-intensive subsistence agriculture that supported not only greater
numbers of people but also large and complex states, yet provided no path to
industrialization.

EARLY MODERN FRANCE

Arthur Young, an Englishman of the lesser gentry, published several books on the agriculture of the British Isles and became the editor of a leading journal on the subject in the 1770s and 1780s. By age fifty, when Young traveled across France at the time of its Revolution, he had become a renowned and respected scholar of agriculture. His thousand-plus pages of notes comprise perhaps the best contemporary commentary on French farming. Some of his most astonishing notes concern the relationship between agriculture and manufacturing.

> The greatest fabrics . . . are the cottons and woolens of Normandy, the woolens of Picardy and Champagne, the linens of Bretagne, and the silks and hardware of the Lyonnais. Now, if manufactures be the true encouragement of agriculture, the vicinity of those great fabrics ought to be the best cultivated districts in the kingdom. I have visited all of those manufactures, and remarked the attendant culture, which is unexceptionably so execrable, that one would be much more inclined to think there was something pestiferous to agriculture in the neighborhood of a manufacture, than to look up to it as a mean of encouragement. [1]

Young wrote that the immense manufactures of Lyon had great renown and that the workshops of the nearby town of Saint-Étienne were among the most flourishing in Europe. But after visiting the countryside, he had little doubt that the Lyonnais was one of the most miserable provinces of France. Young argued that this poverty resulted from the unwillingness of landed classes to imagine better forms of land tenure. Although plots of fewer than two hectares covered the Lyonnais, the largest farms belonged to the privileged classes of the towns, whose leases often required the smallholders to furnish their homes with wood and their tables with dairy products, poultry, fruit, and wine. The leases could require the peasants to do housework in the landlord's urban residence, and to plant and clip young trees and cart hay and straw on his domains. Many of the leases required payment of the seigneurial dues owed annually to the proprietor.

Young recognized that the key reason for these leases "arises very much from the poverty of the French tenantry . . . these poor farmers are *métayers* [sharecroppers], who find nothing towards stocking a farm but labour and implements; and being exceedingly miserable, there is rarely a sufficiency of the latter. . . . Such a tenantry . . . are . . . at the landlord's mercy." [2] Proprietors had little trouble turning a profit on the work of poor peasants in need of rented land to make ends meet. Young found that landlords took about half of their sharecroppers' output and about as much income as did English landowners even though the latter's tenants were far more productive.

Since French landlords secured good returns from the traditional forms of land tenure they had little reason to invest in improvements. In the plains of Forez in the Lyonnais, the landed classes did not devote any income to the development of pasture, fodder crops, and animal husbandry despite the success of experiments with artificial prairies. The landlords defended a profitable, albeit sclerotic, system of sharecropping that restricted the extent of arable land through binding rotations of wheat, rye, barley, oats, and fallow so as to prevent intensive farming and soil exhaustion. Rather than receive abundant nourishment in stables, cows scavenged for it on fallow land and thus generated meager amounts of fertilizer. The domains of the Lyonnais had dreadfully weak yields of two, and no greater than three, times the seeding of wheat, rye, and oats.

Young observed that the Île-de-France, the province around Paris—which offered a much larger market than did Lyon and Saint-Étienne—had excellent soil, rivaling the best of Europe, but poor husbandry and consequently extensive fallow lands. He noted that the domains yielded as much grain as did English ones, but also noted that the spring corn was miserable, nowhere amounting to even 50 percent of what it should. Young wrote that wheat and rye dominated the crop rotations yet did not generate any more of these grains than they would have had these crops appeared less frequently and alternated with barley, tares, or beans. Turnips and clover, Young argued, would have improved the soil for the grains and provided nourishment for farm animals, which in turn would have generated nutrient-rich manure fertilizer and allowed for the elimination of the fallow.

Young wrote that the landowners showed little inclination to develop agriculture by investing in improved rotations of this sort. Their farmers did not spread fertile muds on the land, grow meadows of nitrogen-rich grasses, or advance funds for stables, fences, drains, gates, stiles, posts, or rails, not to mention the periodic repairs. The landlords, calculated Young, invested half as much in permanent improvements as did their counterparts across the Channel. Without the proper farm infrastructure, their tenants had no choice but to maintain the minimum number of oxen needed to work the land and to maintain the farm animals in ways prohibitive of improved husbandry: "the open arable fields of Picardy, Artois, part of Normandy, the Île-de-France, Brie and the Pays de Beauce, are cursed with . . . the rights of common pasturage, commencing on given days, when under corn, and throughout the fallow year."

Young provided an expert description of the substandard agriculture of the Paris Basin yet little explanation beyond the failings of the privileged orders, accustomed to the easy returns generated from the labor of land-hungry peasants. He argued that "the leading mischief, in most of the courses of crops throughout France, is the too great eagerness to have as much wheat or rye as possible. A vast population, and a subsistence which experience has proved precarious, have probably occasioned it: but the blindness of the conduct can, with enlightened persons, admit of no doubt." Young made the case that outlays in improvements would have been exposed to the seigneurial rents of the nobles and clergy and thus rarely saw the light of day. Specialized cattle rearing, Young argued, required investments, which farmers, exposed to rapacious rents, would not risk making. The "blindness" of the nobles also apparently accounted for the persistence, in the Île-de-France, of the "miserable fantastical division of property which seems to have been contrived, for giving an occupier as much trouble and expense as possible in the culture of his scraps of fields. In England we have been making, for 40 or 50 years past, a considerable progress in the allotment and enclosure of open fields."[3]

Young's assessment of French agriculture was a product of his social class and time, which made him see the husbandry of his own country as the natural and logical model for all farmers. He probably would have had difficulty fathoming that the husbandry of England resulted from political acts, from the gentry's capacity to impose its interests on society and reorganize the agrarian landscape to suit its purposes. Young probably would never have recognized that English agriculture was predicated on the dislocation and anguish of rural inhabitants deprived of small farms and common rights. He probably would have had difficulty comprehending that in a different context, such as France, the proprietors might not have found it in their interest to sort out all of the strips of land and make the countryside amenable to forms of agriculture associated with nitrogen-restoring fodder crops and specialized animal husbandry.

Young recognized that French landlords secured as much rent from their tenants as did their counterparts in England. Landlords of the Île-de-France, he wrote, obtained the highest rents in the country. He noted that wheat yields on certain farms of the Île-de-France were as high, sometimes even higher, than those of England. These observations seem odd amid Young's gloomy description of French agriculture.

The only explanation one can offer for the high rents and yields in the Île-de-France is the ingenuity of the rural population. Young repeatedly disparaged the French peasants: "Whenever bad management is found in those rich and well cultivated districts, it is sure to be found on small farms."[4] "Small properties are carried much too far in France; . . . a most miserable population has been created by them, which ought to have no existence; . . . their division should be restrained by express laws."[5] Yet Young was a conscientious observer and never knowingly falsified the record. When he went beyond these sorts of superficial statements he remarked that the smallholders made up for their deficiencies in spring corn with viticulture, that is, the practice of growing grapevines, especially for winemaking. French farmers, Young noted, produced maize, olives, silk, and alfalfa. He noted that Normandy had fine pastures and Flanders a wealth of farm products. Young wrote that Alsace and parts of Artois, as well as the banks of the Garonne, had quality agriculture, rivaling that of England, thanks to plants adapted to the soil. He also observed that enclosures took place in the Pyrenees and other mountainous areas where the communities were the proprietors of the wastes and sold them to farmers eager to cultivate them. This practice, Young observed, invariably led to improvements.

Young implicitly acknowledged the superiority of peasant farming when writing about the contrast between the foregoing examples of progressive husbandry and the waste plains of Bretagne, Poitou, Maine, Guyenne, Picardy, Artois, part of Normandy, the Île-de-France, Brie, and the Pays de Beauce, where seigneurs ceded the use of their uncultivated land for dues and labor services but retained ultimate possession. These plains, Young wrote, remained barren, bereft of fodder crops, and desolate, with fallow land, common pastures, and few farm animals.

Young probably did not delve more deeply into this contrast, because it did not square with his studies in England. There, the agricultural revolution entailed enclosures, the grouping of farms into larger contiguous units, and the eradication of small holdings. What is more, improvements in land productivity in England increased the standard of living, and everything Young saw and measured in France pointed to indigence. His intellectual paradigm did not comprise instances of progressive husbandry coupled with grinding poverty. It did not prepare him to understand the dynamics of French agriculture.

Such an understanding could only come from a historical account rather than a study of the agricultural market and the monetary value of land. In the medieval period, French peasants resisted the feudal claims of the lords, and, by the thirteenth century, succeeded in establishing the inheritability of their tenures and de facto property rights over the greater part of the farmland (see chapter 2). The nobles came to accept the legality of the peasants' plots over the following two centuries yet also began to make periodic surveys of seigneurial inventories to define their rights. Duties that had fallen into abeyance were discovered in the unnoticed implications of customs, others were invented and added to the tangle of levies, and a heavy seigneurial burden accumulated on the peasantry. The peasants also had to pay tax collectors and vendors of essential goods, and often, to make ends meet, had to sell their produce when prices were lowest. After a long period of economic and population growth from the end of the 1400s until the 1670s and 1680s, the peasants faced mounting difficulties, as the subdivision of their plots through inheritances left them with parcels too small to support their households. They faced crushing debts and foreclosures, and the nobles were left with estates as large as three hundred hectares in the Paris Basin amid an overall context of crisis that lasted into the first half of the eighteenth century.

But then the conjuncture turned, as the large estates began to break off smaller farms for peasants, who succeeded in making them viable by dint of the positive examples of labor-intensive husbandry noted by Young. The peasants always had more labor within their households than they could employ productively on and off their plots and consequently moved into labor-intensive lines in which their superabundant capacity for work gave them a competitive advantage. They turned to market gardening in the parishes bordering Paris to the northeast in the decades following 1740. They continued gardening with spades and sickles rather than more productive implements available at that time. Spades and sickles did not accomplish much work relative to the labor expended. Yet the peasant had more than enough hands in their household to achieve yields at least as high as they would have gotten from the latest tools. The benefit of the spades and sickles was that they did not require additional outlays of family income.

Peasants of the Paris Basin also farmed vineyards, which, like the gardens, yielded more income per hectare than did wheat fields. They did not need cattle, animal fertilizer, plows, carts, or other costly inputs to work vineyards, just human labor. In contrast to cereal cultivation and its dead seasons, viticulture filled the calendar year with breaking up the land, layering to multiply the base of the vines, three plowings with hoes, putting in stakes for vine shoots, repairing trellises, pruning and trimming, preparing vessels and basins, harvesting, fermenting, pressing the wine, and many other tasks, which together permitted households to put their stores of labor to gainful use. The peasants had far fewer prairies and woods than did the urban landowners, yet nearly all of the vineyards. The peasants of the Île-de-France took the revenue from their labor-intensive lines and devoted it to the acquisition of tiny parcels of land, even contracting debts to accumulate as much land as possible, in the hopes of attaining self-sufficiency. Later in life, when too old to work, they sold pieces of land to assure their retirement.

Similarly, in the Lyonnais, where the population grew rapidly in the eighteenth century into one of the densest concentrations in the realm, the peasants converted woods and stony soils to vineyards with the aim of complementing their holdings in rye, wheat, hemp, and oats devoted to local use. The Lyonnais became a jigsaw puzzle of tiny vineyards spread through the larger arable fields of the landed classes. The vineyards required hardly any expenditure, beyond stubborn work, and brought in two and a half to five times more income than did fields of grain.

Rural inhabitants of the Lyonnais also generated income working as lumberjacks and in household industry. In the mountains of the Beaujolais, they labored the winter as weavers and spinners of hemp cloth for export. They worked in manufacturing in the parishes around Saint-Étienne. The peasants of the surrounding countryside filled the downtime in the agricultural year with labor in nail forges and with piecework weaving ribbons from the material supplied by merchants. Peasants in the mountainous areas of Forez made dishes, tools, cloth, and wicker chairs in wood workshops. In the area around Saint-Bonnet, the peasants worked in forges and the related lock-making workshops. They had a lively desire to possess land and used the income from manufacturing to purchase small properties. The number of peasant parcels multiplied in this part of Forez through the eighteenth and nineteenth centuries.

The peasants of Poitou, in the west, had from as little as 2 percent of the land around Poitiers to as much as 25 percent in the outlying areas of the Vendée. Yet they had around 40 percent of the land planted in hemp and anywhere from 30 to 85 percent of the land in vines. Hemp was labor intensive, requiring soaking the stems, grinding the dried ones a month later, cleaning and combing the material, spinning it, and then putting the hanks on winders for the making of cloth. Artisans usually worked a quarter of the year in rural cloth workshops, the rest on their parcels of land. The peasants planted turnips after the hemp to bring nutrients to the topsoil and prepare it for rye. This subsistence crop, which predominated on the peasants' arable fields, fetched a lower price than did wheat but did better on lands lacking fertilizer.

The rural households of Poitou gained further subsistence resources by sending members, whose labor was not fully put to use on their farms, off to other parts of the province for harvest work. Large landowners around Thouars, a densely populated region of vineyards, had more day laborers on hand than they needed for the wheat harvests. Peasants left to work in the neighboring Loudunais and then returned when it was time to harvest the grapes. Such migrations increased, as the population continued to grow in the nineteenth century, and later declined when farmers cleared wasteland, suppressed fallow, developed cattle rearing, and ceased to rely on so many laborers to harvest hay, wheat, and cereal stubbles.

Cereals covered at least 70, and usually 80 to 90, percent of Poitevin fields, especially those of the landed classes. They also took up the majority of the peasants' time. Even so, fodder crops, for commercial cattle, began to appear on the plots of peasants and sharecroppers in the wooded countryside with small irregular-shaped fields and many hedges and trees. The smallholders developed crop rotations of buckwheat to clean, loosen, and break down the soil, and then various bushes, leguminous plants, and sainfoin, a plant for livestock feed, farmed with barley and oats, after the harvest of wheat. The bushes on the heaths fixed lime and phosphorous acid (in the same way legumes do) in these soils naturally deficient of such nutrients. Peasants left the broom and gorse on uncultivated paths to be saturated in rain and animal droppings, and trampled by cattle and people. They obtained excellent fertilizer in this way and had fodder to rear about one draft animal per two hectares, a proportion superior to that obtained on the commercial cereal domains and open fields of northern France.

To practice this sort of animal husbandry, the peasants of Poitou tilled plots for several years, abandoned them, and then cleared other unplanted lands. They used hoes to divide the broom and gorse, and to plow several times with the aim of breaking up the roots and taking out the weeds. The husbandry required enormous amounts of labor involving both sexes and all ages. To casual observers it may have appeared to be time wasted, but it actually was an intentional strategy to put excess household labor to use raising yields and so maintaining an increasingly dense population on small farms.

The peasants of the Berry, in central France, reared oxen. Horses did farm work more rapidly but cost more to buy and maintain. Since the peasants did not face pressure to maximize the market value of their time, they saw horses as pointless expenses. They reserved their best land for subsistence crops rather than for fodder, and their oxen thus did not produce optimal amounts of fertilizer. Yet the peasants still had more manure for their fields than the landed classes of the Berry had for their commercial cereal domains, which typically had extensive sheep grazing, fallow, and few bovine animals. The peasants intensively applied household labor to farming peas, broad beans, and turnips, which renewed the soil and increased yields. Fallow receded from their plots long before it did from the large domains. The peasants laid out gardens and vineyards, and farmed hemp for household clothing and sale of the surplus garments. To maximize the soil nutrients going to their plants, they worked with spades and hoes, which went deeper into the soil, and turned, ventilated, and weeded it better than did plows. Spades and hoes required much more labor, but the peasants only had to take wood from the forests to make them and did not incur expenses to maintain and replace them. The peasants saved instead for new parcels to assure their food needs.

The peasants' ingenuity in applying household labor to wring additional resources from their plots and assure their subsistence undoubtedly provides the key to understanding the high yields and rents that Young observed in the Paris Basin. Over the course of the eighteenth century, the population of the region grew by nearly a third, making it the most densely populated in the realm after Artois. The number of peasant households grew, along with their need to put their labor to gainful use.

Some of the benefits of the peasant labor accrued to the agricultural managers of the great lords of Paris and Versailles. These managers paid money to lease estates and then threw their weight around in the seigneur's name, hiring local laborers, engaging artisans, collecting dues, and amassing grain for charity, wages, and other sorts of influence. They often benefited from the lord's fiscal privileges and held much of the local peasantry in debt and dependence. Young probably did not bother to include these farm managers in his notes for the reason that they acquired revenue in much the same way as did the lords. If one looks at the investment patterns of these lease-holders, one finds that they sank their revenue into land purchases, even to the point of taking on debts themselves. Unlike the yeomen tenants of Eng-land, who compulsively amassed surpluses and cut costs, the tenant farmers of the Paris Basin dissipated their capital in attempts to assure landholdings and social respectability for their children, and probably hoped their heirs would one day become noble.

In this way, peasant differentiation proceeded over the course of the eighteenth century yet did not lead to a more advanced form of husbandry. The leaseholders worked under the nobles to exploit the peasants in tradition-al ways, availing themselves of the peasants' eagerness to put the underem-ployed members of rural households to gainful use and bring in the income needed to sustain the dense population. Tenant farmers capitalized on the peasants' experience and knowledge of intensively weeding and farming nitrogen-restoring legumes, and applying all the manure and compost that could be scraped together, to get more out of the land. The peasants used all of the knowledge they had accumulated to obtain wages toiling on the estates of the Paris Basin. They increased output through an even greater increase of labor input. However, because high yields obtained in this way came at lower returns for each hour of work, wages declined relative to the price of leases and grain over the course of the eighteenth century.

In this sense, the increased productivity of the land did not reflect devel-opment. Rising labor productivity was necessary for improving living stan-dards, because it gave the landowners the margins to offer the peasants an increased share of the output thanks to the enlarged economic pie made through the more productive work. But in the Île-de-France, high yields coincided, not with relatively fewer labor inputs, but with even more drud-gery. This phenomenon undoubtedly explains how it was possible for Young to observe high yields and rents amid peasants bowed by hard labor, diets deprived of meat and cheese, and a general state of poverty very different from the appearance of the English countryside.

The peasants of France, then, raised output by devoting extra labor to the fields but had to contend with the demands of urban landowners and seig-neurs. The peasantry provided the towns with textiles and foods but did not purchase items in return. As the population of the Paris Basin grew more dense, it raised output at declining returns for each additional hour of work, and had little discretionary income to sustain a consumer market. Inhabitants raised the productivity of the land but suffered from mounting poverty. Their standard of living declined as their growing numbers competed for relatively scarce resources in land, food, and jobs. Wages failed to keep pace with prices, especially those of grain, and day laborers had to devote larger shares of their household income to food. The vast majority of peasants did not have the farmland and surpluses to sell and benefit from the high prices. While no one actually starved, the population's long-term malnutrition is well documented. A symptom of the economic malaise was the voluntary restriction of births as early as the 1720s, and quite markedly after 1775–1780, in areas of the Paris Basin such as the Beauvaisis. Another was the rising tide of bread riots. The Île-de-France had the highest incidence of rural revolts in the realm, along with the Orléanais, Blésois, Touraine, and Berry, between 1661 and 1789. In that year, the Paris Basin witnessed the greatest peasant Jacquerie, a communal uprising or revolt, in its history, involving more peasants and more destruction of property than the anti-feudal uprising of 1358 described in chapter 2.

In the Lyonnais, the low-cost vineyards did not lay the basis for sustainable growth. Only a third of the vintners owned the minimum of two hectares needed to support a family. The rest had to supplement their incomes in other lines, often as laborers on the arable fields of the landed classes. The growing population, and its reliance on labor markets for income and on grain markets for food, drove up the price of rye, the staple crop of the region, higher than the agricultural wages. Growth came to a halt as a result of the saturation of vineyards in the region of Lyon. Wine prices rose over the course of the century, as the population expanded and consumption caught up with the levels it had attained prior to the crisis of the end of the seventeenth century. But output surpassed demand, as much of the urban population, in years of high grain prices, had to sacrifice wine purchases to necessities. Harvests expanded excessively, brought down wine prices in the decade of 1776–1785, and plunged the regional population into a precarious situation.

After 1770, rising land rents and rural poverty reduced the market for nonessential goods and triggered a severe downturn in artisanal activity affecting all the households of the Poitou-Charentes that earned ancillary income producing hemp cloth. While the prices of grain and other products rose, those of wine and flax fell on account of the oversupply of vineyards and hemp fields carved out of the hillsides and poor lands, places where cereals did not grow. The vintners of northern Poitou saw the value of their plots fall in the 1780s. After-death inventories of eastern Poitou show a decline of fortunes in the last third of the century and a particularly sharp drop among day laborers and plowmen without much property. Those of the Gâtine Poitevine, measured against the regional food grains, show a decline of fortunes between the beginning and the end of the eighteenth century. The livestock markets grew exponentially in the fairs of Fontenay and other towns of western Poitou from 1758 to 1776 but then suffered a brutal recession. The lack of fodder made animal fattening impractical, and peasants had to sell the cattle amid falling prices in their effort to eke out a living. The number of poor and beggars grew in western Poitou, and the population of the district (*élection*) of Fontenay actually declined in the years preceding the Revolution of 1789.

In the second half of the eighteenth century, the high price of grain provoked revolts against tax farmers held responsible for depleting the Poitevin peasants' resources. Insurrections swept across Poitou in the spring of 1789, as the peasants confiscated the contents of grain convoys, broke into granaries, and forcibly lowered prices. Over the following years, 119 anti-seigneurial uprisings, and another 205 subsistence revolts, took place in the west of France. In the Lyonnais and Berry, peasants looted grain depots, took over markets, and forcibly lowered prices in 1789 and 1790. The peasants of Berry rebelled against the troops sent to enforce the tax farms of the Old Regime. They seized common lands occupied over previous decades by lords intent on extending the area for grazing larger flocks of sheep. In a word, the growth of the eighteenth century had not ushered in sustainable development but rather a general social crisis.

LATE IMPERIAL CHINA

Catholic French missions to eighteenth-century China were struck by the immense attention of peasants to tilling, weeding, and preparing the soil. They compared Chinese farming to gardening back home.

> It may be of some use to observe that the little efforts and knacks, the inventions, and discoveries, resources, and combinations, that have created what seem like miracles in gardens have been transported on an increased scale into the countryside, and done wonders there . . . as witness manures, which have become so varied, so multiplied, so abundant, so easy to use, so effective, and so well combined.[6]

Anyone who has tended a vegetable garden knows that the secret to bounty is meticulous work. Hours must be spent preparing and spreading compost and manures, weeding and mulching between the rows, carrying, watering, removing slugs and insects, and pruning, while close attention to seeds and rotations is necessary to avoid disease and pests. To describe Chinese farming as gardening is therefore to emphasize not only its high output but also its back-breaking qualities. In other words, the authors of this report are aware that the Chinese peasantry achieved high yields, at times higher than those of their global contemporaries, but did so at great expenditure of effort.

The seventeenth century was a period of economic difficulties worldwide. A long cooling spell known as the Little Ice Age adversely affected farming throughout Eurasia. Though notably the high farming of England and Holland was relatively unaffected, peasants from Spain to Japan experienced hunger. In China, rural hardship brought on by climate change was made worse by two separate but parallel developments. The first was the increase in population. Between 1400 and 1600 the number of people rose from 90 million to between 160 and 200 million. The land under plow and harvests grew too, but not as fast. The second was changes to the legal and social standing of peasant households, as elites drew upon the authority that came with political office and local clan systems to encumber peasant freedoms, while shifting the burden of the land and head taxes onto them. Caught between shrinking farms and rising exploitation, indebted peasants were pressed into legal bondage that lasted several years, decades, or for life and even extended to children.

For many in the second half of the sixteenth century poverty and legal degradation went hand in hand. Men who signed employment contracts that lasted a year or longer were required to call their employer "master" and were considered inferior before the law. Bonded tenants were unable to leave their allotments, were required to obtain their landlord's permission to marry, and were compelled to provide their landlord with meats, eggs, and other items at New Year's.

Peasant discontent correspondingly grew and by the 1620s the Ming dynasty was wracked by a chain of large and small uprisings in which peasants attacked their landlords, burned their houses, and destroyed debt records and rent books. When they could, landlords fled the countryside for the safety of walled towns. But in spring 1644 an army of peasant rebels seized Beijing, causing the emperor to hang himself and setting the remainder of the Ming court to flight. At that moment a nomadic army from northeast Asia, which had been gathering strength for several decades, successfully broke through the border defenses, drove the peasant army from the capital, and in June 1644 proclaimed the founding of a new dynasty, the Qing.

To establish authority, China's new conquerors—the Manchus—needed both to establish a foothold in the countryside, where the great mass of Chinese lived, and to bend former Ming elites to their will. On the one hand, China's new rulers had no desire to facilitate the reestablishment of landlord regulation of peasant lives insofar as this handicapped the collection of taxes, incited social protest and unrest, and generally challenged the crown's authority over local society. On the other hand, the new state needed the cooperation of the traditional ruling elite, whose expertise and experience in the management of state affairs was key to the urgent task of reimposing political order. When the dust finally settled in the 1680s, rural life was greatly transformed.

For their part, peasants retained their hard-won liberties. They were no longer subject to landlords' arbitrary levies and demands for labor services, they were free to take up and abandon leaseholds as they wished, and many won legal title to land occupied during the period of rebellion and war. Landlords, on the other hand, secured title to whatever holdings they had held on to and retained the right to add to these through legal purchases. Thus, while there was no limit to the size of their estates, landlords were prevented from compelling peasants to work on them.

Eager to gain a hold on local society, the newly proclaimed Qing dynasty, headed by Manchus, encouraged these developments through the imposition of new laws and regulations. It imposed measures that prohibited landlords from exercising punishment against tenants and laborers and thereby declared the crown to be the sole arbiter of all contractual disputes between landlords and peasants and between employers and hired farmhands. While powerful landed men still wielded influence over local society, especially where lineages were strong, the Qing successfully blocked them from forming private bailiwicks from which to challenge the crown. At the same time, the Qing denied peasants any political representation. By breaking the landlords' grip on peasant lives while denying the peasantry a voice, the new rulers cleared the way to taxing all land and firming up the government's fiscal base. Subsequently, all small-holding peasants were taxed household by household on the land they possessed, while landlords were required to pay tax on the land they owned out of their rent receipts, the collection of which the state upheld in local courts.

Though the surnames of powerful households were now entered in the land tax rolls, and their ability to lord it over local society was greatly diminished, these families successfully preserved their long-standing access to state office and the incomes this generated. The revival of the imperial examination system was a significant victory for China's landlord class, which continued to send the bulk of candidates to sit the exam and fill the posts in the imperial bureaucracy. For its part, the Qing dynasty used the revival of the examination system to enhance its legitimacy and win over China's traditional elites to its agenda.

This is where state impingements on rural life stood in the 1680s. In sum, peasants were subject to the direct authority and taxation of the throne, while the landholdings of powerful households were no longer exempt from the land tax; enhanced legal autonomy served to protect peasants against the flagrant seizure of their land, labor, and other resources by the local powerful; and finally, elites retained the ability to collect rents and compete for salaried offices in the state.

These developments subsequently underwrote an expansion of peasant security in land similar to developments in France two centuries earlier. Many came to own some or all of the land they plowed, a condition encouraged by state policies promoting homesteading on vacant land. This was especially true in north China, where ecology and the levels of farming technique also made landlordism less profitable. In south China, where the high productivity of rice farming made for better returns, the peasant population was split evenly between tenants and owner-operators. Where peasants rented their farms, the throne supported the spread of permanent cultivation rights purchased at the moment tenants took up their leaseholds. Under these arrangements, land was said to have "two masters," whereby the landlord owned the "bones" or subsoil (the right to collect rent) and the tenant owned the "skin" or surface (the right to cultivate the land). This distinction debarred landlords from raising rents or replacing tenants at will, leaving them little choice but to wait for tenants to relinquish their leaseholds before replacing them or raising rents and entrance fees. Yet, because tenants freely passed their tenancies on to their children or sub-let them to neighbors, without incurring a fine, entrance fees were avoidable. Consequent to these developments, landlords could not readily raise rents on tenancies that were improved nor levy dues when their tenants added a second or even third annual crop to their portfolio. The rights of tenants were, in fact, so strong that landlords even faced difficulty evicting those who delinquent on their payment, especially during times of hardship when magistrates feared popular unrest arising from landlessness. The benefits to tenants of these developments were enormous. Not only did they bring to an end arbitrary levies and restrictions on their movements, but tenants going forward consolidated their claims over increases in output that came from their own efforts.

The strength of peasant assertions over the land extended beyond titles and permanent leaseholds, as they succeeded in extending customary claims after the point of sale. The most common of these practices were known as *dian* and *zhaojia*. Under the *dian* a peasant surrendered use of his land for a price (a portion of the value of the land), yet retained the right to reclaim it at any time by simply repaying the amount. If he were unable or unwilling to do so, the sale was completed when the buyer paid the difference between the initial price and the full value. The seller's rights did not end at this time, however. After any sale of land the seller had the right to return to the buyer and demand new payments or the *zhaojia*, on the grounds that the value of the land had risen in the intervening years. Extraordinarily, under custom there was no limit to how often or how many times a seller could demand and receive the *zhaojia*.

By means of permanent tenure, fixed rents, the separation of rent from use rights, and the customary and judicial acceptance of partial alienation, peasants had by 1700 established conditions that shielded them from having to select crops on the basis of market returns to effort. Because there was no competitive requirement to cut costs, peasants pursued avenues that incurred little expense yet took advantage of their relatively abundant and cheap labor. Improvements were irregular and on the whole labor intensifying. Not under constant pressure to build up their savings and to search out and to employ the latest cost-cutting tools, the less adept held on so long as they met their basic subsistence needs. It is little wonder that two centuries later only one in ten rural households was landless. But, by this time the size of the typical farm was a fraction of what it once was.

Security in land not only alleviated peasants of the need to match prices, but supported fathers in their hopes that sons and daughters marry and begin bearing grandchildren early. Girls were commonly married out as young as fourteen and most were married by eighteen. Boys married in their late teens but remained at home with their wives to work alongside their fathers and brothers, to support their parents in old age, and to perform the rites and sacrifices necessary to care for the ancestors' spirits. But raising a son to adulthood was not easy. In the comparatively advanced economy of 1920s Taiwan (under Japanese rule), one in ten children still died in the first year of life, and two out of five died by age ten. Consequently, to ensure adult children, couples strove to give birth early and to continue having children for as long as possible. Those who failed to have children early tried hard to make up for lost time once they started.

To facilitate family formation, peasants practiced partible inheritance. Each son received an equal share of land as well as an equivalent share in movable property, tools, and livestock. Even bowls and chopsticks were divided fairly. Because daughters had no role in supporting parents or in ancestor worship, they typically received nothing. A small amount of cloth might go with brides at the time of marriage, but typically less in value than the price paid by the groom's household to her parents. To underscore fairness, each son received an equivalent share of land measured both in quality and quantity. This produced not only small holdings, but noncontiguous farms composed of many tiny fields scattered pell-mell across the village. Individual strips were similarly bought up as the opportunity presented itself, as peasants scrimped and saved in their effort to build up their holdings in preparation for dividing them among their adult sons. As in France, early and universal marriage led to slow but steady population expansion. Despite high infant mortality, and the sixty million deaths from rebellion and war, China's population reached 150 million in 1700 and 400 million by 1900.

The first families to experience the pressures of mounting population lived in the longer-settled areas where population was already great. These included the north China plain, the middle Yellow River and Yangtze River plains, Jiangnan, and Lingnan. The frontiers of course were not immune to these developments, though they unfolded later after a period of heavy settlement.

Sixty years after the establishment of Qing rule, the Kangxi emperor noticed in south China "that the wealth and plenty of villagers were far less than before. . . . The population rises daily. Consequently the food supply becomes gradually insufficient." On conditions in prosperous Jiangnan, he noted that "the people are very limited in their savings and have no means for the famine emergency." Ten years later, Kangxi's son the emperor Yongzheng explained, "Our country has been peaceful and has rested for several decades. The number of homes and people have multiplied from time to time. But the amount of land is limited. So, unless we can direct the whole force of the farmers to expend their strength on cultivation in order to multiply the harvest of different crops, how can we expect to find families and houses with plenty and satisfaction?" The emperor suggested that the situation could be alleviated if "in every village we choose one or two old farmers who have been industrious and diligent to give them a high grade of rewards in order to encourage farming works."[7] Despite expressions of imperial concern, peasants for the most part were on their own and how they responded shaped and reshaped farming.

Many peasants escaped hardship by migrating to sparsely populated Guangxi, Yunnan, Sichuan, Manchuria, and Taiwan. In some frontier regions the state facilitated homesteading by offering security, tax breaks, and even supplies. Sichuan, where the population was decimated by conquest and rebellion, was repopulated by migrants from central, southeastern, and north China. Taiwan was colonized by Cantonese and Fujianese, and Manchuria was settled by peasants from the north China plain. Elsewhere, families moved upland, carving terraces into hillsides to retain water and build deep beds of soil, or reclaimed marshes and lakes, floating paddies on rivers, and constructing polders and dikes to hold back the water along tidal flats and lakesides. In one of the most extraordinary feats of grassroots engineering, thousands of hectares were drained along the shore of Dongting Lake in central China, creating a flood-prone ecosystem of dikes, polders, and sluice-gates.

Families also took up the growing of New World crops, especially those that raised the population-carrying capacity of the land. Maize spread to southwest, central, and northern China and into the hills where it grew well on unimproved land. The sweet potato followed and also spread to Taiwan, Guangdong, and Fujian, where it became a staple alongside or replacing rice. In addition to changing the Chinese diet, the adoption of these crops altered the farming landscape. As maize moved upland, peasants removed the dense tree cover only to find that the soil eroded quickly. Forced to move on, they left the exposed earth to wash downhill, where it caused rivers to break their banks and filled irrigation canals. The spread of sweet potato in south China allowed peasants to live on less land than before. For those already on marginal land, the sweet potato filled stomachs while freeing labor for tobacco and sugarcane.

In the low lying districts of Guangdong the mainstay of the peasant diet switched from rice to sweet potato, which had the advantage of yielding more calories per hectare. By reducing the area devoted to food, these households freed up valuable land for sugarcane. Both crops required considerable work, but peasants could avoid stretching their effort too thin by carefully managing their time and fields. From cut sections of planted sugarcane, healthy and productive shoots or ratoons sprouted each year for up to seven years. The labor thus saved by not planting the cane every year was diverted instead to preparing and planting sweet potatoes. In the late summer, before the potato harvest, the cane was cut and processed in simple mills managed by four or five neighbors cooperatively. Immediately following the extraction and conversion of cane juice into raw sugar, the potatoes were dug up and stored. The sugar was exchanged for rice, to make up for food shortfalls. On tiny farms of a hectare or less, a family could thus survive. Peasants moving into the Fujian highlands made up for their meager plots and marginal soils by putting down gardens planted in sweet potatoes or clearing cover to plant maize. With their basic sustenance met, they devoted the remainder of their effort to growing and preparing tea. Thus, like their French counterparts, peasants with access to markets were able to make ends meet by growing cash crops alongside their food.

On account of their tiny farms, however, the incomes of cane and tea growers remained close to subsistence levels and left them at the mercy of merchants for food and other goods they could not secure on their own, as well as for loans with which to buy them. At the end of each year, after feeding their families, making necessary purchases of salt, cooking oil, and cloth, and paying off debts, their incomes were too small to afford expensive improvements. Rather than devote their energy to buying new tools, they preferred to use their labor to acquire more land in the hope of adding more overall income regardless of returns to work. Consequently, among cane and tea growers neither farming nor processing underwent significant changes in technology, in sources of power, or in the scale and type of organization that might otherwise have raised the productivity and hourly earnings of their labor.

Since neither migration, the adoption of New World crops, nor cash cropping fully alleviated the growing problem of land scarcity, peasants had little choice but to embark on a back-breaking period of agricultural intensification. Those living in south China extended the farm year by adding a second crop. Jiangnan families that farmed paddy rice added winter wheat, while in Guangdong families added a second rice crop selected from early-ripening strains. In north China, where the growing season was shorter, peasants followed their fall harvest of sorghum, millet, and barley in the traditional manner with a winter planting of wheat, which they harvested in the spring and then followed with a summer crop of fast-growing beans. In this fashion, north Chinese squeezed out three crops over two years. Though the additional work added income, there were associated costs.

More intensive use of the land and the addition of commercial crops such as sugarcane and cotton drew huge amounts of nitrogen and water from the soil. Peasants had little choice but to add more fertilizer. But because their plots had long grown too small to afford putting fields in leys for pasturing or plowing nitrogen-fixing legumes back into the soil for added organic matter, and because they could not afford the grain or hay needed to corral large manure-producing animals, they were forced to expend great effort gathering and preparing fertilizers from other sources. They diligently collected and composted farm sources of vegetable and plant waste, fowl and pig manure, and their own night soil. Those close to towns purchased night soil from street collectors. To these they added organic matter gathered from beyond the farm. They went to distant hillsides or meadows to cut and gather green grass or expended even greater energy carting to their fields the heavy nutrient-rich river, canal, and pond sludge called *oufei*. Pits were dug and these materials were left to ferment over the winter and then spread in the spring and again as chase fertilizers over the course of the growing season. Given the lack of large draft animals, one can only imagine the enormous effort needed to make the applications of twenty-eight tons of mud-compost mix per hectare observed by a Western traveler on the farms of Shanghai.

Describing the care in manuring the wheat planting that followed summer rice in the Yangzi Delta, the chronicler Mr. Shen wrote in the seventeenth century:

> When one is planting wheat, the covered reservoir for manure must be full. . . . One waters it [with liquid manure] once at the time of planting, and once again in spring. Each transplanting clump contains five to six stalks. One applies liquid manure to them twice, as is the standard practice, and also banks them up with cattle manure, covering this over [with mud] shoveled out of the [adjacent] ditches. Colza (an oil-bearing seed) would be given twice as much liquid manure as wheat, and perhaps also household garbage or cattle manure. One digs mud from the adjacent ditch and once again applies liquid manure to force blossoms.[8]

A hundred years later, histories of the same region noted that "whether one is planting wet-land or dry-land fields, chase fertilizers are important. Human manure has a beneficial power and ox manure has a long-lasting effect." If manure was unavailable, then the author recommends that "rearing sheep or pigs is a convenient supplement. . . . Without any effort one obtains a large quantity of chase fertilizer. . . . For sheep, though, if one has to hire someone to chop the hay, then this can really waste one's reserves."[9] The commentary notes too that theft of manure was a widespread problem.

A German agronomist noted that "the Chinese use the greatest care in gathering of animal dung as much as for human. To this end the peasant goes off on the roads in the winter, or at other times in the year when he is idle, with a basket on his shoulder and a spade in his hand, and looks for manures."[10] In Zhejiang, where peasants grew mulberries for their silkworms alongside their rice paddies, muddy earth from the paddies was occasionally exchanged for soil from the mulberry orchard, but only after first layering the soil along canal banks to absorb lime, phosphoric acid, and potash.

Gathering and preparing fertilizer was hard work and added greatly to the intensity of farming, which is why richer households turned to commercially available and nitrogen-rich oilcake fertilizers made from the pressings of oilseeds, oil-bearing beans, and peanuts. The cost of seed and bean cake fertilizers, however, mounted across the nineteenth century because manufacturers did not respond to demand by raising production or innovating to lower cost. In the mid-eighteenth century, the cost of bean cake in Jiangnan already equaled the value of the added wheat crop, which had made the addition of fertilizer necessary in the first place. Increasingly, bean cake manufactured in north and central China went to those peasants growing sugarcane in the far south who were better able to afford it, and consequently Jiangnan grain yields stagnated and even richer peasants had to make do with composting their own fertilizer.

Despite all of these efforts, peasants found that their plots had simply fallen below what was minimally necessary to feed their families. They found that the addition of the second crop yielded less total output than the first and yet increased the overall amount of labor expended, much of it going to the application of fertilizer. Those adopting cash crops found that they had to work harder for each marginal increase in income. Sugarcane growers, for example, earned twice as much as rice growers, but they put in more than twice as many hours of work. This effort may have allowed them to survive on a plot that was too small to support them in rice, but it did not raise their standards of living.

The same was true for Jiangnan peasants, who faced a particular problem when they added wheat. Paddy farmers had long benefited from the productiveness of wet rice because of a process known as podzolization, in which the constant raising and lowering of the water level precipitates iron from the soil and leaves a hardpan. Once constructed, this pan establishes a new water table that prevents irrigation water from passing through. The continuous addition of canal, pond, and river mud, as well as lime, prevents the paddy from becoming overly acidic from the iron. While centuries of podzolization established a highly productive rice-growing system, it created problems for Jiangnan peasants who added wheat, a crop that grows poorly in water-laden soils. To prevent the roots of the wheat plant from rotting, peasants in low-lying areas had first to drain their paddies. They then broke down the retaining walls and used the earth to raise the bed high enough that the roots did not rot. The added work entailed, whether in field preparation, spreading fertilizer, or weeding and hoeing, diminished the daily returns from wheat in Jiangnan to well below that of rice and probably below what wheat growers on the dry fields of the north China plain received.

This reduction in daily returns to labor was experienced across China as peasants extended the working year in the face of shortfalls from their shrinking farms. To be sure, annual returns were greater than if they had done nothing, but because the extension of the work year came in response to diminished farm size, there was still very little room to accumulate capital at the end of the day. Cheap labor and lack of capital inevitably meant that costly, labor-saving innovations of the sort associated with capitalist farming (even before the industrial revolution) did not materialize. Farm implements remained inexpensive and geared to the needs of labor-intensive methods. There were therefore many varieties of small hand tools such as hoes and sickles and various digging implements, each designed to suit the meticulous work that small fields demanded. The broad blade of the Chinese hoe, for example, was angled to draw parallel to the surface, cutting shallow while dropping the soil back in its original place, thus ventilating, weeding, and mulching the soil at the same time.

Conversely, there was no place for innovation in the heavier, more expensive, and most-labor-saving tools. Between the fourteenth and twentieth centuries, the plow and seed drill, for example, saw no remarkable changes, and the latter was not commonplace. The Qing versions were for the most part equivalent to the best of the Han dynasty. The northern plow in use in Shandong, Hebei, Shanxi, and Shaanxi was so light that it could be carried by a man on his shoulder to and from the field. Cheap and affordable, it was not capable of the deeper plowing associated with well-manured and organically rich soils of more productive farming systems. Even where heavier tools had been adopted, there was a shortage of draft animals, the number of which declined most in densely populated areas where the land was at a premium. Peasants in Guangdong, Fujian, Jiangnan, and Zhejiang, who needed the heavier plow to turn their water-laden paddies, were forced to share oxen.

As land grew relatively more expensive, first in long-settled districts and later on the frontiers, peasants found it to be in their best interest to substitute labor for tools in every effort to assemble the precious funds needed to buy land, which often included taking on heavy debts. Yet the substitution of labor for capital was not restricted to the poor. On the north China plain, where some managed to build up the size of their farms to as much as twenty hectares, commercial farming took form on the basis of the deep pool of cheap labor. In a situation analogous to self-exploiting peasants, these managerial farmers covered the costs of their larger holdings by cutting back on expensive tools and draft animals wherever possible and instead made profits by hiring more laborers and plowing money into land purchases. Yet, no matter how successful, these social-climbing farmers constantly looked beyond commercial farming. When their estates grew sufficiently large to live well on rent alone, they abandoned management. Instead, they pushed their

sons to sit the imperial exam, or take on employment at the county government, in search of the greater income that came with state office.

For those at the bottom of village society, however, self-exploitation on
the farm only went so far. The added work implied in second crops, higher-
returning but more labor-demanding cash crops, and the more exhausting
management of soils and fields in general, was constantly countered by the
shrinking of family farms and the rising amount of idle or underemployed
rural labor. The circumstances that pushed peasants into handicraft production were summed up by a Qing government official, who wrote that since
"farming only suffices to feed the village people for the three winter
months[,] they begin weaving in the spring, exchanging the cloth for the rice
they eat." Emphasizing the connection between poverty and handicrafts, he
added that "in villages where the soil is very poor, both men and women
work exclusively at spinning and weaving."[11]

In this regard, silk manufacture was one option. But again this was very
labor intensive and the returns were exceedingly poor. A typical silk-
manufacturing family might raise two hundred thousand silkworms, which
over the course of three weeks consumed 2,700 pounds of hand-picked mulberry leaves. They were fed by hand every two hours and the baskets on
which they lived were constantly cleaned of droppings to maintain their
health. The work was so time-consuming that it was said men and women
neglected their toilette. "Day and night they would be nervously preoccupied
with the business of their cocoons," because if the worms failed to become
moths, then families suffered and parents might have to sell their children.[12]
After eighteen days of constant care, the worms cocooned, the cocoons were
boiled, and the threads reeled into yarn. Despite the effort, peasants had no
choice but to forgo the higher wages earned by weavers because they could
not afford the fine machines needed to work the delicate silk threads into
cloth. Describing the industry in the nineteenth century, a Western observer
noted that sericulture "can be successfully carried out only where there are
dense populations who are content to give long wearisome hours for a small
money return."[13] The typical yearly earnings of a silk spinner would feed her
family for less than a month.

Not surprisingly, therefore, comparatively higher-returning cotton manufacturing was far more common. Cotton arrived in China in the thirteenth
century, probably from India, and a peasant woman named Huang Daopo is
credited with teaching its cultivation, spinning, and weaving. Though cotton
was initially grown to clothe the family, as farms and available farm work
shrank, cotton by-employment grew to occupy more time and effort. It
spread to north China when families figured out that working up the raw
cotton in underground cellars kept the air moist enough to produce good-
quality yarn. The great advantage over silk was cotton's greater tensile
strength, which suffered the cheap looms that peasants could afford. Rather

than take the lower incomes that went to silk and cotton spinners, poor households could afford to work up higher-value cloth. Even so, households could not afford the equipment for finishing and dyeing, thereby assuring that the greatest returns went to urban artisans and the merchants who bought and sold their products. At the end of the day, the relatively low price of cotton cloth, and the low level of technique, inevitably meant low earnings. A Chinese observer noted in the eighteenth century that "the labor is great, the profit is small—not enough to feed even one individual. A young woman [weaving] would find it difficult to avoid starvation."[14]

There is little doubt that hourly earnings from farming, however meager, were greater than those from household manufacturing and that peasants would have preferred to focus their efforts on raising crops than working handicrafts. But they were hampered by the small size of their farms. For a time, the more sparsely populated frontiers sustained a steady stream of cheap grain exports that fed the spinners and weavers of places like Jiangnan and the silk and sugarcane growing areas of Guongdong. But as the frontiers filled with people, they had fewer surpluses to ship. Inevitably, the cost of grain rose faster than manufactures and the earning power of handicraft workers tumbled. By the 1850s weavers had to work up twice as much cotton cloth to achieve the same hourly earnings received a century earlier. Had they increased hourly output, they would not have lost ground. But they didn't. Instead, men joined women spinning and weaving and lengthened the overall time bent over looms in an effort to make up for depressed earnings. In the absence of an agricultural revolution, rural manufacturing had reached a dead end as grain prices grew faster than mass manufactures.

The poverty of families is evident in their failure to respond to falling cloth prices by mechanizing to cut their costs and raise their hourly output. Even though weavers would have benefited immensely from the increase in yarn that would come with the mechanization of spinning, and despite the wide availability of water and the knowledge of how to apply it to power geared machines, there were no significant innovations in this direction. Instead, cloth production remained captive to the hand spinner who could never forward enough yarn to keep the weaver at work for more than a few months in the year. Similarly, no technologies were forthcoming to raise the hourly output of peasant weavers to compensate for falling cloth prices. The simple fact is that these kinds of technological innovations, though perfectly feasible and often known, were uneconomic given that rural households had abundant cheap labor and very little to no capital on hand.

Women who wove were regarded by the state as virtuous for supporting and clothing their families. "I especially pity the women of Xiang[yang]," wrote one Qing official. "They have no way to develop specialized work of their own and thereby affirm their commitment as faithful wives."[15] Yet, the conditions and arduous nature of this work belied such gendered and deeply ideological sentiments. The discipline required of pre-adolescent girls who sat and spun day after day was staggering. It seems that common folk took up the elite practice of footbinding to enforce it. Foot-binding artificially shortened a girl's feet by breaking the arches and then binding the toes under by ever-tighter degrees. It very rendered fieldwork very difficult. Thus the Scottish investigator of Chinese tea production, Robert Fortune, observed Jiangnan women hoeing cotton fields with bound feet, but qualified his account by noting that only women with unbound feet could manage such heavy work as turning a water wheel. Binding began when girls were old enough to spin yarn, at the age of six or so. At this age they possessed the necessary finger dexterity but certainly not the aptitude for long days of forced drudgery indoors, especially as their young brothers ran amok outside. By binding their feet, mothers and grandmothers were better able to elicit long hours of sitting and to squeeze enough yarn from their young daughters to keep the family's loom clicking.

In the eighteenth century there was already very little surplus food in China. As early as the 1750s, permanent grain deficits had opened up in former exporting regions such as Guangdong and Jiangnan. These places had to look elsewhere for grain. First, they turned to neighboring regions. But as those areas, too, filled up with people, the folks of Guangdong and Jiangnan had to go further afield. Having exhausted the surplus of Guangxi, Guangdong imported grain from Taiwan and Southeast Asia. Jiangnan imported grain from as far as Sichuan and Manchuria. In Guangdong and Jiangnan, peasant diets had to change to include less-appreciated foods such as sorghum, millet, and sweet potato as rice grew scarcer. Not surprisingly, the fraction of people living in urban areas, which was already tiny, had no way to grow. Only one in twenty lived in towns and cities by the 1820s.

By the 1820s the national grain surplus was a mere one out of every ten liters harvested. With such margins, the slightest shortfall could only have tragic consequences. In the mid-eighteenth century, hundreds of thousands were displaced by famine and millions died in north China. The state bought up grain in surplus years and released it during times of scarcity. It admonished profiteering merchants, though this probably had little effect. The environment also took a beating. Hillsides were deforested and peasants were reduced to gathering the woody stems and roots of their field crops as well as collecting grass from graves and hillsides to fuel cooking and heating. Cleared of ground cover, upland soil washed downhill where it silted up rivers and canals and threatened fragile dike and polder systems. In vain, government officials prohibited migration upland.

Signs of social unrest became increasingly common. China experienced its first large-scale rebellion in a century in 1800, propelled by messianic buddhism. A half-century later, the failed scholar and self-styled brother of Jesus Christ, Hong Xiuquan, proclaimed the founding of the Taiping Kingdom and launched a devastating fourteen-year rebellion. The Taipings began in the ecologically fragile region of south China, among a disenfranchised minority known as the Hakka, but soon spread to the Han majority, and drew its force from the wellspring of peasant hardship. It promised the redistribution of property to the poor and even advocated for women's right to inherit land. The twenty million deaths that followed were a macabre respite from mounting demographic pressure. But by the early twentieth century the population had recovered, and the resultant poverty was compounded by the worsening international context of rising Japanese militarism and the global economic downturn of the 1930s, leaving China politically weak and shattered.

We began our discussion of the peasant agriculture of China with a quote from the French mission. We will end with one, too. Here, the missionaries described how difficult conditions had become despite the huge efforts to make the land productive and the great lengths to which families went to occupy idle hands.

> The large population, something so much desired elsewhere, is here [in China] a scourge, and the foremost cause of all revolutions. Whether the farmers cultivate their own lands, as most do, or those owned by others, they barely have enough on which to live pleasantly, even when the land responds in the optimal fashion to their care for it and hard work. This care and hard work are not enough to keep most of them busy around the whole year, especially in the southern provinces. This has caused the extension of the crafts of necessity and of painstaking toil into the countryside.[16]

Just as Arthur Young puzzled over the poverty of France's peasants despite their exertions, so this anonymous author strained to understand how so much hard work by the Chinese yielded only minuscule gains. In our discussion of peasant agriculture we have seen how the reluctance to specialize shielded pre-capitalist farmers from the risky and costly requirement of cutting costs, while leaving them free to pursue other highly prized goals. We have seen too how those goals were underwritten by the peasants' ability to defend their farms against outsiders. Peasants certainly showed ingenuity in making ends meet as their growing numbers diminished the size of their farms. They turned to intensive market gardening, viticulture, sericulture, double cropping, and animal husbandry; they made Herculean efforts to scrape together additional fertilizer and keep the overworked soils productive; and they added manufacturing sidelines in order to leverage the market to their advantage.

These trends prevented the social differentiation evident within the peasant communities of France and China from leading to any qualitatively different path of development. The successful and ambitious peasants, we have

Table 4.1. Chief Differences between Capitalist and Peasant Farming in the Early Modern World

	Capitalist farms	Peasant farms
Dominant relationship to the farm	Commercial and regularly adjustable leaseholds	Outright ownership, permanent tenure, nonadjustable rents
Inheritance rights and practices	None to leaseholds	Partible and among all sons for all or most land
Farm	Large, contiguous, and growing	Small, fragmented, and shrinking
Primary source of farm labor	Hired wage labor	Family labor
Tools	Increasingly complex, expensive, and designed to save labor	Simple, cheap, family-made, and suited to absorbing labor
Cropping practices	Specialized and changing with prices	Diversified for household consumption and changing according to family needs
Marriage and family formation	Delayed	Initially early and universal
Sideline manufacturing	Abandoned	Used to absorb underemployed labor
Large livestock (cattle, oxen, and horses)	Many and increasing in number and size	Few and declining in number as farms shrink
Yields	Growing	Growing slowly or not at all
Labor productivity and wages	Rising	Stagnant or declining

seen, adapted to the overall context of farming for practical uses, rather than money reserves, as well as to the overall context of extractive rents, taxes, and sharecropping agreements. Better-off peasants became dues collectors and lease enforcers. Rather than storing cash, they spent their wealth on titles, offices, and lands for offspring. And as the peasants accumulated debts in their efforts to bring more land into productive use and assure their subsistence, the well-to-do villagers took advantage of the rising land prices to realize speculative profits in sales, and in doing so further fragmented the countryside into an uneconomic mosaic of scattered plots.

In this way, despite the peasants' security in land, they only succeeded in testing the limits of their respective Malthusian development paths. Because the innovations pursued in farming did not produce increases in hourly labor productivity, the entire economy remained hostage to high and rising grain prices. The resulting cheapening of peasant labor not only further discouraged cost cutting on the farm, but allowed peasants to underprice urban manufactures even to the point of lowering their hourly incomes. It is little wonder therefore that despite markets and the sometimes voluminous circulation of goods, no division of labor between town and country developed to foster competition for workers in general and lift wages. There were no industrial revolutions, in other words.

In the chapters that follow, we examine the ways in which rural surpluses will be extracted and redistributed in the modern era. Like the novel capitalist modes of obtaining wealth explored in chapter 3 on England and Japan, and like the non-market taking of rural surpluses explored in chapter 2 on the dynastic states, in the modern era, the particular ways in which the dominant classes obtained their wealth varied in accordance with the contingent character of the political struggles over land and labor required to grow and process the crops.

NOTES

1. Arthur Young, *Travels in France during the Years 1787, 1788 and 1789*, ed. with introduction by Jeffry Kaplow (Garden City, N.Y.: Doubleday, 1969). Abridgement of the 2nd ed. of the author's *Travels during the Years 1787, 1788, and 1789*, published in 1792 (1st ed.), 432–33.

2. Ibid., 285–86.

3. Ibid., 299.

4. Ibid., 310.

5. Ibid., 323.

6. Mark Elvin, *The Retreat of the Elephants: An Environmental History of China* (New Haven: Yale University Press, 2004).

7. Mabel Ping-hua Lee, *The Economic History of China with Special Reference to Agriculture* (New York: Columbia University Press, 1921), 415, 417.

8. Elvin, *The Retreat of the Elephants*, 213.

9. Ibid., 213–14.

10. Ibid., 469.

11. Francesca Bray, *Technology and Gender: Fabrics of Power in Late Imperial China* (Berkeley: University of California Press, 1997), 224.

12. Elvin, *The Retreat of the Elephants*, 213.

13. Sucheta Mazumdar, *Sugar and Society in China: Peasants, Technology, and the World Market* (Cambridge: Cambridge University Press, 1998), 266.

14. Susan Mann, *Precious Records: Women in China's Long Eighteenth Century* (Palo Alto: Stanford University Press, 1997), 158.

15. Ibid., 163.

16. Elvin, *The Retreat of the Elephants*, 466.

Chapter Five

The New World

Planters, Slaves, and Sugar

European colonization of the New World fostered the expansion of old and new ventures. Alongside the men and women who cleared farms to support their families in a manner reminiscent of peasant Europe, there were those who intended to farm for profit. Experimenting with different cash crops and labor systems, some eventually put together a highly commercial farm regime based not on capitalist rents and wages, as in England, but on plantations and captive labor. In its reliance on slaves, these ventures were distinct not only from capitalist farms but also from the most commercially oriented peasant operations of the old world.

Although driven by profits and demonstrating remarkable responsiveness to the market, as they switched in quick succession from tobacco, to cotton, to sugarcane, New World planters were not capitalist farmers. The planter's dependence on slaves undoubtedly alerted him to the cost of labor, and by implication to the value of their output. Yet, as we shall see, the slave-master relationship did not incur systematic cost cutting and improvements along the lines seen in early modern England and Japan.

Rather than reduce labor costs through productive investment in tools, planters favored extending the slaves' working day as well as the intensity of his effort. Slaves were supplied with the crudest and cheapest of farming implements. Undoubtedly, the commercial tenants of eighteenth-century England were also aware of the need to get as much work from their hired laborers as possible. They too looked out for shirking and when necessary had laborers work as many hours as needed. But the similarities ended there. Just as England's commercial tenants were remarkable for their investment in labor-saving tools and methods, so plantation masters were remarkable for their ability to organize and direct highly coercive systems of labor supervision and discipline.

Highly commercial agriculture, as this chapter shows, was therefore not exclusive to agrarian capitalism, nor as we shall see was it a guarantee of rapid technological change. The key difference was often the state of labor, which was free to allocate itself to where wages were highest in England—forcing employers to raise output while cutting costs—yet was locked in place on the New World plantation—prompting planters to raise output by squeezing more effort out of the slaves.

Most of us are familiar with the tale of Robinson Crusoe's misadventures as an island castaway. We know of his struggle to survive apart from civilization, and his triumph over nature has been adapted and retold so many times that the story of Crusoe, as the self-made and independent man, strikes a common chord. Less familiar, because it is often omitted from the retelling, is the prelude to his misfortune. In Daniel Defoe's novel, Crusoe is shipwrecked while on a slaving venture between Brazil and West Africa, having set sail to secure labor for his sugar plantation.

Crusoe arrived in Brazil's sugar country in 1651 and, according to the novel, was "recommended to the house of a good honest man like myself, who had an *Ingeino* as they call it; that is, a plantation and a sugar-house. I lived with him some time, and acquainted myself by that means with the manner of their planting and making sugar, and seeing how well the planters liv'd, and how they grew rich suddenly, I resolv'd [that] I would turn planter among them." Crusoe "purchased as much land that was uncur'd [uncultivated] as my money would reach, and form'd a plan for my plantation and settlement." He began with staples, and after two years his estate was large enough to support some tobacco and some land ready "for planting canes in the year to come." Though less profitable than sugarcane, tobacco required less labor and was a common starting crop for commercial adventurers in the New World.

When Crusoe turned his full attention to sugarcane, however, he found his own labor wanting. He sent back to Europe for more capital and, when it arrived, "I bought me a *Negro* slave, and an *European* servant too," and "went on the next year with great success."[1] As his plantation grew larger, so too did his need for workers. Monopolies in the Atlantic trade put the cost of slaves beyond his purse, he complained. So, with the experience of sailing with merchant vessels to Guinea, he set sail on his ill-fated journey to acquire slaves for himself.

Defoe's story, though glossing over details of the plantation, and seemingly blind to the barbarity of slavery, nonetheless captures key aspects of the growth of the New World sugar plantations. Like Crusoe, colonial planters were compelled by the expense of acquiring land, constructing the sugar mill, and acquiring labor to draw heavily on capital from Europe. This was especially so on the English plantations in the Caribbean, a history with which Defoe and his readers were probably familiar. Stories of the fortunes made in sugar were commonplace in the streets of London and Bristol and the informed public knew that great sums were needed. Like Crusoe, early planters experimented with a variety of commercial crops, including cotton, indigo, and tobacco. Earnings from mixed commercial farming were invested in the construction of the more costly sugar plantations. Finally, as in the book, the turn to sugar monocropping strained the supply of workers, pushing planters to experiment with native labor, indentured European servants, and African slaves. At times they combined all three. But from the mid-sixteenth century, reliance on African slaves deepened until they became the predominant source of labor in the sugar economy.

Once committed to African slavery, the planters' willingness and desire to exploit it knew no bounds. Some eleven million Africans were transported to the Americas. Just under nine and a half million made it to the auction blocks. To these souls we must also add the millions of African parentage born into slavery in the New World. When the seventeenth-century cleric Antônio Vieira wrote, "Whoever says sugar says Brazil and whoever says Brazil says Angola," he expressed succinctly the connections between Europe's demand for sugar, the ambitions of the planters, and the exploitation of Africans. [2]

In retrospect, the intimate association of sugar and African slaves came late. Sugarcane came to Europe in the hands of Muslims in the early Middle Ages, and it was soon grown in Egypt, Syria, Sicily, and southern Spain by peasants. Grandee landholders built irrigation systems to support the expansion of cane cultivation and constructed mills to transform the cane into sugar.

Medieval Europeans were in the habit of using honey to sweeten and preserve their food. The beehive was common in the countryside, with some lords requiring that tenants pay rent in honey. But bees are finicky. They transport poorly and output is constrained by their life cycle and access to wild nectar. Modern hives require an acre of sown field each and produce only 150 pounds of honey annually. Cane sugar provided a cheap and viable alternative. Though considerable up-front investments were needed, limits to its production were fixed only by the availability of land and labor.

As the Muslim presence in Europe receded, Christians eagerly filled the vacuum and took up sugarcane. In the fifteenth century, following the *reconquista*, Spaniards manufactured sugar on a large scale in Valencia and promoted the cultivation of sugarcane across the Mediterranean. Iberians then introduced it to the Atlantic islands—the Canaries, Madeira, the Azores, Cape Verde, and São Tomé—and in so doing unwittingly set a new course.

Rivalry with Spain spurred Portugal to colonize the uninhabited island of Madeira in the 1430s. Lords directed settlers to clear brush, lay irrigation, and build farms. In the early days peasants favored the mix of crops and animal husbandry that they brought from home. In 1452, however, the first water-powered sugar mill was built and by the end of the century, the island was devoted almost entirely to the commercial production of cane sugar. Madeira's transformation from an enclave of peasant-based mixed farming to commercial monocropping ballooned local demand for labor. Unable to persuade Europeans to make the crossing in sufficient numbers, Portuguese authorities experimented with alternative sources before settling on the importation of slaves from North and sub-Saharan Africa, as well as the neighboring Canaries.

Though the Portuguese cut their teeth in slave-based farming on Madeira, they did not build up large plantations of the sort associated with slavery in the American South or the Caribbean. The scale remained small. The typical operation employed only a handful of slaves, who often worked side by side with wage and indentured laborers. The basic components of the New World plantation were first cobbled together on the isle of São Tomé. Located in the Gulf of Guinea, with easy access to the African slave trade, European settlers aggregated large estates by the standards of the day. Free from having to deal with existing communities of agriculturalists, but unable to secure workers, they turned to the slave trade. In the island's heyday, five to six thousand enslaved Africans produced two thousand tons of sugar annually for export to markets as far away as Antwerp.

At the end of the fifteenth century the São Tomé model was introduced to the Caribbean by Christopher Columbus, who as a young man traded in Madeiran cane sugar and whose father-in-law held a captaincy on Porto Santo. Realizing the potential for profits, he brought cane plantings on his second voyage to Hispaniola. While the first effort failed, subsequent experiments followed and, after fits and starts, and with the financial support of the Spanish crown, sugar growing took hold. By the 1520s, some forty sugar mills (*ingenio* in Spanish, *engenho* in Portuguese) processed locally grown cane for Europe.

To encourage the spread of sugar production, the crown granted up to fifty square miles to anyone demonstrating the ability to make use of it. Financing made its way from Europe, with Columbus' fellow Genoese merchants prominent among early investors. Because technological change was slow, and because there were few if any economies of scale to early sugar production, plantation owners could only raise incomes by acquiring more land on which to put their slaves to work. As the cost of production rose so did the price of entry, fostering the emergence of a wealthy estate-holding elite. Commanding large estates, owning significant numbers of slaves, and dominating the levers of local government, these planter grandees formed a narrow class, whose descendents would guide colonial development in the Spanish Caribbean and American mainland for centuries.

The increase in scale of sugar production that accompanied the emergence of planters stretched thin Hispaniola's labor supply, at a time when the native population was succumbing dreadfully to old world diseases and the physically exhausting demands of the plantation taskmasters. A staggering 90 percent of the island's native population died by the 1530s. There were no immediate sources of labor to make up for such a catastrophic decline. Laws prohibited the forced removal to the Americas of any Europeans apart from convicts. Few migrated voluntarily and those that did often died early. Trials with Indian wage labor were not particularly successful and, while military raids against neighboring islands secured new slaves, these people too suffered from high mortality. Desperate to profit from their land grants, but stymied by their inability to find an adequate supply of labor, planters quickly drew upon the experience and lessons of the Atlantic islands and tapped into the established slave trade. By 1540, slavers had deposited fifteen thousand Africans on Hispaniola's shores. Not only were the constituent parts of the New World slave plantation now in place but so too were the political and social organizations and trading networks that would secure the new labor regime for several centuries.

Given the intimate association of cane sugar and slavery after 1450, one might conclude that premodern commercial sugar production required slaves. In the narrowest sense, this was true. But it was so only because New World planters found that recruiting labor through other approaches posed a series of insurmountable problems. In Portuguese Brazil, for instance, early planters and *engenhos* used native Indians enthusiastically. Though they were recognized to be less productive than Africans, their cheapness made up for any deficiencies in output. By the 1570s, however, the combination of rebellion, high mortality, and the Church's anti-enslavement laws foreclosed this route to commercial success. Unwilling to surrender their ventures, Brazilian planters eagerly turned to African slaves. By the 1580s they made up one-third of the labor force in the Pernambuco region and one-half by the 1620s.

While planters in British North America and the Caribbean also ended up relying exclusively on African slaves, their journey took a different route. In early days, servants from the British Isles filled the gap when the sparser native labor proved unreliable or unavailable. In the seventeenth century, 350,000 indentured workers made their way to America, the vast majority going to the "tobacco coast" (Maryland and Virginia) and Barbados, where cotton, tobacco, and indigo competed with sugar for the planters' interest. Before 1775, perhaps half of white colonists to North America arrived as servants. On Barbados, first settled in 1627, the supply of whites proved insufficient as early as the 1640s. A boom in sugar prices encouraged planters to abandon early the mixed export economy of sugar, tobacco, cotton, and indigo and focus solely on sugar. High profits lured investors such as the Noell brothers, who arrived from London in 1647 and acquired six hundred acres in five plantations with the goal of sowing and processing sugar. Entrepreneurs such as these rapidly extended sugar cultivation to 40 percent of the island by 1645.

This swift transformation predictably strained the labor supply. For a time, West Indies planters had no recourse but to raise wages and improve the terms of indenture. They also secured servants from further afield, in poorer Scotland and Ireland and among political and common prisoners. The island gained an unsavory reputation: "The island is inhabited with all sortes: with English, Duch, Scotes, Irish, Spaniards thay being Jewes; with Ingones, and miserabell Negors borne to perpetually slavery they and thayer seed. . . .This island is the Dunghill wharone England doth cast forth its rubidg: Rodgs. Hors and such like peopel," wrote Henry Whistler in 1655.[3] In the end, African slaves offered Barbadian planters a solution to the labor crisis, just as they had in Hispaniola and Brazil. Their number grew quickly. They accounted for two-thirds of the population in 1680 and four-fifths by 1710, while their continued import extended sugar cultivation to 80 percent of the island by 1767.

The question remains why planters did not continue in Africa the practice in Europe of recruiting indentured servants and wage laborers. In all likelihood, such a scheme would not have drawn many Africans to the New World because, as we saw in chapter 2, Africa did not have a large landless population that could be persuaded to make the journey to work for wages. Moreover, planters would have faced the problem of blacks establishing farms and removing themselves from the labor market once their contractual obligations were fulfilled. Karl Marx commented sardonically on this "dilemma" in a much later instance, after the freeing of slaves in the Indies.

> *The Times* of November 1857 contains an utterly delightful cry of outrage on the part of a West-Indian plantation owner. This advocate analyses with great moral indignation—as a plea for the re-introduction of Negro slavery—how the Quashees (the free blacks of Jamaica) content themselves with producing only what is strictly necessary for their own consumption, and, alongside this "use value," regard loafing (indulgence and idleness) as the real luxury good; how they do not care a damn for the sugar and the fixed capital invested in the plantations, but rather observe the planters' impending bankruptcy with an ironic grin of malicious pleasure, and even exploit their acquired Christianity as an embellishment for this mood of malicious glee and indolence. They have ceased to be slaves, but not in order to become wage labourers, but, instead, self-sustaining peasants working for their own consumption.[4]

While the immense profit in plantation agriculture conjured demand for a large reliable labor force that could not be obtained from Europe, the impracticality of alternative labor regimes could not bring forth the New World slave economy on its own. Still other conditions were necessary. In the first instance, the planters had to pacify numerically superior native populations in order to assemble and defend their plantations. Historical advances in weaponry, shipping, and political organization facilitated this task. In the second instance, planters could use slaves only so long as propitious conditions in Africa permitted. In a word, fragmented African polities and a slaving tradition provided Europeans with avenues for not only purchasing slaves but enlarging their supply. First, agricultural practices that left Africans less productive at home than in the New World assured their relative cheapness to planters. Second, as the slave trade grew, the institutions and technologies for capturing and transporting slaves improved and brought costs down further. Third, early attempts to enforce trade monopolies and set prices fell apart or were abandoned as interlopers from England, Holland, and France entered the market, and as planter interests overcame those of merchants enjoying privileges within the monarchies of Europe. Consequently, the cost of slaves fell by nearly a third between 1670 and 1720.

In the final analysis, New World slavery came about because of the particular social and political struggles in the western hemisphere, Europe, and Africa. We have, for example, seen instances of peasants combining household labor, small plots of land, and a little capital to grow and process sugar for sale in southern China. We will see too that peasant cultivation was separated from milling and effectively bound to industrial-scale processing on Taiwan in the 1910s and 1920s. While other ways of finding labor to profit from sugar were clearly possible and practiced, what the slave plantation offered was a means for a small number of landholders, far from home, to accumulate unprecedented fortunes and influence. All in all, the appearance and longevity of slavery rested on the coincidence of initially autonomous developments: the capacity to expel natives and construct plantations in the colonies; the inability to exploit native or European labor; and the steady capture of African slaves. The French liberal and apologist for slavery, Montesquieu, captured that history with typical precision: "The peoples of Europe, having exterminated those of America, had to make slaves of those of Africa in order to use them to clear so much land."[5]

The cultivation and processing of cane was bound to shape the pace of work and the natural environment. Managed correctly, a plantation kept slaves working six months of the year in the Caribbean and nine months in Brazil. That work revolved around a perennial tropical grass that sends up sugar-bearing shoots. The first cane harvest after planting is called the "plant" and subsequent harvests are "ratoons." Agriculturalists learned to periodically root up and replant or suffer falling yields. To plant a field in the sixteenth century, land was cleared and divided into squares of three and a half feet. Field hands dug trenches a few inches deep, into which they placed cuttings selected from standing cane that had grown tall and narrow and would thus yield little juice. Wide easements were left for the heavy carts that transported plantings, fertilizer, and the harvest to and from the fields. Describing the work Bryan Edwards wrote,

> The negroes are then placed in a row in the first line, one negro to a square, and directed to dig out with their hoes the several squares, commonly to the depth of five or six inches. . . . The negroes then fall back to the next line, and proceed as before. Thus the several squares between each line are formed into a trench of much the same dimensions with that which is made by the plough. . . . An able negro will dig from sixty to eighty of these holes for his day's work of ten hours. . . . The cane holes or trench being now completed, whether by the plough or by the hoe, and the cuttings selected for planting, which are commonly the tops of the canes that have been ground for sugar . . . two of them are sufficient for a cane-hole. . . . These, being placed longitudinally in the bottom of the hole, are covered with mold about two inches deep. [6]

The method of dividing and bordering a large field into small squares—an innovation of the Caribbean plantations—reduced the soil erosion that otherwise plagued planters after the natural forest cover was removed, while the addition of "mold" (manure) restored soil. To reduce the number of slaves required, planters divided their estates into fields and directed their overseers to spread planting over many months. Taking advantage of the long season in this way not only staggered the hard work of planting, weeding, and harvesting, but also delivered to the mill a constant yet manageable quantity of cane as fields ripened in waves.

Shoots appeared fourteen days after planting. Cane took fourteen to eighteen months to mature, reaching as high as eight feet tall. The punishing chore of harvesting was done with a simple sharpened handbill, with which the field worker removed the cane top, stripped off leaves, and cut through the base. On many plantations men wielded the bill while women bound the cane for removal. While Caribbean planters required their slaves to work a ten-hour day during the harvest, in Brazil it was common to assign quotas that, when completed, left the slave free to work for himself. The second year's crop—the ratoon—grew from the same plant but needed only ten months to mature. Planters typically got seven harvests before replanting. Our Jamaican planter, Edwards, wrote that the labor saved by ratooning compensated for the weaker yields.

> In most parts of the West Indies it is usual to hole and plant a certain proportion of the cane land in annual succession. This . . . is frequently attended with great and excessive labour to the negroes, which is saved altogether by the

system we are treating of. By this latter method, the planter, instead of stocking up his ratoons, and holing and planting the land anew, suffers the stoles to continue in the ground, and contents himself, as his cane fields become thin and impoverished, by supplying the vacant spaces with fresh plants. By these means, and the aid of manure, the produce of sugar per acre, if not apparently equal to that from the best plant-canes in other soils, gives perhaps the long-run full as great returns to the owner; considering the relative proportion of the labour and expense attending the different systems.[7]

Labor saved by ratooning was put to other work around the plantation. The most persistent task was weeding. The same tropical climate that sustained cane also nurtured unwelcome plants that stunted cane growth, shaded venomous snakes, and cut into profits. Less attentive overseers relied on the closely planted cane to squeeze out the weeds. But the profit-minded planter made hoeing the weeds a year-round chore. Describing the Barbadian sugar plantation in the 1650s Richard Ligon wrote: "The first work to be considered is Weeding, for unless that be done, all else (and the Planter too) will be undone, and if that be neglected but for a little time, it will be a hard matter to recover it again, so fast will the weeds grow there." He continued,

And the best husbands, command their Overseers to search, if any weeds have taken root, and destroy them, or if any of the Plants fail, and supply them; for where the Plants are wanting, weeds will grow; for, the ground is too virtuous to be idle. Or, if any Withs [creepers] grow in those vacant places, they will spread very far, and do much harm, pulling down all the Canes they can reach to. If this husbandry be not used when the canes are young, it will be too late to find remedy, for, when they are grown to a height, the blades will become rough and sharp in the sides, and so cut the skins of the Negroes. . . . which they will not endure.[8]

Intensive weeding began a month after planting and continued so long as cane grew. The more vigilant planter dispatched daily teams to hoe fields after completing the most urgent tasks of the day. He would also direct them to remove suckers growing from cane joints that drew nutrients and water but produced no usable cane juice.

Another task that required much time and labor was "dunging," or spreading manure. Hoping to squeeze as much out of their land as possible and cover their costs, planters rarely rested or rotated their fields. On Barbados, fields were "grubbed up" and left to fallow after many harvests and never long enough to counter the toll of intensive monocropping. Planters in the Caribbean thus spread as much cow or ox dung as they could get their hands on. On Jamaica, the intensive application of manure was introduced from England, where—as we have seen—it already played a role in the agricultural revolution. Bryan Edwards wrote:

The necessity of giving even the best soil occasional assistance is universally admitted. . . . But the chief dependence of the Jamaica planter in manuring his lands, is on the moveable pens, or occasional inclosure before described; not much for the quantity of dung collected by means of those enclosures, as for the advantage of the urine from the cattle (the best of all manures), and the labour which is saved by this system. I believe, indeed, there are a great many overseers who give their land no aid of any kind, other than that of shifting the cattle from one pen to another, on the spot intending for planting, during three or four months before it is ploughed and holed.[9]

In Brazil growers unconvincingly boasted of getting thirty years from a single cane planting and insisted that their soils remained vital. Nevertheless, their consistently poorer yields and lower profits suggest they would have benefited from the "high farming" methods of Barbados.

The work of gathering, composting, and spreading manure was great. In 1689, Edward Littleton wrote that thirty cartloads of manure were needed per acre. He advocated the construction of terraces downhill to catch the mix of dung and soil that washed off fields so that it might be re-spread. The rapid succession of small and big tasks kept slaves so busy that Littleton notes his "Negroes work at it like Ants and Bees."[10] The rapid expansion of sugar cultivation on the islands reduced pasture, however, and soil exhaustion set in much like it had in late medieval Europe. In 1708 John Oldmixon reported that "when sugar was first planted on this island, one Acre of Canes yielded more than now, for four, five, six, or seven Years together, without any further planting or dunging." But Oldmixon complained too that "the Soil is so impoverish'd, that they are now forc'd to dung and plant every Year; insomuch that 100 Acres of Cane require almost double that Number of Hands they did formerly." He added that weeds proliferated from the "frequent Dunging."[11]

Careful management of work was required to balance the planter's need to maintain yields under the stresses of monocropping while managing his expenditures on slaves. If poorly done, a planter would either exhaust his slaves or accumulate unsustainable debts acquiring too many. The key to success was organizing work in ways that minimized costly slave purchases and yet completed all necessary tasks.

Planters thus favored filling the downtime in cane cultivation with gainful work that covered some of the cost of maintaining their estates as well as their workforce. Toward this end, they put aside land on which slaves grew food and fiber. Richard Ligon described his partner Sir Thomas Modyford's Barbadian plantation in the 1650s:

There was imployed for sugar some what more than 200 acres; above 80 acres for pasture, 120 for wood, 30 for tobacco, 5 for ginger, as many for Cotton wool, and 70 acres for provisions; viz, Corn, Potatoes, Plantines, Cassavie, and

Bonavist; some few acres of which for fruit; viz. Pines, Plantines, Milions, Bonanoes, Gnavers, Water Milions, Oranges, Limon, Limes, etc, most of these only for the table.[12]

Similarly, planters in Brazil, where wood was plentiful, gave slaves daily quotas of 1,600 pounds of cut and stacked firewood, which was used in the boiling of the cane juice. It cost the planter little to nothing to use his slaves to their fullest extent and, given the large numbers employed on a typical Barbadian plantation (the average was two hundred in the late seventeenth century), the pressures to do so were great.

The seasonally uneven requirements for labor posed a problem if left unattended. The Jamaican planter Edwards spoke of the "methodical arrangement and distribution of the labour with which [plantations] are conducted, as it is unquestionably more severe and constant than that on any other species of landed property in the West Indies."[13] Robert Ligon wrote, "canes are to be planted at all times, that they may come in, one field after another; otherwise, the work will stand still. And commonly they have in a field that is planted together, at one time, ten or a dozen acres."[14] Later in the same account Ligon added, "For, you must not plant too much at once, but have it to grow ripe successively, that your work may come in order, to keep you still doing; for, if it should be ripe all together, you are not able to work it so; and then for want of cutting, they would rot, and grow to loss."[15] A planter with an eye on profits therefore kept his slaves on the move constantly, shuffling them from task to task: weeding, dunging, planting, cutting, and hauling as well as building and repairing the estate. The mature plantation was an extremely complex and integrated system that, in the words of Edwards,

> ought to be considered as a well-constructed machine, compounded of various wheels turning different ways, yet all contributing to the great end proposed; but if any one part runs too fast or too slow, in proportion to the rest, the main purpose is defeated. It is in vain . . . to plead in excuse the want of hands or cattle; because these wants must either be supplied, or the planter must contract his views, and proportion them to his ability; for the attempt to do more than can be attained, will lead into perpetual disorder, and terminate in poverty.[16]

Even with the best forethought, however, the strain on labor at milling time was tremendous. The pace of work induced exhaustion, giving birth to the Brazilian saying "as sleepy as a sugar-mill slave." The sight of this activity enthralled and terrified European observers for whom, not yet accustomed to the pace and brutishness of factory work, the novelty of the scale and violence of the mill captured the imagination. It even gave some pause, as in Padre Vieira's oft-cited description:

And truly who sees in the blackness of the night those tremendous furnaces perpetually burning; the flames leaping from the apertures of each through the two mouths or nostrils by which the fire breathes; the Ethiopians or cyclopses, bathed in sweat, as black as they are strong, feeding the hard and heavy fuel to the fire, and the tools they use to mix and stir them; the cauldrons, or boiling lakes, continually stirred and restirred, now vomiting froth, exhaling clouds of steam, more of heat than of smoke . . . the noise of the wheels and chains, the peoples of the color of the very night working intensely and moaning together without a moment of peace or rest; who sees all the confused and tumultuous machinery and apparatus of that Babylon can not doubt though they may have seen Vesuvius or Mount Etna that this is the same as Hell. [17]

The planter Thomas Tyron described with equal measures of shock and awe the same process in seventeenth-century Barbados:

To live in a perpetual Noise and Hurry, and the only way to render a person Angry and Tyrannical, too; since the Climate is so hot and the labor so constant, that the Servants night and day stand in great Boyling Houses, where there are six or seven large Coppers or Furnaces kept perpetually boyling; and from which with heavy Ladles and Skimmers they skim off the excrementitious parts of the Canes, till it come to its perfection and cleans, while others as Stoakers, Broal as it were alive, in managing the Fires, and one part is constantly at the mill to supply it with canes night and day, during the whole season of making sugar, which is about six months of the year. [18]

The work was treacherous. Scarred and limbless slaves were a common sight on plantations: an ax was kept handy at the stone rollers to sever the limb and save the life of any unfortunate slave whose hands or feet got caught as he fed cane into the machine.

Once it started up, the mill ran until the harvest was done, with a few hours of rest daily when the machinery was repaired and readjusted. Mills operated 270 to 300 days a year in Brazil and 120 to 180 days in the Caribbean. As long as there was daylight and cane to cut, it was bundled and hauled to the mill. It was fed between the large stone rollers as fast as it was delivered. The released juice flowed into channels for collection. It was passed through five to eight copper kettles to be boiled each time, as impurities were skimmed off and the syrup thickened. At the correct moment the concentrated syrup was decanted into clay forms, where it remained for four to six weeks as a damp clay seal drew out more impurities. When ready, the forms were broken and the outer white, and more valued, sugar was separated by hand from the cheaper brown sugar at the center. After grading, it was packed for sale and shipping.

It required skill and experience to gauge the right moment to transfer the juice from kettle to kettle and to transfer the syrup to the forms. Because a mistake at this time might waste months of work, these tasks were entrusted to an experienced slave known as a "sugar master." But field and most mill work required little skill. There was little technique to planting and cutting the cane, to bundling and passing it between the millstones, ladling and transferring the syrup between kettles, skimming off adulterations from the bubbling juice, stoking the fires that heated the kettles, and decanting and filling the forms.

Like the owner of the modern factory, experience led the planter to break up and simplify tasks, to reduce the skills needed for the bulk of work. Profitability rested in large part on simplification such that the planter might easily substitute slaves. The reason was straightforward. Because beating and injury were integral to the routine of plantation work, it was important that one slave should easily stand in for another. Maltreatment not only put slaves out of work but made for high mortality and low life expectancy. Male slaves born in nineteenth-century Brazil could expect to live only eighteen years, while the seventeenth-century slave population on Barbados would have declined without steady replacements from outside. Plantation owners had every incentive to simplify tasks and impart the few necessary skills to a select group of better cared for slaves. This thinking was expressed with grim clarity by an Antiguan planter to the slave trader John Newton in 1751: "it was cheaper to work slaves to the utmost, and by little fare and hard usage, to wear them out before they became useless, and unable to do service; and then to buy new ones, to fill their places."[19]

Simplification had the added benefit of reducing the slave's leverage over the work pace. All planters had a good sense of the optimal productivity for each task and could insist that slaves match it. Unskilled slaves were substitutable and thus poorly positioned to strike or bargain over the pace of work. Skilled slaves had greater control over their conditions. The kettle man who supervised the heating and purification of the cane juice and the sugar master who judged when the syrup was ready to form, as well as the African slave driver who managed the pace, could not be worked like other slaves, and thus plantation owners sought to limit their numbers. On a Jamaican plantation in the 1750s, of 258 slaves only 29 possessed skills: 4 drivers, 6 mulemen, 6 carpenters, 4 coopers, 3 distillers, 2 masons, 2 wheelwrights, a boiler, and a rope maker.

The dilemma at the heart of the plantation was that it was a labor-intensive business reliant on a reluctant workforce. Very few slaves ever became free, many faced an early death, and the threat of unemployment was absent. Unable to fire his slaves, as in the capitalist enterprise, planters relied on compulsion. Overseers on horseback carried pistols and whips to enforce work discipline. Beatings were so common that colonial administrators and legislators formulated special codes to grant and clarify the planters' rights to administer them. On Barbados, the island's legislature passed its first comprehensive code for regulating servants and slaves in 1661, at the moment when blacks became the majority. Under the law, Africans, who were "an heathenish, brutish and an uncertaine, dangerous kind of people,"[20] could be whipped for offering offense to any Christian. The planter was permitted to slit the nose and burn the face of repeat offenders.

When Barbadian slaves converted to Christianity, the legal parlance changed to distinguish between "blacks" and "whites." Legal trends in other English colonies hewed closely to developments on Barbados. In 1662, the Virginia Assembly determined that baptism "does not alter the condition of the person as to his bondage or freedom," and in 1667 the same assembly absolved masters of any crime if they killed a slave when delivering punishment. In 1660, the English Council of Foreign Plantations, while declaring that servants were either "Blacks or Whites," went on to affirm that whereas blacks were slaves, to be bought, exchanged, and held in perpetuity, white servants were employed for the duration of their contract. In most colonies, such laws went against the general trend at home, where states were busy monopolizing legal powers.

In Brazil, by contrast, slave owners were legally prohibited from beating slaves to death, and after 1688 slaves could legally denounce a sadistic owner to civil and ecclesiastical authorities, though the laws were rarely enforced. While the Church criticized planters who made their slaves work on church holidays, in contravention of ecclesiastical law, more often than not it turned a blind eye. Governors, clerics, and planters shared a general disdain for Africans and the former rarely intruded upon plantation affairs, sharing with planters the belief that constant chastisement was needed to overcome the slave's innate superstition and indolence. Similarly, though the application in Haiti (Saint-Domingue) of France's 1685 *Code Noir* gave slaves the right to sue their owners, the code was first and foremost designed to regulate slaves. It clarified and defined rights over slaves and their children while setting down the appropriate punishments for slave offenses. Its provisions allowed planters to execute slaves who struck them or made repeated attempts to escape. In short, legal frameworks underwrote the profitability of plantation colonies and, so long as privately administered corporal punishment kept blacks working and secured white rule, laws and practices supported it.

The "slave gang" and accompanying whip might well be the most recognizable expressions of planter power. The gang set the work tempo and the whip sustained it. The slave gang was, however, a fairly late development. In early operations, planters assigned tasks and quotas. When the quota was met, the slave was free to do other things, which often included tending a small garden. Quotas were of course set with profits in mind. Harvesters were expected to cut 4,200 shoots per day, a number expressed in hands and fingers for easy enumeration. Ten fingers represented ten sheaves containing twelve shoots and a slave was expected to harvest "seven hands" a day.

Tasking and quotas were particularly common to Brazil, where farming remained small-scale and planters typically owned fewer than ten slaves.

Ganging slaves was common to Barbados in the early eighteenth century, when holdings were both large and incorporated mills. The Barbadian Henry Drax is reported to have remarked that it was "the best Way I know of to prevent idleness, and to make the Negroes do their work properly will be upon the change of Work, constantly to Gang all the Negroes in the Plantations in the Time of Planting."[21] We are told by William Belgrove that on Drax's plantation slaves were divided into five or six gangs according to their strength, gender, and age, ranging from the ablest and best for "holing and the stronger work" to "the ordinary Negroes in a gang for dunging," down to the children's gang assigned to weeding. During milling season, another gang kept the boiling kettles fired. Drax entrusted a slave to keep each gang working and required that this man maintain a "list of the gang under his particular care that he may be able to give a particular account of everyone, whether sick or how employed." These lists were brought to him fortnightly so that he could check on the performance of every slave and "identify lazy Negroes absenting from their work." Ganging was thus a recognized means for keeping large numbers of slaves constantly busy (see the description of the slave gang at work in the U.S. south in chapter 6). One Barbadian slave acutely remarked, "The devil was in the Englishman that he makes everything work: he makes the negro work, he makes the horse work, the ass work, the wood work, the water work, and the wind work."[22]

Reverend Walsh, in his description of gangs in Brazil, expressed the benefits to planters derived from improved invigilation:

> In a large fallow . . . were from eighty to one hundred negroes of both sexes; some with infants strapped to their backs, in a rank, breaking up the ground for fresh crops with hoes. . . . With this [hoe], they all struck with the regularity of soldiers drilling for the manual exercise. . . . Over them presided a tawny-colored driver, in a cotton jacquet and a large straw hat, with a long rod in his hand by which he directed their industry, and punished the idle.[23]

Military-like drills had ganged slaves work in unison, repeating the same simplified action, often accompanied by satirical and rhythmic singing. The cadence was set by the slave driver who, mounted on his high horse, could spot any slave who fell out of tempo, the same way a sergeant major spots a private who missteps on parade. A threatening word or lash of the whip quickly put the slave straight.

Getting the most from one's slaves was essential to all plantations, but especially to the large West Indian ventures, on which slaves constituted a major part of the capital costs. In 1695, a slave on Jamaica sold for twenty pounds. A crew of fifty was worth the equivalent of ten years' earnings of a prosperous English farmer. The planter needed to recover that expense and make a profit over the course of a slave's working years. With fifty to a hundred slaves to manage, losses could be expected if the planter was not vigilant.

From the perspective of the planter, slaves were "tools" and plantations had to be run like machines to be used up before they wore down. Because idle time was lost money, planters everywhere were tireless in their drive to maximize slave output. They thus sought to cut plantation costs by keeping slaves busy when not needed for the commodity production. Working slaves directed their children and elderly to tend the gardens and joined them when their tasks were completed. As added incentive, slaves were permitted to sell items they grew and use the cash to meet other needs at local markets. According to the planter Edwards,

> The practice which prevails in Jamaica of giving the Negroes lands to cultivate from the produce of which they are expected to maintain themselves . . . is universally allowed to be judicious and beneficial; producing a happy coalition of interests between the master and the slave. The negro who has acquired by his own labour property in his master's land, has much to lose, and is therefore less inclined to desert his work. [24]

These arrangements, Edwards argued, had the double benefit of reducing the amount of food purchased while encouraging work among slaves, whose supposed proclivity to "idleness" was a constant complaint. In this manner, the slave's hunger was added to the many ways of disciplining and raising profits.

The persistence of tasking in Brazil, where planters embraced the slave gang late and partially, can be explained by the tenacity of small-scale farming and the separation of farming from mill work. Brazil was similar to Cuba in that wealthy settlers controlled the *engenho* or mill and used patronage and their control over land to secure cane from tenants and small operators known as *lavradores de cana*. Drawing upon their privileges, the *engenho* propagated contractual arrangements that at once removed them from the management of the land while guaranteeing their mills an adequate supply of cane. By contrast, the *lavradores* arrived to the New World with very little capital and, lacking political connections, became dependent farmer-planters. Some took on debt to acquire land, tools, slaves, buildings, and animals, and were thus bound from the start to farm commercially for *engenhos*. *Engenhos* imposed on some land a customary obligation to farm cane for their mills. Sharecropping *lavradores* grew "captive cane," half of which they paid in rent and another one-eighth to one-sixth in milling fees, and were further obligated to provide firewood and pay for any improvements to the mill. Independent *lavradores* could choose their mill but paid a heftier price for the service.

Under these conditions most Brazilian cane growers could not piece together the capital needed to build the integrated farming-milling complexes that required large numbers of slaves. The average planter had only four slaves in the seventeenth century and only seven as late as the 1810s. A planter with seven slaves would be hard-pressed to put one gang into the field. Yet by using quotas the Brazilian planter kept himself abreast of the work pace and day-to-day progress and, as the manager of his own slaves, he was on hand to make necessary adjustments. Only when plantations grew large enough to support and require significant numbers of slaves was ganging readily adopted.

Such was the case on Barbados, where, by 1680, 175 planters or 7 percent of the property-owning population controlled half of the island, had on average two hundred acres of contiguous farmland, and possessed half of the servants and 60 percent of all slaves. These enterprises far exceeded in scale anything found in Brazil and led the way in experimentation, combining the growing and processing of cane in single integrated agro-manufacturing complexes.

Seventeenth-century Barbadian planters benefited from the growing world of English transatlantic commerce, at the center of which was a body of well-capitalized and highly flexible London merchants. Many successful West Indies planters came from this merchant background; others benefited from the relatively cheap capital these men willingly advanced to colonial ventures. In the 1630s, wealthier or yeoman farmers led the way in settling Barbados. They began the clearing of the dense forests and experimented in cotton, indigo, and especially tobacco farming. When steep competition out of the North American mid-Atlantic colonies drove down tobacco prices, they searched for a new cash crop. Dutch merchants had already introduced sugarcane from Brazil and it proved to be highly profitable. Beginning in the 1640s, farmers on Barbados began to focus greater effort on its cultivation and processing, and with the promise of profit London merchants became more involved in the colonial venture. Some bought land and recruited representatives to run their sugar operations. Others, like the aforementioned Noell brothers, made the journey to the Indies as merchant-planters to run their ventures directly. Still others managed to make their way into the ranks of planters from more humble yeoman beginnings.

Regardless of their origins, these new operators ratcheted up the scale and intensity of production. In 1647 alone, twenty-one English merchants purchased 1,654 acres in Barbados, some acting alone and others in company. In some cases they acquired established plantations and in others they took possession of vacant land. But everywhere they augmented the scale of production, bringing in more labor (servants and slaves), livestock, and tools.

Robert Ligon reported, with some embellishment perhaps, that the typical cost of a Barbadian plantation in the late 1640s was fourteen thousand pounds. The great expense of the plantation stemmed from the fact that, while Brazilian *engenhos* let planter-farmers bear the cost of delivering the cane, by the 1660s the Barbadian planter was already experimenting with the integration of mill and farm. When it became clear that the integrated plantation was most profitable when the mill sat on a farm of one to two hundred acres, the cost of entry skyrocketed.

These capital-intensive undertakings were predicated on England's dynamic merchant community, whose members were already implicated in the North American colonies, investing in plantations, moving goods, and trafficking in African slaves. The vibrancy of the merchant community was in turn predicated upon the prior emergence of capitalist farming examined in chapter 3, which had given England a unique advantage in the emerging world system of trade and colonial adventure. Adam Smith was thus correct in his claim that "the prosperity of the English colonies has been, in great measure, owing to the great riches of England, of which a part overflowed, if one may say so, upon those colonies."[25]

As shown in the earlier discussion of England's agricultural revolution, developments particular to the sixteenth and seventeenth centuries had given rise to a class of landowners that received its income from commercially contracted rents rather than from venal offices or seigneurial jurisdictions. These developments, moreover, produced a state dominated by this same landed constituency, which, because it preferred not to levy taxes on itself, fostered overseas adventures as a source of government revenue. In this context, England's commercial classes took on a new color, as those previously protected by political privilege and patronage were superseded by interloping merchant adventurers. Excluded from the traditional trading routes, these men forged new ones in the emerging buccaneer world of the Atlantic.

In origin, these merchants were city retailers, ship captains, and colonial settlers who saw the need for close and even direct management of colonial undertakings. They pioneered tobacco, cotton, and later sugar, while developing the trade between Africa, Virginia, and the West Indies in foodstuffs, horses, and slaves. They made speculative land purchases and invested for the long term—it was two and a half years before they realized profits. They benefited from low interest rates that fell to 10 percent by 1700 and continued to decline across the next century. Thus, it was an exceptionally vibrant commercial environment, predicated upon England's agrarian transformation in the prior century, that gave its colonial planters an edge. The rapidity of development on Barbados was for this reason quite astonishing. By the late 1660s, twenty years after sugar production was taken up in earnest, the value of Barbadian sugar exports already exceeded that of Bahia, where the Portuguese *engenho* had been at it for a century.

Yet for all of its success and novelty, the West Indian plantation complex was slow to cut labor costs. As we have seen, the Barbadian sugar plantation chased profits by raising the slaves' workload and extending the working year rather than improving tools or land. The slave gang was its chief innovation. Addressing the logic of slavery, Karl Marx quoted the Irish economist J. E. Cairnes: "It is accordingly a maxim of slave management, in slave-importing countries, that the most effective economy is that which takes out of the human chattel in the shortest space of time the utmost amount of exertion it is capable of putting forth. It is in tropical culture, where annual profits often equal the whole capital of plantations, that negro life is most recklessly sacrificed."[26] Slavery was embedded in arrangements that both encouraged and allowed the planter to drive his slaves to the point of exhaustion.

Marx understood that industrial capitalists also wanted longer hours from their employees. But he also understood that under capitalism labor was a variable cost that had to be cut by provisioning it with labor-saving tools. The ability of labor to move to better employment was a break on the capitalist's capacity to squeeze more effort from his workforce, while price competition forced him constantly to seek ways to get more value from every worker. Capitalists therefore both managed their workers closely, in a manner similar to planters, and introduced new tools with dizzying speed and repetition to reduce their outlays in wages.

Planters, by contrast, could not afford to dismiss their workforce without suffering declines in profits. The workforce moreover was not free to reallocate itself. It was on this account highly ambivalent, and could not therefore be trusted to use tools economically. Planters found, therefore, that they could only improve competitiveness by getting more effort from their slaves while provisioning the simplest and cheapest of tools. Technical innovation on the slave plantation was thus infrequent, often labor extracting or intensifying, and usually slow to take hold (see the discussion of slavery in chapter 6).

The most commonly noted innovation on the sugar plantation was the three-stone roller mill. This new arrangement aligned three rollers vertically so that each bundle of cane was pressed twice rather than once. Because the weight of the stones no longer pressed on each other, and because the distance between them could be more precisely adjusted, the mill turned faster, broke less frequently, and extracted more juice. But its adoption probably had as much to do with cutting back on waste as it did with reducing the cost of labor. Because the traditional horizontal double roller applied less pressure, slaves had to spend time preparing the cane before pressing, and to extract all the juice they passed the cane through the mill several times. All this took labor, but it also slowed manufacturing down at the moment when planters were eager to cut and crush their cane before it spoiled in the field.

The peasant cane growers of Asia, with their small holdings and harvests, were usually content with less efficient mills because they had less to mill. But New World growers and mill owners operated on scales that called for alleviating this bottleneck. Undoubtedly, the adoption of the three-roller mill saved labor, but it did so in ways that reduced crop wastage and compensated for declining yields—the result of soil exhaustion—by extracting more juice from each cane shoot.

Tellingly, all other significant innovations on the sugar plantation lengthened the workday or increased the intensity of work. Tasking, ganging, and gardening were ways to get the slaves to work longer and harder, but without attention to output per hour worked. The most dramatic example of this technological backwardness was the ubiquity of the hoe. Acknowledging the benefits of plowing, planters were nonetheless universal in their preference for this back-breaking instrument. Bryan Edwards' exhaustive accounting of the expenses of the typical Jamaican plantation does not list the plow, but does list hoes. He emphasizes that West Indian planters universally issued hoes and put slaves to work in gangs, or as he called it the "old laborious mode,"[27] while acknowledging that a plow team would have prepared the land in a shorter period of time. Yet there was no incentive to reduce labor costs in planting and weeding, since the slaves were already purchased and their number was determined by the year's most labor-intensive tasks— harvesting and milling. It made no sense to put forth costly outlays on plows and draft animals, or to develop the skilled labor to operate them, for doing so would have rendered idle the capital already invested in slaves whose labor would be needed soon enough. So, while West Indian planters eagerly took up a new strain of sugarcane acquired from Asia, which released more cane juice, they preferred the whip to new tools. Plantation fieldwork continued to operate with the simplest equipment, much of it harking back to antiquity.

In short, there were few to no economies of scale to be had through technological innovation in sugar production. A common seventeenth-century maxim in Brazil went straight to the point: "Whoever wants to profit from his Blacks must maintain them, make them work well, and beat them even better; without this there will be no service or gain."[28] The Antiguan planter similarly told Newton that it was best "to wear [slaves] out before they became useless . . . and then to buy new ones."[29]

Though New World slavery was far removed, European society was acutely aware of its institutions. The English readers of Defoe's *Robinson Crusoe* would have known of the West Indian sugar plantation. Thinkers of the day wrote and talked about slavery constantly, though there were few voices opposed to it. The most prominent defenders of slavery, and certainly the most influential thinkers of their epoch, were liberals. Best known for their defense of the rights of individuals vis-à-vis the state, Pierre-Victor Malouet, Hugo Grotius, Thomas Jefferson, Antoine Barnave, and many others all supported slavery and the rights of slaveholders.

John Locke, arguably the father of modern liberalism, had little problem reconciling his arguments against tyranny with his support of slavery in the Americas. Though the opening line of his seminal *Two Treatises* begins, "Slavery is so vile and miserable an estate of man, and so directly opposite to the generous temper and courage of our nation,"[30] he was himself a shareholder in two slaving corporations, the Royal African Company and the Bahama Adventurers. He served briefly as secretary of the Council of Trade and Plantations (1673–1674), where he participated in the drafting of the legal convention governing slaves in the Carolinas. A central tenet of that convention was that "every freeman of Carolina shall have absolute power and authority over his Negro slaves, of what opinion or religion soever."[31] Citing the apostle Paul, Locke wrote that "conversion did not dissolve any of those obligations they were tied in before but . . . the gospel continued them in the same condition and under the same civil obligations [under which] it found them."[32] Locke went further to justify slavery by arguing that because "horses and slaves" were both purchased by "bargain and money" they constituted inviolable property. The slave had no history before his purchase. This fact gave the planter "absolute dominion . . . legislative power over life and death," and even "arbitrary power."[33] The equation of slaves with work animals or tools was part and parcel of the system.

The English legal scholar William Blackstone turned to natural law and geography to explain away the contradiction between freedom in Europe and slavery in the Americas. He argued that "the law of England abhors, and can not endure the existence of, slavery within this nation" and "this spirit of liberty is so deeply implanted in our constitution, and rooted even in our very soil, that a slave or a negro, the moment he lands in England, falls under the protection of the laws, and with regard to all natural rights becomes *eo instanti* a freeman."[34] Liberty, it was argued, was given in England by tradition and nature and thus not applicable elsewhere. Echoing Blackstone, Montesquieu wrote in *The Spirit of Laws*, "There are countries where the heat enervates the body and weakens the courage so much that men perform an arduous duty only from fear of chastisement: slavery there runs less counter to reason" and "one must not be surprised that cowardice of the peoples of hot climates has almost always made them slaves and that the courage of the peoples of cold climates has kept them free."[35]

For the preeminent philosophers of the day, slavery was the natural condition of some peoples, given to them by climate, geography, and contract. In making these assertions, liberals defended slavery in the New World and Africa and inoculated Europe and Europeans from its "tyrannical" effects. Thus, at the moment of classical liberalism's founding, here were arguments in favor of slavery made on the grounds that majority rule was mob rule, private property was sacrosanct, and state regulation was tyrannical: in other words, slaves were rightfully gained property, and it was tyranny to compel their freedom.

NOTES

1. Daniel Defoe, *The Life and Adventures of Robinson Crusoe* (New York: Penguin, 2001).

2. Stuart Schwartz, *Sugar Plantations in the Formation of Brazilian Society: Bahia, 1550–1835* (Cambridge: Cambridge University Press, 1985), 339.

3. Henry Whistler, "Extracts from Henry Whistler's Journal of the West Indies Expedition," in *The Narrative of General Venables*, ed. C. H. Firth (New York: Longmans, Green, 1900), 146.

4. Karl Marx, *The Grundisse* (London: Penguin Books, 1993), 325–26.

5. Montesquieu, *The Spirit of Laws*, ed. Ann Cohler et al. (Cambridge: Cambridge University Press, 1989), 88.

6. Bryan Edwards, *The History, Civil and Commercial, of the British Colonies in the West Indies*, vol. 2 (1793), 216.

7. Ibid., 213.

8. Richard Ligon, *A True and Exact History of the Island of Barbados* (London: Peter Parker, 1673), 88.

9. Edwards, *The History, Civil and Commercial, of the British Colonies*, 255.

10. Russell Menard, *Sweet Negotiations: Sugar, Slavery, and Plantation Agriculture in Early Barbados* (Charlottesville: University of Virginia Press, 2006), 140.

11. Ibid.

12. Ligon, *A True and Exact History*, 22.

13. Edwards, *The History, Civil and Commercial, of the British Colonies*, 128.

14. Ligon, *A True and Exact History*, 55.

15. Ibid., 88.

16. Edwards, *The History, Civil and Commercial, of the British Colonies*, 219.

17. Schwartz, *Sugar Plantations in the Formation of Brazilian Society*, 144.

18. Menard, *Sweet Negotiations*, 15.

19. Ibid., 84.

20. Ibid., 117.

21. Peter Thompson, "Henry Drax's Instructions on the Management of a Seventeenth-Century Barbadian Sugar Plantation," *William and Mary Quarterly*, 3rd series, 66.3 (July 2009), 578.

22. Robin Blackburn, *The Making of New World Slavery: From the Baroque to the Modern, 1492–1800* (London: Verso, 1997), 334–35.

23. Schwartz, *Sugar Plantations in the Formation of Brazilian Society*, 139.

24. Edwards, *The History, Civil and Commercial, of the British Colonies*, 131.

25. Adam Smith, *An Inquiry into the Nature and Causes of the Wealth of Nations* (n.p.: Alex Murray & Co., 1872), 463.

26. Karl Marx, *Capital*, vol. 1, ch. 10, sec. 5. The original is found in John E. Caines, *The Slave Power: Its Character, Career, and Design* (London: Parker, Son, and Bourn, 1862), 110.

27. Edwards, *The History, Civil and Commercial, of the British Colonies*, 203.

28. Schwartz, *Sugar Plantations in the Formation of Brazilian Society*, 133.

29. Menard, *Sweet Negotiations*, 84.

30. John Locke, *Two Treatises of Government* (London: Whitmore and Fen, 1901), 1.

31. *The Statutes at Large of South Carolina*, vol. 1 (1838), 55.

32. Locke, *Two Treatises of Government*, 147.

33. Locke, *Two Treatises of Government*, 24.

34. William Blackstone, *Commentaries on the Laws of England* (1765), book 1: 119–23, 157, 237–38, 243–44, 411–13.

35. Montesquieu, *The Spirit of Laws.*

"October," engraving by Jacques Callot, 1609. From a collection of seasonal vignettes titled Les Mois (The Months), "October" foregrounds a French peasant broadcasting seeds by hand. The lord's castle is perched on the hilltop in the distance, overlooking a church and village. In the distance, a peasant prepares the fields with the simple horse-drawn hook plows and another man scatters seeds across freshly plowed furrows. The Latin text reads: "October entrusts the seeds of Ceres [i.e., grain] to the tilled earth, breaks up the clods and levels the ground. The corn crop is more prosperous as it grows in a regularly harrowed field, but ominous Scorpio hinders the sowing." *Source*: Bibliothèque nationale de France.

French peasant sowing field by hand, photographed by Jacques Boyer, 1920. Taken two years after the end of World War I, the picture shows a scene that is almost biblical. Rather than employ a costly seeder plow, the peasant carries seeds in a cheap bag and sows them broadcast. The field has been rudimentarily prepared with only shallow furrows and low ridges. Compare with the early sixteenth-century engraving created by Jacques Callot, "October," on the previous page. *Source*: The Image Works.

"Andean Peasants Sowing Potatoes and Oca," from Felipe Guaman Poma de Ayala's *New Chronicle and Good Government*, 1615. A peasant uses a wooden foot plow or *chaquitaclla* to prepare a hole into which a woman drops seed potatoes. The third figure holds a mallet to pulverize the earth clods before covering. According to a description cited in our text, "By lowering their ploughs at once they can raise clods of earth so large that anyone who has not seen it could hardly credit it. . . . The women work opposite the men and help to lift the clods with their hands, turning the grass roots upwards so that they dry and die, and the harrowing requires little effort."

"Buffalo Plowing, Dry, San Yuan Dien," photographed by Sidney Gamble, 1917. A man guides his water buffalo through a rice paddy in Sanyuan township, Sichuan, China. This image is testament to the slow pace of technological change. A comparison with seventeenth-century printed wood-carved images in Chinese agricultural treatises shows that the method of plowing and the structure of the plow (a wooden hook plow with an iron share) is unchanged. *Source*: Sidney D. Gamble Photographs, David M. Rubenstein Rare Book and Manuscript Library, Duke University.

"Men Pulling Plow, Peking Western Hills," photographed by Sidney Gamble, 1924. Poverty coupled with the shrinking of farms through partible inheritance left peasants without land to support draft animals. In this case, a north China peasant household must make do with a very simple wooden plow, much like an ard, designed to be pulled by human rather than animal power. Capable of only the shallowest of plowing, such methods must have produced low yields. Such a plow would not have worked, however, in the much more productive paddy farming of south China, where a water buffalo was essential. *Source*: Sidney D. Gamble Photographs, David M. Rubenstein Rare Book and Manuscript Library, Duke University.

"Plowing with a Primitive Native Plow: How the Russian Peasant Tills His Leased Fields," photographer unknown, circa 1915. The image shows a peasant on the eve of the Russian Revolution preparing land for planting. He expertly drives a simple wooden sokha or hook plow through a field that has been left in fallowed grasses, perhaps to fatten cattle. The sokha was a light wooden plow with two iron-tipped shares. It had no moldboard or landslide for turning the soil. Though it had the advantage of being cheap to buy and operate (it required a single, small horse to pull), its light weight and inefficient design precluded deep plowing and breaking up earthen clogs. *Source*: Library of Congress, LC-USZ62-100634.

"Cutting the Sugar Cane," from "Ten Views in the Island of Antigua" by William Clark, 1823. A slave gang cuts and bundles ripe cane for transportation to a wind-powered mill, seen in the distance. The adult men and women in the foreground are shown using rudimentary "cane knives." They are supervised in this case by a black "driver," shown holding a whip, and a smartly dressed white overseer (perhaps the plantation owner) mounted on a horse. A child too young to work is visible next to its mother. *Source*: The British Library Board, 1786.c.9, Pl IV.

"Planting the Sugar Cane," from "Ten Views in the Island of Antigua" by William Clark, 1823. Under the supervision of two black "drivers," slaves wielding simple hoes and wooden poles place cane cuttings into prepared trenches. The trenches described by Bryan Edwards on Jamaica were dug to half a foot deep and covered with "mold," or a mix of manure, compost, and soil. *Source*: The British Library Board, 1786.c.9, Pl III.

"A Woman at a Spinning Wheel, Dinan, Brittany, France, c. 1922." Household manufacturing or handicrafts were an essential part of peasant life everywhere and spinning yarn and weaving cloth were among the most common forms. The technology and technique were relatively simple and cheap, allowing all but the most destitute households to acquire them. The raw materials were either grown by the household (such as cotton, silk, or flax) or acquired from local merchants. The materials produced clothed the family and provided cash earnings to buy oil and salt, pay taxes and rents, and acquire grain. The work was typically performed by those too old or young to engage in farm work, as in this image, or when times were difficult by all family members after the fields were tended. So long as productivity in farming was low, the manufacturing of cheap everyday goods remained trapped in the household. *Source*: The Print Collector/Alamy.

"Faucheurs, Somme," photographed by Eugène Atget, 1923–1924. In a scene most certainly recognizable to any medieval French villager, a peasant harvests his wheat by hand using a simple scythe. That the picture was taken in the supposedly advanced farming region of France's Somme department in 1924 is telling of the laggard pace of development in nineteenth-century French agriculture. Compare with the North American wheat farm shown on the next page.

Source: Library of Congress, LC-USZ62-105724.

Mechanical harvester-thresher, photographer unknown, 1923. A large team of mules pulls an automated harvester-thresher through a wheat field near Pullman, Washington State. The harvester was distributed by International Harvester Company (later Case IH)—a firm formed by the merger of McCormick Harvesting Machine Company of Chicago and Deering Harvester Company of Milwaukee in 1902. IHC was one of the new agro-industrial manufacturing firms that built large and small labor-saving machines suitable to a variety of terrains and farm sizes. In this image, the blades extending from the right of the carriage cut the wheat as an oil-powered engine drives the thresher to separate the grain from the stalk. Typically mule-drawn carriages rode alongside to collect and cart away the threshed grain. *Source*: Wisconsin Historical Society, WHS 3972.

A Taiwanese farmer manipulates a hand or walking tractor. These small machines were suited in cost and working capacity to the small farms of postwar Taiwan, just as the lawn tractors and moto-mowers of France were adapted to the comparatively small farms there. According to Taiwan's Joint Commission on Rural Reconstruction, which oversaw rural modernization, "The era of farm mechanization in Taiwan began in 1954 when JCRR imported seven garden tractors of 1.5 to 10 h.p. from the United States and introduced two small Japanese power tillers of a tractive and a rotary type. Power tillers now in use number 18,500 units of which 79 per cent are locally manufactured. The local manufacture of the corn sheller, jute decorticator, sweet potato digger, grain dryer, soybean planter, peanut thresher and sheller and tea cutter is paving the way for large scale mechanization of agriculture. The rice transplanter has revolutionized the method of rice planting" (The JCRR, 1948–1968. Taipei, Taiwan, 1968).

Source: Liang I Chang.

This page and opposite: "Slaves at Work in a Coffee Plantation at Vale Do Paraíba," near Rio de Janeiro, photographed by Marc Ferrez, 1882. The first photograph shows slaves working on a steep hillside picking the cherry coffee. Once picked, the cherries are carried in a basket back to the drying floor. The second image shows slaves collecting coffee beans with simple rakes that have been sun-dried on a hardened flat floor. After picking, the cherry coffee was spread four to six centimeters deep on a compacted earth surface and had to be stirred up to four times a day until it lost 60 percent of its moisture content. It was then bagged and shipped to the coast for further processing, or for export. The raking was done mostly by men, while women collected the beans in baskets. The overseer on the far left directs the work. *Source*: Marc Ferrez/Gilberto Ferrez Collection/Instituto Moreira Salles Collection.

"Gang labor" harvesting carrots in California's Imperial Valley, photographed by Dorothea Lange, 1939. *Braceros* at work. The original description reads, "Gang labor, Mexican and whites from the southwest. They pull, clean, tie, and crate carrots for the eastern market for eleven cents per crate of forty-eight bunches. Many can barely make one dollar a day. Heavy oversupply of labor and competition for jobs is keen." As in the slave plantation system, labor on the vegetable and fruit farms of central California was ganged to a task. In this case, they were paid by the crate in an effort to maximize returns to labor and get a perishable vegetable crop to the market when it was ripe. *Source*: Library of Congress, LC-USF34-019195-E.

"Mass Soybean Harvesting at a Farm in Campo Verde, Mato Grasso, Brazil," by Alf Ribeiro, 2008. The scale of soybean farming in the Brazilian Cerrado has grown massively in the past two decades. State land policy has encouraged the formation of 10,000 acre farms, managed by corporations and employing vast amounts of capital in machinery to cut labor costs. Each of the Case International Harvester combines pictured here is capable of cutting and threshing one thousand bushels (sixty thousand pounds) of soybeans every hour. The expansion of soybean cultivation accounted for the removal of 10 percent of the Amazon forest between 2001 and 2005 alone. Today, more than half the Cerrado has been cleared for crops and cattle and in the process 275 million tons of stored carbon dioxide were released between 2002 and 2008 alone. *Source*: Alffoto/Dreamstime.com.

Chapter Six

American Farming

Agrarian Roots of U.S. Capitalism

J. Hector St. John de Crèvecoeur's *Letters from an American Farmer*, published in 1782, made him a famous author among his French contemporaries. Though classically trained in the Jesuit tradition in France, he married and raised three children on a farm in rural New York, where he worked the land for almost a decade until the vicissitudes of the War of Independence forced him to flee America. His *Letters* affirmed that North America held out hope to Europeans, because it offered the opportunity to own land and assure one's livelihood. "What should we American farmers be without . . . the soil? It feeds, it clothes us, from it we draw . . . our best meat. . . . No wonder we should thus cherish its possession, no wonder that so many Europeans who have never been able to say that such a portion of land was theirs, cross the Atlantic to realize that happiness."[1]

Crèvecoeur put into writing the assumptions of the people of New England in the colonial era in the seventeenth and eighteenth centuries. They had land and food security, and developed agricultural practices suited to subsistence farming. The inhabitants of New England looked after a diverse production of crops, livestock, and handicrafts that spread the work of family members across the year and averted the price uncertainties, high seasonal labor demands, and potentially catastrophic blights involved in economic specialization. As late as the 1840s, the farmers of Massachusetts cultivated a variety of wheat, rye, corn, barley, oats, pulses, and hay. They continued to set land aside for flax so that they could make their own clothes. The more land and security enjoyed by the household, the more diverse was its array of crops.

To round out their needs, families took advantage of their abundant land to raise pigs, milk cows, and beef cattle. Meat made up a regular part of people's diets, and the milk was used to make cheese and butter. Households obtained hides and skins, tallow for candles, and bristles and other animal by-products for local use. Livestock also served to even out harvests. In good years, farmers used grain surpluses to fatten cattle and pigs for slaughter or for export to Boston. In bad years, they lacked animal feed and slaughtered their livestock for food or to gain extra income for provisions by selling the dried meat. After 1800, farmers began to raise sheep and broom corn (sorghum), which had market as well as local uses. Sheep supplied wool for cloth, and meat for consumption or sale. Broom corn was used primarily to make and sell brooms but could also be allowed to run to seed for cattle feed. Thus, farmers remained wary of products that committed them in advance to a single economic line.

Rural communities provided the context for these subsistence strategies. People set up households in specific areas in order to form part of linguistic and/or religious communities rather than pursue narrowly economic ends. Crèvecoeur remarked that the people of America "are a mixture of English, Scotch, Irish, French, Dutch, Germans and Swedes." Some observers, he wrote, wished that the unmixed descendants of Englishmen in the eastern provinces intermingled in the other communities. But Crèvecoeur preferred "it much better as it has happened," the "great and variegated picture."[2]

These different patches of settlement relied on local exchanges in the form of barter. Poorer inhabitants typically traded labor services for food produced on the farms of better-off landowners. Almost all households accumulated debts payable over many years in labor, crops, or cash. The debts were sometimes forgiven and rarely contracted at interest. Crèvecoeur wrote that the European immigrant, "instead of being employed by a haughty person, . . . finds himself with his equal, placed at the . . . table of the farmer . . . [H]is bed is not like that bed of sorrow on which he used to lie: if he behaves with propriety, and is faithful, he is caressed, and becomes as it were a member of the family."[3] If this laborer demonstrated "progress . . . in the rural arts, honesty, sobriety, and gratitude" he could lease "an hundred acres for any term of years . . . and make it more valuable. . . . By that means he may, with what little money he has, buy a plough, a team, and some stock. . . . [H]ad he two or three sons as able as himself, then . . . he [would be] more eligible . . . to purchase the fee simple." Crèvecoeur posited that the honesty of this newcomer to America "procured him friends, and his industry the esteem of his new neighbors. One of them offered him two acres of cleared land, whereon he might plant corn, pumpkins, squashes, and a few potatoes." When he had "neither mowing nor reaping to do . . . the time was come to build his house; and . . . for the purpose [Crèvecoeur] would . . .

invite the neighborhood to a frolick; . . . thus he would have a large dwelling erected, and some upland cleared in one day."[4]

In this manner, the inhabitants of colonial New England participated in a system of intra-community exchange of goods in kind, labor of family members, and loans of plows, horses, and other equipment, all drawn from the crops and livestock of their farms. Cash represented one item among others to be bartered for its uses. Owners of large farms in Massachusetts profited from the sale of swine, sheep, grains, and apples, and they used cash, accounting, paid laborers, the legal system, and written instruments with interest attached. Yet until the 1850s, they also produced much of what they consumed, and maintained a dense network of neighborly trade in beef, hides, shoes, dung, pastures, and carting services. Their finances included barter entries with no monetary value ascribed, as if they did not calculate debts and expenses as two antithetical acts, but rather saw the debts and expenses as one act involving two people in need of the concrete labor or practical goods of the other. They accepted wheat, rye, flaxseed, and other grains, along with money, as payment.

Much of the trade and landlessness recorded in colonial New England reflected the cycle of land accumulation for the purpose of establishing offspring. Crèvecoeur wrote that the immigrant, "having received his own and his family's wages . . . would willingly have land of his own, in order to procure him a home, as a shelter against old age: that whenever this period should come, his son, to whom he would give his land, would then maintain him, and thus live all together."[5] Family members joined forces to generate a marketable surplus and build up and enlarge their farm. The acreage owned by heads of households swelled through their forties and fifties and then shrank in their sixties, as they distributed it to children. To be young, in colonial New England, was to be landless or in possession of insufficient land to support a family, as parents held on to property to ensure their well-being in old age. The family remained the focus of existence. It offered training and capital for new generations, as well as comfort and security in old age. No other institution provided these indispensable services. People worked with their families to secure their subsistence until the appearance much later of schools, insurance, banks, industries, and other non-familial social, economic, and political organizations.

The farm surpluses, generated with the aim of procuring land for offspring, never dominated the economic activities of households. Farmers did not purchase necessities or obtain much income from marketed crops. Specialization in a commercial crop could lead to disaster in the event of insufficient yields, inadequate prices, or excessive costs of subsistence items. Pennsylvania farmers, even in the vicinity of Philadelphia, preferred to grow a wide variety of crops and make their own household items rather than specialize their output. Towns on the eastern coast of Massachusetts grew rapidly in the 1760s and 1770s, and nearly half of the farm households of Essex County had to purchase much of their food. But the agricultural response to this market demand was negligible. Even though the price of wheat rose substantially between 1750 and 1800, little of the total farm products of the northern rural communities were sold on markets even as late as 1820.

Farming for local use, in short, existed not because of the absence of opportunities favorable to commercial farming, but because of traditions secure in their rationality, traditions resistant to market dependence. On the eve of the American Revolution, inequality had grown in all regions of North America but did not entail the mass poverty common to Europe at that time. A growing sense of well-being pervaded prerevolutionary America, especially among landholding farmers. They grew taller and healthier than did their contemporaries in other parts of the world.

In reading the letters of Crèvecoeur, one gets the sense that the success of subsistence farming was due, in the last analysis, to the absence of a ruling class. New England "is not composed, as in Europe, of great lords who possess everything, and of a herd of people who have nothing. Here are no aristocratical families, no courts, no kings, no bishops, no ecclesiastical dominion."[6] Thanks to the absence of rulers, Crèvecoeur suggests, immigrants from Europe were free to obtain land and decent returns on their labor.

> Pleasant farms present themselves; [the European immigrant] may purchase what he wants, and thereby become an American farmer. Is he a labourer, sober and industrious? He need not go many miles, nor receive many informations before he will be hired, well fed at the table of his employer, and paid four or five times more than he can get in Europe. Does he want uncultivated lands? Thousands of acres present themselves, which he may purchase cheap.[7]

Colonial New England, of course, like all civilizations, was stratified by social class. Older and wealthier households involved in long-distance trade controlled the colonial legislatures and administration. Yet these rulers, Crèvecoeur implies, did not have a presence in all of the villages—as did European lords, and the English gentry—or have the power to prevent settlers from occupying the potentially lucrative borderlands. Many pioneers established legal freeholds in the Connecticut River Valley, Vermont, New Hampshire, and Maine. The colonial militia was not a national army and could not be used to enforce government claims to the frontier. The wealthier inhabitants of North America thus did not have the means to control the unimproved land, raise its price, enforce taxation, enmesh the households in obligations, and constrain them to produce for the market.

The only region in which landlords had power over thousands of acres was the Hudson Valley. Large landowners and speculators dominated New York more than they did any other colony. They owned nearly all of the land outside of Long Island and monopolized the frontier. Ten or eleven men owned three-quarters of the province in 1700. Eighteenth-century governors gave millions of acres to favorites and helped themselves imperially. As staple prices rose in the decades after 1750, many landlords forced tenants to sign short-term leases, raised rental rates, and demanded payments in wheat. These leasing practices played a part in provoking rioting against the manors of colonial New York in the 1750s and 1760s.

But elsewhere, Crèvecoeur observed, rural households had the lands and communities to see to their existence, and did not rely on commodity production. They did not have to match the prices of competitors or face pressure to keep pace with the innovations made on other farms. For this reason, the inhabitants of New England had no reason to fixedly rationalize their time to get the maximum monetary value out of it or obsessively accumulate surpluses and adopt the latest agricultural equipment. Instead, they farmed the same fields in traditional ways until the fields no longer yielded decent crops, then moved to other parts of their property, and let the original fields lie fallow for decades. The size of the land they possessed, relative to the family members with which to work it, led them to farm extensively and allow their pigs to roam freely for food. In the late 1770s, typical farmers in inland Massachusetts had much land in pastures and meadows, as well as vast expanses of fallow reserve and unimproved woodland. Their landholdings were much larger than those held at that time by peasants in China or continental Europe.

Agriculturalists obtained yields of twenty-five bushels an acre on the best land and the first harvests in Massachusetts and Pennsylvania, but in general obtained about fifteen bushels per acre for corn and eight to twelve for wheat. These modest yields did not offer many of the farms, apart from the most productive ones, much of a marketable surplus. The economy of New England grew over the course of the colonial era. Yet so did the population. It doubled by natural increase every quarter century, growing from less than 250,000 to almost 2.5 million from 1700 to 1780. Economic and population growth thus offset one another with the result that the per capita value of livestock, crops, tools, and output remained stationary.

Although this farming did not have an inherently developmental dynamic, it did represent a radical change from the former types of land use. The myth of the noble savage has led to depictions of the Native Americans as carefree, contented peoples enjoying a rich life of leisure, happy with the fruits of relatively little labor. This picture no doubt idealizes the Native Americans yet still contains an element of truth when one compares them to the European settlers. This is not to say that European methods were inherently better than those of Native Americans. We saw in chapter 2 the difference between the intensive subsistence agriculture of feudal Europe and the extensive contemporaneous farming of the Americas. Native American women saw to the farming and plowed with hoes and their hands. The farmers from Europe used oxen and horses that worked the soil more deeply than it ever had been before and wiped out the native plants. The settlers changed the landscape by way of a new habitat of domesticated species. Their animals permitted them to farm a larger area and cultivate a given stretch of soil more regularly. The animals, in this way, led to soil erosion and deforestation, and ultimately, as a consequence, to recurrent flooding.

For these European settlers, the large reserves of unimproved land, the expansion of livestock rearing, and the more systematic exchanges of labor within families and communities improved productivity and maintained the stability of subsistence farming. In the early decades of the nineteenth century, domestic manufacturing for local merchants supplemented incomes and helped maintain viable communities largely bereft of impoverished rural workers. Much of the landless population of New England went west of the Hudson River in New York State and from there into Ohio, Indiana, Illinois, and the rest of the Midwest in the hopes of working their way up the agricultural ladder from laborer, to tenant, and then to freeholder. As a consequence, population density never became as acute a problem as it became in contemporaneous France and China, and most farmers never had to exploit themselves through increased drudgery at declining returns to their labor.

Poor farmers migrated to new lands on the frontier. They defended their holdings from the claims of land speculators, remained debt free, did not have to produce for the market, and by and large succeeded in reproducing the pattern of independent households of New England of the previous two centuries. Cash was sparse, roads were poor, and costs between the farms and the markets were high in the region of Springfield, Illinois, in the 1840s. Rather than buy and sell commodities, farmers devoted their energies toward subsistence production for domestic use and household security. Probate records and reports of farmers show that they made their own wood tools just as settlers had since colonial times. Households farmed corn and devoted smaller fields to oats and wheat. They raised several score of hogs, a dozen heads of cattle, oxen and milch cows, a small flock of sheep, and assorted poultry. They had gardens for vegetable and root crops, patches of flax or cotton, and orchards of apples or peaches. The women of central Illinois made cheeses for sale in Saint Louis.

The households saved the income to buy land and enhance their economic security. Some farmers slaughtered their hogs and marketed thousands of pounds of pork. Yet, in spite of their great earnings, they continued to plant crops to meet the food and fiber needs of their households and bartered for extra-household labor with pork, corn, and portions of their arable land. The laborers used this land to grow their own subsistence crops. Well-off farmers of central Illinois, ones who sold large surpluses, used the profits to purchase land in the 1840s and 1850s. Their holdings grew several times larger than the typical farms of New England. Wealthy farmers invested in land clearance, draining, fencing, manure, and other improvements. Yet despite the difficulty of securing workers they did not invest in new mowers or other sorts of mechanization. The conditions remained conducive to the establishment and maintenance of self-provisioning households, and the farmers perceived no need to invest in inputs that would augment the marketable surpluses.

In these ways, although the expansion of the population and market in New England diminished the availability of land, increased its prices, and obliged its farmers to take on debt, these natural forces, so to speak, did not bring subsistence farming to an end. Rather, concrete political acts, taken by the foremost lawyers, land speculators, and investors in large-scale coastal and wholesale trade, compelled the inhabitants of New England and the Midwest to change their economic behavior. Political leaders had long sought to expand commodity production through investment in roads, canals, and railroads, as well as through mortgage lending and other forms of land speculation. They had long sought to regulate the use of public lands in order to prevent the spread of self-reliant farms, replace kin and communal bonds with contractual relations, and augment the sphere of market exchanges. But it was only in the 1780s and 1790s that they organized politically to impose fiscal policies and property rights on the frontier and close off avenues to self-sufficiency.

During the War of Independence, state officials requisitioned food and clothing, and army contractors roamed the countryside offering cash for food, horses, and wagon transport. The war increased agricultural prices and encouraged farming for the market. Rural households devoted labor to commodity production, did not produce all their consumer goods locally, and borrowed from store owners to purchase necessities. After the war, English commercial houses and wholesalers called in their debts in cash from New England's urban merchants who in turn put pressure on store owners and traders in the countryside. These rural traders insisted on cash payments for the debts their neighbors had formerly repaid over many years in cash or kind.

Meanwhile, land speculators and merchants fought against rural households to build up governmental institutions capable of forcing farmers to pay debts and taxes. They opposed the emission of paper money liable to downgrade their loans to state governments and undermine foreign trade. The 1781 "Consolidation Act" converted the war debt of Massachusetts into legitimate tradable documents proving ownership of credits not subject to depreciation. A high rate of taxation facilitated the repayment of the debts in specie by 1788. The Massachusetts General Assembly refused to grant stay laws to inhabitants of the central and western part of the state driven into insolvency through falling prices, rising taxes, and debts. In the 1780s,

The creation of the machinery of exploitation

groups of irate farmers fought against tax collectors, rescued the property of neighbors from sale at auction, and freed oxen confiscated by constables from defaulters. Shays' Rebellion formed part of a larger struggle of rural inhabitants against tax collectors, merchant-creditors, and land speculators across Maine, Vermont, Pennsylvania, and Ohio through the 1780s. The Constitutional Settlement of 1787 consecrated the defeat of these struggles by establishing the political dominance of investors and merchants, a permanent fiscal officialdom, and a federal army to enforce legal titles.

At the close of the Revolutionary War, merchants began in earnest to promote turnpikes, canals, and bridges. They channeled larger portions of their wealth into loans for public works projects. The wealthier inhabitants of New England held more and more shares in banks and insurance companies relative to their traditional farm assets. Investors poured money into western lands during and after the Revolutionary War in anticipation that victory would open new vistas for rapid settlement.

The inhabitants of New England thus became ensnared in liabilities for debts and taxes, fretted over the cash needed to stave off bankruptcy and expropriation, and reluctantly devoted labor to market production. Once down this road, households had little choice but to adjust their farms ever more precisely to consumer demand, improve methods and implements to cut costs, immediately adopt any improvements developed by economic rivals, and thus raise aggregate productivity. Over the course of the colonial period, equipment and techniques remained largely unchanged, and production expanded extensively. But from 1785 to 1815, the percentage of improved plows and output per farm grew in upstate New York. Crop rotations of pastures and meadows, associating arable land and animal husbandry, along the lines of the tenant farmers of England as early as the sixteenth century, enhanced labor and soil productivity in the northeastern United States in the early 1800s. Per capita wealth, and social inequality, increased. It required enormous amounts of capital to settle and farm the land west of the Appalachians in the nineteenth century, and much of this wealth came from the transformation of agriculture in the East, where growers worked for wages and saved for the purpose of land purchases, commodity production, and monetary surpluses. The profitability of eastern agriculture, and the wages it generated, made possible the movement of capital westward.

Commercial farming came to prevail in the territories west of New England, not as a result of market opportunities but rather as a result of the actions of land speculators and money lenders backed by the state. Frontier farmers required draft animals, livestock, and fencing to clear, break, and mark out the land. They needed seed, farm implements, transportation to the West, and a house, all prior to tilling the land and acquiring income from the first harvests. In the years following the War of Independence, settlers put their savings into these improvements in the hopes of establishing viable farms. Federal officials, however, hoped to sell the western lands, shore up public finances, and bind the buyers to the state as the guarantor of their investments. Congressmen did not see the squatters as the industrious, moral, and orderly sort liable to develop the region in the proper fashion. Just as the Taiwanese state of the 1950s, studied in chapter 9, obligated farmers to produce for the market through a land reform, which saddled them with mortgages and fees, American legislators, in the early nineteenth century, resolved that frontier farmers would have to purchase the property directly from the federal government or more commonly from speculators. Businessmen had purchased large tracts of land with the aim of selling farms to squatters. These settlers on the trans-Appalachian frontiers had little revenue to pay the companies that acquired the land and after evictions ended up as tenants or debtors to moneylenders representing banks and businessmen in the East.

Over the course of the nineteenth century, large insurance companies and private investors in the eastern states oriented their businesses around loans to farmers in the West. Banks did not face any federal oversight or direction, and could thus advance vast sums speculatively and drive up land prices rapidly. Investors from eastern cities and Europe enticed people to western Pennsylvania with descriptions of extensive luxuriant meadows but did not mention the Indian wars, the weather, the terrain, and, above all, the fact that the best land would have to be rented or purchased from its owners.

By 1810, in the Northwest Territory, nearly half of Ohio's population was landless, while about 1 percent of it owned nearly a quarter of the state. Needless to say, the landholders had an interest in infrastructural projects that would raise the value of their assets. A dozen great land speculators, holding influential state offices, blamed the economic panic of 1819 on the weakness of governmental institutions and pressed ahead with improvements in transportation to integrate Ohio into the federal economy and state. Over the subsequent decades the calls for public outlays on internal improvements reached a fever pitch, as political leaders across the Midwest came to associate this infrastructure with the growth and prosperity of the nation.

The purchases of western settlers, and especially of the speculators eager to anticipate their needs, made the public land sales of the 1830s the largest in American history. Of the 38 million acres of public land sold in 1835–1837, 29 million were acquired for speculation by bankers. Subsequent waves of boom and bust made it difficult for farmers to ever pay off their debts to landowning companies and attain economic security. Many lost their assets with the onset of economic depression in 1837 as a large number of customers withdrew cash from deposit accounts and depleted bank reserves. The downturn then dissipated as commodity prices rose, immigration quickened, and capital surged back into the region in the 1840s. But banks foreclosed many mortgages again in 1846. Thousands of farmers lost their homes, and people either went elsewhere to attempt to settle again or became tenants upon their old claims. Propertyless tenants, day laborers, and farmers who repurchased the land at a higher valuation made up about a third of Indiana's voters in 1846. By mid-century, the vast majority of Iowa farmers had purchased the bulk of their land from the state's realtors, lawyers, government officials, and other land speculators.

The commercial depression of 1837–1842 created fiscal and revenue crises for the states. Bankers and merchants in the US and Britain, as well as government bondholders, pressured the states to restructure their tax systems, raise revenue, and meet interest payments. All of the northern states, except Michigan, eventually met their obligations in spite of the opposition of local farmers. Tax rates increased 650 percent in Illinois from 1841 to 1848. The actual amount of taxes collected rose 959 percent in Ohio from 1836 to 1851. A growing number of state surveyors, land-office administrators, and tax collectors, backed by the federal army, bore down on the inhabitants of the Midwest. These farmers lived in dispersed settlements and, in comparison with their peers in New England, lacked the traditions of communal land and water usage. They did not have the wherewithal to take collective action against land speculators and tax collectors. Farmers west of the Appalachians had no choice but to market their output with the aim of gaining the income needed to comply with their fiscal obligations and service their debts.

Farmers thus became dependent on the market on account of debts and taxes and were obliged to improve production with the aim of matching the competitive prices of other commercial farmers. Rising productivity and output forced down commodity prices and further compelled farmers to augment output, contract debts, and obtain better equipment and breeding stock despite the financial strain. The pressure to enhance output relative to labor time raised productivity sharply in the 1840s and 1850s. Capitalist farmers accumulated labor-saving implements, as the shortage of workers, due to the accessibility of land, gave an impulse to mechanization. The compulsion to lower costs and match the competitive prices of other capitalist farmers accelerated the diffusion of the horse-drawn steel plow, developed by John Deere, to cut through the tangled roots of prairie grasses. Reapers, threshers, and other equipment, produced by industrial concerns such as the McCormick Harvesting Machine Company, became steadily more efficient and mechanized from the 1840s into the twentieth century. The rate of labor productivity compounded every decade, rising faster than that of industry.

The obligation to compete to survive economically propelled farmers in the Ohio Valley and Great Plains to specialize in wheat and steadily bring down its market prices. They also specialized in corn to feed commercial hogs and cattle. Midwestern agriculture involved a distinctive corn-hog nexus, as pigs absorbed surplus grain, raised farm income, and increased fertilizer production. The period saw social differentiation, as the viability of farms depended on the ability of producers to meet the high capital costs necessary for economic survival. The most advanced capitalist farmers, possessors of already large farms by world standards in the 1870s, more than doubled their acreage. Less competitive growers lost their holdings, while wage laborers experienced difficulty securing land and entering commodity markets.

Low-cost production in the Midwest made grain and beef unsustainable among eastern farmers who had become dependent on the market after 1800. Agriculturalists of New England could not match the low prices of the capital-intensive farms of the Midwest and had to specialize in other lines such as peas and beans, fruit, and other products of market gardening, as well as potatoes, dairy goods, and oats for horses used in the cities. They turned to tobacco farming, whose value tripled in western Massachusetts in the 1860s and 1870s. When the demand for tobacco fell in the 1870s, the area suffered the worst reversal in fortune of the 1800s until prices revived in the 1890s. Rural inhabitants who did not have much land labored to a greater extent in outwork and became wage earners in regional manufactures.

This transformation of eastern agriculture to dairy, market gardening, and tobacco comes across in the memoirs of Anne Sneller about her family in Cicero, in the middle of New York State not far from Lake Ontario, in the second half of the nineteenth century. She expressed the uncertainty and anguish generated by the debts required to make farming viable. "My father was a proud and happy man when at the end of seven years he was able to buy a farm . . . twenty acres for three thousand dollars. He had to go into debt for it. . . . He implanted in Ethel and me a horror of debt that never left us."[8] The memoirs give the sense that the debt was contracted for the purpose of commercial farming and was necessary to achieve social standing and to avoid relegation to an outcast group of economic failures.

> There were various reasons that led father to buy another farm. He wanted more land for raising tobacco and grain; the apple orchard on the new farm promised a good cash crop; and the farm was located on a hard gravel road that made going to market much easier than the mud of the sideroad in spring and fall. Underlying all of these sound reasons was his undeclared wish to improve his social position. The main road separated him more definitely from all that was Dutch on the Mud Mill Road.[9]

The mental universe of the Sneller family was clearly one of commercial farmers forced by competition to make cost-cutting investments.

> Father had . . . a passion for machinery. As fast as a new farm machine was put on the market he was eager to try it and see if it made life easier. All kinds of farm tools and machinery were undergoing rapid changes . . . ; each change meant that more work could be done better and faster. This was especially true of plows, mowers, and reapers. Father's first reaper was a triumph and the

sound of it music to his ears. He bought a tobacco setter before most farmers
had heard there was such a thing. [10]

The Sneller household aimed to make its time productive of market value.
"Tobacco was the big money crop that paid off the mortgage. It was a
precarious crop, for a sudden hailstorm in August could cut it to pieces or an
untimely frost destroy it without remedy. Crop insurance was unknown.
Raising tobacco, father said, took more out of the land and more out of the
men than any other crop." [11] Sneller's father started farming the tobacco early
in spring. He mixed the tiny seeds with other substances to make them visible
and then sowed them by scattering them with his hand. The seedbeds had to
be meticulously prepared with the best soil and with embankments of boards.
A light woven cotton material was extended over the seeds to protect them.
The Sneller household devised a method of suspending boards over the seedbeds so that one could crouch and weed them as the sprouts emerged.

The tobacco setter economized on the time spent by family members and
hired workers planting the seedlings in rows. But much work still had to be
done hoeing to keep down the weeds as the plants grew. Once the plants were
three feet high, six to eight inches were broken off the top so that they grew
broad leaves rather than unsellable nicotine blossoms. Shoots grew at the
base of the leaves, and much labor was expended going up and down the
rows taking them off. Family members also had to expend time removing the
tobacco worms attracted to the soil. The farmers later took down the plants
with shears and laid them out in lines across the field for them to wilt
sufficiently to be gathered into piles without breaking the brittle leaves.

The tobacco plants were heavy, and once they could be safely handled, it
required considerable effort for the farmer and hired laborers, with the aid of
family members, to string them up on laths. The plants were thus hung on
poles in the shed separate from one another so that they would not touch,
suffer poleburn, and ruin their texture and color. Sheds had to be appropriately constructed to permit ventilation for curing the leaves to the proper color.
"But curing was not the end. It was the halfway mark when the farmer could
say, 'So far, so good.'" [12] Sneller's father would choose a moist day in the fall
for him and the hired hands to take down the plants, strip the stalks, and
begin the long process of sorting them into the different elements used in
cigars, pipes, and chewing tobacco. A pan of water was kept burning on a
stove in the barn to prevent the tobacco from drying out during this work.
Glazed paper covered bundles of the finished products before they were
cased and packed, nailed, and labeled in strong wooden boxes.

Tobacco buyers arrived from New York or elsewhere in early winter to
inspect the tobacco and negotiate a price. "Ill feeling often arose when one
man's crop sold for much more than another's. . . . One never-to-be forgotten
year father's tobacco check was twenty-two hundred dollars. . . . His face

was shining and he said triumphantly, 'This will cover the last payment on the mortgage. The place is ours.'"[13] By the end of the century, as market prices changed, farmers in the area had to turn from tobacco to cabbage, and the tobacco setter was transformed with little work into a cabbage setter. Cabbage entailed less work and risk.

Sneller's memoirs are especially instructive in their description of the women's work required to make the farm economically viable. Anne Sneller, one of her aunts, and her mother put in skilled and tiresome labor making cheese. They carried big pails of milk from the stable, lifted them to a vat, and then saw to the long process of taking care of the curds and whey. They got the cheese in and out of presses, turned it on the shelf, greased it, and provided it with other attentions crucial to the flavor and texture. Most of the cheese was sold in Syracuse.

Sneller's aunts spent much time making shirts for the men and some of the cloth for the bedding. When the family purchased a sewing machine, it lessened the toil yet "increased the number of things to be sewed."[14] "But most of all and worst of all for women were the washings and ironings."[15] On Sunday night, women put the soiled work clothes to soak in water pumped from the cistern or well and heated on the kitchen stove. "Monday was a day of carrying, bending and lifting."[16] The tubs were emptied in the morning, and the clothes were placed in a new supply of heated water to be rubbed on the washboards. More water was heated, this time with soap shavings, and the clothes were boiled, while the women moved them about with a stick to get them thoroughly clean. These two steps of rubbing and boiling had to be done once for whites and again for colors. The clothes next went through a stage of sudsing and then one of rinsing. Women had to thoroughly cook starch and get it free of lumps or scum that sticks to cloth. They then pegged the clothes firmly to a line. Tuesday was dedicated to ironing. Flatirons were heated over a fire, and using them in July demanded plenty of fortitude. Everything had to be ironed, and Anne Sneller learned the chore when she was fairly young. She confessed to preferring it to other tasks, for once it was mastered, it could be performed even as the mind wandered to other subjects.

The land and the farm capital were eventually divided among Anne Sneller's uncles. She thought it odd that the women made no claims on the inheritance.

> Till middle age and beyond, they had worked as hard as their brothers. Without their unpaid labor the high prosperity of the family could not have been achieved. The hired help was well paid; reduced to its simplest and somewhat deceptive terms, the women got their board and clothes. The Household was generously provided for, but the thrift and saving practiced in its management increased the money that could be spent in improving the farms. . . . The

women were not willfully overlooked in the settlement. It was the custom of the period to disregard the money value of women's work.[17]

Anne Sneller's memoirs give the sense that farmers were major consumers too. Her father bought special hoes, clippers, and other sorts of the latest equipment. He bought special cuts of lumber needed for the various agricultural tasks and for the latest designs of farm buildings. Growers throughout the Midwest snapped up the latest implements, machines, industrial fertilizer, and transportation so that they could farm more acres with their household labor and meet the prices of competitors. The Sneller family seems to have purchased all of their clothing apart from a few tailor-made work outfits. They purchased receptacles, pumps, irons, kerosene lamps, and other metallic goods.

Farmers like the Sneller family sold their crops to cover the costs of land acquisition, supplies, and taxes. Household production of goods for domestic use such as clothes, tools, implements, fencing, meats, and grain declined sharply between 1840 and 1860. Like the population of early modern England examined in chapter 3, the farmers of the United States made up a large consumer market and thus helped spur the development of industrial zones. Farmers purchased vast quantities of seeds, plows, tools, pots, stoves, furniture, and everything else they needed. Manufacturers mass-produced items sold through the Montgomery Ward catalogue. Based in Chicago, Montgomery Ward shipped hats, hardware, guns, athletic goods, musical instruments, and many other commodities to farm households all over the Midwest in the last decades of the 1800s.

In this sense, the industrialization of the United States was closely connected to the expanding spheres of capitalist agriculture. Textbook descriptions of US industrialization start with textiles, shoe and boot manufacturers, and railroads, which called forth machine making and innovations in iron production. One longtime Chicago resident more accurately stated in 1893, "The cities have not made the country, on the contrary, the country has compelled the cities. . . . Without the former the latter could not exist. Without farmers there could be no cities."[18] Food processing, to take a case in point, amounted to the leading sector of industrial growth. It included grain milling, hog butchering, distilling, and brewing industries in Milwaukee, Minneapolis and other cities of the Midwest. These industries represented much more than intermediaries between grain farmers and eastern consumers. They emerged at the outset of the agricultural settlement, went through technical innovations, and became machine-based industrial enterprises. Flour milling constituted the first national industry in terms of the total value of output between 1850 and 1880. Meat packing ranked fourth nationally in the total value of output in 1880 and first in 1905.

The industries producing agricultural machinery, tools, and supplies also stood at the forefront of the industrial revolution. The early manufacturers of the Midwest, with close links to iron and coal industries, encouraged agriculture. Companies such as John Deere and the McCormick Harvesting Machine Company churned out plows, harrows, hoes, seed drills, and reapers. The manufacture of agricultural implements accounted for over a quarter of the value of all US machine production by 1870. Manufacturers also produced seeds, wagons, carriages, harnesses, fertilizers, and saw timber and nails for fence rails and buildings. The early manufacture of iron in places like Pittsburgh was largely oriented toward farming and rural household products such as stoves, kettles, skillets, ax-heads, horseshoes, plowshares, hoes, nails, and rifle barrels. The competitive pressures to cut costs, gain market share, and keep pace with rival farmers created a mass market for agricultural inputs and household supplies, as agriculturalists devoted more and more time to productive labor in the fields.

All in all, the expansion of capitalist agriculture westward constituted the motor of economic growth. It drew in ever-larger investments of bankers, insurance companies, and industrialists. More and more Northerners, through participation in this expansion, came to value a society in terms of the work ethic, social mobility, wage labor, diversification, and the nationwide benefits of a broad and developed economy. All of these qualities contrasted with their views of the slave economy of the South. Northerners were naturally drawn to the Republican Party, as it emerged in the 1850s, in the hopes of spreading their values to the nation as a whole.

In this way, the idea took hold that the western territories ought to be a place where people of European descent could find a home and better their circumstances free from the degrading competition of slave labor. Citizens of the North looked on with apprehension when Southern leaders imposed a blockade against abolitionist propaganda. They became even more alarmed in 1854, when the way was opened for slavery to spread westward after the annulment of the 1820 prohibition on slavery in the Louisiana Territory north of the 36°30′ latitude line (with the exception of Missouri). It then became clear that to win elections in the North, one had to unequivocally oppose the expansion of slavery. The Republican Party campaigned for offices on the theme of a strong resistance to Southern domination. This platform implied a subordinate status for slavery within the country as a whole. The capitalist agriculture of the North had an expansive dynamism and led Southern slave owners to deem it impossible to coexist within the United States.

The judgments and considerations of the slaveholders emerged from a distinct civilization that first emerged in Virginia after the early 1600s amid a lack of internal consumers, an abundance of land, and a consequent high rate of withdrawal from the labor market, all of which constituted inducements for investors to turn to forced labor and staple exports. This economic orientation entailed subsistence farming for the coerced labor force, the export of investor profits in luxury consumption, and the monotonous cultivation of the same commodities over the long term.

Slave agriculture was highly commercial, driven by profits, and responsive to markets. The strong demand for exports gave plantation owners the means to increase the number of slaves, create a high ratio of workers to the land, and cut supervision costs. The masters developed means of wringing maximum labor from their slaves through multiple tasks every day and year, as well as through the development of tasks for the children, elderly, and women. Beverly Jones related the story of a fellow Virginian slave, Jake, who said, "Just come to tell you Massa, that I've labored for you for forty years now. And I done earned my keep. You can sell me, lash me, or kill me. I ain't caring which, but you can't make me work no more."[19]

The management techniques used to compel the incessant labor needed to make slavery profitable developed out of the experience of the wealthy planters, who, in the eighteenth century, founded their power on patriarchal families and dynasties of political leaders in the colonial assemblies of Virginia. The Virginian planter William Byrd described it this way in 1726:

> Like one of the Patriarchs, I have my flock, and my Herds, my Bond-men and Bond-women, and every soart of Trade amongst my own servants, so that I live in a kind of Independence of everyone but Providence. However, this soart of life is attended without expense, yet it is attended with a great deal of trouble. I must care to keep all my people at their Duty, to see all the Springs in motion and make everyone draw his equal Share to carry the Machine forward.[20]

The period from 1750 to 1775 saw high tobacco prices and easy credit, and the planters improved their lands, houses, and barns. On the eve of the American Revolution, the average wealth of whites in the Southern colonies was higher than it was in the North. It was inequitably distributed, however, and to acquire it, one had to purchase land and slaves, and produce for the market. Despite the common practice of leaving land fallow for twenty years, soil quality and tobacco yields began to decline in the Chesapeake by the early eighteenth century, and cultivation moved to the coastal plains and into the piedmont regions of Virginia, the Carolinas, and Georgia between 1720 and 1770. The price of land, farms, and slaves mounted and made inheritance crucial to a man's success. The whites who did not own slaves struggled to maintain themselves as independent farmers amid the growing plantations or sought to improve their status by migrating to the frontier.

Between 1790 and 1820, 250,000 whites migrated to the Lower South with 175,000 slaves. The whites remaining in the Upper South sold many slaves and switched to grain, as tobacco markets declined. Yet this evolution never freed the economy from the wretched labor force. Julian Niemcewicz, a Polish poet, spent two weeks in Mount Vernon in 1798, and described the huts of George Washington's slaves.

> [They are] far more miserable than the poorest of the cottages of our peasants. The husband and wife sleep on a miserable bed, the children on the floor. . . . A small orchard with vegetables was situated close to the hut. Five or six hens, each with ten or fifteen chickens, walked there. That is the only pleasure allowed to negroes. They are not permitted to keep either ducks or geese or pigs. They sell the chickens in Alexandria and buy with money some furniture. They receive a peck of Indian corn every week, and half of it is for the children, besides twenty herrings in a month. They receive a cotton jacket and a pair of breeches yearly. The general possesses 300 negroes, excepting women and children of which a part belongs to Mrs. Washington.[21]

Farming subsequently improved in Virginia over the following decades. The sale of slaves to the Lower South offset the losses from tobacco and financed the acquisition of fertilizer, equipment, and livestock. Progressive farmers sought to diversify crops and improve livestock. The reduction of the labor force reduced supervisory costs and permitted versatility. Yet these reforms depended on the income gained from the sale of slaves and thus from the expansion of labor-intensive plantation agriculture in the Lower South.

This region has a perfect weather pattern for cotton in that the rain increases from the spring to midsummer and then progressively decreases in a manner allowing roots to take hold and then the cotton flower to remain intact and dry for the picking. Farms in the Cotton South were on average over twice as large as those of the Northwest. This average was entirely due to the cotton plantations, rather than to the non-slave farms, which were slightly smaller than their Northern counterparts. The Gini coefficient, which measures the income distribution of a nation's residents, reveals much more inequality in every one of the cotton regions than in any of the Northern states. The dissuasive costs of labor made it impossible for Northern farmers to cultivate fields beyond what their family members could work, whereas the only limitation on farm sizes in the South was the amount of slaves money could buy.

Growers in the North and slave owners in the South both had to sell their output on the market for the income needed to pay creditors and avoid foreclosure on their farms. Yet while Northern farmers responded to this pressure by investing their surpluses in labor-saving implements with the aim of increasing output per time worked, slave owners invested theirs back into the original outlays on land and slaves. Masters had to calculate the cost of slaves, and other plantation expenses, relative to the overall output. The capital sunk into slaves entailed further costs in feeding and maintaining them. While the masters kept these costs to a minimum, they nonetheless represented a constant drain on profits and encouraged the masters to offset them by keeping the slaves busy at all times. The plantation owners thus complemented cotton with corn, whose peak labor requirements in planting, cultivation, and harvest came on either side of cotton's and permitted the masters to keep the slaves at work producing the consumption goods of the plantation and cutting down on expenses.

This system did not offer the slaves a humane diet. "All that is allowed them," according to the slave Solomon Northup, "is corn and bacon. . . . Each one receives, as his weekly allowance, three and a half pounds of bacon, and corn enough to make a peck of meal. That is all—no tea, coffee, sugar, and with the exception of a very scanty sprinkling now and then, no salt."[22] The food nonetheless provided sufficient nourishment for the slave population to increase. North America had always been farther than the Caribbean and Brazil from the slave markets in Africa. After 1808, federal law prohibited merchants from importing slaves into the United States. Slaves thus had a higher capital value in the US South than they did elsewhere in the world. The wealth of US slave owners consisted principally of their human chattel. Thus, while the masters were compelled to keep slave rations to a minimum, and drive the slaves to constant toil, they nonetheless saw to the slaves' reproduction. This practice contrasted with the rest of the Americas where the owners found it profitable to work the slaves literally to death and then purchase younger ones.

Despite this difference, in all parts of the Americas, the principal impediment to development was the same one examined in the last chapter on slavery in Barbados and Brazil. The masters, unlike capitalists, could not expel laborers to make way for labor-saving tools and machinery. To expand production and reduce costs in the face of world-market competition, the masters' only option was to increase the intensity and pace of work, and to add slaves and land, especially in more fertile areas. Geographical expansion, rather than the development of productive equipment, became necessary for the growth of slave agriculture. Calculations show that the plantations had a good deal less equipment and land per worker than did small farms of the South, and the implements used on small farms in the South were much less advanced than were the ones used by their capitalist counterparts in the North.

Productivity undeniably advanced in the South. On the one hand, the spread of cotton farming onto more fertile lands westward, and the adoption of new plant strains amenable to picking, enhanced the labor productivity of slaves four times over from 1800 to 1860. New strains of cotton did not require additional supervision to make the investment profitable. On the other hand, the sullenness of the captive labor force, recognized by all, though never admitted publicly by masters or slaves, discouraged the planters from entrusting valuable tools and livestock to their workers. It was not worth the cost to manage the slaves and make sure they used advanced implements appropriately.

Instead, to enhance cotton output, harvest the crop as soon as it was ready, and meet the exigencies of their creditors, the masters perfected the art of keeping as many slaves busy on as much land as possible. Northup's description of the brutal logic of the cotton fields bears a striking resemblance to the gang system used against the slaves of the sugarcane plantations of Barbados examined in the last chapter. The slaves of the Cotton South had to hoe the fields four times at about two-week intervals to prepare the furrows and eliminate weeds, grasses, and deficient plants. "During all these hoeings . . . the fastest hoer takes the lead row. He is usually about a rod in advance of his companions. If one of them passes him, he is whipped. If one falls behind or is a moment idle, he is whipped. In fact, the lash is flying from morning until night, the whole day long. The hoeing season thus continues from April to July."[23]

Work breaks amounted to lost income, and for this reason, according to Northup, it was an offense "invariably followed by a flogging to be found at the quarters after daybreak. Then the fears and labors of another day begin and until its close there is no such thing as rest . . . with the exception of ten or fifteen minutes, which is given at noon to [eat]. . . . [Slaves] are not permitted a moment idle until it is too dark to see, and when the moon is full, they often-times labor until the middle of the night."[24]

Then at the end of the day, "a slave never approaches the ginhouse with his basket of cotton but in fear. If it falls short . . . he knows that he must suffer. And if he has exceeded it by ten or twenty pounds, in all probability his master will measure the next day's task accordingly." In cotton-picking season, "it was rarely a day passed without one or more whippings. . . . The delinquent whose weight had fallen short, was taken out, stripped, made to lie upon the ground, face downwards, when he received a punishment. . . . It is literal, unvarnished truth that the crack of the lash and the shrieking of the slaves can be heard from dark till bedtime . . . any day."[25] Yet from the master's perspective, this violence could only enhance productivity so much without harming the labor force and undermining its ability to work. Slaves were the masters' most valuable assets, worth too much for them to be permanently maimed. Slave agriculture, on the whole, thus had a finite capacity for growth.

Slavery also retarded the development of industry and population. Wealthy investors in high-priced slaves had little to gain from free labor immigration. Since slaves could be used as strikebreakers in towns, and may have depressed wages, they accentuated divisions between the white propertied and non-propertied classes, and played a major role in discouraging immigration to Southern cities. The presence of slaves in the labor force made it difficult for Southern manufacturers to recruit labor. Northern investors, unlike slaveholders, imported immigrants to break strikes and, more generally, stood to benefit from the growth of the free population and its salutary effect on property values, urban growth, and the railway business. By contrast, the internal market of the South consisted primarily of the plantations, which the masters kept self-sufficient apart from cheap slave clothing, cotton gins, a few crude agricultural implements, and rope for cotton bagging.

Thus, it was not so much the overall economic growth that benefited the Southern potentates as it was the slaves themselves, whose very value offered normal rates of profit even for wasteful masters. Slaves, rather than farm improvements or public infrastructure, constituted the main form of property speculation and the basis of social status. They could be transferred to wherever their work proved most profitable and thus, as a form of property, did not require a framework of fixed investments to enhance their value. Rising slave prices led to levels of wealth truly staggering in comparison with the averages of other groups of the US population.

In sum, the civilization of the South, built on the relations of master and slave, did not follow a capitalist course of development. In the absence of the Civil War, it would never have led to the cotton farms seen today in the United States, where all operations are mechanized, including the harvest done with mechanical pickers, and no labor costs weigh on the grower. Slave owners were a ruling class of masters and, as such, would never have relinquished their slaves even when offered compensation.

Slavery, rather, represented a way of life to which the master class had become accustomed. An anonymous Northern visitor to a plantation wrote, "I soon hear the tramp of the laborers passing along the avenue. . . . All is soon again still as midnight. . . . I believe that I am the only one in the house that the bell disturbs; yet I do not begrudge the few minutes loss of sleep it causes me, it sounds so pleasantly in the half dreamy morning."[26]

The obverse side of this pleasantness of the civilization of the South was the slaves' dissatisfaction with their condition. Even though slaves seldom attempted to revolt or escape, and even though they seldom admitted their unhappiness, they nonetheless constituted a resistant malcontent workforce. Class conflict, manifest simply in the slaves' dissatisfaction, shaped the political evolution of the country as a whole, even if it did not appear in many overt acts.

For one thing, this class conflict helped forge the political alliance, characteristic of Jeffersonian Democracy, of independent farmers and slaveholders. Slaveholders garnered their wealth from their human property, not a class of peasants or workers. They could sing the praises of agrarianism and egalitarianism, and reach out for the support of poorer citizens, because they exploited black slaves rather than white farmers. Slaveholders and Democrats in the South insisted that all must have equal rights to the fruits of their labor and the political participation to maintain these rights. The Jeffersonian legacy obscured the fact that some would have the right to the fruits of the labor of slaves by merging the slaveholder with the farmer in general. Blacks never figured into this conception even though they made the wealth of the slaveholders and made possible the alliance with nonslaveholding whites. The cohesion and stability of Virginia, the relative harmony among the voters, rested on slavery.

The Jeffersonian legacy to the Democratic Party helped the slaveholders bring much of the white population under their leadership. Whereas Northern investors obstructed the spread of independent rural households, which, we have seen, compromised property values and raised labor costs, slaveholders eulogized the farmer. Thomas Jefferson doubled the size of the country through the acquisition of Louisiana, whereas John Adams and most of the Federalists sought to diversify the economy by restricting the availability of land. Wealthy Northerners found the Democrats' rhetoric, their fulminations against the Federalists for encouraging social inequality, crude and demagogic. Their rhetoric on racial difference cemented the loyalty of whites to the slaveholders' government. Their rhetoric on moral autonomy underlined the citizen's right to choose to own slaves. Their egalitarian individualism had genuine appeal even to white Americans in the North.

In the South, farmers in both the up-country and the plantation belts purchased few of their consumption goods. They feared subjection to the market and loss of independence. As long as the Democrats did not challenge the political rights of these farmers, levy taxes on them, build roads, establish banks, or aid merchants, the wealthy slave owner could continue to emphasize local and individual autonomy and remain a partner of the subsistence and semi-subsistence farmers. Limited government also reduced the potential threats from the federal government to slavery in the South.

In this way, the slaveholders, through the Democratic Party, exercised leadership over the nation as a whole until the 1850s. Members of the party openly expressed their dislike of bankers and merchants, and even campaigned on this dislike and implemented policies harmful to commercial elites. Andrew Jackson destroyed the Second Bank of the United States, the largest commercial institution in the country, and some states ridded themselves of all banks. At the same time, Democratic politicians might oppose slavery but could not mingle such views with policy positions. If they did, they met with resistance and likely expulsion from the party. Jackson held that the Constitution made an explicit provision for slavery, and the case was therefore closed. For the Democrats of the 1850s, Jefferson had provided the legacy of the expansion of territory, democracy, and liberty. The path charted by Jefferson and reaffirmed by Jackson had no place in it for slaves. These disappeared from view. Democrats thus reacted fiercely when this sectional issue intruded upon politics, and anyone who agitated over it, knowing the potential instability of such agitation, was a traitor to the nation.

But while class conflict, manifest in slavery and its discontents, made it possible for the masters to win the support of nonslaveholding whites, it also made them pursue destabilizing policies. The arguments in favor of free soil in the West would not have portended emancipation, or seemed threatening to slaveholders, had the slaves been content with their status. Abolitionism would not have proved so difficult for Southern leaders to handle, and would not have led them to curb free speech after 1830, to the horror of Northern nationalists, had slaves felt loyalty to their masters. The crisis generated by the Mexican war would not have emerged if slaveholders trusted their slaves. Senator John C. Calhoun of South Carolina argued in 1844 that Texas ought to be annexed in order to protect slavery, which was of incalculable value to the nation. If Great Britain captured Texas, he argued, it would expose the western frontier to abolitionists, and agitation against slavery in Texas would open the way to a race war in the South and the rule of the barbarians. Slave owners feared the prospect of abolition in Texas, just as they did in the District of Columbia and the black belt coastal regions of South Carolina. Southern Democrats initiated expansion into Texas, and the party's responsiveness to their interests turned the issue into a national conflict.

Most importantly, Southern leaders would have remained indifferent to the Republican ascendancy over the federal government had their workforce been reliable. The leadership of the Republican Party had made abundantly clear that it would not interfere with slavery where slavery already existed. The Republicans sought rather to prevent the spread of slavery to new states in the West. Yet the discontent of the slaves made it imperative for their owners to control the federal government.

For this reason, the victory of the Republicans led the slaveholders of the cotton districts of the Deep South to set in motion the momentum for secession. They made clear that they left the Union in order to preserve slavery. Geographical expansion to more fertile areas did not present much hope within the US South. Slaveholders looked to frontier regions where they could shift to new lines of production. The Midwest prairies attracted planters as a place to grow corn and raise pork. Others viewed areas conquered from Mexico in 1848 as places where slaves could mine metals, and graze cattle and sheep. Still others hoped for the annexation of Cuba and other Caribbean islands where slaves could grow sugar, cotton, and other tropical staples. The Democratic leaders deemed slavery a positive good and their civilization the finest. Accepting the Republican Party's stated intention to limit slavery to where it already existed, even with the party's pledge to uphold it there, entailed a rebuke to the slaveholders' society and system, the acknowledgment that slaveholding constituted an evil. The free-soil argument struck at the core of the slave owners' pride and self-belief. Containment of the system was intolerable, for it seemed to portend the end of the moral and political existence of the Southern ruling class.

Underlying this fear of Republican control of the federal government was the fact that the price of slaves rose to stratospheric heights in the 1850s. Masters thus became exceedingly sensitive to political and economic expectations. The value of their property in slaves made them seek to eliminate potential threats to its legality. The Republican victory in the presidential election, many feared, would raise doubts about the future. It might lead slave owners in the Border States to put their slaves on the market, lead the timid in the cotton states to do the same, lead buyers to take note and bargain accordingly, and then send slave prices tumbling downward. Credit and investment in the expansion of Southern agriculture depended on perceptions of the permanence of slavery. Thus, to maintain their wealth, political power became paramount to the slaveholders, if not over the federal government, then at least over the independent Confederacy.

In the Upper South, the sale of surplus slaves required the expansion of the plantation system to the south and west. The money for investment in improved farming in Virginia presupposed the exhaustive agriculture of the Lower South. The interregional slave trade held the system together and made the expansion of slavery a central part of it.

Yet this same increase in slave prices in the 1850s made it difficult for Southern whites to obtain them and started to cause divisions within the Democratic Party. The forces strengthening the economic incentives of slave owners started to undermine support for the institution among non-slaveholders of the South. Slave owners as a proportion of the population declined, especially in the Border States, and the institution became concentrated more and more in the Cotton South. Southern unionists typically hailed from the ranks of independent nonslaveholding white farmers. Many counties in Louisiana, northern Alabama, and northwestern Texas boasted more troops in the Union armies than in the Confederate ones.

For this reason, the states' rights leaders of the Lower South forced secession on the rest of the population. In Florida, Governor Madison Perry stated that it was unwise to wait for an overt act of the Republicans. That was the mistake, he argued, of the white inhabitants of Saint-Domingue (Haiti) whose fate the inhabitants of the South would share if they did not secede. Florida lawmakers defeated a proposal for a delay or plebiscite, and voted immediately for secession. The Alabama Legislature refused to submit a vote on the issue of secession to the people. In Mississippi, by contrast, blacks made up a majority of the population, and almost half of the white population held slaves. Whites felt that threats to slavery endangered the very fabric of society. In South Carolina, commercial growth reinforced the dependence of the wealthy on slavery, and even though competition from the more fertile lands in cotton states to the west led to difficulties, the success of some planters focused the aspirations of other farmers. Slaves moreover made up the majority of the population. Many therefore harbored anxiety about emancipation and saw secession as the only conceivable option.

In this way, slave agriculture did not evolve whatsoever toward free labor and capitalist farming. By the 1850s, Southern investors gained more wealth from slavery and became more dependent upon it than ever before. They channeled an ever greater portion of their profits into land and slaves, and adopted increasingly aggressive policies to defend the economy of the Cotton South.

Agriculture in New England and the Midwest initially developed around cohesive communities of subsistence farmers resistant to capitalist agriculture and to dependence on commercial crop growing. Investors had to regulate the access to, and the cost of, new lands in the West, raise taxation in support of internal improvements, and replace barter relations with contractual debts in order to oblige the farmers of the Midwest to farm for exchange rather than for their own use. Once subject to market discipline, Northern farmers began to specialize their production to suit the fluctuations of consumer demand, and the relative shortage of labor gave momentum to a very technologically advanced agriculture and to the rapid growth of Northern industry.

The drive toward increasingly large and profitable investments in land and industries, as agriculture spread westward in the North, made the political class ever more critical of the efforts of slaveholders to claim power and territory for a system seemingly inimical to economic opportunity. When Northern politicians laid claim to the federal government and the overall direction of the country, the antagonisms between divergent economic systems came to a head. Southern slaveholders perceived a grave threat to the slave economy and saw no choice but to secede.

NOTES

1. J. Hector St. John de Crèvecoeur, *Letters from an American Farmer* (Carlisle, Mass.: Applewood Books, 2007), 27.
2. Ibid., 51.
3. Ibid., 77.
4. Ibid., 110–14.
5. Ibid., 106.
6. Ibid., 49.
7. Ibid., 75.
8. Anne Gertrude Sneller, *A Vanished World* (Syracuse, N.Y.: Syracuse University Press, 1993), 138.
9. Ibid., 141.
10. Ibid., 144.
11. Ibid.
12. Ibid., 146.

13. Ibid., 147–48.
14. Ibid., 152.
15. Ibid., 153.
16. Ibid., 155.
17. Ibid., 286.
18. Quoted from William Cronon, *Nature's Metropolis: Chicago and the Great West* (New York: W. W. Norton, 1991), 97.
19. Julius Lester, *To Be a Slave* (New York: Puffin Books, 2000), 126–27.
20. Patrick Henry, *Economic, Political, and Domestic Life in Late Eighteenth-Century Virginia* (Washington, D.C.: National Park Service, 1989), 36.
21. Lester, *To Be a Slave*, 62–63.
22. Ibid., 73.
23. Ibid., 66–67.
24. Ibid., 71.
25. Ibid., 71–72.
26. Ibid., 74–75.

Chapter Seven

New Imperialism

Colonial Agriculture in the Age of Capitalism

The era of New Imperialism, when vast areas of Africa and much of Asia succumbed to colonial rule in the decades after 1870, disrupted the livelihoods of millions of peasants who previously had relied on local exchange and village customs to farm for their own needs. Colonial powers sought to make newly conquered territories profitable for investors in shipping companies, agribusiness, and other overseas ventures. They tightened control over local populations as capital flowed in greater amounts than before from the financial centers in Europe, North America, and Japan and settled in investment in mines, railways, and plantations. Raw products flowed back to the processing plants and factories. The disruption to existing ways of life was on display across the global south.

The rulers of Belgium, France, Germany, Great Britain, Japan, and other countries sought to make the African and Asian peasantry farm for the benefit of investors in the imperial countries. Yet this peasant labor was largely reluctant to work for wages or to farm for cash. Great effort was therefore expended by colonial administrators to capture it and direct its efforts toward the gathering of forest products such as rubber and lumber and the cultivation of cash crops such as cotton and sugar. This chapter is devoted both to the policies pursued by the colonial powers to spur the indigenous populations to till the land for the benefit of Europeans and Japanese and to the native responses to these policies.

To highlight the very local character of the struggles between colonial powers and indigenous people, and to demonstrate the very uneven nature of the outcomes of these struggles, we have elected to examine a wide range of cases. We discuss Belgian, Portuguese, British, and French colonies in Africa, British rule in India, and the Japanese rule over Taiwan, and conclude with a discussion of the similarities and differences in these imperial outcomes.

AFRICA

Jean Elima, a witness of events of the 1890s in Bokuma, a village in the Congo Free State, a colony founded and owned by Leopold II, the king of Belgium, told an investigator in 1953:

> When you Whites arrived, you did not arrive with the intention of fighting, but of buying ivory . . . you fought against us because we provoked you. We called you "bambulumbulu." . . . The Whites passed in a small boat. . . . They fired on a river person, and he died. The name of this person is Iluwa. It was the beginning of the war between us and the Whites, because Iluwa fired arrows at them.[1]

Pierre Lokuli, another African observer in Bokuma, told the investigator:

> We saw the White of the State, Ikoka, Mr. Coquilhat . . . but he only passed by. Seeing that, our fathers said: "Look, this fool flees from us. . . . Let's take his pearls and drown him with his dugout canoe." But when Ikoka saw that they were beating the gongs and drums and church bells, he turned the canoe around and fired above our heads. The struggle wasn't strong this time. But a lot of men died.[2]

François Bombute, a former African judge and servant of an Italian doctor, told the same story but claimed that "there were not many deaths, because they fired in the air, to scare the people."[3]

Whatever the precise events involved in the arrival of colonizers in Bokuma, all of the testimonies concur with Lokuli's as to what happened next.

> Two Whites Ntange and Wilima imposed the rubber harvest. They placed sentinels in the villages. . . . At the time of Ntange and Wilima the killings were at their height. Extermination of people. There was nothing to eat, there was no way to live in the village. If the sentinel found someone who had eaten, if he found a bone of a fish or animal, he immediately fired and death followed. . . . My father came out of the forest . . . to make peace. . . . [The sentinel] agreed with him and told him: "Good, but call your family in order to get rubber."[4]

Bombute stated: "This history of rubber is terrible and sad . . . we endured bad weather and hunger in the forest . . . the sentinel . . . exterminated us. . . . When the rubber was insufficient, he killed the people. . . . If there were bananas in the banana tree only he cut them. If he found that you ate bananas he killed on the spot."[5]

Jean Elima testified:

> We got the rubber. We took the rubber sap and rubbed it on our stomach. When it coagulated, we rolled it into a ball. . . . There were three Whites for whom we got rubber and to whom we had to bring human hands. They were Ntange, Wilima and Ikomakoma. . . . [Bokuma] had to deliver four baskets of rubber. And with each delivery they killed four men, and with each basket of rubber they added four hands of men they had killed . . . the people of [Bokuma] were unhappy and mad about these killings and fled, the village died out completely.[6]

Describing these same events to the investigator, the witness Joseph Ekuku affirmed that people were killed when villages furnished less rubber than had been demanded. "Each soldier had to cut the left hand of his victim to make the count." Villagers, he added, had to carry the rubber two hundred to three hundred kilometers. Ekuku also described a revolt. Villagers went to see a shaman who made them invulnerable to bullets. "The soldiers killed many people with their rifles, but the villagers killed many soldiers with javelins."[7]

King Leopold II, the instigator of this terror, had portrayed himself as an altruistic humanitarian on a disinterested mission. Knowing that Europe would not permit him to carve out a new colony in the heart of Africa, he set up the International African Association in 1876 in order, he claimed, to end the slave trade in the Congo, welcome Christian missionaries, and foster investment in public works for the benefit of the Africans (Leopold II publicized outlays of his personal fortune). At that time, many middle-class Europeans attended meetings to learn about, and seek an end to, the small-scale wars that continued to fuel slave markets. Forces of the African Manyeman Empire, in the second half of the 1880s, raided villages, took captives, and released them in return for ivory. Once they saw they could obtain no more ivory, the forces agglomerated the territory into the empire and obliged villagers to enroll in the armed gangs. Some of these gangs enforced justice through mutilation to prevent theft.

Leopold II took advantage of reformist sentiments in Europe against African violence and slavery to legitimize his ambitions. Initial reports from the Congo swelled his goals and desires. Half of the Congo was covered with vines of rubber, a material of soaring value on account of the industrial production of bicycle tires and insulation for electric cables, and the Congo Free State, established by Leopold II, invented the fiction that most of the territory, previously used for shifting cultivation and hunting, was vacant and therefore belonged to the public domain. From 1891 to 1892, the state started to harvest rubber in this area through a tax collected in labor from the native population. This work was overseen by *la Force Publique*, a mobile army of local mercenaries, the largest military in central Africa, created to occupy the country and police labor from its command over the rubber-collecting posts.

Agents of the companies to whom Leopold II granted rights to the rubber in various regions of the colony received 2 percent commission on all of the raw material collected at their posts. This money could amount to eight times their annual salary. They therefore had every reason to bring in as much rubber as possible. Company agents recruited and armed free villagers and slaves, and stationed them in the rural communities. These sentries had the power to coerce the rural population into placating them with wealth, good housing, and sexual favors. They forced the rural population to harvest rubber in order to maintain these advantages.

The quantity of rubber due per male amounted to about full-time work away from home in the forest. According to the testimony of one of these rubber gatherers, "should the creeper have already been tapped, the man must climb into the supporting trees at more or less personal risk and make an incision in the vine high above the ground where the sap has not been exhausted; and there he will remain, perhaps the whole of the day, until the flow has ceased."[8] Additionally, rural inhabitants had to provision the administrators in Léopoldville (today Kinshasa). They had to harvest, prepare the food, and take it there by foot on their backs and heads. Under threat, people had to change their work and farming schedules, previously geared toward satisfying their own needs, in order to provision the colonial administration.

A Protestant missionary remembered a case he witnessed in 1894 when a village did not fulfill the food requisitions. Soldiers surrounded the village while the inhabitants were sleeping, and as they sought to flee, the soldiers pitilessly shot down men, women, and children, and destroyed their village. To enforce the rubber quotas, the sentries stationed in the villages took women, children, and the elderly hostage until the inhabitants complied. In cases of defiance, the military used rape, torture, mutilation, cannibalism, surprise raids, and summary executions in a psychological war of terror to oblige the peasantry to collect rubber. European officers suspected that their ammunition might not be used properly and demanded a severed hand for each empty cartridge. The sentinels cut hands from living people in order to keep bullets for hunting. The hands even began to serve as war trophies, signs of bravery. A pastor witnessed the severing of the hand of an old man killed for refusing to collect rubber. When the pastor complained to the district commissioner, he was threatened with expulsion if he continued to involve himself in such matters.

The ultimate reason for all of this savagery was the Africans' resistance. When Leopold II's colonial state began to build the headquarters for the Abir company in 1893, the Lulonga and Maringa valleys rose in revolt against the rubber impositions and two agents were killed. This inauspicious beginning served as the prelude to the constant hostilities that lasted until the company departed in 1906. It took the company until 1898 to drive the Manyemans out of the region, and the local population continued to show hostility, preferring the irregular demands of the Manyemans to the rubber regime imposed by the Congo Free State. Jean Elima, Pierre Lokuli, and Joseph Ekuku, the African witnesses to the rubber terror mentioned above, each stated that the violence escalated when the village population revolted. Even in areas where the state's military dominance was established, Africans continued to resist demands for labor and produce through outright rebellion, murder of state and company agents, industrial sabotage, and evasion of duties through migration and flight. The Congo Free State also faced a series of mutinies within its military and had to contend with at least twelve major guerrilla wars. Even after Belgium took over the colonial administration from Leopold II in 1908, it still had to send the military into battle because of the Africans' refusal to submit.

Africans lucky enough to avoid the whips, prison sentences, and other aspects of the violent pacification of the colony had difficulty cultivating the fields. Men went away to collect rubber and could not clear new agricultural lands in the mode of swidden farming (see chapter 2). Women then had to farm the same fields at reduced fertility and declining yields. Compounding the crisis, sentries confiscated animals and raided gardens. The result was a steadily worsening famine from 1899 onward. Smallpox, sleeping sickness, and especially lung and intestinal diseases, attributed by a missionary to the exposure involved in rubber gathering, killed many people from 1893 into the early 1900s. The Congo probably had around twenty-five million people in 1880. In 1925–1926, when an official census was taken, the population had fallen to little more than ten million people. From 1880 to 1908, about thirteen million lives were lost. The violence does not match the current definition of genocide in international law: "Acts committed with intent to destroy, in whole or in part, a national, ethnic, racial or religious group."[9] But the loss of so many people no doubt amounted to a veritable holocaust.

The terror only subsided when it came to the attention of the European public. From the outset, commercial houses of Europe had opposed the monopolies granted by Leopold II to concession companies as a means of channeling all of the profit to himself and associated investors. The success of Abir, one of these companies, in collecting rubber denuded the entire Maringa-Lopori basin of productive rubber vines by 1904, and from then until the fall of 1906, when the company left, it was caught in a downward spiral of declining productivity and increasing violence. This violence came to light thanks to ex-state officials, travelers, and especially missionaries, whose testimonies strengthened and then superseded the opposition of the merchant companies excluded from the colony. The international humanitarian movement publicized the brutality of the Congo Free State and made it a subject of international politics.

But before the disclosures could have an effect, the Congo Free State provided Leopold II with funds free from any oversight of the legislature, public opinion, or even civil servants. He used them to build up the armed forces. The merchant house of Bunge, like the handful of other international businesses associated with the commerce in Congolese goods, and with Leopold II's dynastic and national projects, turned Antwerp into the world's leading market in rubber and ivory. The riches from the Congo made colossal family fortunes and elegant villas in Wallonia and Flanders. Hardly any of it went into public buildings, roads, or factories in Africa. The Congo did not even have a hospital prior to World War I.

Leopold II's rule over the Congo may have made up the grimmest episode of the new imperialism, but its system of labor was copied after 1900 by the German authorities of Cameroon, the Portuguese of Angola, and the French of Congo-Brazzaville. The rubber companies relied on whips, chains, hostages, forced labor, burned villages, and paramilitary sentries, and about half of the population of these colonies perished. Even after Leopold II died, things did not change drastically in the Congo. His colonial officials and la Force Publique stayed on as employees of Belgium. Many of them had investments in the Abir rubber company.

Taking rubber profits necessarily required violence, because the relatively small workforce, examined in chapter 2, made up the critical variable in the African economy. In 1910, Congolese peasants worked only about one-thirtieth of the arable land. They provided for themselves and had no interest in harvesting rubber or any other commodity profitable to the colonizers. Their use of machetes, axes, hoes, and other outdated labor-intensive tools limited the land under cultivation, contributed to labor scarcity, and yielded very little taxable income.

Consequently, coerced crop production—like the feudal obligations foisted on European peasants around the year 1000—became a feature of imperial agriculture in Africa. The difference from the feudal logic examined in chapter 2 was the extraordinary growth of the world market during the nineteenth century. The competitive dynamic inherent to capitalism constantly forced down the rate of profit and compelled investors to counter by cutting costs through ever-cheaper raw-material inputs. Manufacturers in Europe and Japan, concerned about access to inexpensive cotton after the defeat of slavery in the American South, pressured their governments to exert control over foreign lands. To stimulate production for world cotton markets, observers recognized that imperial states would have to dominate territories. Japan sought control over north China, where cotton was already grown by peasants. Imperial Germany set up gins throughout the bush-growing areas of its colony in Togo so that growers would not have to separate the seeds themselves or carry heavy raw cotton over long distances. The administration distributed seeds scientifically developed specifically for the Togolese environment. It established minimum prices and dispatched purchasers all over the colony to reduce the risks for native growers. The German authorities built a railroad from the cotton-growing areas to the coast and thus cut the travel time from a week to a couple of hours by 1907. They even brought in African American experts from newly founded Tuskegee Normal and Industrial Institute. Yet despite all of these incentives, German officials bemoaned the fact that "unlike America [see chapter 10], the peasant here is not dependent on cotton growing for his subsistence. The latter always has access to other crops, and his needs are so low, that he can live without any cash income for extended periods of time."[10]

To avoid the setbacks faced by Germany in Togo, the Belgian parliament, which had taken control of the Congo from Leopold II, continued to authorize coercion, no longer so much to collect rubber, but to grow cotton. Around 1920, the authorities charged agricultural agents from Europe to oblige two to three thousand rural households to work sixty days a year on cotton plots in two vast zones of north and south Congo with appropriate climate and rain patterns. Each household could only do business with one of twelve concession companies responsible for the region. The main difference with the former rubber regime was that the methods used to enforce the cultivation of cotton were more discreet and tactful so as to avoid provoking a new international campaign of denunciations. For this reason, the British company Lever was invited to invest in cotton cultivation, and the Belgian government offered it enormous advantages to get it to consent. The state forced a few hundred households to farm for the companies in 1917, but then hundreds of thousands, in subsequent decades, in vast areas covering hundreds of thousands of hectares. The concession companies, like the modern sugar mills we will see in Japanese Taiwan, did not obtain farms but rather monopoly rights to the peasants' cash crops. But whereas Taiwanese cane growers enjoyed other liberties, the Congolese could neither withhold sales, grow other crops, or seek better prices from different companies.

Authorities had various means of getting the peasants to farm for the companies. Films, festivals, plays, and other propaganda were intended to instill a new work ethic and values. The state rigidly allotted more land to cotton than it did to other crops, forced down the prices of other agricultural commodities, and increased those of cotton in an effort to stimulate production. The Belgian Congo had great mineral wealth (especially gold) and a number of plantations owned by settlers. From the 1920s to 1950, the authorities limited labor recruiting, in areas of low population density, to the peasants whom officials deemed troublesome farmers liable to set a bad example. By permitting mining companies and settlers to draft these peasants, the authorities intimidated the rest into compliance with the cotton regime.

In 1938, the Portuguese state adopted the Congolese model for Mozambique. It granted concession companies monopoly rights to buy cotton from peasants at low fixed prices. The authorities dictated the size of fields and the amount of cotton due at the markets. They relied on African police, local chiefs, and headmen but still did not have enough loyal functionaries to force the peasants to meet production targets. The state therefore had recourse to spectacular acts of terror and intimidation. Overseers of the concessionary companies vested with police powers made the rounds of the fields and kidnapped babies, imprisoned recalcitrant peasants, sent them off to plantations owned by Europeans, and sexually abused rural women. They used rhinoceros whips to beat growers whose fields seemed inadequate. In the Congo, when peasant women failed to fulfill production targets, they and their children were taken hostage, and their kinsmen and husbands temporarily had to return from their work at European companies in order to liberate their families.

Congolese peasants spent hours felling trees and clearing land for the cotton fields. Hoeing lasted from April to the end of August and involved breaking up the soil and grassland, making furrows, and spacing the plants. Belgian agronomists instructed them as to the obligatory work schedule of planting, seeding, weeding, and harvesting. Peasants had to burn the stalks of cotton plants to clear the natural habitat of parasites. It took twenty workdays to seed a hectare of land. Peasants had to weed several times over the course of fifteen weeks and faced jail time when the authorities deemed their efforts inadequate. Peasants had to spend time removing pests and bollworms. The intensive painful work of harvesting, done amid the hot climate and flies, amounted to the longest operation of the cotton cycle. On top of all this work, the peasants labored sixteen additional days, for each hectare of cotton, sorting, drying, and readying the crop in baskets for the market.

Congolese peasants, in the 1920s and 1930s, had to travel from three to over ten days every three or four weeks to official cotton markets as far as a hundred kilometers away. This travel deprived them of the best times for hunting and fishing, and diverted them from childcare, collecting edible caterpillars, and taking trips. The weeding, harvesting, and postharvest tasks prevented women from growing eleusine, millet, and other crops favorable to infant nutrition. Women turned to New World manioc, which grows on arid marginal soils and gives the highest yield of carbohydrates per cultivated area (apart from sugarcane and beets), in order to divert less land from cotton. But their diets then suffered a malnutritious loss of protein, vitamins, and minerals.

Portuguese officials in Mozambique estimated that it took 140 to 180 days a year to perform all of the labor-intensive work for one hectare of cotton. This work included three to four obligatory rounds of weeding in the spring. To avoid physical punishment, peasants had to do additional unremunerated work repairing bridges and roads. These labor services did not leave them time to farm any crops besides the manioc, sorghum, and corn needed to survive. To make matters worse, officials prohibited the intercropping of beans, sorghum, and peanuts among the obligatory rows of cotton despite the peasants' inclination to do so, because fields planted according to the peasants' customs looked backward and seemed to perpetuate behaviors the Portuguese believed uncivilized. The cotton regime thus undermined the custom of growing sorghum, beans, and peanuts in elevated mounds, and caused subsistence crops to dwindle in the 1940s.

In the southern zones of the Congo, Belgian authorities divided people into crews under the supervision of a village headman responsible for production targets of food, cotton, and labor for the mines. A network of supervisors toured the countryside making sure the crews kept at cotton farming. The authorities verified that the peasantry performed forced labor for the African chiefs. The peasants had to prepare the chiefs' plantations by digging holes, seeding, weeding, and harvesting their cotton. The chiefs received cash premiums for cotton exports.

Mozambican chiefs had an ambiguous status. The colonial police made sure they enjoyed a relatively advantageous position by forcing villagers to work their fields. Yet the chiefs faced humiliating harangues from the administrators and overseers about unmet quotas, and occasional beatings brought home the fact that they too were colonized Africans. They most likely worked on behalf of the concessionary companies because of the lack of alternatives to obedience.

In both the Congo and Mozambique, the state, missionaries, African chiefs, and concessionary companies privileged male heads of households and paid earnings from cotton sales to them as much as possible. Congolese men used the money for bride prices, gramophones, bicycles, and sewing machines. The state imposed the power of chiefs and males, and thereby exploited all of the Africans, though the peasants were more adversely affected than were the chiefs and the women more than the men.

Peasant incomes increased in the Belgian Congo from 1936 to 1959. The price paid to cotton farmers of Mozambique doubled in real terms, and rose at an even faster rate than did the price charged by the concessionary companies to their customers, over the course of the 1950s. Life became bearable for farmers who gained the new status of *agricultores*, about 40 percent of the total, and thus became eligible for technical assistance, bonuses, relocation to planned communities, and exemption from conscript labor on plantations, as long as they cultivated cotton on areas as large as the rest of their fields. Production more than doubled in northern Mozambique. This growth did not result from technological gains yet still amounted to an increase in productivity of about 150 percent, as it went hand in hand with a slight decrease in the area under cotton. Real earnings more than doubled for northern growers during the 1950s. In the Belgian Congo, output rose to over a hundred thousand tons of cotton a year by the 1940s and fluctuated thereafter before peaking on the eve of independence in 1960.

Nevertheless, all of these advances resulted from the use of force. It required coercion to assure that sale prices for Mozambican peasants remained well below the export prices of raw cotton. In the Congo, the Belgian authorities had assumed that a "civilizing" education and the benefits of market production would diminish coercion. Strong-arming, however, remained the norm until the final years of the colonial period. In 1947, 10 percent of the adult male population of the Congo had spent time in jail, mostly for opposition to the cotton regime. Because Africans remained reluctant to labor in cotton, coercion was necessary to assure the profits of the concession companies.

Moreover, the Portuguese administration proved particularly negligent with regard to the natural environment. In other African colonies, extension officials charged with education discouraged farming on slopes, encouraged tie ridging, and saw to the reforestation of land taken out of rotations. In Mozambique, thirty years of the cotton regime, and the absence of any conservation efforts, depleted soil nutrients and prompted the state to encourage the clearing of forests with the aim of making way for new cotton fields. Abandoned land, devoid of nutrients, had little vegetation, eroded, and caused long-term problems for Mozambican food production.

In this way, and many others, coercive crop production never yielded optimal results. In Mozambique, just as, we will see, in colonial Taiwan and Brazil, farming remained enmeshed in peasant subsistence agriculture, and the authorities never completely overcame the farmers' efforts to privilege their own crops over cotton. Colonial administrators could not measure every field to make sure it met the requirements. They could not keep tabs on when and how the peasants worked, or whether the peasants harvested the entire crop. Some peasants grew cotton among better-paying, or subsistence, crops despite the interdiction. In the early 1940s, administrators found that only two-thirds of the peasants actually cultivated cotton. Violent disciplinary measures often provoked even more resistance. Peasants boiled seeds or fled, and commonly gave the state less cotton than it demanded. Peasant flight, protests, and localized, clandestine, and highly effective sabotage eventually became intolerable to Portuguese officials and textile industrialists, who ended the system of concessionary companies in 1961.

In West Africa, the capitalist drive for cheaper inputs within the metropole economies of Europe absorbed and reinforced servile labor systems in Africa. The Asante Empire dominated central Ghana, a frontier area between the Upper Guinea forest and its adjacent savanna, from 1700 to 1900, when its population crested at about five hundred thousand. Given this sparse settlement, the Asante rulers found few people in need of extra work and thus came to rely on slavery. We saw in chapter 2 that the West African rulers provided a steady stream of slaves to the planters in the Americas. But around 1900, the British state prevented them from bringing new slaves into the Asante lands at the same time that it commandeered native labor for colonial projects. In this context of labor scarcity, Asante chiefs took advantage of their special rights to the forced work of pawns, slaves, and peasants to plant cocoa trees which bear cocoa beans used to make cocoa mass, cocoa powder, and chocolate and helped the chiefs to profit from the markets of the British Empire. Slavery was abolished by the colonial administration in 1908 against the wishes of the chiefs and free subjects of Asante, as well as of the British officials in the colony, all of whom recognized that the generalized access to land precluded the existence of a labor market.

Yet as the cocoa trees grew, they proved lucrative and encouraged free Asante subjects to make use of the virtually unrestricted access to land within the territories of their ancestral chiefs. While the farmers did not have individual titles to the land, their cocoa trees amounted to marketable capital assets in the way annual food crops never could, and thus represented the collateral for moneylenders to advance the funds for new plantations. The earnings enabled the farmers to afford wages high enough to attract voluntary laborers. The opportunity to earn wages, or farm cocoa for themselves, encouraged slaves to leave their masters. In the earliest days, up to about 1910, the ranks of laborers included Shai, Anum/Boso, and others who lacked the finances to buy land, but who succeeded rapidly in saving money for plantations of their own. In this way, slavery came to an end, but a reliable pool of landless laborers never emerged, as migrant workers, like indebted Asante farmers, continued to have access to land.

The women and children of Asante households cleared the land for the cultivation of manioc, cocoyam, and plantain, which provided shade for the cocoa seedlings and carbohydrate subsistence for the five to fifteen years needed for the trees to produce marketable crops. The forests made protein available in the form of game and edible snails. Women and children of the conjugal family thus provided the crucial domestic labor for the men to prepare new plantations beyond those of neighboring farmers. In this way, the land-extensive growth of cocoa output owed much to the subsistence farming of the women. Additional marriages increased a male's productive assets, and pawn-wives, loaned as a marriage payment, remained numerous as late as the 1940s.

From the 1930s through the 1950s, the area of cocoa farms spread, immigrant laborers and farmers arrived, and the domestic economy, and market for food crops, expanded. These economic opportunities helped women become more autonomous. The number of women among the commercial cocoa growers increased both absolutely and proportionally. Women also found opportunities cooking food and trading other goods in local markets.

Girls, in view of these conditions, no longer accepted being pawned out by their households.

In Nigeria, British imperialism provoked a more sudden and dramatic dissolution of slavery, and left in its wake a system of debts and taxes, which benefited merchant conglomerates and indigenous elites, but which coerced the inhabitants into export crop production. The African elites descended from the Sokoto Caliphate of the Sahel, the largest state of the continent prior to British conquest in 1903. The caliphate drew on a large market for human chattel from its tributary emirates. It depended on slave labor as the mainstay of production and the basis of aristocratic incomes. Slaves, in possession of lands and houses, comprised half the population and worked in the hundreds, even thousands, for the caliphate's landlords and officials.

The Sokoto Caliphate did not cover an economically prized territory, and Great Britain only occupied it to prevent the French from doing so and to satisfy the ambition of the first high commissioner, Sir (later Lord) Frederick Lugard, who proclaimed the protectorate of Nigeria on January 1, 1900. Many slaves took advantage of the avowed abolitionism of Great Britain to flee or renegotiate their status. They threw a wrench in the plans of the British cabinet, which had planned to maintain the caliphate within a system of indirect rule. Lugard exhorted village headmen to prevent the former slaves from acquiring farmland and securing their independence. But given the low population densities of the Kano region, the authorities could not prevent the former slaves from migrating and cultivating the soil for themselves. Unable to block off this route, other modes of capturing their labor were needed.

British administrators in Nigeria drew on their experiences in the Punjab and Burma to establish a form of agriculture similar, we will see, to the one the Japanese imposed on the peasants of Taiwan. In 1910, the Northern Nigeria Lands Committee granted inhabitants the right to farmland in return for a regular tax per measured acre. The system was a pragmatic necessity, because the highly dubious colonial venture only could be justified if it were self-financed and maintained the parsimony of the metropolitan treasury. The minuscule British outlay could only support a diminutive cadre of political officers and no standing army. Almost all of the infrastructure came from private initiatives and local resources. The measurement of landholdings took a long time and remained incomplete, but dramatically increased taxation, in excess of 150 percent in one district between 1908 and 1913. A further change after World War I provided for a single levy on entire peasant communities. In the process, the Lands Committee converted the caliphate's traditional officeholders into salaried bureaucrats financed by direct taxes on the peasants of the Hausa plains.

The colonial authorities collected taxes in sterling and opened the Nigerian market to British shipping companies. British consumer goods extinguished many local manufactures, on which smallholders had relied for ancillary income, and forced them to focus on agriculture for the cash needed to pay taxes. The authorities hoped inhabitants would specialize in cotton farming, but when the Niger Company, John Holt, and other firms opened their business outlets in 1913, the newly built railhead was deluged with groundnuts. Peasants saw groundnut exports, boosted by British demand for the oil, as a more reliable way to get currency. They could consume groundnuts to prevent starvation but still needed to sell them over time. Groundnuts complemented cotton, which did better in the humid climes, especially on the rich laka soils of the southern Hausa plains. Groundnuts did well in the arid northwestern part of Nigeria as well, especially the areas of Sokoto, Katsina, Daura, Kaon, and Borno. After the 1930s, as the colonial tax system stabilized, rural producers increasingly produced for the market, worked for wages, purchased inputs, and grew vulnerable to fluctuations in groundnut prices.

The peasants had to get ever more revenue from the land, as population growth and inheritances, similar again to the process that played out in colonial Taiwan, led to the subdivision of plots. The intensive labor required to make these plots viable profited the United Africa Company, a subsidiary of the Unilever combine, which prior to 1939 presided over an oligopoly of six firms known as the Association of West African Merchants. These firms imported soap, bicycles, kerosene, cotton goods, high-grade salt, cigarettes, and metalware into Nigeria, and handled nearly all of its foreign trade. They advanced huge sums to African agents, brokers, and middlemen, who in turn offered credit to the peasants. These sometimes pledged their crops, at postharvest low prices, for borrowed cash to cover taxes or other obligations. Having diminished the yields of subsistence crops relative to those of groundnuts, and having pledged their harvests to money lenders, the peasants then lacked grain reserves between harvests and had to borrow further funds after the rainy season. Peasant indebtedness helped to discipline producers and orient their farms toward the cash crops from which the trading houses profited.

Hugh Charles Clifford, governor of Nigeria from 1919 to 1925, addressed the Nigerian Legislative Council:

> Agricultural industries in tropical countries which are mainly, or exclusively in the hands of the native peasantry (a) Have a firmer root than similar enterprises when owned and managed by Europeans, because they are natural growths, not artificial creations, and are self-supporting, as regards labor, while European plantations can only be maintained by some system of organized immigration or by some form of compulsory labor; (b) Are incomparably the cheapest instruments for the production of agricultural produce on a large scale that have yet been devised. [11]

From 1915 to 1940, groundnut exports, like cocoa from Ghana and other West African colonies, grew spectacularly. Yet across West Africa most of the benefits accrued to the fiscal bureaucracy, export companies, and marketing boards and little was left to the agricultural population. In Nigeria, in particular, the British state worked through the traditional African class of officeholders paid out of the surpluses taken from the peasants in taxation and debts. The aristocratic class lost a source of surplus with the abolition of slavery but retained control over the free peasants through their positions as revenue collectors for the state and foreign firms. The endemic corruption of this ever-growing non-producing sector, its authority to act arbitrarily, and its bureaucratic controls ground down the Hausa peasants. Four major famines, as well as a litany of localized crises, afflicted Nigeria in the first half of the twentieth century.

In contrast to these regimes of peasant export production in West Africa, Mozambique, and the Congo, the imperial authorities in Algeria, Kenya, and southern Africa expropriated the indigenous peasantry for the benefit of European settlers intent on commercial farming. Algeria, in particular, prior to the 1800s, had large landowners and peasants, as well as shepherds and sharecroppers at the bottom of the productive system, and generally much less social stratification than was later the case under French rule. Inhabitants passed land from generation to generation but did not own it as private property or speculate on its value. The society prized the conservation of the family patrimony rather than the accumulation of monetary value.

The ecology of Algeria is prone to drought and suited to grazing, especially under extensively mobile practices like the ones used by pastoralists prior to colonization. Large herds of livestock deposited dung and urine on the grasses they grazed. Constant movement prevented overgrazing of the plants, while periodic trampling assured protective covering of the soil and facilitated the reintroduction of organic matter into it. The land then better absorbed and held seasonal rains.

The peasants devoted about a third of the land to arable crops, the rest to fallow and pasture. Low-density livestock yielded meat, milk, and hides for local use. The inhabitants of the mountain areas farmed more intensively. They cultivated watermelons, squashes, and onions, and rotated these crops with grains to maintain soil fertility. The inhabitants of the mountainous areas did not produce enough grains and had to trade with the farmers of wheat and barley in the plains. They used the woods for fuel and building material. Farmers had few tools beyond wooden harrows and plows, the same ones used in Roman times, and did not have wheeled transport.

Ottoman taxation took 10 percent of each item of harvests from some Algerians, net payments from entire tribes in areas less directly subject to imperial control, and a market tax from those beyond its reach. Taxation increased in the eighteenth and early nineteenth centuries, yet remained relatively light. The people of northeastern Algeria seem to have had a high standard of living, though one undermined by a cyclical decline in the early 1800s.

Following the French invasion of 1830, a long line of "experts" instilled a narrative about the North Africans' use of the environment. Writers condemned the Arab invaders of the eleventh century for spreading across North Africa and ruining everything in their path through deforestation and the resultant desertification. Nomadism and sheep grazing, the French claimed (contrary to the facts outlined above), sterilized the land, whereas the Romans previously had brought permanent settlements and wheat fields, turning the region into a calm and prosperous granary.

This narrative delegitimized traditional agriculture, justified colonial rule, and laid the basis for moving the North Africans off the best lands and for banning the core practices of their way of life. By 1851, 151,000 Europeans had settled in Algeria, 33,000 in rural areas, and had taken more than four hundred thousand hectares from indigenous people who died or fled during the conquest. The state expropriated land as punishment for rebellion or simply in the name of the public good. Algerian households sold under duress at absurdly low prices when private investors and colonial officials took advantage of the chaos following the invasion to threaten state-sanctioned expropriations.

Colonizers regarded the land as a source of exchange value and determined that land was wasted when not cultivated with the intention of enhancing its sale price. The land could then be confiscated, because, in the minds of the settlers, the native population did not improve its cultivation. The state passed laws restricting nomadic pastoralists to what was required for their "needs," as defined by the colonizers. A statute of 1873 revised an earlier law much reviled by the settlers known as the Sénatus-consultem, which protected indigenous common lands. The revision made all land conform to individual rights as defined by the colonizers. Henceforth, only a single villager's will was needed to alienate collective property from the joint owners and divide it into private holdings. The new legislation fulfilled the settlers' wish to chase Algerians from the centers of imperial rule. Indeed, Jacques Louis Randon, governor-general of Algeria, stated as much when he noted that Algerians had to accept being "driven away, which is in the nature of things."[12] In this way, "unproductive" grazing land ended up, through alienations, in the hands of Europeans.   *manipulation of property laws*

The French state arrogated all the forests thanks to a law of 1851. It reserved only a small area for indigenous Algerians who had relied on the woods as part of their subsistence economy. In the 1850s and 1860s, capitalist production became firmly implanted in Algeria, first in forestry and later in agriculture. The military, colonists, and private companies together cut down nearly a million cork oaks for tannin production. Yet Algerians took *economic modernization destroyed traditional livelihood* [handwritten annotation]

nearly all the blame for deforestation. A law of 1874, which settlers had promoted for decades, made Algerian "tribes" collectively responsible for forest fires, enabling the authorities to punish peasant villages with fines and the expropriation of their livestock or property when fires broke out.

A law passed in 1845 made the Algerians liable to a tax in money rather than in kind and thus forced many of them to sell land and other belongings, and to work for wages. In the 1870s and 1880s, Algerians faced direct taxes, and further "Arab taxes," which towns, dominated by the settlers, spent on things mainly beneficial to the urban areas. Municipal budgets drew to a large extent on the taxation of the Arab population, which, in the early 1900s, sometimes paid more than one-third of the value of a property, and always more than did Indian households, we will see, to the British colonial government. After putting down an insurrection in 1871–1872, the French authorities fined the rebels and expropriated their land for the benefit of the colonists. As a result of the repression, as well as of the other policies of colonial rule, not to mention famines and epidemics in 1877–1881, the Algerian population declined by nearly a third since the early 1800s.

By the first decades of the twentieth century, the indigenous population recovered and outnumbered European settlers several times over. The latter, however, had accumulated the prime farmland, while the number of native Algerian farmers declined sharply, as the dynamics of colonial expansion squeezed them onto ever-smaller parcels of land and taxed them heavily. Nomads reliant on grazing animals declined from about 60–65 percent of the population at the time of the conquest to 18.5 percent in 1911. Poverty forced them to take up fixed residences and wage occupations. Algerians did not have the land to raise crops or livestock in traditional ways and became a rural floating population with high rates of unemployment and little hope for advancement, obliged under the circumstances to work as sharecroppers and wage laborers for Europeans.

Settlers, who comprised only 2 percent of the agricultural population in the 1930s, made cereal production possible in the areas of the high plateau with low rainfall through a three-year cycle of plowing, planting, and fallow. Company-run commercial farming on large tracts of land took off after World War II. Businesses profited from the cultivation of wine, early vegetables, and citrus for export. This farming caused soil degradation by laying open marginal lands to cultivation. It broke the surface of the land, turned over the soil, exposed it to erosion, and allowed its moisture to evaporate. Crop yields declined over time. The Algerians' traditional scratch plows or ards had not been so detrimental because they did not cut deeply into the soil or expose it to heat, aridity, and erosion. The farming of the colonial period reduced the time land spent in fallow and thus depleted its nutrients and moisture. Overall, colonial agribusiness and the introduction of "modern"

European techniques stripped the soil and impoverished it, and led to declining production over the long term.

The British rulers of Kenya, Northern Rhodesia, and Southern Rhodesia (today Zambia and Zimbabwe), similar to their French counterparts in Algeria, dispossessed native peasants to make way for commercial farmers from Europe. In the first decade of the twentieth century, about two thousand settlers monopolized 2.5 million hectares of the Kenyan highlands yet farmed only three hundred thousand hectares, because the point was to confine the inhabitants to the lower-quality land and force them to seek employment. The administration of Northern and Southern Rhodesia used rents, taxes, labor services, and outright eviction to force Africans onto congested native reserves far from the best farmlands and market opportunities even though much of countryside then lay untilled.

In Kenya, the tax system served to make Africans dependent on employment. They had to rent land from white settlers and work for wages on the settlers' farms in order to fulfill their fiscal obligations. In Southern Rhodesia, many peasants prospered growing grain for the markets created by the opening of the Selukwe gold mines around 1900. Administrators interpreted this prosperity through the lens of imperial prejudice. "In Victoria there is a huge Native population of which only a very small proportion ever work at all. They are a contemptible race of men, weak, cowardly and indolent, relying on their wives to till their fields, gather their crops, and earn for them the hut tax which they are too lazy to earn for themselves."[13] With the aim of undermining independent rural households, the administration of Northern Rhodesia granted settler farmers monopoly rights to provision mining areas, which were the principal internal market of the colony. The administration of Southern Rhodesia bypassed the African agriculturalists of the Victoria district when it built the Gwelo-Salisbury railway to the gold-mine area in the first years of the twentieth century. Native peasants were thus deprived of their source of income for the hut taxes and had to seek employment.

During World War I, Kenyans faced food and livestock requisitions that depleted their surpluses and combined with drought to cause famine in several parts of the colony. Great Britain conscripted thousands of them into the military. The settlers, by contrast, profited from the high export prices for the coffee, sisal, and maize grown on their plantations. Yet amid the low prices in the 1930s, in Kenya, Northern Rhodesia, and Southern Rhodesia, African farmers produced maize for the mining areas, townships, and other markets more cheaply than did the settlers despite the crop research stations set up to aid the European settlers, not the subsistence peasants, and despite the commercial farmers' investments in modern inputs, dams, and mechanized processing. In each of the three colonies, the British administration reacted with acts and ordinances that created procurement stations favoring European growers, but ignoring African farmers. The policies enforced dual pricing schemes with better terms for the settlers.

Nonetheless, though the assured prices kept large-scale white farmers of Northern Rhodesia viable through the 1930s, they also gave an incentive to indigenous farmers, permitting the peasants of the Tonga plateau of Northern Rhodesia to continue cultivating maize for their subsistence, while selling surpluses on the market, and thereby enhancing their food security. Similarly, Kenyan entrepreneurs began to form companies and enter retail by the 1940s. The government increased controls to protect European farmers. But the maize grown on the plots of fewer than five hectares was cheaper than was the grain grown on large European farms even when the government facilitated the latter's sales. The small farms of Africans were intensively tilled by family members, who could deprive themselves and lower prices below those of settlers obliged to meet the costs or agricultural implements and hired workers. The settlers subsequently enlisted the authorities to expel 250,000 squatters from the highlands and turn them into forced laborers on mechanized farms. But this policy helped provoke the Mau-Mau rebellion of 1952. Great Britain used deportations and concentration camps to separate inhabitants from the insurgents and defeat the insurgency. Yet this episode, combined with the cheaper maize available from African farmers, led Great Britain to begin distributing millions of hectares to the Kenyans, to provide them with research, extension, and aid programs, and to lift restrictions on the indigenous production of cash crops. The administration of the Baringo district turned most of the grain trade over to African businesses, which then dominated regional trade and transport. Agricultural output tripled over the following decade.

In South Africa, Dutch settlers known as Boers paid nominal fees for as much land as they pleased in the early decades of the 1800s. Farms were enormous, well over six thousand acres on average. Settlers could graze them bare and then move to new areas without regard for the soil's long-term productivity, and no economic development took place for much of the 1800s. The British who ruled the Cape colonies after 1807 were wary of the Boers' aggressive stance toward neighboring territories and of the unrest that might ensue. The Boers, however, were unwilling to compromise and forcefully laid claim to the lands beyond their original settlements.

The Boers' primary concern was the labor for their land. Slave emancipation in 1834 led some on the Great Trek north where they founded the Free Orange State and compelled African chiefs in Natal to provide low-wage laborers for public works. The Boers used "pass" and vagrancy laws to obtain labor in the Eastern Cape and child apprentices in the Transvaal. But in just about every area of the country, the common means of obtaining farm hands was a feudal sort of arrangement by which African squatters continued living on the land in return for rent or for 90 to 180 days of work a year.

Social taboos on manual labor originated in these times and persisted into the twentieth century. Blacks did the farm work, and whites lived by and large as a leisure aristocracy.

Markets sprung up after the late 1860s when gold and diamonds were found to be exploitable en masse for profit. Investment poured into South Africa and compounded the labor shortage. Africans used the land for subsistence and could not easily be turned into pit workers or commercial farmers for the needs of the mining population. Militarily independent African societies prevented the British authorities from gaining control over the labor needed to make investment in mining profitable. To overcome this problem, Sir Bartle Frere, the special high commissioner of the colonial secretary Lord Carnarvon, seized on the opportunity offered by drought, and the consequent weakening of indigenous and Boer populations, to crush the defenses and rebellions of the Xhosas in the Cape in 1878. But in 1879, the Zulus annihilated 1,600 British soldiers at Isandhlwana, inspired the Sotho and Pede peoples to protracted resistance, and gave the Boers the confidence to retrieve their independence at Majuba Hill in 1881. The Boers discovered the Witwatersrand's mineral wealth in the following years. The British Empire retaliated against the Zulus with tactics bordering on the genocidal, including home arson, cattle seizure, and destruction of the economic foundations of their homeland.

In Natal, settlers began to recruit indentured servants from the Indian subcontinent. After five years of servitude, the Indians could stay in the country, buy land, and have their families join them. For the Orange Free State and Transvaal the authorities passed the *Plakkers Wet*, or Squatters' Law, in 1895. They thus prohibited more than five African families from residing on the lands of settlers. The goal was to distribute the population across the land and improve the labor supply. The law undercut the Africans' bargaining power and forced them to accept disadvantageous agreements. The white growers also benefited from the greatest farm subsidies in the world after 1890 and through the first decade of the 1900s.

Yet the settler farmers constantly complained about the scarcity of labor. They asserted that raising wages, rather than attracting labor, only reinforced the natives' idleness. The administrations of the Cape Colony, Natal, and the Boer Republics created an array of taxes and labor obligations in an effort to increase the labor supply in the last decades of the nineteenth century. Yet squatting and sharecropping on white-owned estates still shielded most Africans from having to seek wages. With the expansion of mining capital and the demand for cheap foodstuffs, the colonial administration, in 1913, passed the Native Lands Act. A small portion of the country was thus set aside as Native Reserves, and Africans could not purchase land in the remaining white areas.

Africans in the reserves, as well as in the territories that later became Botswana, Lesotho, and Swaziland, enjoyed prosperity in the mid-1800s and the following decades. The peasants of the Transkei, for instance, a fertile area receiving adequate rainfall in eastern South Africa along the Indian Ocean, raised enough food to feed themselves and sell surpluses. They selectively accepted wage labor when they needed additional income. Some peasants on the borders of the region took advantage of the diamond boom by selling wool, grain, hides, cattle, vegetables, fruit, and dairy in local towns and villages. In 1893–1894, the Cape Labor Commission commented on the natives' land, their ability to grow what they pleased, and their limited wants. The president of the Chamber of Mines stated, "The tendency of the native is to be an agriculturalist, who reluctantly offers himself or one of his family as an industrial worker for just so long as the hut tax can be earned, and expects the industrial demand to give him work when his crops are bad. He cares nothing if industries pine for want of labor when his crops and home-brewed drink are plentiful."[14]

But in the Transkei, in a process similar to what unfolded in other reserves, the east coast fever decimated herds, pauperized the inhabitants, and forced many to rely on wage labor in the early decades of the twentieth century. The peasants took on debts and had difficulty buying back cattle put up as collateral. Colonial legislation led to the eviction of peasants elsewhere in the Cape. Commercial farmers, moreover, began to dispense with the quasi-feudal relations that had previously provided Africans with land owned but not occupied by whites. These trends, combined with natural demographic growth, added several hundred thousand people to the Transkei around the turn of the century. This population growth, together with the debts, diminished the viability of subsistence farming. In these ways, the reserves, which formerly had been food-exporting areas, became teeming slums with declining agricultural productivity, dependent on food imports financed through the remittances of migrant laborers.

In this way, the Native Lands Act of 1913 effectively inhibited the expansion of the class of African commercial farmers able to compete with European growers. Africans instead came to rely, to an increasing extent, on offering the labor of their households, for a certain period of the year, in return for the right to reside on, and work, a portion of a farmer's land for subsistence. Money wages increased between 1866 and 1966 but much less than they would have had it not been for the settlers' long-standing preference for coercive means of obtaining farm hands rather than the allurement of the free market. The truth, discovered by investigations by independent commissions at the beginning of the 1890s, is that when farmers paid a little more, they obtained all the labor they needed. In the 1930s, a farmer from the Orange Free State offered laborers four-room cottages, a cash wage, a food ration with meat, an arable morgen of land (0.856 hectares), a vegetable garden, a shilling per bag of harvested maize paid into a common pool to be shared among the workers, and the right, as a group, to hire and fire staff. This farmer had financial success and no labor troubles. But the standard view appeared in a letter to a Johannesburg newspaper in 1947, the year before apartheid.

> To speak of better wages and housing is nonsense. All the wages and housing schemes will not change the native. He will remain dirty, lazy and thoroughly dishonest. He does not understand decent civilized treatment. He can, and does, understand a good hiding. If we want the natives to be law-abiding, let us speak to them in the language they understand: the language of the sjambok, administered frequently and with vigor.[15]

All the way into the 1960s, South African farm laborers remained isolated without the traditional social ties existent in the reserves or the wider experience of African residents of the towns. White agricultural workers made five times what blacks did in 1866 and eight times what they did in 1952. Farm owners enjoyed all of the amenities of modern life by 1960, including private tennis courts, cars, and even airplanes, whereas their black workers, in most cases, had wattle and daub shacks in compounds, no electricity, wells where water could be fetched in buckets a distance away, and lavatories, if they existed, of a pit type.

BRITISH INDIA

In India, the political leaders of Great Britain created extensive railways, standard currency, weights and measures, contract law and individual property rights, and regional and national markets for food grains, commercial crops, and other bulk commodities. They expected economic development to follow. Grain production rose steadily from the 1850s to 1914, at about the same rate as the population increased. But after 1875, demographic growth began to overtake food production, and from 1891 to 1941 yields per acre of food grains declined, especially after 1921.

The arable surface expanded to the point that the supply of quality land dried up in much of western India by the 1870s. Peasants denuded hillsides of shrubs and forest cover in some areas of the Bombay Presidency. One of the reasons they strove so intently to add farmland was the competition they faced, in traditional craft lines, from the industrial imports. Millions of inhabitants, who had manufactured wares for the people of their area in the past, had to focus on farming. The pre-colonial economy had been much less agricultural.

Colonial forest policies compounded the pressure Indian peasants had to put on the land. Whereas 20 percent of India consisted of forests open to public use in 1870, all of it became enclosed and protected by armed agents of the state before the end of the decade. The colonial authorities intended to assure the diminishing stores of wood for shipbuilding, urban construction, and especially railroads. The Second Indian Forest Act of 1878 added all village common land to the protected forests. It deprived Indian peasants of collective terrains they needed to obtain dry grass for fodder, shrub grass for rope, wood and dung for fuel, leaves and forest debris for fertilizer, clay for plastering houses, and clean water.

British taxation further compelled Indians to seek income from farming. The East India Company, which governed the territories until 1858, did not introduce major economic changes. The company copied the land tax of India's previous rulers and retained duties on internal trade and taxes on artisans, though it collected these funds more rigorously. The company, for instance, collected nearly twice as many rupees from Orissa province than had the prior Marathas conquerors despite the latter's reputation for exactions. Famine overtook the districts of Bombay and Madras when they came under direct British rule at the end of the 1870s. The governor continued to press and ruin the rural communities when deferring the land tax might have kept mortality to a minimum. The taxes collected by the government, largely from villages, were spent at an average of 33 percent on the army and police. The government also spent revenue on official salaries. Only 2 percent returned to rural areas in investment in agriculture and education and 4 percent in public works. Independent states of developing countries today spend much more on education, famine relief, and public health.

The most disruptive colonial policy may have been the land settlement, which required the registration of property in the name of the individual head of household for the purpose of taxation. All adult males had claims to a portion of the inheritance in western India in pre-colonial times. They had a right to a plot in both Hindu and Muslim law, as well as in the peasants' informal practices. In practice, however, the land remained within the joint household divided among the individual family members. The land settlement, conversely, caused the joint household to disintegrate and made it possible for individuals to start a family once they had an inheritance. Women and children constituted a work team at no monetary cost to a family. Marriage and biological reproduction became key facets of the family economy and ensured a high birthrate. The population rose as the barriers to landownership fell.

The result was a proliferation of plots registered to the heads of households that formerly worked the land as part of the larger joint family. Statistics from the Bombay Presidency show that while hardly any small farms existed in the late 1800s, dozens, sometimes hundreds, of them appeared within each village in the twentieth century. On the old canals in the Poona district, the fragmentation of the land led to many field shapes and sizes prohibitive of effective irrigation. Wells fell out of usage after their division among heirs. Small parcels of land raised the relative cost of investment in household plots, especially since these could be divided subsequently among inheritors. It became unwieldy for peasants to transport cattle, heavy plows, and irrigation, all necessary for productive wheat farming, to each one of their plots of land. They instead used tools suited to small and scattered holdings, not iron plows suited to improved dry-farming.

The fragmentation of farms made peasants waste income in numerous borders to protect fields from animals and birds. The borders, after subsequent property divisions, could only yield coarse grains or went out of cultivation. More commonly, the peasants found it too costly to close off and watch over their lands and therefore allowed one another's cattle to range over the fields after the harvest. Doing so, however, imposed common uniform farming, across the villages' arable land, of crops for human consumption, and sometimes of crops that could also be fed to livestock, so as not to diminish the available resources for the community's subsistence. The rotations discouraged innovation and specialization in the most lucrative crops and animal feed and prevented a second seeding after the initial grains and fodder.

Frequent droughts and famines in the Bombay Presidency wiped out farm reserves, ruined businesses reliant on local sales, diminished employment opportunities, and gave the peasants practical experience of the need to bring as much land as possible into rotations of crops for local consumption. They thus increased arable land relative to pasture, with the result that the number and quality of cattle declined, stocks of manure dwindled, and soils eroded in many places. To eke out income, peasants often sold their rich manure wastefully as fuel to urban purchasers.

For all of these reasons, the technical base of agriculture deteriorated, and gaping alimentary deficits appeared by the first decades of the twentieth century. Inhabitants regularly purchased grain grown elsewhere, and large volumes of imports were needed in times of drought to avert starvation. These trends drove up the cost of living much higher than any wage increases in the hinterlands of Bombay and Ahmedabad in the 1910s. Peasants suffered from poverty and chronic protein deficiency. In short, the individual property rights established by Great Britain did not make for rural development within the peasant context of subsistence farming in the Bombay Presidency.

Nor did they lead to capitalist growth in the southern Deccan Plateau, where large landowners profited from soaring cotton prices during the US Civil War, but then ceased to engage in agriculture and profited from it instead by switching to usury and commerce. Growers benefited from rising living standards in the 1860s, but then world market prices declined, especially after the onset of the global depression in 1873. Although the price of cotton fell by half relative to millet, the peasants of the Deccan continued to farm cotton and buy millet on the market. Even in periods of low prices, cotton brought in higher returns per acre than did millet, had higher yields when more labor was applied to it, and thus helped land-short peasants to earn subsistence. Cotton's share of the land of the Deccan thus increased between the 1870s and 1911. Families labored assiduously, as customary crop rotations with long fallows and numerous oxen gave way to a congested agricultural cycle filled increasingly with human labor rather than animal traction. The quantity and quality of the cattle, relative to the cultivated land, steadily declined from 1850 to 1930. Peasants suffered from the vagaries of the weather and world-market prices set in the US South. They had a hard time repaying loans and covering fiscal liabilities amid falling prices, as the profits of their intensive labor went to large landowners in interest payments and rents. Per-acre food production fell between one-third and one-half from 1870 to the years after World War II. Life expectancy fell 20 percent between 1872 and 1921.

The region of Berar, to the northeast, had a subsistence economy with household workshops largely shielded from world markets in the 1850s. But high international prices during the US Civil War stimulated the planting of cotton and diverted it from the Indian spinners and weavers who had previously transformed it into yarn and cloth. Heavy taxes levied on local woven goods, combined with cheap English imports via the Great India Peninsular Railway, ruined local artisans and forced them into farming. The area under cotton doubled, as more of this commodity flowed into England from Berar than from any other area of the empire. Moneylenders and grain merchants controlled tax collection and cotton marketing, and profited from the transactions between the villages, Calcutta, and Manchester. Subsistence farming on the poorer soils of Berar and Deccan, and districts of Poona and Sholapur, to compensate for the land devoted to cotton—a crop that takes nutrients from the dirt, crowds out nitrogen-restoring legumes such as gram, and constantly demands virgin land—led to soil erosion, diminished water retention, and increased susceptibility to drought. Berar suffered from famines in 1876 and 1899, the latter killing about 8.8 percent of the population. The greatest percentage of deaths occurred in the districts most given over to cotton farming.

To the north, in the Central Provinces' Narmada Valley (part of Madhya Pradesh), the administration of Sir Richard Temple encouraged malguzars (landowners) to produce commercial cotton, and especially wheat, at a time when the Bombay-Calcutta railroad permitted cloth from England's industrial Lancashire region to flood the area and ruin local handicrafts. Rising wheat prices in the years after 1870 made large-scale cultivation profitable and induced the malguzars to lay hold of as much land as possible rather than leave it to the peasants in traditional leasing agreements. The malguzars appropriated the superior soils and forced the peasants onto marginal lands more sensitive to deficient monsoons.

The wheat boom in the Narmada Valley, generated by the construction of the railway and the purchases of exporters on the western coast, broadened farming onto the thinner inferior soils vulnerable to the unreliable monsoon. Merchants fanned out to the countryside, and together with the malguzars, sought to control the peasants' output through advances of cash and seed. The export of grain to England helped stabilize prices there and permitted commercial agents to profit from re-exports to the European continent. But in the Narmada Valley, these trends led to soil mining and crushing household debt. When the rains failed, the peasants could only continue production by going perpetually into arrears and subordination to moneylenders. Famine overtook the Narmada Valley in the 1890s. But the effects of inadequate monsoons varied, as the superior lands suffered a relatively marginal decline of output. The fact that prices increased meant that the owners of these lands gained even more income than they did in periods of adequate rains, high output, and lower prices.

In the Punjab, the British state coordinated infrastructural projects similar to those of the Japanese in Taiwan described later in this chapter. The construction of canals facilitated the colonization and population of the region. British administrators regulated the allocation of water and property so as to win over the landholding peasants as a source of stability. The peasants of the Punjab provided more soldiers to the British Army than did the inhabitants of any other Indian province. Their lands also yielded the largest portion per unit of the Punjab's fiscal proceeds.

Prior to 1912, the British state, which served as landlord, restricted bequests to one offspring. This policy ran counter to customary law and the sentiments of the peasantry. The issue led to agitation in the canal colonies in 1907, and the authorities then yielded to demands for proprietary rights with free succession. Great Britain ceded to the uneconomic practices of the peasants in order to avoid political opposition and assure its control over the Punjab.

But at the same time, the authorities relied on the landholders, whom they favored with additional grants of land, to control the province. These prominent families provided the government with commissioners and honorary magistrates. Large landowners of the Punjab did not organize production, seek improvements, or invest in farm inputs. Rather, they leased land in return for half of the output and lived as rent-collecting absentee owners. Much of their land contained canals and afforded influential families, such as the Nun and Tiwana, great power in their regions. They thus helped raise soldiers and other contributions for the British in World War I and fought against independence movements in the 1930s and 1940s. In return, the authorities offered them assurances regarding their property rights to the canals and dropped plans to build the Shahpur Branch, which would have undermined their monopoly. In this way, Great Britain tolerated an outmoded irrigation system, and the semi-feudal social relations over it, in order to placate a political ally and perpetuate imperial rule.

Although measures of the cultivated area, output, marketing, and trade showed impressive growth, they all resulted from the spread of settlement over barren and sparsely populated areas of western Punjab, not from improved farming. Rail-borne traffic was the springboard to a well-developed trading network, and exports flowed to other parts of India and overseas. While the canal colonies of the Punjab became one of the leading areas of commercial agriculture in South Asia, and the peasantry became one of the most prosperous of the continent, the farms were small and labor-intensive. The larger grants of land were rented to subtenants and continued to be farmed with non-mechanized customary implements.

In East Bengal, the population and cultivated area grew in 1860–1890, just as they did in the Bombay Presidency, amid the proliferation of farms. Agriculture reached extensive limits in many parts of the region in 1890–1920. Peasants migrated to lands of lesser quality on the floodplains of Brahmaputra in neighboring Assam. The new intensive farming of jute as a cash crop offset the diminishing returns on these lands.

Under the pressure of population growth and the reduction of farm sizes, the mass of Bengali smallholders saw cash crops as a better bet for ensuring their subsistence than growing insufficient quantities of rice. One observer had the impression that about half of the peasants had an acre or less in the jute-growing district. The turn to cash crops in these circumstances did not enhance productivity or raise the standard of living. In this respect, developments were similar to those experienced in France and China in the eighteenth and nineteenth centuries, where peasants turned to intensive viticulture, sugarcane, and cotton, in addition to household manufacturing, as farm sizes diminished. Some parts of Bengal actually saw declining output, and even the parts with growth saw per capita declines. All in all, population grew 0.8 percent per annum, as agricultural output grew 0.3 percent, from the 1920s into the 1940s.

The peasantry did all of the extra work of double cropping and jute growing without any technological improvements. Instead, families put a premium on the reproductive capacity of mothers and the unremunerated work of women and children. Farm operations other than crop cutting became ever more feminine for about a century after 1860. Paid labor outside the family, in tasks such as dehusking paddies, could not compete and dwindled as a source of income. Males sought to maintain their levels of consumption by reducing those of female family members. The exploitation of women and children allowed the peasants to hang on to their subsistence plots. Women suffered higher rates of destitution and death in the great famine of 1943.

Local moneylenders benefited from the intensification of agriculture and the expansion of jute production for the world market. Although the peasants had secure rights to the land, debt burdens prevented them from enjoying any independence. The volume of loans increased from the 1880s to the 1930s, not on account of creditworthiness, but on account of increased need. Peasants contracted debts to obtain seeds, repair homesteads, replace cattle, pay for labor and marriages, and get food in lean periods of the year. Over four-fifths of the peasant households had debts in 1930. The moneylenders—trader-mahajans and talukdar-mahajans—preferred to hold the peasants in permanent debt rather than expropriate them. The moneylenders thus constrained the peasants to cultivate jute for their benefit. Creditors nurtured the peasants as they impoverished the peasants, for though they offered the credit needed for the peasants to survive and work, the usurious interest helped keep the peasants destitute.

During the worldwide economic depression of the 1930s, the restriction in credit led institutional lenders associated with the colonial administration to withdraw from the rural loan business. Mahajans and talukdars were deprived of liquid cash, and their vital role to the peasants, in seeing them through lean months and bad years, vanished. As the benevolent garb was lifted, the peasants refused to show deference, banded together to withhold interest payments, repudiated debt bonds, and demanded subsistence loans. The crisis lasted through the 1930s and 1940s, as the peasants marked out the rent collectors and grain dealers as the targets of their struggle. Their resistance to zamindars and talukdars of East Bengal eliminated the debt relations that siphoned off their surpluses. But at the same time, food moved out of the credit market into the commodity market and a famine overtook the region in 1943.

This context helped the populist faction of the Muslim League attract support in East Bengal. Demands for an independent Pakistan encapsulated not only the Muslims' aspiration for dignity but also the peasants' economic objectives. The Hindu elite's power stemmed from moneylending, not landownership, and thus lost its spell over the Muslim peasants in the credit crisis of the 1930s. The peasants' individual farms divided them from one another on their similarly sized holdings. Religion held together the social base for their political demands. In the final decade of colonial rule, upper-class Muslims capitalized on this cultural aspect of the peasants' resistance to the moneylending elite to seize the political fruits of their agrarian struggle. Hindu landlords and traders departed after the partition in August 1947.

TAIWAN

In 1894 Japan went to war against China and won decisively. Under the terms of the peace treaty that followed, it acquired the island of Taiwan. Japan's victory, and the acquisition of its first colony, signalled to those at home and abroad the success of its efforts to modernize and join the exclusive club of imperial Great Powers.

Less than thirty years prior, in 1868, a clique of modernizing samurai toppled the Tokugawa shogunate, euthanized remnants of the feudal order, and embarked on the mission to lift Japan into the ranks of industrialized nations. They abolished the privileges of the samurai class, pensioned off the daimyo, removed the feudal domains and established modern prefectures, created a conscript army, built modern schools, and enacted a German-styled constitution with the Meiji emperor at its head. Following the creation of a national bank in 1882, commercial and industrial policies were drafted that deepened the gains of Japan's rural capitalists and nursed the formation of modern industrialists.

While the news of military victory over China was well received in Japan, the domestic mood was far from buoyant. Facing shortfalls in public revenue at home and mounting diplomatic pressure abroad, many worried that the costs of Japan's first colony outweighed foreseeable benefits. Some urged the government to sell the island and invest the money at home. Parsimonious politicians agreed. Pro-empire elements within the cabinet were, however, reluctant to surrender this highly symbolic prize. They were eager to leverage Japan's newfound military prowess and rising industrial strength to abrogate thirty-year-old treaties that impinged on national sovereignty. After much debate, Taiwan was kept but colonial administrators were told that the island would have to pay for itself.

Conditions on the island were far from promising. Taiwan was without modern industry, its infrastructure was beyond antiquated, and local capital was concentrated in the hands of native merchants and landlords who showed no interest in modernizing agriculture or investing in new industry. As for the peasantry, they were bereft of capital despite the long hours of work they put in every day—circumstances vividly described by one observer:

> Farming in Formosa is very hard work, and only by the strictest economy can it be made even fairly remunerative.
>
> The entire farm of a family in Formosa would make but a garden for an agriculturalist in America. The owner of eight or ten acres is looked upon as in easy circumstances. The farms are all small and are entirely without fences. A rice-farm is divided into little irregular plots for the purposes of irrigation. These plots are made by throwing up around each low mounds of earth, by which means the water is retained at the required depth.

As two crops, and sometimes three, are reaped every year, the farmer is kept busy from spring to autumn. During seedtime and harvest his wife rises at three o'clock in the morning, cooks rice and salted vegetables, prepares hot water for the men to wash with, and about four calls them up to breakfast. The men are in the field about five o'clock and work until ten, when a lunch of boiled rice and some salted vegetables is carried out to them. At noon they return for dinner and rest for an hour and a half. In the afternoon the same kind of lunch is taken to the field. At seven o'clock they return, wash their breasts and limbs, and sit down to a better meal, generally consisting of a tiny cup of hot liquor, pork, and fresh vegetables boiled with rice. At nine they retire.

The farmer's lot in North Formosa is not altogether an unhappy one. He works hard and is generally thrifty and economical. His wants are few and easily supplied. There is monotony, perhaps, but then he knows nothing of the "nameless longing" that fills the breasts of much-read farmers in the restless West.[16]

In the face of such unpropitious conditions, the colonial administrators who were eager to prove the worth of the colony were left little choice but to tax and levy fees on the native population and use a portion of the proceeds to finance growth. Consequently, the colonial government created monopolies in opium, camphor, tobacco, salt, and alcohol; it imposed excise duties on imports and exports; and while it sold bonds to the Japanese government, and less unsuccessfully sought Japanese investors, the lion's share of revenue was generated through the land tax.

In one of its first major acts on the island, the colonial government surveyed the productivity of all farmland with the intent of taxing it. The process was so thoroughgoing that the journalist and imperial booster Yosaburo Takekoshi wrote in 1905, "There is no town or village in the island the exact position of which has not been determined, no field or plantation, however small, which will not be found upon one or other of the prepared maps."[17] With tax obligations registered and an efficient collection agency established, government coffers swelled with the addition of three million yen annually. But impositions on the countryside did not stop there. As the government mapped fields, measured output, registered landowners, and clarified tax obligations, it also rationalized the byzantine property system. Two centuries of colonization by Chinese settlers had laid down complex and layered claims on the agricultural surplus, which the colonial administration wished to simplify and in some cases replace with its own.

The government began by reforming the inherited system of tenancy and subtenancy. At the very top of the property structure sat the chartered households that had acquired in the eighteenth and nineteenth centuries possession of entire districts from the Qing government. Rather than make the journey to Taiwan, these men remained on the mainland and collected rents from families they recruited to settle. After clearing the native population and constructing their farms, these early settlers often added to their estates and sought tenants of their own, while continuing to meet their fiscal obligations to the chartered households. Whether initial settlers or later migrants, all tenants acquired the same irrevocable or permanent rights that characterized tenancy in the mainland. These not only protected them against increases in rent but also allowed them to sublet. Thus, after a generation or two a single piece of land might have four private claimants, each taking a share of the harvest, extending from the actual farmer to the original chartered household.

In their effort to capture more of the agricultural surplus, and reform what they considered "uneconomical" practices, Taiwan's new masters abrogated the rights of charter holders, fixed lease terms at twenty years, and enshrined in law the landowners' right to remove delinquent tenants. The reforms ended the customary practice of retaining residual claims to land after sale that, as noted in chapter 4, was universally recognized by communities in late imperial China.

There was little to no resistance to these efforts. The harshness of Japanese rule no doubt dampened enthusiasm for protest, just as the creation of an island-wide constabulary, supplied with the complete records of every household and its members, enhanced surveillance and the enforcement of social order. Charter holders on the mainland had of course no legal recourse in colonial Taiwan, while those chartered households that had migrated to the island received government bonds as compensation. Landowners undoubtedly felt the collection of taxes to be burdensome, particularly since the Qing had failed to register more than half of all land and was unable to tie its land tax to actual output. But proprietors soon benefited from colonial efforts to raise yields and from the predictability of Japan's buoyant demand for Taiwanese rice and sugar. As for the Japanese, they were unencumbered by local class interests and therefore free to approach land reform as a purely technical problem.

Having streamlined property rights and enhanced tax collection, the colonial government focused on raising farm output and agricultural exports in its effort to transform the island into an exporting colony capable of paying its own way, attracting Japanese private capital, and importing Japanese goods. To be sure, exports and cash cropping more generally were not unheard of before the arrival of the Japanese. Pre-colonial tenants had sold their crops to earn cash to pay rent, and landlords who collected their rents in kind marketed the rice and sugarcane to merchants. Nevertheless, so long as commercial activity was more or less an expression of rent extraction, and so long as agriculture was subordinated to the peasantry's desire to self-provision in general, avenues for commercial expansion were limited. When the Japanese took control of the island, some two centuries after Han migration to the island began in earnest, only a tenth of farmland was devoted to growing rice and sugar for export, a mere 14 percent of all rice made it to the market generally, and the annual volume of sugar exports had stagnated at and below forty thousand tons since the 1870s.

The colonial government understood early on that reforming the property and tax system was not enough to transform agricultural practices. That required direct intervention, for which colonial officers had a model in Meiji Japan. The key, they understood, was lowering risks in order to encourage private savings and investment on the one hand, and restricting outlets for farm labor to avenues designated by the state on the other.

The colonial regime began by taking on costly public investments that would lower the cost of cash cropping. It constructed modern ports and connected these to interior towns with thousands of miles of modern roads and railways. It built and managed a massive water control system that eventually tripled irrigated farmland, enhanced protection against flooding, and delivered hydroelectricity to towns and rural processing plants. It forwarded to peasants cheap private loans for purchases of chemical fertilizers, tools, draft animals, and storage. It founded educational extension services to deliver new and more productive cultivars of rice, sugarcane, and sweet potatoes as well as bananas and pineapples suitable for canning and exporting. Finally, Japanese capitalists were offered opportunities to invest that virtually guaranteed returns.

Taiwanese peasants responded to the lowered costs. With irrigation ready and cheap, they expanded paddy cultivation from less than half to 60 percent of all farmland, brought new land under cultivation, and delivered water to their sugarcane fields in record volumes. They applied ever-greater quantities of chemical fertilizer to their fields and they adopted improved cultivars. Introduced in 1922, the Ponlai strain of japonica rice was designed to be highly responsive to modern fertilizers, suited to Taiwan's tropical climate, and compatible with Japanese tastes. It raised yields by one-fifth and fetched a price in Japan 5 to 10 percent higher than traditional Taiwanese cultivars. The Japanese-managed Taiwan Sugar Research Institute freely distributed millions of cuttings of Rose Bamboo and Lahaina sugarcane from Hawaii and Stripped Tanna from Java. As early as 1911, the Japanese had managed to convert 96 percent of cane fields to the resistant and high-yielding Rose Bamboo cane. The effects on farm output were remarkable. The total rice harvest grew 50 percent between 1915 and 1940, when the island produced nine million *shi* of rice. Total sugar production more than doubled while the sweet potato harvest grew by nearly as much. All in all, the productivity of the land increased 80 percent under the Japanese.

In the absence of modern birth control, and with the continuation of traditional household formation practices alongside strengthened property rights, the growing food supply and improved health in general had a predictable effect. As the death rate, especially among infants, declined, the population doubled from three to six million by 1943. Given the continued practice of partible inheritance, and natural limits on the amount of arable land, farms remained small and relatively undercapitalized. Nine out of ten farms were fewer than three hectares, half were fewer than one hectare, and three in ten were less than half a hectare.

Against this backdrop, there were clear limits to what could be achieved. As the labor force in farming grew, purchases of fertilizers, tools, and equipment peaked, and households extended their working hours to wring more out of the land. Consequently, the productivity of farm labor hardly budged and increases in output came largely through greater effort. Rather than use precious cash to purchase the full complement of chemical fertilizer, households met one-third of their needs by gathering and composting their own despite the greater efficacy of modern inputs. Rather than enjoy the gains that would come from specializing entirely in cash crops, they continued to devote household labor and land to growing their own food and reducing their bill. Taiwanese peasants hoped that by scrimping and saving in this manner they could hold on to what little land they had and save toward land purchases or new leaseholds and stave off impoverishment. In this regard, at least, they were very successful: landless laborers never constituted more than 6 percent of the total agricultural labor force.

Thus, despite unprecedented state intervention and impressive gains in output, it is evident that the organization of production and peasant behavior more generally weighed on the economy. In response, the colonial regime, like the Belgian and Portuguese authorities in central and southeastern Africa, took action to suppress rural consumption even further and to squeeze and capture more of the rural surplus. An examination of Taiwan's sugar industry shows just how focused and determined Japanese efforts were.

From the outset, the colonial government was eager to increase and improve sugar manufacture to capture the Japanese market. Journalist Yosaburo Takekoshi noted, at a time when sugar imports accounted for half of Japan's trade deficit, that "the possession of such a good sugar-producing country as Formosa will be of inestimable benefit to us."[18] Yet sugar manufacture under peasant control was not only unsuited to the Japanese market but grossly inefficient. "The Chinese method of manufacturing," noted the American consul, "is undoubtedly the most crude and wasteful process in existence anywhere in the world. Their primitive appliances yield only half the sugar that can be obtained by the most modern methods known."[19] To pave the way for the modernization and rationalization of the industry, the colonial regime outlawed native sugar mills in 1905. It then assigned all sugar-growing peasants to districts and required that they sell their cane to the single modern mill permitted to operate within their district. Coupled with the expansion of irrigation, increase in chemical fertilizers, and the successful promotion of higher-yielding cane varieties, conditions on the island proved irresistible to Japanese capital. Japan's largest trading house, Mitsui, was easily convinced to form the Taiwan Sugar Refining Joint Stock Company, with additional financing from Japan's imperial family and the Sumitomo, Mori, and Suzuki zaibatsu groups, and within a short time nine modern refining companies processed all sugarcane on the island in 115 mills.

These investments demanded a steady supply of high-quality cane, yet peasants were free to plant whatever they wished, including paddy rice. Thanks to improved irrigation, new fertilizers, and better rice cultivars, rice farming was becoming quite profitable. Colonial planners solved the need for cane by disrupting the market. Each year, before the harvest, planners set the cane price relative to rice at a level that promised cane growers higher incomes. Simultaneously, the colonial government took steps to lower the risk of converting paddy land to cane fields by requiring mills to buy whatever cane was grown in their district at the fixed price. Guaranteed a good price and a market, supplied with free cane shoots for planting, and able to take out cheap loans to buy whatever chemical fertilizer was needed, peasants happily converted fields. Even so, cane growers remained wary of devoting all of their energy to a cash crop. Their timidity was an expression of the fact that food prices had their own dynamics and that increasingly these were shaped by Japan's demand for food.

A sudden jump in the price of Japanese rice in 1918 sparked urban riots that shocked both industrialists and the government. Since wages were linked to the cost of this food staple, both parties were eager to address the problem of long-term supply. In 1920 Japan's government liberalized rice imports and required improvements in its cultivation in the colonies. Moreover, to placate the rural sector, domestic rice prices were allowed to rise slowly, creating a windfall for Taiwanese growers. Between 1925 and 1935, Taiwan's contribution to Japan's rice imports rose from just below one-fifth to one-third. Predictably, Taiwan's food prices rose as the rate of increase in rice exports exceeded that of yields. Once again, factories were threatened by higher labor costs and the economy and government faced a slowdown in investment. The colonial government responded by restricting increases in rice prices on the island and also requiring mills to pay cane growers additional cash, which amounted to as much as 30 percent of the total cane price, to make up for unexpected increases in the rice price.

Henceforth, colonial planners performed a delicate balancing act, setting prices for cane and rice at levels that encouraged sugar production without driving up food prices to levels that would slow the general cycle of capital accumulation on Taiwan or in Japan. Their policies proved successful and the economy on Taiwan not only expanded across the 1920s and 1930s, it grew faster than Japan's. Between 1903 and 1929 sugar exports rose nearly fourfold, from 216 to 798 million kilograms, and topped out at 850 million kilograms in the mid-1930s. Nevertheless, its high rate of growth came at a cost to Taiwan's workforce, which colonial administrators continued to squeeze. Rice consumption on the island was reduced from 130 to 100 kilograms per person per year (the typical Japanese ate 160 kilograms) and rice shortfalls were made up by a switch, pushed by colonial planners, from rice to cheaper and less desirable sweet potatoes. This began with cane growers, who were encouraged to grow sweet potatoes because they freed up land for cane, producing more calories per hectare than rice, but soon spread to rice growers as the colonial government encouraged the release of rice to the market.

While there was clearly slack to be exploited in the peasant economy, there were also limits to what could be gained. Relentless cajoling and squeezing by colonial masters could not overcome the fact that in the absence of improvements in labor productivity, especially in food production, Taiwanese peasants had no choice but to withhold significant quantities of land and labor from the market. Sugarcane farmers continued to provision half of their food needs from their own labor and land, while paddy farmers consumed half of their rice. As we will see in chapter 9, it took the concerted effort and investment by a new government in manufacturing and appropriate farm technology to draw labor away from farming and break the cycle of growth through labor intensification. Even with price controls and massive subsidies in startup costs, sugar mills could not depend upon peasants to grow enough cane. To make up for shortfalls, they resorted to buying and managing cane fields. By 1940, sugar companies owned as much as half of all cane-growing land. What they couldn't farm with imported field workers from the Pescadores, they leased to tenants who paid rent and met loan payments in cane.

In their effort to turn the colony into a profit-making venture, capable both of paying its own way and provisioning Japan with low-cost resources, colonial administrators were forced to go to great lengths to bend peasant production to the market. At great expense, they lowered costs, guaranteed incomes, suppressed consumption, captured labor, and encouraged investment. In return, peasants got modest improvements to their living standards, longer life expectancy, and better diets. At the same time, landlords saw their incomes rise and along with merchants benefited from growing trade, new schools, modern clinics, public sanitation, electrification, and Japanese cosmopolitanism. They worked closely with their colonial masters and strove to send their children to Japan to study. A complex and hybrid economy had emerged by the 1940s that paved the way for postwar growth yet remained grounded in small-scale peasant production relying only on household labor.

There was slack to be exploited, but only through the extraordinary effort of a powerful state, unconstrained by the economic interests of Taiwan's landlord and merchant class, were conditions established conducive to peasants devoting greater energy and resources to cash cropping. In other words, much like the slave economies of the Caribbean, in the absence of market compulsion on individual economic behavior, it took extraordinary expenditures and the close supervision of Taiwanese labor by technocrats, sugar mill operators, police, and various local agents to raise the level of commercialization above customary levels.

In comparative terms, the mildness of Japanese colonialism is striking. The colonial state no doubt subordinated the well-being of Taiwan's population to the interests of the Japanese. It encouraged and pushed Taiwanese peasants into rice and sugarcane cultivation to enhance the profits of Japanese food processors and trading companies, as well as slow the cost of basic commodities and workers' wages in Japan. Yet in contrast to the outright compulsion visited by the colonial regimes on the peasants of the Belgian Congo and Portuguese Mozambique, Japanese policies entailed a mix of incentives and mild coercion. Consequently, Taiwanese peasants maintained a degree of independence from the market without risking their physical well-being and that of their families, let alone suffer anything approaching the rubber terror.

To explain Japan's divergence from the Anglo-European pattern of colonial rule we must look to Japan's own route to modernity. While there can be no doubt that Japan benefited tremendously from the appearance in the eighteenth century of the highly productive system of agriculture on the basis of commercial tenancy discussed in chapter 3, and the accompanying development of rural industry on the basis of free labor, its economy nonetheless lagged far behind those of England and the US, as well as the emerging industrial powerhouses of Belgium, Holland, and Germany. In the hostile late nineteenth-century environment framed by interimperial rivalries and wars, catching up with the leading industrial nations was a geopolitical necessity yet entailed a unique set of problems.

Briefly stated, the global terms of competition were set by the advanced economies, whose advantages accumulated over time and over which Japan had no control. Leading firms benefited from their proximity and ease of access to suppliers, a pool of skilled and flexible labor, machine builders, distributers and wholesalers, specialized financial institutions, and superior infrastructure. The "bloc" of capital embodied in mature industrial districts such as England's Manchester offered manufacturers huge discounts and cost advantages that outweighed their much higher wage bills and to prolong their lead in older and less capital-intensive industries. To invest in manufacturing in this environment was full of risk for Japanese firms. Japan's solution was to leverage the power of the state to mitigate the danger. It forwarded cheap capital to industrialists, who invested in raw materials, energy production, and industries producing intermediary products. It also threw up trade protections, provided subsidies to exporters, controlled inflation, and encouraged the development of large manufacturing banks. To guide policy, the state recruited technocrats skilled in law, government, and economics and housed them in government agencies charged with guiding the economy.

This model of state-guided growth was exported to Japan's colonies in Taiwan, Korea, and Manchuria, where Japanese colonial states saw opportunities to develop local economies in ways that complemented and quickened the pace of growth in Japan. Had Japan's colonial planners been required to invest capital in ways that suited the needs of the Taiwanese landlord and merchant classes, traditional paths of development would have continued. But planners did not have to answer to the native populations. Drawing on tools used to force and accelerate growth in Japan, they went to work building Taiwan's economy as they wished. They were free to eliminate sectors of the landowning class, terminate customary rights, and reduce the landlords' take. Moreover, they were free to tax the population and invest in long-term developmental goals without worrying about short-term returns or driving traditional merchants out of business. In Taiwan coercion and exploitation proceeded hand in hand.

By contrast, colonial development under the Anglo-European powers was left entirely to private interests, with the state offering military protection. In some European colonies such as British Nigeria and India, population densities led the colonizers to dispense with coercive policies. Great Britain established its property laws and levied taxes. Yet its reluctance to invest adequately had catastrophic consequences for peasants who had to produce commodities in order to meet their fiscal obligations in a context of colonial property law that precipitated the subdivision of landholdings and the creation of uneconomic plots of land. Hausa and Indian peasants could no longer supplement their agricultural resources with manufacturing for local markets, because Great Britain opened its colonies to merchandise produced in the metropole, and indigenous artisans found it difficult to earn any income. The peasants of West Africa and India became deeply indebted to indigenous elites and administrators serving as intermediaries for banks in London. In contrast to the heightened sensitivity of Japanese planners to rice supplies on Taiwan, British administrators took a laissez-faire approach to grain shortfalls in India and provoked a series of famines from about 1870 to 1945.

Elsewhere, the efforts to make colonies useful to the imperial countries led to the expropriation of indigenous populations for the benefit of European settlers in Algeria, Kenya, and southern and South Africa. Great Britain and France sought to make the colonies profitable for individual citizens willing to settle in their African domains.

In all of these instances of colonial agriculture, as cruel as they were to the indigenous populations, these populations still had the capacity for autonomous actions that constrained and shaped the policies of the imperial powers. Most famously, the anti-imperial uprising in Algeria from 1954 to 1962 forced the French settlers to leave the best arable land of the country for its original inhabitants. The Mau-Mau rebellion in Kenya helped convince British rulers to reverse course, cease favoring settler farmers, and begin encouraging the agriculture of the indigenous peasantry. The rebellion of the peasants of East Bengal in the 1930s and 1940s undermined the hierarchy of authority through which Great Britain had ruled this region of India. Mozambican peasants passively resisted the cotton regime, prevented the Portuguese state from ever meeting its production targets, and eventually led it to abandon forced cotton growing in 1961. Peasants of Ghana, Kenya, and Northern Rhodesia economically outperformed the settlers and made Great Britain abandon its plans for European-owned plantations.

Finally, colonial administrators, who saw in the peasants' demand for more land and lower rents an opportunity through land reform to introduce commercial farming, were disappointed to see that while peasants wanted land of their own they avoided dependence on the market. Only the political application of limits and pressures got Taiwanese peasants to orient more of their efforts to commercial farming. Even then, the peasants continued to engage in subsistence agriculture and thwarted the plans of the Japanese authorities to lower commodity prices to the levels they would have liked.

NOTES

1. E. Boelaert, H. Vinck, and Ch. Lonkama, "Témoignages africains de l'arrivée des premiers blancs aux bords des rivières de l'equateur (rd congo)," *Annales Æquatoria* 16 (1995), 652/317–18.

2. Ibid., 650/312–13.

3. Ibid., 651/314–16.

4. Ibid., 650/312–13.

5. Ibid., 651/314–16.

6. Ibid., 652/317–18.

7. Ibid., 669/351–53.

8. Quoted from Robert Harms, "The World Abir Made: The Maringa-Lopori Basin, 1885–1903," *African Economic History* 12 (1983), 133.

9. United Nations General Assembly, Resolution 96(I), The Crime of Genocide, December 11, 1946.

10. Quoted from Sven Beckert, *Empire of Cotton: A Global History* (New York: Alfred A. Knopf, 2014), 371.

11. Quoted from Michael Watts, *Silent Violence: Food, Famine, and Peasantry in Northern Nigeria* (Athens: University of Georgia Press, 2013), 180.

12. Quoted from Diana Davis, *Resurrecting the Granary of Rome: Environmental History and French Colonial Expansion in North Africa* (Athens: Ohio University Press, 2007), 48.

13. Quoted from Ian Phimister, "Peasant Production and Underdevelopment in Southern Rhodesia, 1890–1914, with Particular Reference to the Victoria District," in *The Roots of Rural Poverty in Central and Southern Africa*, ed. Robin H. Palmer and Neil Parsons (Berkeley: University of California Press, 1977), 262.

14. Quoted from Frederick Johnstone, *Class, Race, and Gold: A Study of Class Relations and Racial Discrimination in South Africa* (London: Routledge & K. Paul, 1976), 127.

15. Quoted from Monica Wilson and Leonard Monteath Thompson, *The Oxford History of South Africa*, vol. 2: *South Africa 1870–1966* (New York: Oxford University Press, 1969–1971), 162.

16. George Leslie MacKay, *From Far Formosa: The Island, Its People, and Missions* (Edinburgh: Oliphant Anderson and Ferrier, 1896), 209–10.

17. Yosaburo Takekoshi, *Japanese Rule in Formosa* (London: Longmans, Green, 1907), 128.

18. Ibid., 242.

19. James Davidson, *The Island of Formosa: Historical View from 1430 to 1900* (London: MacMillan, 1903), 455.

Chapter Eight

Socialist Agriculture

Collectivization in Three Countries

What made each of the revolutions in Russia, China, and Cuba unique was not only the preexisting rural economies but also the extent of participation of peasants and rural workers in the socialist transformations. In Russia, prior to 1917, and China, prior to 1949, millions of peasants, within hundreds of thousands of rural communities, farmed with the purpose of assuring a stable existence. Landlords, with varying success and to varying degrees, used political influence, and their relatively larger share of the soil, to take labor and farm output from the peasants. Cuba, by contrast, had a much smaller peasant population prior to the Revolution of 1959, while most of its rural inhabitants worked for wages on farms run by tenants, who themselves fell under the sway of sugar companies.

While Russia and China had roughly similar agrarian structures, their revolutions were very different. While the peasants of the Russian Empire joined the revolution late to eliminate the landlord class, free the rural sector from burdens, and consolidate their control over agriculture, the political character of the socialist transformation was determined in the cities by the Bolshevik Party. In China, conversely, the revolution developed out of the countryside as a prolonged armed struggle of poor and middling peasants under the leadership of the party. Whereas the Communist Party of the Soviet Union (the Bolsheviks changed their name to the CPSU) eventually developed an adversarial relationship to the rural communities, the Chinese Communist Party, it will become apparent, proved much more responsive to the peasantry. For this reason, the agrarian sector of China, in the long run, has proved much more dynamic than has the Russian. In Cuba, the revolution began in the countryside, not among the plantation workers, but among the smaller class of peasants and sharecroppers. Its success resulted from the swift collapse of support for the government in the cities. The revolution quickly won the approval of the rural wage workers by pursuing radical policies to make life more secure for plantation labor.

In all three cases, we will see, revolutions made to end exploitation led to a new sort of unequal society stratified by new classes. Bureaucratic planners and state managers in control of government institutions enjoyed relatively privileged lives thanks to the work, inefficient by capitalist standards, of the rural population. At first small, the industrial proletariat grew with state investment in manufacturing and it soon came to enjoy relatively higher standards of living afforded by urban life. These similarities resulted from the model of rural collectivization established in the Soviet Union in the late 1920s and 1930s, designed to extract farm surpluses on a large scale for investment in industry.

In making these points, we will address a series of questions about the dynamics of socialist transformations in the countryside. How did the peasant economies of Russia and China, and the sugar export sector of Cuba, evolve prior to their respective revolutions? How did the peasants in Russia and China, and the rural workers of Cuba, influence the policies of socialist leaders in the revolutions' aftermaths? What problems did the rural populations pose for the leaders' goals of industrial development? How did the Communist regimes respond to these problems? In seeking to develop their countries, what new forms of class exploitation did the leaders bring into being? And finally, what were the long-term consequences of these forms of exploitation for the respective economies? But before answering these questions, we must first examine tsarist Russia to fully understand the model for collectivization established in the Soviet Union.

SOVIET COLLECTIVIZATION

V. I. Lenin, the head of the Bolshevik Party and of the November Revolution of 1917, before becoming the leader of the Soviet Union until 1924, argued, in his 1899 study *The Development of Capitalism in Russia*, that after the liberation of the rural population—the serfs—from bondage in the 1860s, the generalization of cash rents, the growth of urban industry and commodity production, and the increasing use of money together led to the differentiation of the peasantry. He documented the rising inequality in rural areas, but claimed additionally that the modernization of lending practices led to investment in agricultural production and, by implication, to economic development.

Lenin presented a wealth of research and detail, and if one sifts through the data it becomes apparent that from the 1860s to the late 1890s the countryside experienced pauperization rather than economic expansion. In contrast to the courses of development described in chapters 3 and 6—on seventeenth-century England, eighteenth- and nineteenth-century Japan, and the American Midwest in the 1850s, characterized by mounting rural investment, technological advance, and a rising standard of living—Russia evolved in a manner similar to eighteenth-century France and China. Lenin showed that a growing mass of poor peasants squeezed more income from scraps of land, often in an utter state of ruin, by replacing spring grain with potatoes and flax. Potatoes required more work than did grain but yielded more calories per unit of land. Flax also required much labor in farming and especially in extracting the fiber from the stalks. But its sale price procured the income with which the peasants obtained more food per unit of land than if they had continued to grow grain. Potato and flax yielded less income per labor expended than did grain but yielded more food per unit of land at no cost, apart from drudgery, to poor peasants with much unused labor within their households.

Even after making their bits of land more productive, many peasants still had to find remunerated work in the vicinity as unskilled farmhands and building workers. These impoverished households split their time between farming the landowner's estate and tending to their own family plots and livestock. Since they obtained some of their provisions by working their plots more intensively, and since tens of millions of them hunted for wage-paying work in their localities, the landed classes did not have to pay them much. This growing mass of poor peasants took up the worst jobs characteristic of the labor-service system in which remuneration consisted more of medicine, schooling, and flour milling than of money. Landlords thus faced no pressure to invest in farm improvements and economize on expenditures on labor.

When the dust settled after the revolutions of 1917 and the civil war of 1918–1921, the balance of forces in the countryside was turned upside down. The Communist Party of the USSR formally established soviets in rural areas, but real power was held by the traditional peasant communes. These emerged stronger than they had ever been thanks to the expropriation of the nobles' estates and the New Economic Policy (NEP) of the 1920s. This policy granted economic autonomy to the villages, where the overwhelming majority of the population lived. The peasant communes redistributed immense amounts of land in 1918 and continued to do so, at a much reduced rate, in the 1920s. They fixed and imposed taxes for collective local needs even though these taxes were illegal. Some communal gatherings even collected state taxes in the old system of collective responsibility, a practice that had been abolished as long ago as 1906.

Better-off, more aggressive members of the communes made decisions that were then ratified by acclamation. Poor peasants were silent or absent. But these made up a small, irrelevant group. Prior to 1917, since nearly the entire rural population owned at least some land, fewer than 1 percent were fully dependent on wages. The number of rural wage workers grew smaller still as a result of the land expropriations of the peasant revolution, and nearly a decade later remained smaller than it had been under the tsar. The largest group in the countryside, a group that grew as a consequence of the revolution, consisted of households in the middle peasantry, owners of six to eleven hectares. The communes were thus fairly cohesive and defensively conservative. The Communist Party, by contrast, consisted overwhelmingly of townspeople who could only to a very limited extent mobilize any of the peasants.

Maurice Hindus, a Russian-born American journalist, who spent time in Bolshoye Bykovo, his native Byelorussian village, in the first months of 1930, argued that the peasants' control over the land and work had harmful consequences for agricultural production.

> Between 1917 and 1927 the number of individual farms had leaped from seventeen million to twenty-seven million. This automatically removed from cultivation millions of acres which were taken up by the buildings and the yards of the new households, and by the ridges and the dead furrows which in Russia, in the absence of fences, have since days immemorial divided one strip of land from another. . . . One scientist estimates that these Russian "fences" take up 7 percent of the land, and another reckons that their aggregate acreage, if properly tilled, would raise enough bread to supply the yearly need of half the total population of Russian cities. [1]

Peasant agriculture, in this way, not only took land out of production but also made labor less productive. As Lenin's figures demonstrate, the rural population far exceeded the requirements of agriculture. Even at the peak demand at harvest time in August, the supply of labor still surpassed what was needed. The number of rural inhabitants became even more excessive during the civil war of 1918–1921, when the urban population declined and the number and similarity of landholdings increased. Soviet studies of the 1920s show that the peasants did not expend anywhere close to their capacity for work.

In many rural households short of land, the members intensively used this excess capacity for work to scratch out a living at falling rates of return per labor input. The peasants of western Ukraine, a densely populated area relative to the rest of the country, introduced potatoes, which were of lower profitability than were oats, but yielded more calories upon extra labor inputs. By 1928, potato production vastly exceeded the level of 1913. Many of these peasants also began to cultivate beets, hemp, and other labor-intensive industrial crops even though they brought in less revenue than did grains per hour of work. Hemp and beets had the advantage, however, of higher yields the more intensively they were farmed, and thus increased the returns to rural smallholders by dint of the greater overall output.

During the 1920s, the peasants of the western districts shifted some of their land away from three-field rotations with fallow in order to make all of the soil productive. They did not spend household funds on threshing machines, because family members could separate grain from the stalks and husks themselves, whereas purchasing machines depleted peasant incomes and entailed further depreciation costs. By 1928, the metal plow had replaced the ard or scratch plow on the overwhelming majority of farms, but nearly half of the harvesting was still done with sickles and scythes, and an even greater proportion of the sowing was done by hand. The peasants avoided outlays on labor-saving implements that would leave family members idle. They instead satisfied their consumption needs by doing all the necessary work with unpaid household labor.

In more sparsely populated regions of the Soviet Union, the peasants tended to household gardens around their cottages and enjoyed the harvests of strips of land within the three-field rotations of the village commune. The peasant assembly decided for the entire village the crops to grow and the times for plowing, sowing, and harvesting. Even communities endowed with good soils and market locations did not grow in wealth. Seeing the increased returns to their labor, the peasants worked less, and satisfied their requirements with decreased economic activity, trading drudgery for leisure.

Because of this peasant rationality, the twenty-five to twenty-six million farmsteads, which accommodated about 120 million people and 80 percent of the Soviet population, did not bring down food prices for the growing urban population. In 1926, grain output nearly equaled, and overall agricultural output surpassed, the levels of 1909–1913, even though the area tilled stood a bit below what it had been. Per capita output declined slightly. What is more, marketed grain in 1926–1927 stood at only 17 percent of the total harvest as compared with 22–25 percent in 1913. Prior to World War I, the landlords profited from market sales of grain appropriated by means of usury, low-paid work, and labor services. But once the peasants took over the land, they fed much of the grain to livestock because of the low prices offered by the state. The rural population preferred to sell more lucrative meat and dairy products. By 1926, the number of cattle almost equaled the level of 1914, and it continued to rise in 1927 and 1928. The cattle weighed more than they had prior to World War I. Had grain exports not amounted to only a quarter of what they had been prior to the war, urban food consumption would have declined to dangerously low levels.

According to Hindus, the peasant "saw value chiefly in goods, and whenever he sold grain, a calf, a pig, he wanted to buy something. But the Soviets were unable to supply him with the amounts of goods demanded; the capacity of their factories was limited."[2] The greater part of the Soviet economy thus revolved around what was useful to the peasantry rather than any drive to accumulate money. The decline in the terms of trade—namely the scarce and expensive manufactured goods—did not offer the peasants incentives. Had the peasants farmed solely in response to what the market encouraged, rather than in response to their household needs, one would have seen reductions in the harvests and sown area. Yet after the early 1920s, these nearly recovered to prewar levels, whereas the marketed surpluses did not rise proportionately, because the peasants used the land for the requirements of their families and communities. Similarly, had the aforementioned increases in the total output in beets, potatoes, and the like yielded more surplus, peasants would have seen their cash incomes grow and the supply of food would have moderated urban prices. But the peasants of Ukraine ate the increase in potatoes and used income from hemp and beets to cover household needs.

The increased output thus did little to fulfill the aspirations of the Communist leadership for industrial advance and urban growth. The first Five-Year Plan was launched in 1928, and Joseph Stalin's regime required supplies of food for the towns and exportable surpluses to pay for industrialization. But the 1927 harvest came in below the previous year's. The government collected less grain in 1928 and 1929 than it had in 1926–1927 despite raids on peasant houses and other arbitrary measures. Better-off peasants then cut down on sowing, and the authorities failed to make good the reduction by increasing the farm area of the rest of the peasants. In the spring of 1929, the government had to introduce ration cards amid a looming famine.

Given this crisis, collectivization appeared as a means to overcome peasant resistance, appropriate the grain, and, at the same time, eliminate traditional agriculture, increase productivity, and modernize the countryside. The experience of the civil war and famine of 1921–1922 impressed upon the Soviet leadership that no attempt to take grain from the peasants could succeed so long as it remained their property. Communist leaders therefore contemplated alternative means of obtaining foodstuffs without having to pay for them. The leaders must have noticed that while only 2 percent of the land was in collective or state enterprises in 1927, this accounted for 7.5 percent of the marketed output. If Soviet leaders augmented the surplus by pushing collectivization, they could resell the captured grain at a higher price and get the peasants to shoulder much of the burden of industrialization. If they were to take control of agriculture, they could orchestrate the movement of labor from village to town as forecast in their Five-Year Plan. Many Soviet leaders, in any case, regarded the peasants' attachment to their land as petty-bourgeois hostility to socialism.

Nevertheless, one should not regard collectivization as a historical necessity. No Bolshevik leader had advocated anything akin to the obligatory pooling of landholdings, liquidation of the prosperous peasants, and destruction of the entire market sector. These policies seemed so aberrant that the Soviet leadership continued to tout private farms and markets as the correct policy of socialist construction in spite of what everyone saw around them when collectivization was in full swing in 1931.

To account for collectivization one must consider the errors of Soviet leaders in allowing the urban food shortages to develop. The party had made cooperative farming a major theme of propaganda but took no concrete steps to encourage it. The leaders instead applied their efforts and resources to internal political struggles and other sectors of the economy. Tens of thousands of families on the collective farms suffered neglect, struggled to maintain themselves, and faced obstructionist attitudes from the authorities. As the Chinese path up to 1958, examined later in this chapter, suggests, a better-developed cooperative movement, an adequately maintained state and collective sector, and agronomic assistance to the peasants could have prevented the grain crisis of 1928.

Up to this time, Stalin aligned himself with the majority of the Soviet leadership against any policy liable to move the country away from peasant farming. His reluctance to press on with industrialization made it impossible for the towns to offer many shoes, clothes, or farm tools in return for peasant output. Then, in the crisis of 1928, Stalin urged grain requisitions despite the resentment they would arouse in the countryside. In the Five-Year Plan presented to the Sixteenth Party Congress the following spring, he reversed course and came out in favor of rapid industrialization. Stalin resolved to confront the rural population at a time when the USSR was internationally isolated, workers lacked bread, industry lacked skilled labor and machinery, and machinery lacked fuel and raw material whose supply depended on peasant farming.

According to the Five-Year Plan, 20 percent of the farmers were to join collectives by 1933. In the period from June through October 1929, the area of the kolkhozes (collective farms) grew from 3.9 to 7.6 percent of the arable land. Hindus described the administrative methods used during these months. The Soviet organizer

> outlines in detail the numerous privileges the government extends to members of the *kolhoz*. There is the question of taxes . . . the *kolhoz* and its members are exempted from all levies on food-producing stock. . . . There is the question of credits. Again the *kolhoz* enjoys superior advantages. . . . To the women he holds out the lure of nurseries and children's homes and, therefore, increased leisure for play and diversion. To the young he emphasizes the advantages of playgrounds, entertainment, freedom of education in all schools and colleges and possible advancement to positions of highest responsibility in large Soviet enterprises. To . . . the aged he offers assurance of security and care in times of illness and disability. . . . He can and does remind them . . . of the difference in the taxation of the individualist farmers and of the *kolhoz* and of . . . their hopeless position when they attain the stature of *koolack*.[3]

These incitements on the one hand, and warnings to the kulaks (the so-called independent capitalist farmers) on the other, did not make for a spontaneous rush to join the collectives. Yet they did not, in most cases, amount to coercion either. No doubt this initial success ought to have been encouraged and consolidated prior to any further advance.

In 1929, the Soviet leaders Nikolai Ivanovich Bukharin, Alexei Ivanovich Rykov, and Mikhail Pavlovich Tomsky submitted proposals to the executive committee of the Communist Party for slowing the pace of industrialization and retaining the free market. They stated that Stalin and his supporters employed "military-feudal" exploitative policies and destroyed democracy in the party. Bukharin then lost his position as editor of *Pravda*, the official newspaper of the Communist Party, and Tomsky lost his as head of the trade unions. Public attacks rained down on them and their allies. The defeat of Bukharin's bloc opened the way for the Stalinist regime. The industrial drive exceeded all limits, and calls went out for the completion of the plan in four, even two, years. The authorities began to use force against the peasants in the fall of 1929 and made it their main weapon in the winter.

The Unified State Political Administration (USPA), the successor to the Cheka secret police, wrote orders from Moscow at the beginning of February 1930:

> To carry out the liquidation of the kulak as a class in the most organized manner and to decisively suppress any attempts by the kulaks to counteract the measures . . . for the socialist reorganization of agriculture . . . a devastating blow must be delivered to the kulaks as soon as possible. . . . The implementation of this historic task will demand exceptional intensity in every area of party and soviet work. . . . What will be demanded of our organs more than ever is . . . determination, and perseverance, an exceptionally rigorous class line, and efficient and swift action. The tasks that have been set will be successfully carried out only if there is unconditional support for them from the majority of landless laborers and poor and middle peasants. [4]

Exhortations of this sort blared across the USSR, and all caution was thrown to the wind. Red Army units and secret police troops, along with a quarter of a million workers and party members, fanned out across the countryside. The urban volunteers, backed by the state, took over local administrations, dismissed reticent officials, and imposed themselves on more than half of the peasants in a matter of weeks in the winter of 1929–1930. They urged local party organizations to beat all records of collectivization. Pressure from the politburo to show results created rivalries between regional authorities. Individuals perceived prospects for promotion or demotion, and vied to outdo one another. Some local party offices started to proclaim they had collectivized half or more of the rural households without any regard for whether the people were ready to join the kolkhozes. Members of the central government were deluged with the news they wanted to hear and then increased their effort to achieve maximum results.

The campaign collided with the refusal of the peasant masses. According to Hindus,

> These peasants had never believed anybody's words; they had always distrusted the whole world. . . . And now they were to give up their individual land, their horses, their cows, their farm buildings—the things that had given them bread, protection against starvation, the very security they needed to hold body and soul together—all on the mere promise of a youthful agitator that this would enrich their lives![5]

State agents escalated coercive measures to overcome resistance. The USPA issued a report in January 1930 that, in the villages of Mosolovka, Saburovka, and Pervaia in the Anna Raion, an administrative unit in southwest Russia, party cadres alleged disruptions at meetings in order to initiate arrests even before organizing the kolkhozes. "The party members then announced 'We have come to build a collective farm, and we will put whoever is against the collective farm on the road to the moon.'"[6] Most villagers left the meetings, and the remaining ones voted in favor of the collective farm.

> Rounds were made of households, property was confiscated, and peasants were instructed to sign without question a statement that they had "joined the collective farm." Those who were unwilling to sign were arrested. . . . As for the organizers . . . , they went on drinking binges with the wives of the arrested men. . . . In the village of Sadovoe 35 people were arrested at one time, including women with babies. All of the arrestees were held without charges. . . . By these methods, collectivization in the raion rose from 26 percent to 82.4 percent in 10 days.[7]

By the end of 1930, the police imprisoned or executed at least sixty-three thousand heads of households, and caused hundreds of thousands to leave their villages. The orders issued by the USPA for the liquidation of the kulaks in February 1930 called for the deportation of tens of thousands of families to Siberia, the Urals, Kazakhstan, and the north of European Russia. When transmitted to party members, the USPA's orders exhorted them to "decisive" "devastating" action, and they responded by deporting even more peasants than planned. A police chief reported to Stalin at the beginning of 1932 that over a million kulaks had been deported since 1929. Many of them literally froze in mid-winter in unheated freight cars.

The peasants felt shock and revulsion at the inhumanity of the state agents, who reduced once-prosperous peasants to outlaws in their own country. Many villagers preferred the so-called kulaks to the local ne'er-do-wells allied to the party officials. The kulaks seemed like conscientious, successful villagers liable to run rural affairs responsibly. The peasants demonstrated their disgust, over the course of 1929, in a rising tide of arson, murder, and violence against chairmen, secretaries of rural officials, Communists, village activists, and members of procurement brigades. Collectivization provoked at least 1,600 cases of armed resistance.

Party leaders began to fear a rupture in the agricultural cycle and a collapse of farm production. Stalin signaled a retreat in the article "Dizziness from Successes" published in *Pravda* in March 1930. He blamed the setback on overeager officials. The Central Committee of the All-Union Communist Party "determined that leading organizations of regions (Middle Volga, Northern Caucasus) are incorrectly implementing the . . . directive, rushing with the arrest and exile of kulaks, disregarding the plan and schedule for exiles issued from the center, and thereby creating a danger of anarchy and uncoordinated actions."[8] Mamaev, who wrote one of the last criticisms of Stalin to appear in print within the USSR until the leader's death in 1953, asked in a *Pravda* article, "Whose head got dizzy?" and sarcastically stated, "It appears 'the tsar is good and the local *chinovniki* (officials) are useless.'"[9] Mamaev suggested that the conditions were not ready for collectivization, that the country did not have an agricultural machine industry adequate to the requirements of large-scale farming, and that the middle peasantry did not want the kolkhozes.

But once an agricultural collapse was averted the Communist leadership pressed forward. Stalin avoided any sign of weakness that might set ablaze the smoldering hatred in millions of rural huts. He named all resistance to collectivization "kulak" even though resistance involved the greater part of the rural inhabitants. The party recognized as much by coining terms such as "kulak hireling" and "kulak choirboy." In a report written in March 1931 about "the forms and dynamics of class struggle in the countryside" the USPA stated that

> the kulaks' methods of struggle have varied and have become increasingly diverse . . . kulak youth . . . are implacably hostile toward Soviet power and represent a ready-made reserve for counterrevolutionary work in the countryside. Some of the young people in rural social-class strata that are close to us— the poor peasantry and the middle peasantry—are also being lured into counterrevolutionary work.[10]

Peasant resistance manifested itself most clearly in the slaughter of livestock. The peasants consumed their cattle rather than see them seized by the state for the collective farms. The slaughter proceeded in an unstoppable downward spiral and left the countryside with dwindling supplies of manure and draft animals. The decline in the number of workhorses erased nearly 75 percent of the traction power in agriculture.

Slaughtering cattle was the least risky form of resistance. In the face of state violence, the peasants reluctantly joined the collective farms over the next few years. By April 1, 1932, most households and plots had been brought into the collectives. Many peasants, it seems, felt conflicting interests, calculations, and sentiments, and village unity crumbled when the party displayed its determination. Cold reflection showed some peasants, and many poor ones, that they might seize the opportunity, and benefit from the dispossession of the well-to-do and the pooling of resources, especially when it was clear who was winning the day.

The collective farms should have adopted a modern agriculture reliant on tractors, machinery, and new buildings. But Stalin and party leaders deemed heavy industry a higher priority than agricultural investment. The Central Committee resolved to make the machine-tractor stations (MTSs) the leading force in the mechanization and operational direction of the countryside. It obliged the collective farms to make large payments in kind to the MTS for spring plowing and the harvest. Rather than make these payments, the rural inhabitants harnessed the remaining malnourished cows and oxen to the plows. Soviet agriculture continued to rely on horses in the 1930s, possibly even more than in the previous decade, even though their deficient numbers could only till a fraction of the land. Party officials refused to acknowledge the declining productivity. They estimated the size of the crop—based on maximum theoretical yields applied to the maximum arable area—named the share of the harvest for the state, and then intensified the coercion to farm the kolkhozes and meet the projected procurements.

The Communist leadership especially distrusted the peasants of Ukraine, because they farmed the most productive arable fields in the Soviet Union and potentially had nationalist claims to the output. The party thus proceeded more rapidly and violently in Ukraine than in the Russian Republic. By 1932, the state collectivized 70 percent of Ukrainian villages as opposed to only 59.3 percent of those in the Russian Republic. Ukrainian farmers harvested 27 percent of the USSR's grain yet were forced to make 38 percent of all deliveries to the state. Officials took a third of the Ukrainian harvest in 1930, demanded 42 percent in 1931, though they could not collect this much, demanded over half in 1932, and still suspected the peasants of withholding produce. Brigades of grain collectors took everything they found in house-to-house searches and left nothing to eat. Leaders in Moscow rejected the complaints of local party members, and their agents arrested the Communists suspected of aiding or protecting peasants. The party liquidated independent Ukrainian Communists and nationalist intellectuals. All the while, the government exported grain—far more than the modest amounts of the 1920s—in order to acquire capital for industrialization.

Food shortages reached their nadir in early 1933, when corpses lined the roads of Ukraine and even instances of cannibalism were reported. German, Jewish, Ukrainian, and Russian villages of Ukraine all suffered famine, which also occurred outside Ukraine in the North Caucasus and Volga regions. The per capita loss of life in Kazakhstan, where the state forcibly settled nomadic tribes, exceeded that of Ukraine.

Officials formed a separate caste over and against the community, lived in houses commandeered from kulaks, and ate specially delivered rations. They set up roadblocks to stop starving peasants from entering towns and begging for bread. The goal was to keep the famine secret not only from foreign journalists but also, as far as possible, from townspeople. An estimated five million people perished before the famine abated in May 1933, when the state replaced requisitions with a grain tax, permitted grain trading, and ended collections.

The brutishness of collectivization made for sullen peasants hostile to the regime that had taken their land, horses, and grain. Village factions and families fought over positions of power and meager resources. Corruption, drunkenness, and violence became endemic to rural areas. Agriculture could not flourish without farmers in a mood to make it work. The demoralized farmers diminished the quality of the soil by applying manure carelessly. The state only made artificial fertilizers available for industrial crops. Yields per acre, as well as total farm output, especially grain and food production, tended downward, as a result, during the 1930s.

Favorable weather improved the grain harvest of 1933. The increased output of this year partly resulted from the extension of the arable surface. Officials sought to offset the declining productivity on collective farms by plowing up the arid regions of the North Caucasus, east of the Volga, in Siberia and Kazakhstan. They created extensive grain farms as large as several hundred thousand acres and appropriated most of the output for industrial areas. By 1933, agriculture began to recover rapidly through the stabilization of the collective farm system and the increased supply of machinery, but output still barely exceeded the level of 1928 and declined per capita. Subsequent gains in output were no larger than the growth of the population all the way down to 1950.

Party leaders, however, regarded collectivization, first and foremost, from the angle of procurements. These doubled in 1932–1933 from what they had been six years previously. The marketed surplus of cotton, flax, and wool grew even more. In 1938, the procurements exceeded the level of the ten previous years by two and a half times. It took coercion to obtain this result. The kolkhoz lacked intrinsic coherence and would have disintegrated into private farming had the state not applied doses of terror at all seasons of the year to enforce plowing, sowing, harvesting, and delivering the food.

This terror implicated the party leadership and probably the whole party. The regime was responsible for the criminal and economic calamities culminating in the famine of 1932–1933. People must have noticed the savaged livestock, deaths of millions of people, and declines in production. Collectivization instilled hatred and despair throughout society. The birthrate plummeted and population growth slowed to a snail's pace. Yet it became obligatory to tout collectivization as a success of the Stalinist leadership. The party's public media departed from reality, depicting a beautiful, better, and more cheerful world. Boris Pasternak wrote in the novel *Doctor Zhivago* that collectivization turned into a disastrous mistake "and so it was necessary to teach people not to think and make judgments, to compel them to see the non-existent, and to argue the opposite of what was obvious to everyone."[11] The discrepancy, atypical in the pre-Stalinist period, between Soviet claims and social realities, sucked the vitality from the party and weakened its resistance to the terror that fell upon it. The expansion of police repression involved in the collectivization and the forced-labor camps set up in 1929–1933 provided the training ground for the institutions and methods later applied in the large-scale police surveillance, suspicion of "saboteurs," purge of the Communist Party, government officials, and Red Army leadership, and mass imprisonments and executions of 1936–1938.

Although the Communist Party touted collectivization as a policy to end exploitation in the countryside, it actually begot and ossified social inequalities. At the top of the collective farms was the white-collar elite appointed by the district officials to act as chairpersons, board members, brigade leaders, and administrators. The chairpersons of the kolkhozes referred to themselves as "khoziainin" bosses. In regard to the headquarters of the kolkhoz, Hindus exclaimed, "What historic audacity it symbolized! What incomparable power it commanded! Surely no peasant could pass it without in his heart of hearts feeling that it had become the very arbiter of his destiny."[12] Some of the peasants, who accommodated themselves, rose into administrative positions, gained training as mechanics and tractor drivers, or worked at the machine-tractor stations that controlled the large farm equipment. The majority class at the bottom received less pay for labor akin to the serfdom from which it had emerged seventy years earlier. These peasants worked in the fields against their will and performed required labor on roads. The state refused to issue passports to the peasantry when they became compulsory for changes in residence in 1932. The kolkhoz chairmen, in these ways, fixed the peasants to the land, and forced them to work it.

By asserting power over the peasants, the party was able to transfer population from agriculture to industry. The deportations, expropriations, attacks on religion and culture, and decline of the rural standard of living led many peasants to leave for the factory districts. The structure of the kolkhoz also served this end. Under the NEP, the peasant household, as mentioned above, expended only a small portion of its labor capacity. But in the 1930s, when peasants faced pressure to work for the local cooperative or another state firm, the underutilization of workers became visible and prompted the reallocation of the labor surplus to industry. Whereas the overall Soviet population grew slightly from 1926 to 1939, the number of rural inhabitants declined,

and the actual agricultural population declined even more. The urban population doubled, while the famine following collectivization and deaths during
World War II reduced the number of rural inhabitants by seventeen million
between 1928 and 1950. Over the following decades, the number of collective farms diminished to a fraction of what it had been in the 1930s, each one
covering about six times as much land.

Nevertheless, labor productivity still lagged well behind the rates attained
in other industrialized countries. Days worked in Soviet agriculture remained
high, because collective farms remained the employer of last resort providing
a meager subsistence to women, children, seniors, and the infirm. Soviet
farms did not have to compete to survive or produce in response to demand
and, with little in the way of support from the state, managers had little
choice but to throw more labor into the fields to meet the targets of the
production plan. Managers aimed for the unbridled growth of their unit in
order to enhance their reputation and improve their chance of promotion
through the state/party hierarchy. They thus hoarded as much material and
labor as possible, and withheld information about their units from the planners.

The only productive farms of the Russian Soviet Republic were the private plots authorized in the 1930s to help revive output. Rural families obtained almost all of their potatoes, vegetables, milk, meat, and eggs from
these household plots. Peasants of the USSR worked most of the time on the
collective farms for less than half of their income. This should come as no
surprise, for the collective farms, we have seen, were designed for the express purpose of redistributing resources to the state through procurement
quotas and payments to the MTS. When these duties were fulfilled, and seed
was stored for the next year, the remaining crops and income were paid out to
the members of the collective farm proportionate to their contribution to it.

The gap between the opportunities and lifestyles in urban and rural areas
touched every aspect of social existence. Down to 1965, farm workers were
excluded from social security, old-age pensions, benefits in cases of illness,
and maternity leave. Rural areas had few educational institutions, and these
were of poor quality. The lack of services, daycare, consumer goods, and
cultural amenities made life particularly difficult for rural women. Stalin,
Kalinin, and other leaders had made statements about liberating women from
the patriarchal family. They regarded the traditional peasant commune as a
threat to Soviet power and an obstacle to industrialization. Males dominated
the communes, and their control over women's labor was seen as an obstacle
to economic expansion. Soviet leaders therefore put women in official positions of the kolkhozes in the early 1930s. But in a sequence of events nearly
identical to what took place in Communist China in the early 1950s, examined below, the Soviet Communist Party's plans for gender equality unrav-
eled after a few years. The chairpersons and administrators appointed from

on high lost their positions; peasants were allowed to have private plots and cows, and to work for wages off of the kolkhoz; village culture reasserted itself; and an increasing proportion of kolkhoz chairmen came from the local male population.

Deep-seated prejudices deprived women of opportunities. The number of female chairpersons of collective farms and directors of state farms mounted to over a quarter of the total near the front or in German-occupied areas in 1943, but then diminished to nearly zero in the 1960s and 1970s. Men held almost all of the better-paid positions involving mechanized operations. Young men could learn skills, work in the MTS, and move to city jobs. Women, by contrast, could not get training on account of assumptions about male and female labor. Hardly any women studied in the technical-vocational schools for farming. They were therefore stuck working the subsidiary household allotments, on which the national economy depended, milking, herding swine, working with poultry, and growing vegetables. Women made up the majority of the farm laborers in the most physically demanding work planting, cultivating, and harvesting.

The subordination of women constituted the core element of a lifeless agricultural sector that rarely fulfilled the output targets of planners. These envisaged optimum meteorological conditions, whereas the vagaries of weather usually diminished the harvests. Planners often made unwise decisions about crop growing, because farming's infinite variety makes it less amenable than other branches of the economy to rational central direction. The rural population had the nominal right to elect the leaders of their kolkhozes. But the leaders were actually appointed by higher levels of the state hierarchy and were regularly removed in order to keep them reliant on the bureaucracy and make them more likely to watch over the farm workers and the procurement of the output. Farmers could not choose to leave and set up production on their own. If one could have ever hoped for the collective farms to become successful, the state would have had to permit them to acquire personality and pride in their initiatives.

Instead, Nikita Khrushchev, the first secretary of the party from 1953 to 1964, sought to bolster crop production on the collective farms by restricting the time rural workers could spend tending to their private livestock. Highly political planning and output targets, pitting regions against one another to double or treble the production of certain items, led the kolkhoz chairmen to begin the agricultural cycles at senselessly early dates. Khrushchev launched campaigns to reduce the area under grass and oats, and substitute maize for sugar beet. Many collective and state farms sowed maize beyond what crop climate rotations would bear. The policies bred resentment among the peasants whose income actually declined in the late 1950s.

Khrushchev's successors reversed his policies and publicized arguments in favor of the peasants' material self-interest. Pay rose sharply after 1965, as the kolkhozes retained 45 percent of their gross revenue for payments to the members and a further 15 percent for bonuses based on results. From 1953 to 1967, the standard of living on the kolkhozes rose 311 percent, as the peasants' earnings from the collectives, rather than sales from their private plots, provided their main source of income. Peasants obtained parity with urban workers in terms of old-age pensions and retirement at age sixty for men and fifty-five for women. The state provided health insurance, in 1970, for the kolkhoz members, though not as generously as it did for urban workers. In sum, a political and economic regime built on the exploitation of a defeated rural population could not gestate a class of farmers for the capitalist era. As the Soviet Union disintegrated at the end of the 1980s, the rural areas harbored an aging workforce generally reticent to embrace competitive farming and enhance productivity.

PEOPLE'S REPUBLIC OF CHINA

Less than a year after coming to power, China's Communist Party (the CCP) laid out new property rules for villages in the 1950 Agrarian Land Reform Law. This legislation was first and foremost a set of rules for redistributing land from landlords to their tenants and from richer peasants to poorer peasants. It was constructed on the one hand to fulfill the compact, fashioned over the long course of the revolution, between the party and its rural base. But it was also designed as an instrument for transforming village life in preparation for the construction of a new socialist society. Its implementation was expected to undo the authority of China's traditional rural elite, to mobilize popular support for the new regime, to lay the groundwork for rural modernization, and to direct rural savings to industry and defense.

Surveying the countryside in 1950, the CCP leadership recognized that rural poverty was the greatest obstacle to socialism. They observed that incomes were weighed down by underemployed labor; that farming was undercapitalized and labor productivity suffered for lack of tools; that rural elites took a great part of peasant savings in rent and labor yet did little in the way of productive activity or investment; and finally that centuries of market development had failed to bring about growth in agriculture, let alone industrialization. Lastly, the party understood that rural development required investment but that peasants could not be induced to acquire labor-saving technologies in the absence of economies of scale. In other words, the ubiquitous smallholding was a structural obstacle to both growth and socialism.

The extent of food and fiber production reached its limits in the early 1900s. Advances in farm technologies had long stagnated, while growth by colonization had all but ended (with the exception of Manchuria, there was no uncultivated yet sustainable farmland left). Tried and trusted labor-intensive techniques were running up against fertilizer and water shortages and there were dramatic signs of a tortured ecology. The involutionary growth path that characterized the premodern era, conditioned by the constant subdivision of farms and capital, and made worse by the parcellation of fields, had exhausted the means to raise yields and prevented a technological breakthrough. The average farm in China's northern wheat-growing region was a fraction above one hectare in 1930, with half of farms under one and a third hectares. In south China, the typical farm was under three-quarters of a hectare and more than half of peasants worked less than two-thirds of a hectare. Compounding matters, the typical farm consisted of five to six scattered fields, while one-fifth of farms were combinations of six to ten.

Despite the labor-intensive farming that followed from these small farms, and in light of underdeveloped manufacturing, rural underemployment remained pronounced. The economist John Lossing Buck's survey of 1930 rural China showed that while nationally three-quarters of adult males worked in agriculture, just over a third were fully employed. Fifty-eight percent had only part-time work, while another six percent were either minimally employed, entirely unemployed, or too sick to work. All in all, adult males were idle for an average of seven weeks each year. A related consequence of rural poverty, and one that contributed to underemployment, was the small number of livestock. In the 1930s, there was on average one water buffalo for every four farms, two oxen and one donkey for every five farms, and one hog and four chicken per farm.

It was uneconomical to invest in new tools or more draft animals under these conditions because any labor saved, or gains in output achieved, were unlikely to match let alone surpass up-front costs. It made much more sense for families to save or borrow to buy land in the hope of making up for shortfalls in food and fiber. But most farmers were unable to add land. With no qualitative improvement in methods, farm yields and returns on traditional technologies stagnated. Rice yields in the most productive region of China averaged two and a half metric tons per hectare in the 1930s, up only 7 percent from the seventeenth century. These yields were of course significant achievements insofar as they supported more people. Yet they were achieved through ever greater drudgery and, at the end of the day, the standard of living remained very low. At the time of the CCP's victory in 1949, the average Chinese consumed half a kilo of rice a day and less than 0.08 kilos of tea a year, and had enough to buy a new pair of cheap footwear every five years. Even at these meager levels, between two-fifths and one-half of rural households incurred debt to meet daily household needs.

As we have shown, the roots of this rural poverty are traceable at least to the seventeenth century, when peasants with the state's assistance strengthened their rights to the land and thereby secured for themselves the ability to subsist without recourse to market exchange. On this basis, the rural economy remained remarkably under-commercialized three centuries later: grain accounted for the largest share of the largest sector of the economy, yet only 10–12 percent made its way into the marketplace after peasants had their fill. Under no pressure to cut costs, labor productivity stagnated and then fell as households responded to their rising numbers and shrinking farms by working more for smaller and smaller gains. With the path to agricultural transformation blocked, Chinese manufacturing fell behind. Nineteenth-century imperialism, political instability, and finally civil war and invasion depressed the standard of living further still. By 1950, GDP per capita was one-tenth that of western Europe and under 5 percent that of the United States.

In describing the economy as "semi-feudal and semi-colonial," the CCP captured significant problems facing the country. Colonial enclaves in cities such as Shanghai and Tianjin had produced manufacturing growth, but at the expense of Chinese sovereignty and the workers' standard of living. Largely untouched by the modern Treaty Port cities, rural areas remained under the control of landlords, the heads of kinship groups, village bullies, and exploitative merchants, whose interests were antithetical to the requirements of growth. On the basis of this historical judgment, the CCP rejected the market economy of western Europe, North America, and Japan and chose to follow the planned economy of the USSR, which had not only grown faster between 1920 and 1950 than the leading capitalist economies but recently defeated the most technologically advanced society in Europe. Under the Soviet model, managers, planners, technocrats, and accountants set annual output targets to meet five-year national production goals and invested capital accordingly.

Because the bulk of national "savings" were tied up in farmland, livestock, and farm implements, any development plan had to begin by expanding farm output and then diverting the surplus for investment elsewhere. This required in turn the creation of more economical farms that would enable the adoption of labor-enhancing tools and methods. Like many Third World countries after World War II, China began its transformation of the economy with land reform (see the discussion of Taiwan in chapter 9). The experience was more tempered than earlier experiments in large part because the CCP leadership concluded by 1950, contrary to Stalin, that China's rich peasants (its version of the kulaks), with their larger farms, better tools, and stronger draft animals, were needed to drive growth, while poorer peasants would only achieve comparable advantages in scale through voluntary cooperatives that pooled tools, labor, livestock, and eventually land. The main target of the PRC's land reform was landlords, a class that accounted for a mere 3 percent of rural families yet owned over a quarter of all land and, in some regions, in excess of half. Their property would go to the bottom two-thirds of families, who before the revolution owned only 22 percent of farmland.

Land reform began with the arrival of a team of party cadres whose first task was to organize poor villagers into a Peasant Association. They began with a simple rent reduction campaign during which class designations were assigned to all adult villagers based upon their property holdings. Under party definitions, landlords owned land but had not personally engaged in essential activities such as reaping, plowing, or planting for at least three years. Landlords' land (including uncultivated fallow, hillsides, ponds, etc.) as well as their draft animals, farm implements, surplus grain, and extra rooms or houses were confiscated. Rich peasants by party definition farmed at least four months but employed wage laborers to assist. Under land reform, they kept all land that they managed but had to surrender any that they rented out. Those who paid rent, received wages, or worked small plots were labeled "tenants," "wage laborers," and "poor peasants." Finally, those who garnered the greater part of their livelihood working their own land using household labor were registered as "middle" or "small" peasants, depending on the size of their holdings.

As stated, land reform had two goals. The first was to repay poor peasants for their historical support of the party. The second was to invert power relations, elevating the poor to leadership positions and in the process building a permanent party presence. For the first time in history, an employee of the state was in every Chinese village. Land reform was therefore a very public act in which the poor were encouraged to recall past mistreatment and denounce the powerful, and elites were publically shamed and cowed. According to one recollection, "when land reform came to this area, no one dared to move against the landlords. . . . But Chen Sumei knew who were the poorest and who could be organized to do what. He got together some poor peasants who'd speak out, who dared to do things, and he got them to organize against the landlords. . . . He helped lead the peasants to be masters of their society."[13] When land reform was done, former landlords were a pathetic sight, relegated to the village bottom to be dragged out for repeated abuse with each new political campaign.

While everywhere village politics was thus turned on its head, land redistribution did little to alleviate the economic conditions of the very poor. Two-fifths of farmland was reassigned and 60 percent of the rural population saw their holdings augmented, yet the typical poor peasant's holding was still less than one-tenth of a hectare. To be sure, the proportion of households considered middle peasants rose from a third to just under two-thirds, while the poor peasantry fell from 57 to 29 percent. The share of income of the top one-fifth fell from 42 to 35 percent. Yet the poor's share of all income stopped at 11 percent. These outcomes could hardly be called radical.

After property confiscations, there was a mere 0.11 extra hectares available per entitled peasant and less than two-hundredths of an animal and under a quarter of a tool for redistribution to every adult. The decision to preserve the rich peasantry assured these households an average of 2.33 hectares, two draft animals, one plow, and a third of a waterwheel. By contrast, the typical poor peasant owned half a draft animal, a third of a plow, and less than one-twentieth of a waterwheel in addition to his one-tenth of a hectare. It was clear to all, including villagers, that land reform left many households struggling, yet provided no blueprint for raising their incomes.

There was reason to believe that, left to their own devices, rich peasants would take advantage of the stability brought to the markets by the CCP to undo whatever gains had been achieved for the poorest. The better off would capture most of the earnings from grain sales and use their capital to purchase land and equipment from their poor neighbors. The party was, however, bent on preserving the new order and protecting the middle and poor peasants. Consequently, the CCP called on the Peasant Associations to bundle tools, labor, savings, and land in voluntary Mutual Aid Teams (MATs) to allow the poor to improve their market position with greater economies of scale. Comprising a few families, each MAT shared labor, draft animals, and tools, while preserving private ownership in land. Household earnings were then determined by a formula that weighted contributions of capital and labor. To prevent rich peasants from ganging together to create even larger and more productive MATs, the party prohibited rich peasants from forming exclusive teams.

As an organization, the MAT was intended to pave the way to larger voluntary combinations—that is, collectivization by choice. Chinese economists observed that the tiny peasant farms constituted a structural barrier to growth, insofar as they lacked both the capital and scale to invite cost-cutting technologies, and they suggested that peasants who saw the gains to be had from pooling labor and tools would voluntarily go further and pool land.

Indeed, the early MATs elicited improvements. A leader from the Guangdong village of Nanjing related how families in the past were always "short of farm tools and too poor to buy fertilizer," were "not able to finish our farm chores in the proper time," and that under these conditions it was "hopeless to think of increasing production." After forming an MAT in 1952, however, he remarked how "we pooled our labor and farm tools for systematic use and thus overcame the shortage of labor and tools. We obliged every family to collect and accumulate fertilizer, and solved our fertilizer problem. The autumn crop was a bumper crop, and we had surplus grain to buy tools and fertilizer."[14] MATs raised output by overcoming bottlenecks in the supply of labor that had previously prevented the further intensification of farming. By pooling water buffaloes, labor, and tools, villagers reduced plowing and planting from fifteen to eight days, while the purchase of hand-driven winnowing machines sped up the harvest. In south China, the saved time enabled the adoption of a second and then third rice crop. Then, by better managing water flow and fertilizer, the MAT compensated for the greater nutrient requirements of multi-cropping.

While land reform coupled with the adoption of MATs solicited improvements in farming methods, it did nothing to reduce the age-old risks associated with markets. In the absence of reliable markets, there was no guarantee that peasants would specialize and improve on their own. For its part, the state brought stability to exchange in its effort to encourage experimentation but also to capture savings for investment in industry. In 1953, the Unified Purchase and Marketing System was introduced to set prices and effect peasant consumption. Through purchases (17 percent) and the new land tax (10.5 percent), the state collected just over a quarter of the farming output, or an amount more or less equivalent to that previously expropriated by rural elites. By ending speculation, those with surpluses could now only augment their incomes by raising output.

Agricultural output showed signs of growth, expanding at 1.6 percent in the years immediately after land reform. However, yields swung wildly. Whereas the 1953 rice harvest was 3 percent up from the year before, it fell in 1954. Wheat stagnated in 1953, yet rose 28 percent in 1954. Cotton production declined in 1953 and 1954, though planners had called for increases. The MATs encouraged gains from the rationalization of labor and the more effective use of the draft animals and tools on hand. Certain water conservancy projects and the closer planting of crops were achievable because peasants lost nothing if they withdrew from the MAT subsequent to these changes. But this was not the case for costly water conservancy projects and certainly not for capital-intensive mechanization, without prior agreement that these investments would continue to be shared if the MAT broke up. Even then, peasants were very wary of sinking their savings in cooperative projects that might go sour. There was also a tendency for middle peasants to exclude poor peasants from their MATs, on the grounds that the poor brought their labor but no capital. When required to accept poor households, better-off households butchered or sold their draft animals rather than share them.

The leadership became aware of these problems when, in late 1954, the countryside experienced serious grain shortages. As state procurements outpaced grain harvests, livestock suffered, the seed supplies were eaten up, and peasants raided granaries and left for the towns. The leadership paused to investigate conditions and reexamine policy.

It was the consensus of part of the leadership that greater economies of scale would encourage mechanization. China's head of agriculture, Deng Zihui, explained:

> The swift advance of the development of agriculture demands that the existing scattered small farms, which use draft animals, are irrigated by manpower, and use only natural fertilizers should step by step be replaced by large farms using machines for cultivation and irrigation and using chemical fertilizers. If we say that the existing small-scale commodity economy of individual peasants is

adapted to the use of draft animals, irrigation by manpower, and use of natural fertilizers, then the future big farms employing machines in cultivation and irrigation and using chemical fertilizers will naturally demand replacement of the present system of private ownership by the system of collective peasant ownership.[15]

In other words, it was thought that the adoption of farm machines would come about slowly as peasants learned through experience that combining assets would raise their standards of living.

Yet China's paramount leader Mao Zedong disagreed. He accurately observed that "although the standard of living of the peasant masses since the land reform has improved . . . many are still in difficulty or are still not well off, there being relatively few who are well off." He continued his analysis, arguing that "as is clear to everyone, spontaneous forces of capitalism have been steadily growing in the countryside in recent years, with new rich peasants springing up everywhere and many well-to-do peasants striving to become rich peasants."[16] There is little doubt that class cleavages persisted. The share of income of the bottom one-fifth of rural households was only 11.3 percent, while rich peasants ate 50 percent more pork than did the poor. For Mao rural poverty was stubborn not because of policy but because of exploitation at the hands of capitalist rich peasants.

Land reform's failure to deliver growth is easy to understand in retrospect. It hardly added to the peasants' working capital: a little land, a couple of tools, and a small share of a draft animal were not about to end rural poverty. Mao concluded that whereas the mechanization and rationalization of land, especially the layout of fields for the introduction of the most productive cropping systems, were needed to achieve further expansion, the organization of farm work within the MATs could support neither. A push of peasants into larger agricultural cooperatives that held land in common was announced in July 1955. Mao argued against naysayers that China would avoid Stalin's errors by moving to collectives in stages, adhering to a policy of experimentation and voluntary association, paying close attention to local conditions and local readiness. Hearing the call to form cooperatives, successful MATs—especially those with politically entrepreneurial leaders—rushed ahead.

Some in the countryside sensed the direction in which the party was leaning and began the transition before July. Fifty-five households (two hundred people) formed a cooperative in the village of Zengbu, Guangdong province, in 1954. In this instance, the land remained privately owned but was farmed collectively. For improvements, each household provided savings for collective purchases, or contributed an equivalent value in draft animals and tools, and planning was shared. The new cooperative immediately ran into trouble, however. Village traditions offered no blueprints for managing production under the new organization, so leaders had to learn on the job. Needless to say, they found their new responsibilities stressful and spent much time persuading villagers of the benefits to be had by pooling more of their resources. Recalling the early days of Zengbu's first cooperative, village secretary Liu Puijin said:

> Using my mutual aid group as the backbone element, I organized a cooperative with 55 households, over 200 people, and 100 labor power units. We had problems initially because, having no experience, we did not know how to assign labor properly or how to apportion the group's income equitably. These problems were solved after much hard work and after I carried out ideological education. We held meetings every night to discuss the cooperative and its problems, and the meetings often lasted well until midnight. Then we had to get up the next day, exhausted, to assign work to the collective's members. It was very arduous and time-consuming work. [17]

By assigning disproportionate weight to labor in the calculation of household earnings, Zengbu's cooperative exhibited what leaders described as greater socialist zeal. Such displays were noticed by those above and these models were held up for national emulation.

With clear support from above, Zengbu's leaders did not pause for long. Within a year the village was organized into what was termed a "higher-level agricultural producers' cooperative." This was deemed fully socialist on two grounds. First, members abrogated all private property, including tools, livestock, fishponds, orchards, and land. Second, wages were assessed solely on the basis of work effort and so no longer took into account the capital brought to the co-op. With the exception of a small garden distributed to each household for growing vegetables and the like, farm work was done collectively. While Zengbu was ahead of the curve, between 1954 and early 1956 team leaders throughout China forged ahead to organize socialist cooperatives. Good harvests in the fall of 1955 convinced leaders, the party cadre, and many peasants to quicken the pace. Between July 1955 and May 1956, the proportion of peasant households in cooperatives rose staggeringly from 14 to 90 percent, and in late 1956 two-thirds of these were described as being "fully" socialist.

The process by and large proceeded peacefully. The equitable distribution of earnings appealed to the mass of poor peasants. Objections from the better-off, which were typically phrased in terms of its effects on family income, not whether land should remain private, were handled by persuasion and ideological work. Such setbacks were anticipated by the leadership: Mao had forewarned cadres to ignore or bypass affluent peasants who were more prone to fear losses, and consequently enthusiasm sometimes gave way to "commandism," as local cadres rushed forward to prove their socialist credentials and curry favor for themselves and their villages. In these cases, they

[handwritten annotation: water-control had been a kind of collective economic work system ... before CCP appeared]

cajoled and bullied villagers into joining. There were reports of confusion and fear. In Zengbu, however, leaders decided to provide extra compensation for households that brought more to the collective for a fixed number of years following collectivization, while those without children to add income or with elderly to support were promised assistance.

In sum, the bulk of peasants welcomed the changes to farming and village life that transpired between 1950 and 1956, as China not only avoided famine but restored production. They first consolidated private small-scale farming, then aggregated to create the MATs, further combined MATs into small cooperatives that distributed income according to work effort, and finally formed large cooperatives that abolished private holdings.

The full collectivization of land resolved significant issues confronting Chinese agriculture. From the planners' perspective these larger units simplified the collection of taxes in grain and enhanced state control of markets. For the peasants, the collectives resolved outstanding tensions between the village haves and have-nots left unsettled. Prior to 1956, remuneration schemes guaranteed clashes between those who brought more land or capital and those who came with only tools and labor. This led to the common complaint that rich peasants were idle and worked less because they received dividends on capital contributions. By one estimate, one of every five dollars earned went to the better-off as compensation for land, tools, and draft animals, an amount that exceeded most cooperative savings by two and a half times. Because of these contradictions poor peasants withheld their labor and harvests suffered.

While resolving these problems, full collective ownership opened the way for greater mechanization, to improved water conservancy, and for larger labor savings as fields previously interspersed across villages were consolidated, boundaries were removed, and land was combined into large contiguous units. As a result, time was saved setting up tools, plowing and tillage were improved, and rotations were better coordinated. Enhanced production meant better diets. Available calories grew as much as twenty-eight percent and their sources diversified as peasants ate more vegetables and pulses. They consumed more preferred grains such as wheat and rice, more cooking oil, and 50 percent more meat. The number of pigs—rural China's preferred meat source—grew from 89 to 180 million. Subsequently, life expectancy improved and infant mortality fell.

These gains, however, were reversed and then some by the events of 1959 to 1961. Reflecting on national and international developments, Mao Zedong concluded in 1958 that the CCP could not take the future of Chinese socialism for granted. He read Khrushchev's 1956 denunciation of Stalin, as well as the Hungarian and Polish uprising of that year, as evidence of counterrevolutionary tendencies. He registered the USA's stated goal to contain and then roll back socialism, interpreting its interventions in Korea, Southeast

Asia, and the Taiwan straits as evidence of America's resolve. Finally, he was unsettled by the directness of complaints voiced by intellectuals.

He concluded that the CCP must accelerate the pace of socialist transformation. "In making revolution, one must strike while the iron is hot, one revolution following another; the revolution must advance without interruption," he argued. As the party convened to discuss the second Five-Year Plan in the summer of 1958, Mao criticized the plan's gradualism and advocated instead that China "strive to go all out to achieve more, faster, better, and more economical results." In August 1958, he called for the full transformation of the countryside and a Great Leap Forward in production and political consciousness. By the end of the year the collectives were gone and all rural families were organized into one of twenty-four thousand massive communes.

Mao's thinking was radically utopian. Unlike Lenin, and even Stalin, who understood that the poverty of rural life was a constraint on economic activity, Mao believed that even the worst material conditions could be overcome by dint of the human spirit. By substituting moral for material incentives Mao argued that the masses' zeal would propel China rapidly through industrialization and on to socialism. What mattered was not technology and planning, but revolutionary action in the economic realm. In 1958, Mao claimed that China would overtake Britain in the production of signature industrial items such as iron, steel, power, and coal in fifteen years. In 1959, he revised his estimate to one year.

At this juncture, euphoria was in the air not only in Beijing but also in hundreds of thousands of villages. Respected local leaders repeatedly promised peasants that the giant communes would yield rapid benefits. Heady from a brew of idealism and faith in the party, many were blinded to the hard challenges ahead. A Zengbu villager remembered: "The people's consciousness was so high at the beginning of the Great Leap Forward that we wanted to do everything in a collective manner. There was no need even for clerks in the stores because people could be trusted to leave the correct amount for the goods they had taken. . . . We had a common dining hall with twelve cooks. Everyone could and did eat three, four, or even five or six times a day if they wanted. To eat as much as one wishes, in bustling company, is a very desirable circumstance."[18] All land was socialized, including gardens.

A typical commune consisted of five to eight thousand household members and merged with local government to administer all aspects of life from production to education and local defense. Families were guaranteed a modicum of food regardless of work, though nonfood income was still fixed by work points, and were assigned for management into smaller brigades and production teams. The brigade was commensurate with the former collective, keeping its administrative structures and now running canteens for the distribution of meals. The production team was made from neighbors working together under a team leader. By building up the commune on existing structures, the state maintained continuity as well as flexibility. It was able to centralize or decentralize decision making up and down the administrative ladder as needs arose.

The commune was a highly effective instrument for mobilizing rural labor. To push women into the fields, nurseries and canteens were built that freed young mothers from childcare and housework. The work point system was adjusted to reward heads of households who encouraged their daughters and daughters-in-law to work in the fields and small workshops. The communes' mobilization of women was a symptom of the greater reliance on labor inputs to lift production in the absence of capital. And China had a lot of labor to put to work. The population had grown from 583 to 695 million between 1952 and 1961 and though initially the proportion of the working-age population was shrinking, it was growing in absolute numbers.

Decisions made by the party to ignore gender inequality are to blame for China's baby boom. Concurrent to land reform, the CCP pursued marriage reform with the 1952 Marriage Law. It banned polygamy and concubinage as well as forced and arranged marriages. It established the legal age of marriage at eighteen for women and twenty-one for men. Women were guaranteed the right to divorce and to custody over children, while the law protected the rights of divorcees and widows to property and girls and women to a share of inheritance. Just as the Land Reform Law was intended to break the back of landlord power, the Marriage Law was designed to end the oppression associated with gerontocracy and patriarchy.

Rural males were not receptive. They objected to the ease with which their wives might divorce. Those households with young daughters were happy to see girls receive as much land as boys during the land reform. However, young men were less happy with the thought of sharing property with their sisters and all men did not want divorced wives and daughters-in-law to take property with them. Facing resistance, the party called for renewed efforts to implement the Marriage Law in 1953. Model families were featured in the media, and the Women's Federation and the Chinese Youth League were drawn into the campaign. Yet, when that campaign ended the Marriage Law was fully implemented in only 50 percent of China. Strong opposition was encountered in 60 percent of the country and the law was entirely ineffective in one-quarter.

As gender inequality persisted, the ability of young women to control their fertility was delayed. China's fertility rate consequently remained at pre-1949 levels (about six births for every woman who survived to menopause), whereas infant and childhood mortality rates declined. The population shot up. For Mao, this was not understood to be a problem. In his view, the masses were an asset. In some respects, Mao's position made a virtue of necessity. Until the widespread availability of farm machines and non-animal power sources, agricultural expansion hung on the mobilization of human labor that became more pronounced as China embarked on the Great Leap Forward.

The Great Leap departed radically from the gradual approach of the Five-Year Plan. It called for the simultaneous investment of large amounts of capital and the mobilization of all available labor. Between 1958 and 1960 capital investment reached new records as it hit 30 percent of GDP. To sustain these remarkable levels of spending, the state had no choice but to pursue policies that restricted consumption. In the countryside one in five adults was diverted from grain fields to giant infrastructure schemes. Water conservation and irrigation projects employed millions, while still more people were put to work building and then laboring in backyard iron and steel furnaces. Predictably, labor shortages arose in farming. Nine northern provinces reported a 50 percent shortfall, with some localities reporting as much as two-thirds. The strain on labor was compounded by the turn to double and even triple cropping in the absence of labor-saving machinery.

The effect on harvests was disastrous. High yields in China were historically sustained by dint of work effort and its sudden removal undermined production. As labor was diverted in double-cropping regions from planting to harvesting, yields shrank because of poor field preparation. In some cases, they fell below what was attainable under a single crop regime. New schemes that held out promise for better yields were not properly supported. When peasants were told to plant seeds more closely, they were not provided with the necessary fertilizers and plants starved. "They pushed a system of planting called 'Sky Full of Stars,'" reported a south China villager. "A field would be so overplanted the seedlings starved. . . . The peasants knew it was useless, but there was simply no way to oppose anything, because the orders came from so high above."[19] At harvest, reaping and threshing was so rushed and poorly executed for lack of labor that grain was left in the fields and on the threshing floors. A national campaign was launched just to gather up the discarded grain. The withdrawal of labor from agriculture led to weed infestation. In the northern provinces hit hardest by labor shortages, 10 to 82 percent of sown acreage was badly affected.

Other problems arose from mismanagement. A call to plant wet rice beyond its traditional southern zone generally met with poor results, at least in the first years. In the search for fertilizer, peasants were told to break apart walls and spread the crumbled bricks across the land. Central planners promoted plowing to a depth of three feet, in the belief that this would aerate the soil better, improve tillage, increase the available organic matter, and promote deeper root growth: "Dig three feet and harvest 10,000 catties per mou!" This was sometimes done so hastily that nutrient-empty subsoil was brought to the surface. Vegetable and pork farming were pushed into factory-scaled production in the expectation of gains from economies of scale, yet floundered from poor coordination, lack of feed, and insufficient storage facilities that left food to rot.

By far the gravest example of mismanagement followed Mao's call to reduce the area of land planted in grain. In fall 1957, Mao had convinced himself of the commune's superiority as both an instrument of planning and a means to unleash hitherto trapped productive forces. Peasants were told to concentrate their efforts by planting less land and spreading fertilizer on the best soils. Peasants were promised a tenfold increase in yield that would more than make up for the reduction in area planted. By the fall, Mao was predicting a harvest of 375 million tons, up from 193.5 million the previous year.

Taking their cue from the central leadership, local cadre put their faith in the commune and suppressed skepticism for fear of being labeled "rightists" or counterrevolutionaries. Team leaders overstated yields, some reporting as much as two thousand catties from land that just a few years earlier was yielding two hundred. Upon hearing the reports, in 1958 Mao summarily declared China's grain problem solved and local cadres were told to plant more industrial crops. Having fallen by 2 percent in 1958, grain acreage fell by another 9.6 percent in 1959. The 1958 grain harvest was 201 million tons, a sizable improvement on 1957. But it did not justify reducing the acreage in grain. Consequently, the 1960 harvest was only 144 million tons. Poor judgment was then compounded by bad weather, as drought spread across northern wheat-growing provinces.

Not yet aware of the nature of the shortfall, the state raised grain procurement targets to pay debts owed to the USSR and to allocate grain to urban areas, where it was sold to raise money for investments in industry. Higher targets met resistance, especially as local cadres leaned on richer villagers within the communes. Peasants responded by hiding grain and brawling with those sent to collect.

Even as procurements rose and grain acreage shrank, the communes made no effort to restrict the amount of food served in the dining halls. By the fall of 1958, there were 2.65 million canteens in place and between 70 and 90 percent of the rural population ate communally. "Open your stomach, eat as much as you wish, and work hard for socialism" was the slogan of the day. By the summer of 1959, rural households were caught between free-falling grain production and depleted stores. When urban grain fell below what was needed to sustain industrial production, leaders irresponsibly transferred extra grain from the countryside.

In 1960 hunger was swiftly followed by famine. Some provinces and regions suffered more than others. In Sichuan, where five million people were mobilized to ship more grain from the province than had ever been transferred before, daily caloric intake fell well below half of what was needed to maintain an adult working in the fields. Too hungry to work, peasants had no choice but to leave fields unattended. They raided granaries, illegally fled to towns and cities, and migrated to neighboring provinces. They abandoned children and under the most extreme conditions resorted to cannibalism. An official military publication reported: "At present what the peasants eat in the villages is worse than what dogs ate in the past. At that time, dogs ate chaff and grain. Now the people are too hungry to work and pigs are too hungry to stand up."[20] All in all, perhaps thirty million perished in the disaster.

The party took swift action once it understood the extent of the calamity and the emerging threat to social stability. Rather than convince Mao to change course, fellow leaders politically sidelined him. The communes were reduced in size to improve planning, and production team leaders who lived in the villages were given greater responsibility for day-to-day management. Private plots were restored and local markets were opened for the sale of garden vegetables and the like. The canteens were abandoned and work points assigned by the production team, where accountants could more readily record work effort, thereby reestablishing the link between work and earnings. By 1962 the situation in the countryside had stabilized.

In the following years, planning was restored and greater effort was made to raise yields through new inputs. Better seeds, chemical fertilizers, and eventually mechanization were introduced. In 1958, Chinese scientists created the high-yielding, hybrid dwarf *indica* variety of rice, which responded better to chemical fertilizers, resisted disease, stood straighter, yielded 5.6 metric tons per hectare, and ripened in only 110 days. Between 1964 and 1977 the area planted in the hybrid went from zero to 80 percent. A second hybrid rice was introduced in 1973. Its improved root structure protected it from drought and waterlogging. It also had greater tolerance for alkalinity, a significant problem in some rice paddies. It boosted yields by 20 percent. All in all, hybrids created by Chinese scientists accounted for one-third of the increase in rice production by 1979. Hybrids in wheat, corn, sorghum, and cotton followed, as did improved varieties of millet, soybean, and barley. To maintain seed quality, communes and brigades took over from villagers the task of selecting and storing seeds.

Improvements also were made to water conservancy and delivery. Whereas the effectively irrigated area fell between 1957 and 1961, it grew by a million hectares a year in the early 1960s, and rose to nearly half of the arable land by 1980. Irrigation helped spread double cropping. Yet it has had a deleterious effect on water tables in north China where well-pumping was a chief source of field irrigation. Rural electrification provided the power needed to drive these new pumps.

Chemical fertilizers were made widely available in the late 1970s. Japan provided technology and support, while investments in petroleum production provided the ammonia. As production gained ground, costs fell and application rose. By 1979, over one hundred kilograms were spread per hectare, far more than the world average. It was channeled to rice, wheat, and cotton. At the same time, petroleum was used to produce synthetic fibers and land in cotton was turned over to food production. To foster appropriate use, the state delivered chemical fertilizer to those collectives that met their grain quotas and even favored those collectives that planted crop varieties known to respond best to its applications. The increased availability of fertilizer, along with tractors, allowed triple cropping in the Yangzi Delta. A veritable Green Revolution was underway.

The application of machines and the introduction of improved tools was a long time in coming. Knowledgeable economists had argued in the 1950s for intermediary technologies that were cheap and suitable to China's labor-rich economy. The Maoist emphasis on labor did not blind leaders (Mao included) to the fact that the intensive use of the land required chemical fertilizers and insecticides, the machines to haul and apply them, and improved water pumps, as well as tractors, planters, harvesters, and threshers to free labor for double and triple cropping.

An ambitious ten-year plan for mechanization begun in the late 1950s was dropped because of the lack of factories to produce field machines and of a lack of capital to import the infrastructure needed to maintain and use them. The question of mechanization was revisited in 1963, at which time planners divided China into eight ecological regions for the purposes of designing appropriate machinery. Local stations devised solutions such as the four- and seven-blade plows, forty-eight-row seeders, land-leveling equipment, and machines to seed and spread fertilizer, all for use in the north. For south China, a ten-horsepower diesel engine was designed to power irrigation pumps and food-processing equipment and to generate electricity, while advances were made in rice-transplanting equipment.

Nationally, more than half a million standard tractors were built between 1961 and 1965. While tractor designs initially came from the USSR, Chinese copies of the English Massey Ferguson designs followed. The way was thus paved for greater mechanization across the late 1960s. By 1973 China had as many large thirty-horsepower tractors in operation as did India, and sixty times as many ten-horsepower hand tractors for paddy farming. Prices for machines were kept low for production brigades, to facilitate the more intensive use of the land as double cropping became the minimal standard on good arable land throughout the south. Consequently, agricultural output grew appreciably from 1965 to 1978, despite the political turmoil associated with Mao's Cultural Revolution. Still, as the countryside was squeezed for capital that flowed into industry, there is little evidence of significant improvements in rural standards of living.

In 1978, the political reformer Deng Xiaoping came to power and set in motion policies that not only opened China to the world but also edged its population into the market, gradually at first but soon with force. In the early 1980s, he allowed rural households to withdraw from the communes. The household responsibility system (HRS) allowed households to contract land from the collective for private farming in return for meeting their share of the collective's grain quota. Families were free to sell what remained. Voluntary at first, the HRS soon became policy. In 2004, the Land Administration Law clarified legal rights, confirming that rural land was owned by the "peasants collective," yet allowing leaseholds of up to thirty years. It is on this legal basis that the state has claimed the economy's enduring "socialist" character. However, since the 2004 law a de facto land market has taken hold that supports private over collective farming in line with developments in the broader economy.

The privatization of farming has forced producers to find ways to be more productive. With only small amounts of capital available to them, however, they have turned to food-processing corporations for capital, market access, and economies of scale. In the most extreme cases, farmers are vertically integrated in long production chains extending from the land to the shopping cart. These so-called "dragon head" combines started in Shandong in the 1990s as part of an experiment that has since spread as far as Yunnan. In these arrangements, farmers either work their own land (under the existing household responsibility system) or farm as tenants and wage laborers for the agribusiness. They face risks associated with market production as well as high outlays for seed, livestock, equipment, storage, and transportation, but their risk and costs have been eased by the corporate distributors at the top of the chain. These encourage farmers to raise everything from vegetables, to fruit, to poultry and wasabi. In Yunnan, the Swiss multinational Nestlé provides coffee trees suited to the climate, technical training, and guaranteed purchases. Xinchang Foods of Shandong provides baby chickens and ducklings, as well as feeding lots and drugs, to ten thousand contracted households, which raise the birds and sell them back when mature. These new enterprises offer reliable markets and affordable inputs to scattered small-scale farmers and, in the process, lower risks and costs to levels that producers can bear.

The process of articulating farming into the market is still in progress, yet has had remarkable success. In 2005 there were a little under 136,000 vertically integrated entities with total revenues of 306 billion yuan. The Ministry of Agriculture's Office for Vertical Integration has especially favored large-scale private agribusinesses, which account for 45 percent of farming enterprises (versus 36 percent cooperatively run). Given China's current regime, the continued expansion of agribusiness can be expected.

CUBA

In the late eighteenth and early nineteenth centuries, land developers from Havana dominated the colonial economy and discouraged the expansion of self-sufficient small-scale farming. They instead exploited the island for the profits to be made from coffee and especially sugar exports. Since the colonial elite relied on slave labor, and since the black population outnumbered the white, anxieties about a racial rebellion delayed the emergence of an independence movement until the 1860s, about half a century later than in the rest of Latin America. When the free and enslaved blacks of Cuba, along with other independence fighters, finally took up arms, they faced the full force of the Spanish Army. They endured horrendous losses of life and destruction of property before the United States Army occupied the island in 1898.

US and Cuban investors accumulated large farms and mechanized sugar production. They controlled the mills, railways, and supply of credit, and thus held sway over the *colonos*—who rented the land and oversaw the farming—and through the *colonos* dominated the much larger population of laborers in the fields. Almost all of the output was exported to the United States. The sugar industry thus shared in the golden age of American agriculture when farm prices rose relative to those of industry in the first decades of the twentieth century.

Inocencia Acosta Felipe, interviewed in the 1960s, described the first eight years of her life in a *colono* family in Matanzas province in the early 1910s, when

> all the colonos were well off. . . . *Papá* rented the farm from the owners of a sugar mill, but a tenant was secure . . . as long as he paid the rent on time. . . . The Zayas family owned the mill and all the land around. . . . They lived in the capital city of Matanzas, but once a year they'd spend a month in the country to take a look at their land. Their country house was very well furnished and had a full staff of servants, just as if it had been . . . in the city. They also had a house in Havana. [21]

The Zayas family seems to have controlled the local economy. Inocencia stated that "the sugar mill made life easier for its colonos by selling them almost everything they needed—cattle and other livestock, seeds, shade trees and different vegetables, fruit, and foods. We'd buy big boxes of codfish from them, and huge sacks of sugar, rice, and dried horsemeat." [22]

"Our sugar-cane farm," Inocencia recollected, "was called Maravilla. It was fairly large, about 167 acres. Quite near the house," she described, "was our kitchen garden, where we grew cabbage, lettuce, radishes, tomatoes, hot peppers, and lots of other things. Farther off were the fields of yucca, corn, sweet potatoes, plantains, and other vegetables; beyond were the sugar-cane fields. The vegetables grew in such abundance we even had enough to sell."[23] The farm was worked without machine tools:

> The sugar-cane farm had about fifteen paddocks, some for horses and some for cattle. *Papá* owned three or four saddle horses, fifty or sixty heads of cattle, oxen for plowing, and ten or twelve dairy cows. . . . We also had a lot of farm tools and three or four Spanish and American made plows. *Papá* had saws, hammers, a hoe, machetes of different sorts—the broad-bladed ones and the large "mountain" blades.[24]

Inocencia provided details about the workforce:

> We had a houseboy and four or five farmhands who lived in a large dwelling with a thatched roof and dirt floor that was also used for storing crops and tools and as a shelter against hurricanes. . . . In the country everyone old enough to do farm work gets up at cockcrow—4:00 in the morning. The hired hand, Ruperto, would milk the cows, then he and *papá* would go off to work in the fields. Most of the days *papá* would already be gone by the time we children ate breakfast at 7:00 or 8:00.[25]

As for the rest of the household, when Inocencia was "eight or nine my main chores were to sweep the floors and burn the trash every day. We girls washed our own clothes, the smaller pieces at any rate, and I had to get up on a stool to reach the high wooden tubs. *Mamá* washed most of the clothes, and we tended the fire in the stove when she boiled them."[26]

Inocencia recalled, in much greater detail, all the time she spent playing with her brothers, sisters, and children of the area. Indeed, the family enjoyed relative prosperity, along with the rest of Cuba, in the first decades of the twentieth century. "In the morning *mamá* gave us milk . . . or else we'd pick ourselves some fruit." For lunch and supper,

> we'd eat things like rice, beans, vegetables, fried eggs, fresh or jerked meat or codfish. . . . We ate a lot of chicken too. I don't mean that we ate meat or chicken every day . . . , but we had one or the other pretty often. We had sweets every day after lunch, because *mamá* loves to make desserts—orange or grapefruit peel in syrup, guavas in syrup or paste, bitter orange paste, also corn pudding or fritters.[27]

"We children were controlled," Inocencia stated, "by scary stories of the bogeyman and witches, and especially blacks. We were told that blacks kidnapped children. . . . The adults would tell us, 'Don't go to that place where the blacks are. Never go near a black or accept anything to eat from him.'"[28] She remembered being "absolutely terrified of blacks. They use blood in their religious rites, and when I was little they stole children in Matanzas for that purpose."[29]

Most of Cuba belonged to mill owners like the Zayas family and was farmed by *colono* families like Inocencia's and their laborers. Some of the land was acquired by townspeople for prestige and income during a period of high sugar prices after World War II. These businessmen and politicians left the land in cane-growing or rent extortion from subsistence peasants, or made it into ranches, though never with a high density of commercial live-stock. They rarely invested in improving the productivity. Instead, the land-owners saved their profits, and banks placed much of the capital abroad, since the economy, bound to the vicissitudes of international sugar prices, exuded a climate of uncertainty and induced rentier habits.

Similar to conditions in Brazil (see chapter 10), the island had relatively few diversified small holdings, as farmers gradually became tenants, subten-ants, sharecroppers, and agricultural administrators. While small holdings accounted for the great majority of farms, they didn't even cover a tenth of the arable land. Small farms generally relied on family members to plant, cultivate, and harvest by hand. Oxen, rather than modern equipment, made up their common source of power. Farmers crafted their plows from forked trees or bought factory-made walking plows. They all possessed a machete, which men used to harvest cane and cut down weeds. They would have worked more rapidly with modern implements but saw no need to deplete household income in the purchase of tools for tasks that could be done by family members.

In 1950, over half of the agricultural labor force, about five hundred thousand people, owned no land and worked on the plantations for wages. Almost a quarter of the active population worked in the sugar industry. Many workers came from China and the Canary Islands of Spain as indentured servants imported by the owners of estates and railroads after slavery came to an end during the War of Independence in the 1880s. The US arranged the immigration of Haitians and Jamaicans to eastern Cuba. The plantation labor force suffered from seasonal unemployment, as technical development re-duced the harvest time from ten months in the early 1900s to three months in the 1950s.

After the 1870s, the world market in agricultural commodities, especially sugar and coffee, was subject to wild price swings. As the beet and cane sugar industries of Europe, the US, and other countries developed, output glutted world markets, and international sugar prices declined in the 1920s. All sectors of the Cuban economy suffered. Inocencia recalled that

in 1920, the country's economy was slow and we were on the way down. I didn't realize it then but the farm was producing less, or maybe the price of sugar had dropped, and we were very short of money. There wasn't even enough to pay the rent. . . . Little by little *papá* had to sell the cattle. When they were all gone he started selling the pigs, then the chickens, until he had very little of anything. I didn't know what was happening, as my parents never discussed their troubles in front of us. . . . After *papá* had sold most of the farm animals, he became a peddler. . . . He'd ride his horse from house to house selling cigarettes, coffee, and matches. It was the last work he ever did.[30]

Inocencia's family then fell into the rural proletariat after her youngest sibling died in 1922.

Papá spent a lot of money to cure the baby, and in 1923 we had to give up the farm. We moved to Felicidad, a hamlet about 20 kilometers from our house . . . where the big landowners had their homes. It had a school, a medical clinic, a general store with clothing and hardware, a large grocery store, and a train stop. We lived nearby in the sugar-cane workers' settlement on company-owned land with the other tenants.[31]

In Felicidad, Inocencia's father passed away, and "*Mamá* couldn't . . . pay the rent. . . . We were left with nothing but a few pieces of furniture and some hens; everything else was taken by the landlord as payment. . . . He himself set the prices, saying, 'This is worth so much and that is worth so much,' until he made up the amount we owed."[32] The family settled "in a town called Retamel, which had a sugar mill and sugar-cane farms." Their house belonged to the owner of the surrounding fields. He "promised to give my brothers—Luis Heberto, who was about eighteen, and Adolfo, who was a mere child—jobs all year round. . . . That landlord exploited my brothers, that's what he did. They worked in the cane field, hoeing, planting, and cutting cane at 1 *centavo* a row, earning only 30 to 40 *centavos* a day."[33] Inocencia and her siblings would go to the fields in midmorning with coffee for Heberto and Adolfo. They would hoe and pile cane so as to give Heberto and Adolfo a chance to rest.

During this time, in the late 1920s, the government lowered duties on raw material and machinery imports, and raised duties on manufactured imports to stimulate new enterprises behind the tariff shield. Agriculturalists began to produce more cheese, butter, and condensed milk, and expanded the beer and livestock industries. Cuban farmers increased the output of salted meat, as imports of beef, fowl, and eggs diminished. Tannery facilities increased output. A new tariff stimulated the production of rice, which with yuca supplanted the more expensive wheat imports. Farmers also expanded the production of fruit, vegetables, and textile fibers.

But as sugar prices in New York fell even more rapidly from January 1929 to June 1933, the US passed the protectionist Hawley-Smoot Tariff Act, and the Cuban share of US consumption diminished. Output plunged partly as a result of an agreement between Cuba and other sugar-producing countries to restrict the supply in an effort to raise the price. The sugar workers' wages fell below those of the early 1900s, while unemployment mounted much higher, and mill owners stretched the annual period of downtime without pay to nine months.

Cuba then signed a treaty in 1934 granting it favored access to the US market and granting US manufactures the same access to the Cuban. The output and value of Cuban sugar increased along with the portion of US imports to the island. These imports impaired the efforts to diversify the Cuban economy, leaving only the sectors complementary to sugar and US industry.

In the 1950s, the sugar industry remained the largest depository of domestic and foreign investment. It generated the vast majority of exports, accounted for over a quarter of GNP, and employed nearly a quarter of the labor force. Yet the industry produced fewer tons in 1956 than it had in 1925. Per capita income declined during the Great Depression, increased during the 1940s, and barely moved during the 1950s. In 1956, the national bank reported that if dependence on sugar were to continue, output would have to expand rapidly over the following years, in the face of falling prices, just to maintain the standard of living of 1947. Given the global glut, it is difficult to imagine where market outlets could have been found to sustain rising harvests of this sort.

Domestic large-scale rice production more than doubled from 1951 to 1957, supplied over half of Cuban consumption, and diminished the market share of US rice growers. These then petitioned the US Department of Agriculture, and the federal government threatened to reduce the sugar quota in retaliation for Cuban subsidies to rice growers. Cuban sugar and commercial interests lobbied their government, the island's national bank ceased to provide credits to domestic rice producers, and the state agreed to imports from the US. Subsequently, the share of national consumption supplied by Cuban farmers declined.

Despite the subordination of the Cuban economy to the US, the high sugar prices of 1900–1920 led to impressive growth rates, and high sugar prices of the 1940s similarly contributed to the well-being of much of the population. Transportation, communication, energy, and construction industries developed rapidly, pushed on by elements of the Cuban elite who benefited from these public investments. By the late 1950s, most of the population had abandoned farming amid the growth of service and manufacturing industries. Cuba had a literacy rate of nearly 80 percent, as well as high rankings in social services, energy consumption, and per capita use of automobiles and communications media. Cuba ranked only behind Argentina and Uruguay, among Latin American countries, in doctors per capita and food consumption. Infant mortality fell while life expectancy rose.

Yet this progress did not encompass the countryside where much of the population still lived. While the sugar harvest required intense labor, demand for it flagged the rest of the year, and many rural inhabitants suffered from joblessness. Illiteracy was four times higher in the countryside than it was in the cities. Whereas most urban homes had electricity and running water, very few rural ones did. Most rural inhabitants lived in palm huts with dirt floors. Farm workers weighed much less on average than did the rest of the population, and about 35 percent of the entire population suffered from malnutrition. High incidences of anemia, tuberculosis, and parasitic diseases resulted from the fact that very few rural inhabitants consumed milk, meat, or eggs. Hardly any doctors spent time in the countryside. Outside the city of Máximo Gómez, Inocencia's brother, a twenty-year-old worker in the cane fields, "got typhoid, and the doctor prescribed a terribly expensive medicine. . . . *Mamá* nearly went crazy. . . . She went to the mayor, and he gave her the money to buy it. But when the prescription had to be repeated . . . she took the prescription from house to house and everyone gave her something."[34] About a decade later, in the early 1930s, Inocencia cut her ties to agriculture, went to Havana, and became the servant of Señora Mérida, the owner of a shop for ladies' dresses.

Rural inhabitants tended to blame foreign property holders for their misery. Angel, an older resident of the area north of Mayarí in eastern Cuba, lived through the building of the American sugar mills, dictatorship, revolution, and socialism. He told an interviewer in the early 1980s: "When the Americans were here, they had these three recreational centers—one just for the Americans; I couldn't put my face in there. In 'Brooklyn' there was a club for the blacks. The Pan-American Club—the one for Americans—had a swimming pool, but of course it was only for them. There was a street on which only Americans could walk, Washington Avenue."[35]

The plantation culture, characterized by the impersonality of wage labor, loosened the ties between workers and employers, and diminished the deference and submission apparent in many other parts of Latin America. The Communist Party and the National Workers Confederation set up committees in the countryside to organize laborers and peasants in the National Union of the Sugar Industry Workers. Sugar workers staged a forty-eight-hour general strike in 1930. Armed bands ambushed trains, cut telephone and telegraph wires, destroyed rail bridges and tunnels, attacked isolated guard posts, and torched millions of pounds of cane.

In 1937, to secure social peace, a law granted the *colonos* secure tenures so long as they paid the landlords 5 percent of the milled sugar, regardless of prices. Increases of other commodity prices thus did not induce the farmers to plant different crops. The plantation proletariat, according to the 1937 law, earned a minimum wage even when they worked in sugar's dead season. Thus, the sugar companies did not have an incentive to plant subsidiary crops the rest of the year, because they had to pay the same wages as those earned at harvest time for the most productive crop during its peak labor demand. For these reasons, the large estates contained vast expanses of uncultivated land at a time of mass unemployment and food imports. Domestic constituencies and the national well-being were too tightly bound to the sugar industry for the government to take bold measures to diversify the economy.

A revolutionary army emerged in the mountains of Oriente Province in the late 1950s amid about forty thousand subsistence farmers of beans and malanga, a tropical vegetable, on rented plots. They differed economically and culturally from the plantation workers of the plains. The rebels consisted of only about 1,200 peasants out of a total Cuban rural population of three million. North of the rebellious area, the peasant *colonos* grew coffee on woodlands held in eight-year leases. The *colonos* only benefited from three harvests, two average and one good, because the coffee trees required four to five years to bear fruit. All improvements to the land accrued to the owners. The *colonos* lived in misery with little or no money beyond a bare subsistence.

Fidel Castro, Che Guevara, and other revolutionaries lived among the peasants of Oriente's mountainous region for about two years, and saw the abject poverty and health problems hidden from the urban middle classes. This experience focused the revolutionaries' vision on rural health, jobs, and social services. They gained the peasants' support, and got food, recruits, and intelligence from them, thanks to a program of agrarian reform, the distribution of land and cattle, and the founding of schools in the area they controlled in the summer of 1958. As news spread of rebel victories in eastern Cuba, the government faced mass defections and swift defeat. Many Cubans had forged a commitment to national independence and social justice in the late nineteenth-century struggle against Spain and felt disappointed by the continued dependence on sugar exports. The upper classes seemed to have a parasitic ignoble place within an economic and political system subordinate to the US.

The revolutionaries issued a decree limiting private holdings to one thousand acres. Land in commercial sugar, rice, and livestock could exceed the limit but only up to 3,333 acres. Properties exceeding this limit were nationalized with compensation provided in twenty-year bonds at annual interest of 4.5 percent. The revolutionaries set up the National Institute of Agrarian Reform (INRA) to implement the decree. INRA granted about 20 percent of the land in minimum allotments of 66.7 acres to two hundred thousand former renters, squatters, and sharecroppers.

The revolutionaries appointed a member of INRA to administer each of the twenty-eight zones of the country and oversee the provision of basic health and educational services. Members of INRA grappled with high unemployment and demands for the right to work on nearby *colono* farms. At the beginning of the 1960s, two-thirds of the laborers still worked, or hoped to work, on private lands. INRA received letters petitioning the state to take over these sugarcane lands, irrespective of their size, for the purpose of making work available and alleviating poverty. Laborers invaded estates on dozens of occasions even though the land reform decree of 1959 stipulated that autonomous land seizures disqualified their perpetrators from land or employment in the cooperatives. Many landowners and professionals fled the country, and many laborers migrated to the cities.

In this context, to maintain popular support, the revolutionary leaders began to envision more radical plans for an activist state on behalf of social justice and economic development. The state passed the Second Agrarian Reform Law of 1963 nationalizing all holdings larger than sixty-seven hectares. The *latifundia*, comprising the great majority of the arable land, passed to the country as a whole as state farms administered by INRA. Revolutionaries used this large public sector to plan production and hoped, in this way, to reduce Cuba's dependence on sugar, the symbol of slavery, oppression, uncertainty, and subservience to foreigners. They hoped to mobilize capital for the modernization of the sugar industry and the adoption of the latest manufacturing technology behind tariff barriers. Unlike in Russia, these hopes for development did not confront a peasant population in control of the land. Most of Cuba's rural inhabitants were agricultural laborers desirous of the security of employment available on state farms.

The revolutionaries confronted problems of a different sort. Almost all of the agronomists working in Cuba in 1959 fled the country. Roughly half of the teachers emigrated, as did nearly a quarter of the professionals and technicians. Half of the physicians and many of the dentists went into exile. Few of the senior medical faculty at the University of Havana stayed on the island. Sugar production began to decline and did not regain the former peak level of 1961 until 1970. Total agricultural output also declined in the early 1960s. Conditions for the poor nonetheless improved, because the state redistributed the wealth of the most affluent Cubans to the poorest 40 percent in the first four years of the revolution. As income levels grew, so did demand for food, and the government instituted rationing in 1962 to assure equal access amid diminishing supplies.

World sugar prices rose in 1963, and the regime scrapped its plan to diminish the country's reliance on sugar. Castro went to the Soviet Union in 1964 and received an agreement on sugar export prices. Sugar and its by-products then became the principal export commodity, as the country imported food, manufactures, and machinery. Cuba ran a huge trade deficit with the socialist countries, particularly the USSR.

In a movement similar to, yet far less disastrous than, the Chinese Great Leap Forward, Cuban revolutionaries made appeals to selflessness and work as the way to purge bourgeois vices and make new "socialist" people. In the absence of capital investments, moral incentives, solidarity, and sacrifice were to heave the country forward. Castro repudiated the use of wage differentials and material incentives. Instead, over a million workers from all sectors of the economy, as well as soldiers and sugar workers, participated in the 1970 cane harvest. The regime planned for a sugar harvest of ten million tons, the largest in human history. Such a harvest, it was hoped, would facilitate the full mechanization of the sugar industry, the expansion of housing and social services, the provision of consumer goods, and reductions to the unfavorable balance of trade with the other socialist countries.

To reach this goal, output would have had to double. Planners allotted more and more land to cane. Harvests of tobacco, beans, yuca, tuber, malanga, tomatoes, and other vegetables declined, even though the economy already generated nowhere near sufficient quantities for domestic needs. Pork, chicken, and milk production fell, while citrus harvests failed to improve much between 1967 and 1970. Widespread mismanagement, a flourishing black market, increasing vagrancy, and worker absenteeism plunged the country into crisis. In July 1970, Castro publicly acknowledged his error in thinking that voluntarism and the idealism of a vanguard, in disregard for the objective conditions, could substitute for competence and investment.

The regime then adopted Soviet planning and management techniques, and offered rewards for increased production. Cuba's well-educated administrators oriented the economy toward efficiency, discipline, and performance. The socialist countries' preferential sugar prices, several times above the world market, facilitated impressive growth rates over the course of the 1970s, and then the fastest ones in Cuban history in the first half of the 1980s. By the end of the decade, the Soviet Union provided massive developmental aid, about four hundred dollars per capita a year and 20 percent of Cuba's GNP. The Cuban government, unlike the governments of many developing countries, reinvested revenue in the countryside. It laid the most advanced infrastructure of any sugar-exporting nation. Tractors largely replaced oxen. Pesticide and herbicide imports soared. Cuban farmers, by the late 1970s and during the 1980s, used much more fertilizer, mechanization, and irrigation than did their Latin American counterparts, even more per capita than did US farmers. The rural population of Cuba declined to nearly a quarter of the total by 1989. Cuba in short had introduced its own green revolution.

Some diversification occurred. Sugar's proportion of farm output and the labor force declined substantially. Food imports also declined. Cubans gained access to healthcare and education, rural electrification, and cultural institutions. The creation of the National Food and Nutrition Surveillance System, used as a model by other countries, worked to eliminate obesity, closely watched mother and infant nutrition, and monitored chemical and biological food contaminants.

At the founding of the National Association of Small Farmers (ANAP) in 1961, Castro pledged "the most absolute respect for the will and the desires of the *campesino*."[36] The ANAP's base committees encouraged cooperation among farm owners and facilitated the use of mechanization, scientific technologies, and large-scale methods. It developed production plans for the farm owners and directed all of their output into the procurement and distribution agency (ACOPIO) at fixed prices immune from the uncertainties of commodity markets. Owner-operators produced a disproportionally large share of Cuban output and exports relative to their numbers, the capital invested in their farms, and the extent of the land they cultivated.

ACOPIO's prices, however, steadily declined in real terms. Farmers had no incentive to cultivate more land. Many of them sought higher prices on the black market. In 1969, the state dispossessed state-farm workers of the plots used for barter and illegal sales, limited private tenures to the lifetime of owners, and encouraged them to sell their land to the state farms. Many of them gave up farming. At the end of the 1970s, a construction worker in Holguín, who formerly had tilled a small plot, was asked if he missed farming: "Are you kidding? . . . What kind of life was that? All that hard work for a little patch of yucca. No, sir. I wanted to come here, where the action is!"[37]

In this way, much of the population lost its taste for rural life at the very moment official propaganda promoted its socialist virtues. Schools built in the countryside in the 1970s housed students in dormitories. The complexes had laboratories, workshops, meeting rooms, libraries, barbershops, beauty parlors, infirmaries, movie theaters, school stores, and swimming pools. The students, aged twelve to sixteen, came from nearby towns and villages, and returned home on the weekend. They farmed citrus, tobacco, bananas, or vegetables. Revolutionary leaders hoped the schools would eventually become self-sufficient and provide an education for all Cuban youths.

Overall, however, Cuba still depended on imports, especially fuel. The US embargo hindered sales on the world market and forced Cuba to rely on the socialist countries. The dependence on sugar for foreign exchange held back diversification. Planners allocated most of the arable land to export crops. Domestic food production declined relative to the industrial growth of cattle and dairy, pigs and poultry, and citrus for export. In the late 1980s, Cuba imported all, or nearly all, of its wheat, beans, livestock concentrates, oil, lard, and cereals. Much of the population's fish, poultry, and dairy products was imported to the island. The nation modernized rice production but still imported half of the rice consumed on the island. In 1989, Cuba had the most collectivized, egalitarian, and externally dependent economy in the socialist world.

It also had a privileged bureaucratic class, similar to those of the Soviet Union and Communist China. Industries did not produce in response to demand or compete to stay afloat. Managers formed part of the ruling group in control of the output. They held back information from superiors and amassed as much material and labor as possible in order to further the growth of their unit. Employees had little incentive to work productively. Managers were not evaluated on these terms. Rather, their prospects for advancement in the political and economic hierarchy depended on fulfilling the targets of state planners. Managers enjoyed preference in educational opportunities and everyday access to products. Party officials received better food, comfortable lodgings, access to high-end goods, uncrowded traveling, and trips abroad to academic or cultural conferences, all the while proclaiming egalitarianism as official policy.

Additional problems resulted from industrial farming, characterized by imports of chemicals and machinery, and the use of large-scale irrigation. Most of the soil suffered from various degrees of erosions, even in the most fertile areas, and some of it suffered from salinization. Farmers and administrators did little to reverse the trend apart from the production of compost and worm humus after 1984. Agricultural productivity and crop yields waned, and rural incomes remained relatively low. Overall GDP began to decline at the end of the 1980s.

Government leaders, in the early part of the decade, sought to stimulate productivity by allowing the extension of the markets that had long served the areas beyond the reach of ACOPIO. Officials had noticed the rising prices on the informal markets and sought, through legalization, to extend state supervision over them. The newly authorized markets thrived, and agricultural goods gained in diversity and quality. But in the absence of an adequate legal administration, speculators bought in bulk and sold at higher prices. Private farmers diverted resources from the government plan on which the population depended. ACOPIO, moreover, failed to efficiently convey the produce to the markets and allowed some of it to go to waste.

These problems worsened after the dissolution of the socialist trade bloc on which the economy depended. Agriculture lost 70 percent of its fertilizers and pesticides, and 50 percent of its seeds. The extension of the US embargo through the 1992 Torricelli Act and the 1996 Helms-Burton Act exacerbated the problem by compelling Cuba to purchase from distant expensive markets, amounting to a virtual tax of 30 percent on imports. Sugar production fell dramatically, and the output of basic foodstuffs plummeted to even more alarming depths. Money for food imports dried up.

Unemployment rose as a result of the closure of industries and the return of Cubans from the former socialist countries. The percentage of the population at risk of poverty more than doubled, though it still remained among the lowest in Latin America thanks to Cuba's high levels of equality. Per capita consumption of calories fell from 2,845 in 1989 to 1,948 in 1994. Cuba, in a word, suffered the worst economic crisis in its history, worse than the 1930s.

The regime had developed plans for food security prior to 1989 but did not implement them on account of the socialist bloc's assurance of Cuba's alimentary needs. It did not heed a number of studies that had shown the relatively high output of smaller private farms. Not until the catastrophic downturn of 1989–1993 did the government change the land tenure system, dismantle the state farms, and turn them into cooperatives. These Basic Units of Cooperative Production (UBPCs) mounted to nearly half of the farmland. Today they own their output but must sell 80 percent of it to the state at prices fixed below the market rate. Between the early 1990s and 1998, government leaders, hoping to stimulate subsistence production, distributed unused farmland in usufruct to families willing to till it. Food scarcity caused the proportion of farmers in the labor force to mount for the first time in decades.

Once the regime settled upon structural reform, it proved capable of innovative programs thanks to the high educational levels prevalent on the island. Cuba has 11 percent of Latin America's scientists as opposed to only 2 percent of its population. The state opened agricultural instruction centers in every municipality after 1991. Basic farming became an option in the curriculum of most primary schools after 1995. The state also encouraged town dwellers to produce eggs and pork in backyards. Employees of urban firms received crops grown on workplace grounds. Though urban gardens have not covered much of the population's needs, and though food imports increased substantially from their low point in 1994, domestic agriculture nonetheless sees to a larger share of the alimentary requirements than it had in 1989.

Independent farmers generally join cooperatives to have access to credit, purchase inputs in bulk, and sell their produce. They enjoy the security of healthcare, land tenure, crop insurance, and education and thus have more easily taken up sustainable techniques than have cultivators in other countries, forced by the bottom line to farm in whatever way enhances income relative to outlays. Interest rates are extraordinarily low through the Banco Nacional de Cuba and nearly every small farmer receives technical assistance from government extension workers or specialists associated with their cooperatives. The state uses price incentives to encourage farmers to cultivate coffee, honey, tobacco, and citrus for export and generate foreign exchange. These farmers obtain dollars and can shop in the official stores for imported goods.

In the 1990s, small farmers began to set aside land for the subsistence of their families and employees. This tendency marked a dramatic shift in a country accustomed to specialization. The change to diversified and subsistence farming reflected the official promotion of food security, the best means for farmers to obtain nourishment and ensure a stable workforce, since salaries alone did not purchase a reasonable supply of food. In September 1994, the state permitted farmers to sell on the open market after fulfilling procurement quotas. Markets came into being across the island, and growing sales enhanced the availability of milk, cheese, fruits, vegetables, and meat. Farmers sell 15 to 40 percent of their output at these markets, generally crops and products that ACOPIO does not purchase. They do not like to disclose the actual percentage, no doubt out of concern that officials might find their sales to ACOPIO deficient and that the state might revoke its authorization of market sales. These independent farmers have expressed favorable opinions about their new line of work.

Since the crisis Cuba has not only seen a growing number of people engage in the cultivation of food crops. It has also seen a migration out of Oriente province, which traditionally has had a lower standard of living. The crisis exacerbated the disparities, concentrating much of Cuba's unemployment in Oriente. Falling imports in 1990 and 1991 diminished the supplies needed to fuel the mechanized farms of Havana province and generated demand for agricultural workers. These workers in the UBPCs experienced increases in their standard of living. The access of UBPC members to food made their standard of living rise faster than that of state employees, when incomes began to rise across the island again after the low point of the crisis in 1994.

The UBPCs generally had difficulty increasing output during the 1990s, because of input shortages, the shoddy labor of former workers on state farms, and especially the low prices paid by ACOPIO relative to those it charged consumers. The UBPCs must devote the greater part of their land to crops purchased by ACOPIO. Members have an incentive to minimize the poorly remunerated output for ACOPIO and maximize their own consumption. They have an incentive to turn to middlemen or sell on the black market at higher prices. Many UBPCs were folded into better-performing ones, and in this way most of them achieved profitability after 2001.

Organic agriculture gained support within policy-making circles when agrichemicals disappeared in the early 1990s. Farmers came to emphasize biological pest control and soil conditioner, microbial antagonists, earthworms, animal and green manures, and compost and other organic enrichers, as well as the integration of grazing animals to supplement scarce synthetic fertilizers. They used resistant plant varieties, crop rotations, and cover cropping to suppress weeds. A sweeping return to animal traction emerged as fuel, tires, and spare parts for tractors grew scarce.

Research centers scattered across the countryside and accessible to all sectors of farming have developed the new organic inputs. A young plant breeder in Havana province visited farmers still producing pumpkins despite nearly a tenfold decline in productivity from the late 1980s to 1993. Upon discovering their knowledge of crop selection, he brought them into his research team. Thanks to their experience in their local farm system, the plant breeder discovered vegetal characteristics hitherto unknown to Cuban agronomists and helped the researchers find pumpkin varieties resistant to disease, drought, and pests. The researchers then rethought their paradigm and, by dint of pumpkin landraces selected by the farmers, these began to obtain, through organic husbandry, yields over three times higher than those of the early 1980s. The farmers' use of energy fell 75 percent thanks to the reduced need for irrigation, fertilizer, and pesticide.

Despite successes of this sort, agrichemicals still form key components of production on most cooperatives. Many farmers do not see organic inputs as practical or modern, and would dispense with them if agrichemicals became available again. Farmers in the province of Santiago, for example, use more oxen and manual labor than do their peers in the province of Havana, no doubt because of their relatively limited access to tractors.

Although economic conditions have improved since the low point in 1994, official statistics show that the results of the transformation of state farms into cooperative and private holdings have not been overwhelmingly positive. Agriculture continues to fall short in animal sources of protein. Cane still covers a large area throughout the country, especially the better soils, yet its output has declined so much that the state imports sugar to fulfill contractual obligations with China and satisfy domestic demand. Inadequate investment in improvements, or even upkeep, combined with deficiencies in management and work organization, has caused sugar output to fall to 1–1.5 million tons in recent years, down from historic highs of 7–8 million in the 1980s. When the price of sugar increased in 2010, Cuba did not have the wherewithal to cash in and lost tens of millions of dollars in potential income.

Much of the land diverted from cane has remained fallow, as the total area of cultivation fell from 1998 to 2007, leaving half of the cropland untilled or underutilized in 2008. The government spent over a billion dollars on food imports in 2006. President Raúl Castro stated in 2007 that agriculture was the regime's number-one priority. It has distributed small farms to growers in usufruct and has relaxed the requirement to sell to the state. Local organizations brought farmers together to hear their needs in machinery, spare parts, equipment, plows, windmills, and other inputs. But while the state distributed most of the idle land, much of it remained untilled. High prices for inputs, resulting from the US embargo, make many lines of agriculture unprofitable. About 70 percent of the recipients had no experience in agriculture. It is hard to find workers for intensive labor in rice cultivation. People hope to earn more in tourism. Cuba's relatively high standard of living and education has led to disdain for agricultural work. The government does not seem interested in immigration of farmers from Haiti. Today, much of Cuban agriculture consists of fruit, meat, and poultry for tourists or export, while scarcity prevails in the state-subsidized neighborhood stores.

These recent developments in Cuba typify the socialist experiments in agriculture. They all ended at an impasse. The three revolutions started out with the support of the rural population, overwhelmingly in China and Cuba and at least tacitly in the Soviet Union. Following the example of the USSR,

China collectivized agriculture and Cuba turned the bulk of the land into state farms, amid widespread popular support. The leaders of these countries were eager to catch up to, and defend themselves from, the capitalist powers. The heads of the Communist Parties of China and Cuba were intoxicated by popular support. All three countries launched breakneck plans to augment output, all of which ended in disaster. Collectivization in the Soviet Union killed millions of people and created a climate of falsity and callousness. The Great Leap Forward led to famine in China, and the campaign to harvest ten million tons of cane in Cuba excessively specialized agriculture and disorganized production.

The underlying problem stemmed from the population's lack of control over production, incentive to work, and motivation to experiment. Ruling groups in control of the economic output led lives different from the rest of the population. They had preferential access to education and consumption (even if they consumed much less than did the ownership classes in the United States, Japan, and western Europe). These benefits stemmed from their command of the economy and its surpluses.

Mao, Castro, and other revolutionary leaders no doubt genuinely believed in the liberating impetus of their regimes. Indeed, Mao's Cultural Revolution began in 1966 as an assault on the new bureaucratic elite within the party and state organs, before its ignoble denouement under the Gang of Four. The drives to collectivize agriculture and augment output ultimately failed, because the systems had no institutional mechanisms to assure the popular involvement needed for an appropriate organization of labor. In the production campaigns of Stalin and Khrushchev, Mao, and Castro, laborers were put to work so long as they created a surplus. The rulers controlled the economies and solely sought to maximize output. The managers had to meet the political requirements of the plans in order to have success within the socialist regimes. They sought autonomy from the planners with regard to their operations and to the accumulation of material and labor, and focused on the growth of their units, since the growth enhanced their reputation and permitted them to maintain or improve their position in the state and party hierarchies. As a result, the socialist campaigns to augment output and catch up with the capitalist powers did not augment productivity and instead ended in disorganization and disillusionment.

Lastly, the different histories of these countries point to their current and future evolutions. The Soviet leadership, especially in the 1930s, created a sullen, demoralized rural population incapable of taking much pride in farming or showing much ingenuity. Agriculture remained stagnant throughout the history of the Soviet Union. The gains of the twenty-first century have resulted from resource extraction rather than productive work. The Chinese Revolution of 1949, by contrast, emerged out of the countryside and benefited from the enthusiastic support of the rural population. The rulers have been able to draw on this dynamism even after the disasters of the Great Leap Forward.

In Cuba, the economy, standard of living, health, and educational level of the population improved during the 1970s and much of the 1980s. The success depended on Cuba's preferential place in the socialist economic bloc. At the end of the 1980s, Cuba suffered a severe depression, as the US embargo prevented it from finding alternatives to the fuel, seed, machine, and chemical inputs formerly received from the Soviet bloc. Cuba's educated population has shown resilience in developing imaginative solutions through organic agriculture and state support for independent and cooperative farms. Yet the country is a victim of its own success. With the US blockade and the end of Soviet subsidies, the experiments in sustainable agriculture are deprived of the latest inputs and instead must rely on the efforts of the population. Cubans, however, have become urban and educated, and shun farming. For these reasons, the country's experiments in organic agriculture consistently fall short of goals.

NOTES

1. Maurice Gerschon Hindus, *Red Bread: Collectivization in a Russian Village* (Bloomington: Indiana University Press, 1988), 58.
2. Ibid., 61.
3. Ibid., 219.
4. Lynne Viola, *The War against the Peasantry, 1927–1930: The Tragedy of the Soviet Countryside* (New Haven: Yale University Press, 2005), 238–39.
5. Hindus, *Red Bread*, 35.
6. Viola, *The War against the Peasantry*, 217.
7. Ibid., 217–18.
8. Ibid., 246.
9. Robert C. Tucker, *Stalin in Power: The Revolution from Above, 1928–1941* (New York: W. W. Norton, 1992), 208.
10. Viola, *The War against the Peasantry*, 352, 354.
11. Boris Pasternak, *Doctor Zhivago* (New York: Pantheon Books, 1958).
12. Hindus, *Red Bread*, 211.
13. Anita Chan, Richard Madsen, and Jonathan Unger, *Chen Village under Mao and Deng* (Berkeley: University of California Press, 1992), 20.
14. C. K. Yang, *Chinese Communist Society: The Family and the Village* (Cambridge: MIT Press, 1959), 206.
15. Vivienne Shue, *Peasant China in Transition: The Dynamics of Development toward Socialism, 1949–1956* (Berkeley: University of California Press, 1980), 146–47.
16. Chris Bramall, *Chinese Economic Development* (New York: Routledge, 2009), 106.
17. Jack Potter and Sulamith Potter, *China's Peasants: The Anthropology of a Revolution* (Cambridge: Cambridge University Press, 1990), 62.
18. Ibid., 71.
19. Chan, Madsen, and Unger, *Chen Village*, 25.
20. Roderick MacFarquhar, *The Origins of the Cultural Revolution*, vol. 2: *The Great Leap Forward, 1958–1960* (New York: Columbia University Press, 1983), 329.
21. Oscar Lewis, Ruth Lewis, and Susan Rigdon, *Four Women: Living the Revolution—An Oral History of Contemporary Cuba*, vol. 2 (Urbana: University of Illinois Press, 1977), 325.
22. Ibid., 325–26.

23. Ibid., 325.
24. Ibid., 327.
25. Ibid., 333.
26. Ibid., 335.
27. Ibid., 333.
28. Ibid., 332.
29. Ibid., 336.
30. Ibid., 342–43.
31. Ibid., 344.
32. Ibid., 346.
33. Ibid.
34. Ibid., 348.
35. Terence Cannon, *Revolutionary Cuba* (New York: Thomas Y. Crowell, 1981), 211.
36. Ibid., 225.
37. Ibid., 227.

Chapter Nine

Late Development

State-led Agrarian Change after World War II

Although the economies of France and Taiwan currently rank among the world's most advanced, they developed, as the title of this chapter implies, late in comparison to England, Japan, and the United States. At the end of World War II, the economies of both countries were still heavily agrarian. Taiwan had only just emerged from decades of colonial rule, which had favored a few agricultural exports but left farming under the control of small-holding peasants. In France, nearly half the population still lived in localities of fewer than two thousand inhabitants and consumed food from their farms or neighboring ones in ways reminiscent of the Middle Ages.

This traditional pattern, however, changed in the 1960s, when the governments of France and Taiwan pursued policies to make people farm for the market and improve the productivity of their labor. The countries then had veritable agricultural or green revolutions. One of the keys to rural development was a set of government policies used to redistribute land to farmers. Reforming land ownership ended a pattern in which landlords exploited, in inefficient ways, an abundance of poor peasants anxious for paid work and channeled the land instead to those liable to use family labor as productively as possible by adopting the latest techniques and technologies and by switching between product lines in search of higher incomes.

Rural development spurred industrialization in France and Taiwan, though in different ways. In exploring this contrast, we will measure the degrees to which the states sought to encourage industry by helping farmers to produce more and improve their standard of living, or alternatively by extracting taxes from them to obtain capital for investment in manufacturing.

We will then examine the newly modernized agricultural sectors to understand the difficulties growers now face in maintaining themselves in a context of ever more productive farming, rising output, and falling relative prices for their commodities. This latter part of the chapter contains an analysis of the benefits and costs associated with the transformations of rural France and Taiwan.

FRANCE

José Bové came to the world's attention in 1999 by leading a group of sheep farmers in dismantling a partially constructed McDonald's in Millau in southwest France. Bové and his companions aimed to draw attention to the US trade barrier erected against many European products, including Roquefort cheese, in retaliation for the European Union's decision to ban the sale of hormone-fed beef. Their action posed the question as to who gets to decide about the quality and integrity of our food: citizens or trade institutions. In an interview the following year, Bové described the process by which France came to this current dilemma. He described the postwar transformation of rural France as

> a real success story. . . . On the strength of the establishment of the Common Market in 1957 and agricultural legislation of 1960 and 1962, the modernization of agriculture . . . leaped ahead. The objectives were clearly outlined: to achieve food autonomy . . . to provide foodstuffs at the lowest cost, and to protect a number of . . . agricultural products—cereals, sugar, milk, meat and wine—from international competition. Another consideration was attempting to guarantee farmers the same income as townspeople. To attain these objectives, France chose to move towards industrialized modernization: specialization, concentration of farm ownership, and the creation of complex chains of production.[1]

As Bové implied, French farms had not shown much capacity for development prior to World War II or even to the establishment of the Fifth Republic in 1958. He also implied that the subsequent agricultural revolution was accomplished politically. The "natural" play of market forces had actually entrenched subsistence farming for use rather than spur farming for amassing money. During the 1850s and 1860s, rising agricultural prices and wages allowed many peasants to buy land, and thus served not to encourage the transformation of husbandry but rather to multiply the number of farms. Peasants planted high-yielding subsistence crops such as potatoes in Brittany, Auvergne, and Provence and maize in the south of the Paris Basin and the Rhône valley and thus could market previously consumed cereals, feed more livestock, and make ends meet on small holdings. In the period of worldwide economic stagnation, in the 1870s and 1880s, the fall in land prices and the low rental values led many landlords to sell land and channel their capital into more profitable investments. These trends led to a slight decline in the number of large farms over forty hectares, and a corresponding expansion in the number of subsistence plots of five to ten hectares, though the dominant trend was immovability in the landholding structure.

Between 1918 and 1939, the state undertook a project of rural electrification and offered loans at 1 percent interest—through the formation of the bank Crédit Agricole—to farmers eager to acquire and improve the land. Yet rates of investment did not accelerate. A large portion of the loans helped the peasants to extend their household plots. Although micro-proprietors, who supplemented subsistence farming in rural industry and wage work, gradually became less numerous, medium-sized holdings of ten to fifty hectares continued to become more common through the end of the 1920s. In this way, while the percentage of the national population residing in the countryside declined, the proportion engaged in farming remained stable, for those that left had supplemented the incomes of their scraps of land in nonagricultural services and manufacturing. Moreover, since the remaining medium-sized farms did not occupy all of the rural population's capacity for work, households did not find it worthwhile to make outlays on labor-saving implements for agricultural tasks their members could perform themselves.

Subsistence agriculture—with a little budgeting for expenditures beyond the basic needs, in addition to taxes—became more viable in the first decades of the twentieth century, as the continuing rural exodus made the lands of smallholders available for purchase or lease and permitted peasants to build up their holdings. In 1945, a third of the population lived on about four million farms, which apart from the arable fields of the Paris Basin and the viticulture of Languedoc were all unique yet analogous. Within the households, the members gathered around the typical fire and table at which they ate the products of the farm from a pot. Many households baked their own bread, while others traded their grain for it at the local bakery. People bought rice, oil, coffee, and sugar, and meat for the holidays, but little else. The cattle ate the fodder grown on the fields and excreted manure back to them. Peasants had the skills of wheelwrights, knew metalwork, and repaired tools, wagons, and carts. If households purchased a machine it was used to fend off disruptions, such as vanishing casual labor, and thus preserve their way of life. Money had a marginal value, used only to buy a new tool, save and buy land, or pay off brothers and sisters at the time of inheritance. Much like the inhabitants of colonial New England, French farmers in 1945 still learned their technical expertise from parents and ancestors.

As an illustration, the population of Loubens, in the grain-producing Lauragais region of the southwest, diminished between 1911 and 1926, as land surveyors, physicians, pharmacists, notaries, and nuns moved to the towns, leaving priests and schoolmasters as the only professionals. From the 1730s to 1948, the pattern of property holdings became reinforced in a manner slightly different from the rest of France, where small farms proliferated. In Loubens, the landlords' share of the soil mounted from 70 to 80 percent. At great cost in energy and time, sharecroppers continued to turn the landlords' fields over with spades rather than plows. The spades went more than twice as deeply into the soil and improved the humus content and yields for the proprietors. For harvesting, in France as a whole, the sickle was only slowly replaced by the scythe, of which there were a mere twenty-three thousand in use on 3.47 million farms at the end of the nineteenth century. Peasants relied on family labor rather than see household income go out the door on unnecessary equipment and maintenance costs. Their spades and scythes were characteristic of this sort of property relation whereby the work devolved upon the sharecropper, while the produce was divided equally.

Sharecropping in Loubens, into the twentieth century, remained a servile bond in which the lessor relished the role of master. Sharecroppers brought the produce to town for the landowners to enjoy at their table. The landlords regarded their sharecroppers as interchangeable parts of the farm and constantly intervened, through their stewards, in the management of the husbandry. The youth of these sharecropper families sometimes felt humiliated upon seeing the elder generation doff their hats when the landlords rode through the fields. Most sharecroppers lived at the base level of subsistence and had to borrow funds from farm stewards to celebrate baptisms, confirmations, and weddings, pay for medical consultations, or send money to kids on military service.

The innovations of the interwar period served to preserve rather than undermine the values and priorities of self-sufficiency. More industrial fertilizer may have been used in Loubens in the ten years after World War I than in the ten years prior to it. But the application of the fertilizer varied from sharecropper to sharecropper and even from year to year on the same farm. The subsequent decade of depression led to a cutback in capital outlays and to technical regression. The variance in the use of fertilizer shows clearly that agriculture did not go along a path of sustained development prior to the 1950s. The landowners could not force the sharecropper to make outlays not specified in the rental contract, and they were loath, by custom, to assume the full bill for fertilizer.

Of all the industrialized countries, France had the highest proportion of self-sufficient farmers in the late 1940s, and things hardly changed over the next decade. The General Confederation of Agriculture (CGA) aimed to modernize husbandry by bringing together all of the farm organizations behind the motive force of technicians tied to the state ministry. But rural areas voted for the Popular Republican Movement (MRP) and other conservatives. Pierre Pflimlin of the MRP, a partisan of the National Federation of Unions of Farmers (FNSEA), became minister of agriculture at the end of 1947, as the CGA lost influence. The prewar leaders of the farm unions and the FNSEA regained their posts. They defended a traditional vision of the peasantry, agriculture, and regionalism as beneficial to the national identity. FNSEA organized big protests in 1956 and obtained the indexing of agricultural prices to those of industry. Landowners were mollified and the countryside seemed set to follow its accustomed course. During these years, agricultural rhythms accelerated but did not undergo transformation. The total wheat harvest did not reach the level of 1907 until 1954. Although farmers started to use tractors and reaper-binders rather than yokes of horses, they still relied on much labor to squeeze in the bales, transport the millstones, thresh, and do other tasks.

But then, after the late 1950s, wheat yields and farm sizes tripled, the number of farms declined four times over, and agriculturalists fell from 30 to 4 percent of the national population. Motorization dramatically changed agriculture. The number of tractors mounted from 140,000 in 1950 to 558,000 in 1958, and nearly one million in 1963. The number of combine harvesters rose from 37,900 in 1958 to 102,000 in 1965. Combine harvesters made labor redundant and swiftly diminished the harvest workforce. Agriculturalists used more than five times as much fertilizer in 1978 as they had in 1946. The number of lawn tractors, moto-mowers, balers, and mechanical seed drills rose in the same proportions. The prolonged seasonal work of threshing in the autumn and winter declined. Productivity thus grew 8 percent a year in agriculture between 1963 and 1967, whereas it grew at 5 percent in the rest of the economy. Labor productivity doubled from 1949 to 1963, rising at an annual rate equal to industry of 7 percent, whereas prior to 1938 it rose about 2 percent a year.

Just as agricultural revolutions in the United States in the 1850s, and Taiwan in the 1970s, spurred the development of major industries of agricultural inputs, so too in France, the mechanization of farming in the 1960s, provided the impetus for a new branch of the metallurgical and engine-building industries. Agriculture also furnished much primary material. Food processing became one of France's principal industries. Factories for meat, sweets, biscuits/cookies, flour, dairy, and other products generated about 15 percent of industrial output by the end of the twentieth century.

Farmers bridged the gap in lifestyles separating them from other social groups. The building of new homes or the remodeling of old ones doubled in rural areas in the 1960s. The farmers' buying power grew every year from 1965 to 1973. Mechanization encouraged the sloughing off of excess labor just as the urban sector's demand for workers was on the rise. France's rural exodus reached its height in the 1960s, when one hundred thousand people left the countryside annually. As a result, the active labor force in farming fell from 20 percent in 1962 to 9 percent in 1975.

These accomplishments could not have been foreseen. Previously, farmers had avoided changes liable to threaten the security of subsistence farming. What wrenched them from the accustomed mode of life was the conscious policies of state administrators eager to bring down the prices of food and raw material, free up rural labor for other sectors of the economy, and develop a market in the countryside for consumer goods and agricultural implements. Charles de Gaulle and his ministers, in a word, sought to make rural France capitalist. Their reports showed the unsustainable weight of agricultural price supports and denounced the archaic character of farming. Georges Pompidou, the adviser of the prime minister Michel Debré, pointed to Europe and the goal of having the common market provide remunerative outlets for agriculture. Industry would rid itself of the hindering weight of the rural sector. The state then suppressed price indexes at the end of 1958. The price equilibrium subsequently came from exports, which grew 22 percent a year within the European common market, and especially quickly in the trade of cereals, sugar, cheeses, fruits, and vegetables.

Growth on this scale resulted from state policy, specifically the laws of 1960 and 1962 intended to augment the size of farms, ensure the survival of the dynamic ones, and encourage the disappearance of the rest. The legislation prevented non-cultivators from hoarding whole chains of farms and operating them with hired labor. It instead favored family farms reliant solely on the labor of two working-age adults using the latest implements and methods. The laws offered lifetime annuities to farmers over sixty-five to cede their holdings for the new usages of land development and adjustments. The laws established a fund for intervention in the land market to preempt sales, group plots together in ways suitable to the latest technology, and offer them to growers eager to establish first farms or enhance the size of their holdings. Previously, the free market had allowed peasants to establish uneconomical farms. The state, through the legislation, took nearly a quarter of the land market from the 1960s to 1986 and sold about a third of its acquired acreage to enterprising farmers. The regrouping of plots, after having slowed down since 1955, developed at a rapid pace after 1960.

The most transformative state policy was to charge the Crédit Agricole, after 1963, with funding modernization by offering thirty-year loans at 3 percent interest. The Crédit Agricole opened branches across the small towns of rural France. To get the loans, growers had to have a minimum farm size, and half of them were thus excluded in some parts of the country. As farmers took out loans to invest in agriculture, make their labor more productive, and cut costs, other farmers had to struggle to keep up by financing the costs of modernization. Debt and the fear of bankruptcy forced farmers, as they had in rural New England and the Midwest in the 1850s, to adopt a new economic focus on matching the competitive prices of their peers. They reduced the ratio of outlays to income through ever deeper specialization, systematic reinvestment of earnings, an obsessive adoption of the latest techniques, and the movement of farm inputs from one commodity line to another in response to changes in demand.

State subsidies in the form of 15 percent discounts on loans for tractors and reduced prices for fuel permitted farmers to plow their fields in a matter of days rather than weeks as in the past. But to get the full value from the investment, farmers had to bring more land under cultivation through purchase or rental. They cut down generations-old fruit and nut trees, and turned the orchards into arable fields, because they needed to get income from as much land as possible. The tractor led growers to make new openings in buildings, to level and widen pathways, and to dispense with horses and oxen. Its adoption forced the reconversion of the artisan, blacksmith, and farrier professions. The tractor permitted cultivators to farm and transport further from their residences and thus contributed to the rise of land prices. Farmers had to get new tools and attachments to enhance the tractor's versatility, new fertilizers to augment yields, and special seed strains to resist diseases. One innovation required a whole slew of changes, which in turn required new loans from the Crédit Agricole. Farmers had to join cooperatives to assure the sale of the wheat as soon as it was harvested and raise the revenue needed to service their debts.

These changes augmented output 1.5 to 2 percent annually after the mid-1960s, whereas demand grew only 0.5 percent and drove down farm returns relative to industrial wages. To maintain the equivalent of the industrial worker's salary, farmers had to grow nearly six times more wheat in 1982 than they had in 1952. Farmers had to take out loans and make investments in order to augment yields and avoid poverty. Buying and maintaining machines, paying salaries and insurance, and purchasing seed, fertilizer, and pesticides required capital at the start of each agricultural year. These expenses mounted from a quarter of the value of sales in 1959 to a half at the end of the century. Households had to practice minute accounting, as their debts grew fourteen-fold from 1960 to 1973. In this way, although the spectacular gains in productivity increased the rural standard of living, the bulk of the gain went in interest payments to the banks.

The government project to increase investment in farming was buoyed by the Christian Agricultural Youth (JAC), and its outgrowth the National Center of Young Agriculturalists (CNJA). In the late 1950s, tension emerged in the CNJA when a tougher, more assertive element from the underdeveloped south and center sought to open the question of drastic structural reform in agriculture. They challenged the CNJA members of the conservative small-farming districts and the sons of large modernized farmers from the northeast. The former group succeeded in putting its representatives Hubert Buchou and Michel Debatisse in the key posts of president and secretary-general in 1959. They publicized the desirability of local self-help, such as the pooling of resources in autonomous technically advanced cooperatives. In the 1950s and 1960s, the CNJA set up a formidable network for general and scientific education, including internships, study days, field trips, and a new overall vision of the profession stressing mechanical expertise and economic knowledge.

François Dufour, a third-generation farmer in La Binolais in Lower Normandy, met his future wife, Françoise Bernier, at a JAC meeting. Together they took over his family's farm in 1976. He had participated in a summer gathering in Larzac in the southern Massif Central with other farmers anxious about rising land prices and about the Departmental Federation of Unions of Agriculturalists (FDSEA), the main farmers' association, which regarded small farmers as "unprofitable and fit for the scrapheap." He and his wife committed themselves politically to change this state of affairs but, on account of the pressures of technology and the demands of the bank, adopted ever more aspects of the intensive farming they intended to combat. They could only obtain the allowances available to young farmers if they sold all their horses, bought cattle, and specialized in milk production. They had to finance six more hectares and build concrete barns for feeding the cattle. Dufour had to spend twice as much time on the tractor, plowing, mowing, and harvesting fodder, as he had previously. He stated:

> On the same patch of land we grew maize intensively, with a very high yield, and ray grass from Italy. We'd smother the ground in nitrogen, to give the maize a kickstart, then cover it with more nitrogen so that we could get grass in the spring. We never questioned what we were doing to the underground water. It was normal practice; if we didn't follow it, we'd lose our backing from the development committee and from the co-operatives. I no longer made decisions according to the needs of the soil or my animals. I was preoccupied with the possibility of managerial errors which could ruin us. [2]

By this time, state programs went through the Common Agricultural Policy (CAP) of the European Economic Community (EEC, founded in 1957). Together the European member states guaranteed prices, offered aid for exports, and enacted limitations on imports. Through most of the 1970s agricultural revenues grew in tandem with production, and France, the country that benefited most from the CAP, emerged as the second agricultural exporter in the world after the United States: a stunning accomplishment for a country whose farming, at the end of World War II, still had much in common with its medieval past.

Yet this economic success, built upon the governmental initiatives of the 1960s, became incompatible with the international economy by the end of the 1970s. According to Bové, the CAP guaranteed cereal growers high prices within the Common Market. . . . Above all, their income from exports was guaranteed at internal prices, any shortfalls of the world price below the European being compensated with subsidies.

This policy soon led to an overproduction of cereals, which had to be sold on the international market. . . . The subsidies given to exports—financed by European taxpayers—were totally perverse, as they fueled speculation on the world commodity exchanges and became a barrier to attempts by developing countries to be self-sufficient in food.[3]

European farmers eventually produced massive surpluses and faced falling prices on markets regulated by stricter international accords. In 1980, Rapport Manssholt, the vice-president of the EEC commission charged with agricultural questions, wrote a report titled "Five Million Too Many Farmers." The report envisaged still larger farms and investment subsidies for the most productive growers with a plan for further improvements to augment their income to the level prevalent in the economic region. Regulations of 1988 envisaged the decrease of the agricultural surface by 20 percent. Subsidies were accorded in proportion to the loss of revenue caused by these new regulations, thus favoring the largest farms able to sustain the removal of land from production. The new CAP adopted in 1992 changed the system from guaranteed prices—which on account of the rigidity of the mechanisms of subventions, it was determined, led to overproduction—to a further allocation of funds to large producers able to put land in fallow and slaughter part of their cattle.

Falling agricultural prices continued to weigh on the smallest French farmers such that by 1993–1995, 40 percent of them had revenue below the legal minimum salary. Farmers, of course, have much undeclared revenue. Yet the low returns stem from the fact that the agricultural population declined more slowly than administrators envisioned. More and more growers marry non-agriculturalists, making the autonomous family farm ever more a myth of the past. Competition has led them to augment their hours of work, complement their incomes through industry and tourism, and go through privations to maintain their lands. French farmers, like their peers around the world, continue to eke out a living on the land even when economic logic points in another direction. Half of the farms have someone working in another sector of the economy. More and more it is women who work as teachers or nurses to add to the farm revenue.

In addition to the precarious economic situation of many farmers, the development of capitalist agriculture since the 1960s has also had adverse environmental consequences. Better equipment for plowing has exposed the soil to erosion. As cattle rearing declines so does the natural restoration of the humus content from animals. Growers thus buy even heavier machines to continue plowing effectively but only compound the problem. The agricultu-

ral revolution, in putting an end to the autonomous self-sustaining system of
the past, has created a perpetual and self-defeating need for industrial inputs.
When asked about maize, a popular crop because of its extraordinarily high
yields, François Dufour pointed out that it

> is very demanding in "inputs" of fertilizer, herbicides, and pesticides. . . . The
> soil, plants and parasitic insects have developed resistances to these chemical
> treatments.
>   Maize, being a summer plant, needs a lot of water. In some areas planted
> with this crop, agricultural irrigation uses 80 percent of the water supply.
>   In winter, fast growing ray grass is sown; this also needs a lot of nitrogen.
> So there's a harvest in October and one in April, creating more work for the
> farmer. Soil that is producing two crops which are greedy for water loses its
> humus, becomes heavier, requires stronger machinery to till, and is more sus-
> ceptible to extremes of weather. Eventually the ground just gets clogged up
> and fulfills no function other than holding up the plants: the rest is done by
> chemicals.[4]

In Brittany, subsistence agriculture reliant on multiple crops, in imitation of
the diversity of natural ecosystems, had been the norm for centuries. Well
into the twentieth century, a dense rural population continued to farm buckwheat and potatoes on lands of shale and sandy loam that would have been
left more economically in grasses for livestock. After World War II, state
officials and the farmers' organizations began to consider this family-
oriented agriculture archaic and its people poor. They organized large cooperatives, associations, and vegetable markets. The state policies of the 1960s,
which made it economically beneficial for smallholders to retire and allow
their lands to be folded into the farms of market-oriented growers, helped
Brittany emerge as a model of intensive, dynamic, and entrepreneurial farming. But as Breton farmers, like those across France, dropped the agricultural
lines in which they were uncompetitive and specialized in what they could do
at lowest cost and highest return, the province became the site of some of the
worst ecological problems. The Breton pork industry, according to Dufour,
generated

B. Lalonde

> animal excrements . . . equivalent to a human population of 35,000 million
> inhabitants. . . . Normally, animal feces are good fertilizer . . . but excrement
> produced by animals in industrial buildings, housed not on straw but on duck-
> board, is more difficult to use. . . . It's smelly, laden with heavy metals, and
> often contains undigested residues of antibiotics. . . . The area of land available
> to absorb it is insufficient. . . . As a result, thousands of tons of nitrogen are
> released into the air (as ammonia). . . . Surface and underground water pollu-
> tion is such that a report in 1995, drawn up at the request of local groups,
> indicates that if present-day farming trends persist, Brittany will have to close
> down three-quarters of its drinking water supply network to meet the European
> norm of 50 mg of nitrates per liter. And that's not a particularly severe restric-

tion—the World Health Organization strongly discourages babies and pregnant women from drinking water that contains only 25 mg of nitrates per liter.[5]

The contradictions between capitalist farming and the ecological equilibrium has also led to foods with negative or badly controlled consequences for health due to pesticides and derivatives of genetically modified organisms (GMOs). New problems emerge as cattle rearing and dairy production decline across the agrarian landscape and become concentrated in the most efficient industrial enterprises. According to Bové,

> antibiotics are essential medicines for human and animal health, but in some husbandry regimes they're used for other purposes: as growth promoters, to resist microbial infections, to compensate for the poor general health of the herd, and because an animal's own immune system has been weakened. In addition, there's the intensification of farm productivity: a cow "pushed" to produce 8,000 to 10,000 kilos of milk a year becomes much weaker, and more susceptible to all sorts of health hazards, than a cow producing 6,000.[6]

Food safety, in a word, can no longer be taken for granted. According to Bové, it was this issue that galvanized such widespread support for the action against the McDonald's in Millau.

> There was so much popular opposition, linked to people's growing anxieties about what was happening to the food chain—mad cow disease, Belgian chickens poisoned with benzodioxin, salmonella scares, GMOs—that the European Parliament actually held firm. When the WTO deadline expired in the summer of 1999, the US slapped a retaliatory 100 percent surcharge on a long list of European products—Roquefort cheese among them. This was a huge question locally—not just for the sheep's milk producers, but for the whole Larzac region.
> When we said we would protest by dismantling the half-built McDonald's in our town, everyone understood why—the symbolism was too strong. It was for proper food against junk food (*malbouffe*), agricultural workers against multinationals.[7]

TAIWAN

Following Japan's defeat in 1945, Taiwan was returned to Chinese governance. Most on the island greeted this act of retrocession with joy, but the ruling Nationalist Party (KMT), under the leadership of Chiang Kai-shek, quickly squandered any sense of goodwill. Acting with a heavy hand, Chiang's delegated governor to the island took charge of all industry as well as key areas of trade. He dismantled and shipped factories and infrastructure to China to be sold or redeployed. He nationalized property belonging to the

Japanese as well as comprador Taiwanese, including the sugar mills and attached farmland. He alienated native elites by treating educated islanders with suspicion and barring them from government service. On the streets the security forces treated the public roughly. Frustration grew when, in early 1947, news spread of the beating of a widowed street peddler at the hands of government agents. When troops fired upon protesters, the local population rebelled. In the weeks that followed some thirty thousand were killed and much of the native political leadership was eliminated. Political repression was then accompanied by rank economic mismanagement. The KMT plundered the Japanese Bank of Taiwan and printed money with abandon to cover the costs of its bloated administration and finance the ongoing civil war at home. Annual inflation soon exceeded 1000 percent.

When Communist forces took the mainland city of Shanghai in 1949, Chiang Kai-shek, along with two million soldiers, officials, national representatives, and their families, departed for Taiwan. By the new year, the KMT's reputation could not have sunk lower as the US cut off support and waited for the People's Liberation Army to take the island. The KMT's strategic value was resuscitated, however, in June 1950 when war broke out on the Korean Peninsula. President Truman ordered the US Navy into the straits separating Taiwan from the mainland and for the duration of the Cold War the KMT's survival was a key element in US Far East strategic planning.

The US, which promoted the doctrine of growth through trade, pressed its allies and satellites everywhere to orient their economies toward its market. Washington, DC, sent economic and technical advisers to the world's capitals to direct industrial, agricultural, and trade policy. It encouraged Taiwan to peg its currency to the dollar, sent millions in development aid, and granted the island's producers privileged access to American consumers. Washington even urged Taiwan to reestablish trade links with Japan.

At the same time, the Pentagon and the US State Department brought Taiwan under its military umbrella and, in the global struggle against Communism, turned a blind eye to the KMT's domestic authoritarian path. From 1948 to the mid-1980s, the KMT single-handedly ran the island. Unifying party and state, it enforced martial law, prevented open and free elections, prohibited the formation of opposition political parties, and imprisoned political opponents. It used its power to maintain control over key industries and the banks and through these instruments the KMT subordinated the economy to its long-term agenda.

What followed was quite extraordinary. Taiwan's economy grew 10 percent annually from 1960 to 1979. In contrast to France, where the agricultural sector grew faster than did the industrial, the main driver of growth in Taiwan was manufacturing, which in the years 1963–1972 expanded annually at 18.6 percent, and in the decades before and after at just under 12 percent. Expansion of agriculture was modest, but still enough to keep the food supply in line with demand, thereby dampening inflation, reducing the import bill, and most importantly releasing labor to the factories. However, the state's persistent squeezing and diversion of agricultural incomes and savings to industry prevented farmers from becoming a significant market for manufacturers. Instead of relying on domestic demand to drive industrial growth, the KMT exploited the much larger and wealthier consumers of postwar North America and, as they recovered, Western Europe and Japan. In short, agriculture served the needs of industrial growth, and that is how the KMT wanted it.

In 1950, before the Taiwan miracle broached the horizon, the party faced a seemingly insurmountable set of problems. Two million refugees—mostly soldiers—had just arrived who, along with Taiwan's already significant urban population, had to be fed, housed, and clothed. Demand for manufactures and food was great, to be sure, yet household incomes were sorely stretched. Manufacturing was underdeveloped on account of decades of Japanese neglect. Agriculture—once the bright spot of the economy—was in disarray: irrigation systems were run-down, modern fertilizers were in short supply, and farming incomes were down because the island no longer had preferential access to the Japanese market.

Despite its problems, farming offered the KMT the best prospects for jump-starting growth. It was the largest sector of the economy by far, producing and employing more than all others combined, and it had proven itself in the recent past capable of sustaining exports and meeting domestic food needs. Yet left to their own devices, peasants were unlikely to make the investments that future development demanded.

For their part, US political advisers, eager to eradicate rural discontent and inoculate the island against Communism, supported the KMT's growth-oriented policies with aid but demanded the eradication of tenancy through a comprehensive "land-to-the-tiller" program. The KMT obliged and one of its first major acts was to lower rent to 37.5 percent of the main crop. The rent reduction campaign pushed the price of land down to levels that afforded many tenants the opportunity to purchase farms and smallholders to acquire more land. The state then capped individual holdings at a diminutive 2.9 hectares and required that land in excess be either rented or sold or sold to the state for redistribution. With rents low, and tenant rights greatly strengthened, most landlords now opted to depart and sold off their land. All in all 140,000 hectares belonging to 106,000 landlords was acquired by the state at roughly 60 percent of prewar prices. Landlords were compensated partly in bonds that yielded 4 percent interest and expired after ten years, and partly in government enterprise shares. At its completion, land reform redistributed one-quarter of all farmland, with a value equivalent to 13 percent of GDP.

Subsequently, the US promoted Taiwan as a model of non-revolutionary reform.

The rigor with which the KMT took up land reform was surprising given its past resistance to it. On the one hand, the price demanded for ongoing US patronage and protection was the thoroughgoing redistribution of land. The threat of complete defeat at the hands of the CCP had galvanized Chiang Kai-shek in 1950 to reconstruct the party from top to bottom, bringing it completely under his control and in the process breaking any resistance to reform. On the other hand, the elected KMT representatives from the mainland, who dominated parliament on Taiwan and had opposed land reform back home, had no vested interest in preserving Taiwan's landholding system. They were also eager to break the native landlords' hold over local society. Thus, these former obstructionists enthusiastically took up land reform in 1950 as a tool against the native opposition. There was of course the added benefit of earning the support of millions of peasants.

While land reform served critical political needs, it was also intended to be a significant piece in the larger puzzle of industrialization. Given Taiwan's poverty (average annual per capita income of one hundred US dollars per annum), and its small population (eight million), supply-side rather than demand-side factors—high savings and high investment rather than domestic consumption—would have to drive growth, at least in the early decades. Yet capital was scarce and mostly locked up in farms. By removing landlords and, in the process, strengthening the state's rural presence, the KMT was by 1952 in a position to siphon off rural savings and divert them to manufacturing and infrastructure. The KMT consciously reintroduced mechanisms perfected by the Japanese—land tax, price controls, and hidden fees and levies—to force and then appropriate savings.

To capture the rural surplus, the land tax was set at colonial-era rates. For every yen of land tax formerly owed to the colonial government, the KMT demanded eleven and a half kilograms of rice and the additional sale to the government of twelve kilograms at a price consistently 25 to 30 percent below wholesale. Thereafter, the government matched the land tax to rising yields, doubling it by the 1960s. Though burdensome, the main instrument for procuring rural savings was not these charges but the KMT's rice-for-fertilizer barter system.

Government-owned enterprises monopolized the manufacture of fertilizer, while the state controlled the importation of essential phosphates and nitrates. On this basis, the government was able to allocate 70 to 80 percent of fertilizer to paddy farmers, where it hoped to see the most gains, but also to charge the peasants above cost. Farmers were required to purchase fertilizer using rice, at an exchange rate fixed by the government. Across the 1950s and 1960s, rice farmers paid the equivalent of 50 percent more for fertilizer than their Japanese counterparts and twice the amount paid by farmers in

Southeast and South Asia. Even as the cost of fertilizer production fell, the government kept the price high. By one estimate the system accounted for 60 to 70 percent of all rice collected by the state. In the 1950s, total state rice receipts from taxes, levies, and the hidden fertilizer charge were approximately 70 percent of the total rice surplus and exceeded annual revenues from the national income tax. In other words, the KMT proved better expropriators than the Japanese, taking an amount roughly equivalent to total prewar rent payments, or about one-quarter of total rice production.

The surtax and barter systems were unpopular but necessary to feed the large non-farming population. About 55 percent of government rice went just to feed military and government families. Another 25 percent was used to stabilize the public market, helping to keep food and wage costs low. Finally, about one-fifth was sold overseas to earn the foreign exchange needed to cover interest on loans and pay for vital imports. At their peak, rice exports contributed one-fifth of Taiwan's foreign reserves.

Like the CCP, the KMT eradicated the unproductive landlord class and took charge of the rural surplus in order to invest in manufacturing. An estimated 25 percent of farm output was transferred through various schemes to the nonfarm sector. As investment in manufacturing rose to new heights, agriculture shrank as a share of GDP. It fell to 17 percent by 1972 and 9 percent by 1980. Agriculture's share of exports fell accordingly from 95 percent in 1952 to 20 percent in 1970 and, whereas half the population was employed in farming in 1950, only one-third remained there in 1970. Remarkably, a transformation that had taken several centuries in Great Britain and a century and a half in the US was over within a couple of decades in Taiwan.

Even as its share of GDP shrank, agricultural output grew. The highest sustained rate of growth was 5 percent. The rice harvest rose 43 percent between 1953, by which time farming had recovered from wartime depression, and 1965. Tea output nearly doubled, the sweet potato harvest rose 37 percent, and banana production grew a staggering 4.7 times. The number of pigs raised for slaughter rose 65 percent. Meanwhile, the cultivated area rose only 2 percent and the double-cropped area only 3 percent. Consequently, whereas in 1946 every hectare of farmland supported 4.2 persons of the agricultural population and 7.3 persons outside farming, by 1966 those numbers were 6.5 and 14.5.

This was achieved while raising caloric intake. The daily per capita consumption of food surpassed prewar records to reach 2,380 calories in 1965 (compared to 3,140 in the US) and daily consumption of protein rose to 61.2 grams, or three-quarters of the Japanese diet. All the while, the export of specialized crops grew. The government on advice from the US promoted canneries in mushrooms, asparagus, bamboo, water chestnuts, and pineapple and farmers obliged by growing these foods until foreign earnings reached eighty million US dollars annually and accounted for nearly 12 percent of total exports. In short, agriculture supported more people, fed them better, and sustained exports, *while* meeting government demands in tax and driving industrial growth.

Had land reform provided Taiwan's peasants with farms but not required that they make their labor more productive (by cutting costs), farmers sooner or later would have succumbed to diminishing returns on their effort and come up against a ceiling much as it had done under Japanese rule. But farmers were denied the ability to withdraw their labor from the market, and to shield themselves from competitive pressures, by the relatively high cost of land. To set up operations, former tenants found themselves having to secure government loans that were strategically priced (the total annual charge of these was an affordable 6 percent of the entire rice harvest) to require cash cropping. In other words, producers had little choice but to grow the crops that brought the greatest return on their total investment, to introduce cost-saving methods, and to expand output. Much as European settlers to the American Midwest were compelled to produce for the market by the debts they took on when buying land, so too Taiwanese households were compelled by interest payments, taxes, fees, and levies to do the same. The extraordinary responsiveness of Taiwanese farmers to market demands was therefore the effect of deliberate policies to prevent the beneficiaries of land reform from either fully withdrawing from the market, or retaining any more land or labor for personal consumption than was minimally necessary.

While land reform obliged tenants to purchase land with loans, the repayment of which was calculated to last a decade or more, government-controlled rice prices along with the new fiscal burdens, in the form of taxes and fees, placed pressure on savings. Squeezed between high costs and low prices, producers had no choice but to reduce their expenditures and raise their output. They purchased new fertilizers because these provided the best gain in harvest for the cost, but they also leaned heavily on their cheapest asset—family labor—searching for ways to expand the working year. Thus, like the villagers of Nanjing in 1950s south China, Taiwanese peasants rushed to buy winnowers and threshers to alleviate pressures on labor at harvest time and allow them to plant a second crop of rice. By the end of the 1950s agricultural households devoted 25 percent more time to farm work.

They also adjusted what they grew. No longer restricted to planting rice, sweet potato, and sugarcane, and forced by new costs to grow what gave them the highest returns, they converted fields to more profitable crops. Correspondingly, regional specialization became more pronounced. Rice and sugarcane were dropped in the north, where farmers focused on perishable vegetables and pork for the Taipei market. Southern farmers added or switched to fruits (pineapple, banana, wax apple, mango, lychee, etc.) and vegetables (mushroom and asparagus) to supply the new canneries. Across the island, the harvest of prewar staples rice and sweet potato fell from 70 to 40 percent of total farm output as vegetables and livestock rose from 6 to 10 and 10 to 30 percent respectively.

In their efforts to raise their incomes, farmers increased their use of bio-cides until the Joint Commission on Rural Reconstruction reported (without a sense of alarm), "Today there are no flies in Taiwan. The new technology requirement for this achievement was very simple. A small spray gun and some DDT powder, which most children can operate."[8] Farmers' associa-tions pushed new cultivars that included rice strains that responded better to chemical fertilizers. All along the way, the government supported smallhold-ers with loans for capital and land acquisitions and plenty of technical educa-tion.

At no point were farmers permitted to rest. Even as they raised yields and earnings, the squeeze on family income continued as the state strategically adjusted taxes, fees, and costs. The pressure on households to raise yields was compounded by the size of their tiny farms, which despite increases in yields left the typical household after consumption only 60 percent of their output to sell. In their effort to stabilize rural society, the crafters of land reform had sidestepped the problem of farm scale and purposely redistributed land to all willing cultivators. "To safeguard the island as a base of opera-tions for national recovery," reflected Governor-General Chen, "we required social stability, and the first prerequisite had to be satisfactory solution of the problem of the people's livelihood." Consequently, though three hectares was regarded as the minimum necessary for successful commercial farming, and farms less than one hectare were not to be expected to make ends meet, the percentage of holdings under one hectare rose from 46 to 63 between 1939 and 1955, while a mere 4 percent of farms exceeded three hectares. The share of farms under one hectare rose higher still to two-thirds in 1965, at which time the average farm was only 1.05 hectares. Adding a further squeeze, the island's population doubled in the 1950s as the death rate plum-meted.

No manner of farming could mop up the excess labor implied by these statistics. However, concurrent developments came to the farmers' rescue. As industrialization took off, capitalists set up manufacturing operations in the countryside to take advantage of the rural underemployed. The poorest families with the least land were the first to send children to work in facto-ries. Soon, those with less than half a hectare took 44 percent of their income in factory wages. In the typical rice-growing town of Xin Xing, in central Taiwan, only 5 percent of working adults earned money off-farm in the 1950s. Yet, twenty years later, two-thirds earned wages off-farm and two-thirds of that income was earned in export furniture and textile factories. As in France, farmers found they could survive only by having household mem-bers employed in other sectors. The structure of rural household income was turned on its head as the source of earnings shifted from 95 percent farming to 85 percent non-farming, until only one in twenty Xin Xing residents self-identified as farmers. As industrial and trade policies paid off, seasonal manufacturing employment became permanent and young folk permanently abandoned their small towns and villages for industrial centers like Gaoxiong and Taipei.

We have seen how peasants in earlier periods rounded out farm income with domestic manufacturing work, often performed in the winter months, and usually deploying low technique. Time and time again, we saw how this route to manufacturing dead-ended, first as grain cultivators failed to cut production costs and then as rising grain prices reduced aggregate demand and drove down manufacturing wages. But conditions were different in 1950s Taiwan (as in postwar France). Combining low wages and targeted import tariffs Taiwan manufacturing took off in the 1960s as Japan, Europe, and North America entered the postwar boom. Despite political efforts to keep wages low, which ranged from outlawing unions to controlling rice prices, extraordinarily high rates of manufacturing investment inevitably soaked up the surplus rural labor and pushed wages up.

With labor leaving the farm at record rates in the late 1960s, those who remained found themselves hard-pressed to tend to their fields. The system of intensive high-yielding farming that followed land reform had always strained family labor at peak times. So long as children worked in factories nearby they could be called upon to return home to help with harvests and planting. But as the young moved into factories permanently, their parents were forced to hire help and, consequently, they bid up farm wages. Across the island, the wage share of total farm production costs rose from 39 to 44.5 percent and the painfully intensive labor methods, which had hitherto proved so successful, were unsustainable.

In the southern Taiwan village of Meinung, noted for both rice and tobacco growing, farmers reported having not only to pay higher wages but also to purchase costly movie tickets, cigarettes, and beer for their farmhands. Having committed to the market, however, these farmers had no choice but to adapt to changing conditions. They pushed to reduce their reliance on hired hands by mechanizing as many tasks as they could. One Meinung farmer reflected on this new phenomenon: "The money to mechanize comes from tobacco-growing. . . . If farmers own machinery it is not necessary to trouble other people or rely on them."[9]

The small size of Taiwan's farms, however, called for appropriately scaled technologies. In the 1950s, hand or walking tractors had proved popular in those households that both double-cropped and made the early leap into off-farm wage work. These relatively cheap two-wheeled, gasoline-powered machines—similar to moto-mowers and rototillers—enhance soil by breaking up earth clods and humus, working over weeds and roots, and aerating the soil to speed up the release of organic matter. Operated by a single man who walked behind and controlled direction and speed from handlebars, these diminutive machines eliminated the reliance on draft buffalo, whose feed costs were rising, and allowed the farmer to reduce his reliance on wage labor at critical times of the year. But the switch to hand tractors only came when labor costs rose. Thus, despite their obvious utility, and their manufacture locally, only ten thousand were in use in 1964. As the labor market tightened that number rose to seventeen thousand in 1967 and forty-five thousand in 1975. Over time, these machines grew in size and horsepower, allowing their operators to speed up their pace and work the soil more deeply and thoroughly. When not used in the field, their engines were adapted to power water pumps for irrigation.

Walking tractors were the most significant but not the only labor-saving tools. Power sprayers for pesticides and herbicides numbered 45,400 in 1974. Power threshers, of which there were 146 operating in 1972, numbered 27,558 three years later. Automated seedling transplanters were introduced and then improved as farmers replaced two-row with four- and then six-row planters. Even miniaturized combine harvesters were introduced. By the mid-1970s the expenditure of human power as a percentage of all energy outlays in farming was cut from two-thirds to one-third, while animal power was reduced from one-third to 7 percent of all outlays. Yields no longer rose as fast, to be sure, but the great reduction in labor inputs implied significant advances in labor productivity and rural wages for the first time. By mechanizing, farmers managed to maintain the high yields achieved by their parents while releasing young men and women to the industrial boomtowns.

There were to be sure regional exceptions, such as the farms along the island's remote and narrow eastern littoral and farming among the island's aboriginal population. Separated by steep mountains from the industrial cities of the west coast, and less touched by industrialization, east coast operations remained less mechanized, more labor intensive, and their communities poorer. Farming among the aboriginal populations was initially of little concern to the KMT, which waited until 1968 to effect change. That year the Aboriginal Reserve Land law abrogated tribal rights to land that was not cultivated. Prohibited by the same law from renting land to Han Chinese, aborigines were compelled either to surrender ownership or abandon slash-and-burn for intensive farming. Land confiscated was leased to corporations for lumber. Gradually, these districts were opened to external forces and compelled to change.

In 1979, the ruling KMT had much to celebrate. Commercial farming was in full swing, requiring farmers to match each other's productivity gains by shifting crops, squeezing out savings at every opportunity, and generally improving their methods. Yet in the 1980s international conditions were changing in ways that required the reorientation of government priorities and policies, while the problem of farming scale remained unresolved. As manufacturing exports grew by leaps and bounds, the government came under pressure—primarily from the US—to address its gargantuan holding of dollars and its massive trade surplus. In response Taiwan acquiesced to partially liberalizing its domestic food market. Despite all of its gains, however, Taiwan's agricultural sector since 1950, unlike manufacturing, had only become less globally competitive. Farming in 1950s Latin America, Australia, and the USA had already secured unparalleled advantages in economies of scale. Those only grew in the decades that followed.

In Taiwan, state planners were aware of the problems of scale in farming as early as the 1960s. But it was only in the 1970s that they introduced policies to encourage the formation of larger operations that were better suited to the adoption of more capital-intensive technologies. Chairman of the Joint Commission on Rural Reconstruction T. H. Shen remarked, "It is generally accepted that the ideal size of a family farm in Taiwan should be about three hectares, with which it would be able to buy a power tiller and other farm machines for its use."[10] Shen and other economists understood that without reforms to affect farm size, the returns on capital invested in machinery would diminish until Taiwanese farmers were caught between falling earnings and the rising cost of capital. As labor and land productivity rose across the 1970s, farm capital productivity did in fact fall.

To overcome obstacles of scale, the government recommended greater cooperation and coordination among farmers. It promoted "crop zones" within which neighboring farmers simulated large operations by planting the same crop while sharing machinery and irrigation. To improve earnings, the government also fostered improvements in rural infrastructure to reduce spoilage and waste. Then, to guard against the deleterious effects of partible inheritance, which over decades fragmented fields and properties, villagers were encouraged to exchange equivalently valued land with neighbors to form contiguous units. To prevent extreme fragmentation, farm owners were prohibited from dividing fields below a quarter of a hectare. But most dramatically, the government raised the cap on farm size and introduced programs that encouraged farmers to augment their operations through purchases. For the first time since land reform, the state actively promoted the absorption of inefficient by efficient operations.

But unlike in France, these policies failed to raise farm size and at best only partially addressed the problem of fragmentation. By 1984 the average farm was still only 1.12 hectares and less than two out of a hundred farms were more than the minimally desirable three. With 73 percent of farms under a hectare, and two hundred thousand farms less than a third of a hectare, 80 percent of households were reduced to farming part-time and just over 50 percent earned more from sidelines than farm work. The results of efforts to promote coordination among neighbors were equally lackluster.

Few farmers joined cooperatives and those that did soon departed, concluding that sharing machines and irrigation was more trouble than it was worth.

Not stopping to reconsider, the government pushed ahead and announced its Second Stage Land Reform, the main goal of which was a reduction in the number of people employed in farming from 1.3 million to six hundred thousand by the year 2000. Providing long-term, low-interest loans, and giving preference to those seeking to buy land bordering their own, or hoping to buy entire farms, the government hoped to oversee the creation of eighty thousand large farms. The plan fell short, however. In 2000, the number of farm workers had fallen to 669,000 but there was no noticeable increase in the size of farms. In other words, farms had managed to shed sons, daughters, and brothers to manufacturing, construction, and service jobs, but had not grown. Consequently, they remained highly vulnerable in global markets dominated by the gargantuan operations of North and South America especially.

In contrast to De Gaulle, who consciously abandoned small farmers for overall gains in scale, the Taiwanese government has since the mid 1970s cushioned them. After two decades of artificially pushing up production costs, in 1973 the government ended the discriminatory fertilizer barter system. It ended compulsory rice sales and instead offered rice growers a guaranteed "reasonable" price, calculated to give a 20 percent return in 1974. Facing a deficit in the food purchase program, the government tried to cap guaranteed purchases at 970 kilograms per hectare. But this crept upward to 1,400 kilograms by the late 1980s, as the KMT tried to win over farmer support at a time when the island was moving toward greater democracy. By 1994, the rice subsidy program had a total deficit of 4.25 billion US dollars.

Subsidies have been accompanied by targeted import protections. Since 1973 the agricultural authorities have approved all farm imports and import regulations have been imposed on all agricultural imports. Tariffs and subsidies have offered some protection for Taiwanese farmers, at the cost to consumers of nine billion US dollars between 1973 and 1990. Over these years the income transfer to farmers totaled 20 to 30 percent of the value of agricultural output and today farm supports are equivalent to 1 percent of GDP. Nevertheless, rural incomes continued to fall behind, shrinking to two-thirds of urban incomes by the 1990s and subsidies have created surpluses that weigh down on prices. The rice harvests exceeded government targets by three hundred thousand tons in the early 1980s, forcing it to dump accumulated stores overseas at a loss of one hundred million US dollars. Meanwhile, domestic consumers have grown wealthier and have reduced rice consumption in favor of more costly foods, especially meat and fruit.

Even so, farmers face growing competition from overseas and new threats at home. The powerful lobby for US agribusiness has pushed Taiwan to open its doors to imports of fruit, pork, and chicken. Taiwan's government acquiesced if only to prevent retaliation against its highly prized industries and to gain a seat at the World Trade Organization. At home, decades of unrestrained growth has damaged the environment. Industrial waste found its way into Taiwan's rice paddies, leaving high traces of heavy metals such as cadmium while unrestrained use of pesticides, including DDT, damaged wildlife and humans.

Farmers have joined social movements to improve their lot. Concern over the environment drove the first sustained wave of antiauthoritarian and pro-democratic demonstrations in the mid-1980s. In May 1988, farmers staged protests in Taipei on a scale not seen since 1947 to demand universal farm insurance, lower fertilizer prices, more price supports, greater control over the hitherto government-dominated farmers' associations, and liberalization of rules regarding land purchases and sales. As democratic reforms progressed, climaxing with the island's first direct presidential election in 1996, farmers shed the long-standing patron-client relationship that had bound them to the KMT and formed independent political parties and organizations to lobby and pressure the government directly. Politicians have responded. Ahead of the 2011 elections, the incumbent president raised the government's purchasing price for rice in an overt effort to curry favor.

One clear example of farmers' political power is the current prohibition on US beef on the grounds that ractopamine used in its beef industry to produce leaner meat is harmful. The compound—known as a Beta-adrenergic agonist—is banned in the EU, and Taiwanese farmers have deftly worked public opinion to keep US beef out: restaurants serving the local specialty of beef noodle soup prominently advertise that they do not serve it. Yet Taiwan's beef production is modest and most of what is consumed comes from Australia, where ractopamine *is* legal. The real worry among farmers appears to be that a liberalized beef market will open the way for greater imports of US pork, which remains an important source of cash for farmers.

Today, farmers are clearly anxious. Rice growers facing low prices have cut costs perhaps as far as they can go given their miniature farms. The most labor-intensive chores such as harvesting are now subcontracted in an effort to offload capital costs. Many farmers are simply managers of their land. Despite these actions, in some areas, only 4 percent of the sale price of rice is profit. Some small-scale producers have tried to switch to organic farming, a growing market given public concerns over GMOs and highly publicized food scandals at home, across the straits in mainland China, and in Great Britain, where "mad cow" disease broke out after farmers fed cattle bone waste to their herds. But established supply chains and infrastructure favor farming in the mode of the "green revolution," and so far the transition to organic production has been difficult. According to one farmer:

My father is in his seventies now. He still grows a small plot of regular rice. My father always tells me to stop growing organic rice. He says, "Your profits are all eaten up by labor costs. You recover your investment little by little when someone buys a pack or two from you. Your money is spread all over. There is no big money. Your kind of money won't make you a man. Look at me, my rice is sold [to intermediary merchants] when it is still wet in the field. But you, you even do your own drying, staying up all night to check the drying machine. You are working yourself to death."[11]

Another farmer explained the problem of supply chains for organic producers:

In principle, every farmer can produce his own organic fertilizer. In reality, without the necessary machinery and equipment, small farmers cannot mass produce compost and cut down on unit costs. Organic fertilizer production needs certain economies of scale, achieved through an integrated factory, for instance. Once the investment is made, the factory also needs its equipment to run without too much downtime, in order to have a decent return on the investment. That's the only way to drive down the cost of fertilizers.[12]

In conclusion, following several decades of improvement, the future is unsettled for Taiwan's small-scale growers. Significant restructuring of the domestic market (its supply and marketing chains) is required to restore profits. The government—regardless of which of the two dominant parties is in power—is bent on meeting international demands for greater accessibility to Taiwan's prosperous market in order to guarantee Taiwan's manufacturers reciprocal access. Manufacturing, after all, continues to drive Taiwan's growth and as of 2004 employed one-third of the working population. Isolated from the international community (Taiwan's government is only recognized by a handful of countries), leaders are concerned that any rejection of global trade agreements, which inevitably include protocols on agricultural goods, would only further weaken the island's international standing. For now, it seems Taiwan's farmers are fighting a losing battle.

In postwar Taiwan and France, the state pursued policies to redistribute land to families that would rely on their own members to work the fields rather than the supplies of labor located in the countryside. The Taiwanese state acted particularly aggressively to break the grip of landlords over the countryside and prevent them from taking investment funds from the actual tillers. It redistributed income to the mass of smallholders and has contributed over the long term to forging a country with much less inequality than many countries of Europe and North America.

The political leaders of Taiwan and France had different goals in mind. Whereas de Gaulle's technocrats sought to make agriculture more productive, bring down relative food prices, spur mechanization, improve rural standards of living, and induce farmers to leave rural areas, the KMT leadership promoted land redistribution in order to uphold social and political stability in the face of ongoing Communist hostility. As a result, Taiwanese agriculture may have had extraordinarily great output per hectare, but its overall costs were higher, and it has not competed as well on international markets as has French farming.

Both Taiwanese and French agricultural development stimulated postwar industrial takeoffs, but did so in different ways. In France, development proceeded from rising incomes by way of mechanization, rising labor productivity, and the development of domestic agricultural implements and food-processing industries. In Taiwan, the KMT taxed farmers and withdrew their savings to fund manufacturing for export markets. Whereas French industrialization emerged thanks to rising productivity and consumption in agriculture, its demand for machines, its new products to be processed, the workers it shed, and the costs of production it controlled thanks to the output of low-cost staples, the success of Taiwanese manufacturers on international markets raised wages and enticed people away from farms that remained small, relatively labor-intensive, and globally uncompetitive.

But it is especially important to note that in both countries agricultural development proceeded by way of rural indebtedness, much as was the case in the United States. But it is especially important to note that in both countries agricultural development proceeded by way of rural indebtedness, much as was the case in the United States. However, unlike the debt undertaken by the peasants of classical Italy, early modern China and France, and pre-revolutionary Russia, which was unproductively extractive, the upshot of peasant desperation, and kept peasants in thrall to landed classes, the debt of postwar French and Taiwanese farmers was both manageable and put to productive use. Farmers were consequently not only obliged to meet the financial burdens of servicing loans, but at the end of the day were left with sufficient means to sustain improvements year on end. In short, Taiwanese and French farmers, after committing their lands to production for the market rather than local consumption, had to compete with other farmers who had also made this leap. They had no choice but to reduce the costs of their labor by reorganizing their farms and mechanizing as many tasks as they could. In both countries today, this relentless pressure to augment yields and output, and obtain the income to keep farms afloat, has led to mounting surpluses, excessive harvests, and difficulties in making a living.

NOTES

1. José Bové, François Dufour, and Gilles Luneau, *The World Is Not for Sale: Farmers against Junk Food* (London: Verso, 2002), 60.

2. Ibid., 46.

3. Ibid., 62.

4. Ibid., 67.

5. Ibid., 109–10.

6. Ibid., 83.

7. Ibid., 200.

8. Sen-chung Hsieh and Teng-hui Lee, *Agricultural Development and Its Contributions to Economic Growth in Taiwan* (Taipei: Chinese-American Joint Commission on Rural Reconstruction, 1966), 103.

9. Irene Bain, *Agricultural Reform in Taiwan: From Here to Modernity?* (Hong Kong: The Chinese University Press, 1993), 262.

10. Hsieh and Lee, *Agricultural Development*, 101.

11. Quoted in Kuei-Mei Lo and Hsin-Hsing Chen, "Technological Momentum and the Hegemony of the Green Revolution: A Case Study of an Organic Rice Cooperative in Taiwan," *East Asian Science, Technology and Society: An International Journal* 5 (2011), 24.

12. Ibid., 18.

Chapter Ten

Corporate Agriculture

Comparing Brazil and the United States

In today's corporate agriculture, the industries supplying the inputs, the trading houses providing market access, and the banks financing capital investment have decisive influence over farmers. It is the product of domestic government policy and international trade and its agreements, as well as developments in science and technology and local struggles over labor regimes and land.

In the case of the US Midwest and West, the struggle to control land and labor was settled by the 1850s. Because farmers had to take on debt to finance land acquisition, they were driven to produce commodities in the most cost-effective manner possible (see chapter 6). In the South, however, the end to slavery and Reconstruction renewed struggles between planters and laborers. To gain value from their vast plantations, Southern landholders sought to capture the labor of free blacks, as well as whites, in new sharecropping arrangements. The result was a debilitating regime made possible by the wholesale political disenfranchisement of blacks and marginalization of poor whites. Planters profited from the export of even more cotton than they had achieved with the output of slaves. However, the repression of the rural standard of living and the disincentive to improve farming caused long-term economic stagnation. While industrialization accelerated in the North, aided in large part by rapid transformations in farming methods, the South remained trapped in agrarian poverty into the 1940s. It took the New Deal reforms, the civil rights movement, and infrastructural investments to extricate the South from its torpor.

In Brazil, the progressive political forces of the late nineteenth century saw in the highly efficient and mechanized farms of the US Midwest a model

for reform and national development. They understood that the slave plantation was a drag on economic and political development and that planters
constituted the chief barrier to modernization. Yet securing alternate sources
of labor for the creation of value from the land posed a significant challenge.
As in the US South, Brazilian planters in the aftermath of slavery sought to
lure and then capture farm workers through sharecropping and debt. On this
basis, they survived the abolition of slavery and continued to profit from
exports of sugar, cotton, tobacco, and especially coffee. Only in the twentieth
century with new government policies did planters begin to modernize their
methods. Today, economic liberalization and beneficial export conditions
have opened the way to the development of corporate farming, especially in
the Amazon. Yet the countryside remains highly stratified and unevenly
developed, with massive commercial soybean and cattle operations coexist-
ing side by side with subsistence peasants and dirt farmers.

In exploring these developments, we proceed by answering a series of
questions. How did the Brazilian pattern of settlement and economic development evolve following the end of Portuguese rule in the early 1820s and
the abolition of slavery in 1888? In the United States, how did the conflicts
between former slaves and planters shape the evolution of agriculture in the
South? In the rest of the country, what sorts of accomplishments and crises
were generated by the competition of capitalist farmers for market share?
What concatenation of economic forces and government policies led to the
unprecedented agricultural breakthroughs in the interior of Brazil, California,
and farming more generally in the United States? Lastly, what new economic
and ecological problems does corporate farming now face?

BRAZIL

> Nothing is so sublime—and nothing pardons our Paulista [São Paulo] pride so
> well—as the sea of coffee trees in rows, placed to substitute the native for-
> est. . . . But the golden tree only produces at the expense of the blood of the
> land. The production of the red pulp is exuberant, but insatiable of humus. An
> octopus with millions of tentacles, coffee rolls over the forest and makes it
> vanish.[1]

> The current agricultural model imposed on Brazil by the forces of capital and
> big business is detrimental to the interests of the people. It transforms every-
> thing into commodities: food, goods of nature (such as water, land, biodiver-
> sity and seeds) and it is organized for the sole purpose of increasing the profits
> of big business, transnational corporations and banks.[2]

As if to underscore its origins as a site of colonial extraction, Brazil is named
after a commodity-bearing tree, the Pau-brazil (brazilwood). It produces a
high-quality red dye that was once in great demand in Europe. Those adven-

turers who gathered the dye called the region where it grew most densely *terra do brasil*, thus making literal Brazil's association with wealth gained by the exploitation of the land.

The dye was the first in a long chain of South American export crops, which included sugar, indigo, cotton, tobacco, coffee, and rubber. In chapter 5, we described the process by which the cultivation and manufacture of sugarcane was brought to the Caribbean and Brazil, highlighting the early difficulty faced by landholders in their endeavor to secure profits from their estates. We noted that these planters turned to African slaves after failing to attract European farm laborers or entice and bend the native population to the rigors and boredom of wage labor and sharecropping. Finally, we showed that after some trial and error, slavery proved highly profitable when managed with an eye to lengthening the time and maximizing the effort of work.

Independence in 1825 did little to change the social character of Brazil's ruling class, or the economic course set by planters and merchants in the seventeenth century. Global demand first for sugar and later for coffee provided the basis for landholder profits, while control of a highly exploitable working population and access to cheap land provided the instruments for realizing them. By the mid-nineteenth century, there were two million slaves in a population of 7.2 million. These being the primary source of their wealth, planters' political interests were narrowly focused. Their reliance on slaves opposed planters to abolition, unrestricted immigration, and political liberalization more generally. With their earnings hanging on trade, however, Brazil's planters also advocated low tariffs and the unrestricted movement of goods into and out of the country. Brazil's first university chair in economics was occupied in 1808 by a champion of Adam Smith and the free market, William Godwin. Political liberals abroad, the planters were ultimately illiberal at home.

To protect their economic position, planters worked assiduously after independence to occupy and influence political office at all levels. They ran for and secured seats in state and federal government and financed the political careers of acolytes. They leveraged for political effect the dependency of local governments on export taxes. Because the robustness of their budgets was bound to the level of agricultural exports, for their part Brazil's politicians were reluctant to implement policies that threatened the plantation economy, even in the absence of pressure from the planter class. They heeded the planters' championing of slavery and other systems of bonded labor, the calls for controlling the migration of Europeans laborers, who would take and drive up the price of land, the arguments for low taxes, and the lobbying for government investment in railways and ports to cheapen the cost of moving the bulky commodities out of the country.

Despite their power, however, planters were not free to choose and impose labor regimes or agricultural systems as they saw fit. They had to contend with resistance from workers, who often included slaves, just as they also had to adapt to changing global appetites and international competition. Slavery remained common to the sugar-growing areas of the North into the 1880s because land remained sufficiently productive, new slaves were available, despite the effects of Britain's 1833 ban on the trade, and because well-established systems of oversight and management were in place to ensure production. However, slavery proved less adaptable to other regions and other crops, forcing landholders to experiment with other labor systems. Yet, they were consistent in their search for means to restrict the mobility of workers in order to squeeze their workforce by political means. The character of this struggle is clear in the development of the rubber and coffee trades, to which we will now turn.

The perfection of rubber vulcanization in the 1840s and the invention of the pneumatic tire presented opportunities for great profit in the industrial West but also in the world's tropical regions (see chapter 7). Yet those Brazilians who hoped to profit from the labor of rubber tappers (known in Portuguese as *seringueiros*) found that the conditions of this work resisted their efforts to manage the labor process for quantity and quality. The Brazilian rubber tree (*hevea*) does not naturally grow in clusters but isolated and separated by considerable distances. Consequently, a single worker at best could tap only 150 trees in a year (many only managed half that number), gathering at most one thousand kilos of latex. The tapper did this by trudging through the forest, locating the trees, and cutting paths between them. He visited each tree every two days or more, cutting into its cambium, and hanging a tin can below to receive the latex. To cure the latex for transportation, the tapper dripped the emulsion onto a rough wooden pole rotated over an open fire until a large, coagulated ball was formed. All of this was done on site in a crude and rudimentary manner. The natural dispersion of the trees, coupled with their modest output, rendered too costly any scheme to oversee the tappers to ensure best methods. Unable to dictate the pace or quality of work, those with the funds were unwilling to invest in slaves or to hire laborers whose living expenses they would have to cover. The problem was succinctly summed up in 1843 by the assembly deputy Manuel Antônio Galvão:

> You want to oblige these simpletons [the tappers] to work? Are these the people that the noble deputy is very seriously going to talk political economy to, inviting them to pick up a hoe and go to work? For them there are many forests, full of fruit and game. . . . Who is to stop these inhabitants of the forest from going a few leagues farther on, from disappearing into the forest and making their clearing when the fog comes, so that the police won't see the smoke, and then remaining there two years planting and contenting themselves with their manioc bread?[3]

This lament expressed the frustration of those who wanted but could not locate a cheap yet disciplinable labor force to work a full day, day after day, at an assigned task, to deliver high-quality latex in predictable amounts. The merchant or landowner wanted something akin to a plantation slave or factory worker, but he found the basic conditions of production to be unamenable. As a result, the best that men like Galvão could manage was to buy the finished latex while developing means to acquire or compel loyalty from tappers. In other words, they had to find a means to discipline work without resorting to oversight.

The rubber buyers or *aviadores* who orchestrated the collection and shipping of latex to the coast were themselves under pressure to secure a steady and predictable supply of good-quality latex. Many had loans to service and they all had to cover the costs of their steamboats and storehouses. To this end, the *aviadores* advanced cash, tools, and basic supplies to the often impoverished *seringueiros* at the commencement of each tapping season in order to obligate them contractually to deliver their rubber. However, because of the ease with which the *seringueiro* absconded or adulterated the product, or simply abandoned tapping for subsistence farming when prices fell too low, the regime was fraught with risk. In the absence of constraints, the *aviadores* resorted to violence and extralegal coercion to ensure deliveries and to keep interloping buyers at bay. In the words of one observer, the rubber trade "imposed greater loss of health, life, and material than an active military campaign, and the human suffering is appalling."[4]

Big rubber merchants at the coast, like their American and European buyers, openly derided the *seringueiro* system. They observed that tappers were insufficiently regimented to produce large volumes of unadulterated product whereas the avaricious and often brutal manner of the *aviadores* undermined any attempt to improve output or quality. Foreign capitalists were at the forefront of efforts therefore to remedy these deficiencies, hoping to wring out higher profits by regimenting labor on plantations. Describing their project, the business journal *India Rubber World* noted first that "conditions existing in the vast and sparsely settled and loosely governed districts in which the rubber trees grow . . . are most unfavorable to foreigners investing their money there." The author continued, "Not the least important feature of the coming development is likely to be the placing of the rubber lands under private control and a more intelligent, systematic and economical supervision of rubber gathering, with the result of rendering supplies more certain and regular, and prices somewhat lower and less liable to fluctuation."[5]

Investors founded Comptoir Colonial Français, Amazon Rubber Estates Ltd., and Rubber Estates of Para, yet the dreams of would-be rubber barons crashed. The distance between naturally growing *hevea* trees kept endemic leaf blight at bay. On the man-made, densely planted estates, however, the blight leapt rapidly from tree to tree, destroying vast outlays of capital in a matter of months. Significant energy was invested in efforts to defeat the disease, but all failed and fortunes were lost. The American industrialist Henry Ford abandoned the eponymous Fordlandia plantation after hemorrhaging twenty million dollars. Goodyear, Dunlop, and Pirelli fared no better. Thus, both big and small native merchants as well as international investment consortiums failed, in the face of significant environmental barriers, to undercut the autonomy of forest workers. Output remained too low and quality too unpredictable to meet modern industrial standards, however. In the end, rubber trees were successfully transplanted to Southeast Asia, where they thrived in the absence of leaf blight. Rubber plantations in British Malay and French Indochina, worked under brutal and disruptive labor regimes, undid Brazilian hopes for a monopoly. By the time petroleum rubber was perfected in the 1940s, Brazil's industry was already exhausted.

Unlike *hevea*, the diminutive coffee tree thrives in dense groves on cleared forest land. It also imposes a very different schedule and work burden. It begins producing marketable beans after only three years and, if well maintained, remains productive for thirty. It requires regular pruning to spur useful growth, careful tillage for soil fertility, attention to weeding, and the constant cutting back of the woody plants native to the forests. The berries, which ripen in waves, must be picked quickly, before they overripen and lose their value. With global prices subject to swift and dramatic swings, managing all of this work efficiently was the planter's only assurance against heavy losses during downturns and sweet profits during the booms.

In the early years of the coffee industry, planters imported slaves, often purchasing from northeastern sugar growers in decline. Some experimented with wage workers as early as the 1840s, but with inadequate labor laws, an under-monetized economy (the upshot of slavery), and shortages of suitable migrants of Europeans, this route was not always feasible. In an effort to create a reliable and manageable workforce, planter and senator José Vergueiro introduced sharecroppers to his large estate near São Paulo in 1847, after financing their passage from Europe, advancing foodstuffs and tools, and providing each a small plot for growing food. Under signed contracts, Vergueiro received half the coffee harvest in rent while his sharecroppers kept what was left after repaying their debts. His neighbors soon copied these methods and within ten years 3,500 migrants worked the famous São Paulo coffee estates.

Vergueiro's method utilized debt to tie sharecroppers to the estates and the interest charges levied on his tenants had the benefit of adding to his income. In the most productive groves, planters found that half of their sharecroppers' income serviced debts, giving them possession of three-quarters of the harvest. The situation was so exploitative that in 1856 sharecroppers from Switzerland revolted, causing the Swiss consulate to protest the treatment of its citizens. A list of grievances included "the calculation of returns from coffee produced, the charging of the commission, the unfavorable exchange rate used to convert their debts into local currency, the charging of transport from [the port of] Santos to the plantation, and the strange division of profits from the sale of coffee."[6] Though planters countered that they were only recouping their costs, both the Swiss and Prussian governments prohibited further migration.

While the sharecropper rebellion was a major blow, and planters reacted in typical fashion by building up the local constabulary to keep labor in its place, of equal concern was the ability of migrants to take advantage of customary law to remove themselves from the labor force by hoving off and settling the unoccupied land of Brazil's vast interior. Brazil's landed elite was especially keen to prevent what amounted to the expansion of the peasantry, which took land out of circulation and drove up the price of both property and labor. The concerns of planters were aptly expressed by Luis Antonio Barbosa, a deputy from Minas Gerais:

> The introduction of free laborers in the country, even if they do not come enslaved temporarily, is always useful; what we want is that our lands should have value, that there should be someone to cultivate them and that our proprietors should have an income. It is indifferent to us whether this value, this income derives from day labor or tenants; what we want is cultivated land and increased production.[7]

Planters sought legal redress. In 1850 they passed laws to abrogate the colonial-era right of squatters to secure ownership to untitled land by demonstrating their productive use of it. The new laws further required states to sell public lands in 120-hectare lots, well beyond the financial means of poor migrants. In short, planters used their political power to stop the spread of the peasantry and to preclude the economic independence of Brazil's small but growing class of free laborers.

Having secured a malleable workforce, planters turned their attention to forcing greater output from it. To resist the planters, sharecroppers devoted greater attention to their food crops and reduced their efforts in the groves. Yields suffered. Some planters responded in turn by searching for another labor regime, one that would, in the words of a critic, "submit [workers] to a profitable system of quasi-servitude."[8] Noting the successful efforts on Cuba to introduce Asian coolies, a group of Brazil's planters looked to China to solve their labor problems They faced critics within the establishment elite. Conservatives argued against coolies on the grounds of "racial degeneration," whereas liberals warned that these workers would be reduced to "a new slavery, as vile, as immoral, and as disastrous as African slavery."[9] Indeed, the earliest contracts signed by Chinese coolies required complete obedience and allowed planters to deliver corporal punishment in ample amounts. There was even an anticipatory stipulation that forbade coolies to demand higher wages upon arrival, when they were sure to discover that even blacks were being paid more. At the end of the day, the Chinese government scuttled this scheme after learning of the deplorable conditions of its subjects in Cuba.

Eventually, the political winds turned against the conservative wing of the planter class. Having lent two centuries of legal support and philosophical succor to slave owners, nineteenth-century liberalism concluded that progress after all sprouted from unfettered markets, not monopolies nor servitude. British industrialists were champions of this shift and the manufacturing conurbation of Manchester lent its name to the newest school of utilitarian economic thought. Whereas a cynic might conclude in the face of this volte-face that liberalism stood for whatever course was most profitable, the implications of its nineteenth-century variant were clear to Brazil's radicals, who unabashedly adopted it in their pursuit of a full-fledged republic. They argued for free trade, a constitution that would undo the long-standing economic privileges of the colonial and planter elite, and the adoption of the fiscally disciplinary gold standard. They promised in return the unleashing of entrepreneurial forces that would industrialize the nation and bring it into the modern era.

As it turned out industrialization did not come so easily to Brazil, yet the radical's moment seemed to arrive with the abolition of slavery in 1888 and the founding of a republic the following year. Planters who had resisted the end of slavery were now compelled to join their more prescient neighbors in search of a new workforce. Swift to pick up on the newest economic ideas, a member of São Paulo's Chamber of Deputies noted, "It is evident that we need laborers in order to increase the competition among them and in that way salaries will be lowered by means of the law of supply and demand."[10]

In other words, what had been individual and often idiosyncratic experiments with wage labor and sharecropping became a national necessity. Free but cheap labor was the slogan of the day. Big proprietors found in the republican government, and especially in the newly created and powerful provincial states, willing partners in their effort. Fiscally strapped and excise-dependent state assemblies were eager to help planters keep up and even boost the exports that brought in foreign exchange and custom revenue. It did no harm that the planters entered the new representative assemblies in large numbers and, with the consolidation of the republic, worked tirelessly to ensure that state power and finance were used to promote their agricultural exports.

State governments subsidized the building of railways and roads, as well as a new bout of European migration. The population of Pará and Amazonas—the heart of rubber country—more than doubled to 695,000 in the last quarter of the century, and rubber exports rose sixfold. Between 1870 and 1920, São Paulo grew from a state of 830,000 people, 139 kilometers of railroads, and 60,000 coffee trees to one of 4.6 million inhabitants, 6,600 kilometers of railway, and 844 million coffee trees. Nationally, nine hundred thousand Europeans—many of them Italian—arrived before 1914. Coffee output, which had reached 3.7 million bags (or 221 million tons) in 1880, leapt to 16.3 million (685 million tons) by 1900, or three-quarters of world output.

The question of how to put migrants to work on the land remained, however. In a country still rich in vacant land, agricultural wages were very high and, in the words of one planter, were "a bleeding that must be stopped before it exhaust[ed] the patient."[11] Suppressing wages, however, was at times self-defeating. The journalist Cesar Chauvin scolded rubber *aviadores* for paying so little that they undid any incentive for the tapper to gather more rubber or to coagulate it well. Tappers were better off returning to "indigenous hunting and gathering," he complained.[12] Similarly, sharecroppers squeezed by planters tended "a reduced number of coffee trees, preferring to plant food crops to supply their homes and cover their need."[13]

The solution to labor problems on the coffee estate was a modified form of wage work known as the *colonato*. Recruited male workers (*colonos*) received monthly wages for tending a specified number of trees, a further piece rate per kilo of coffee harvested, and enough land from which to feed their families in grains, vegetables, and meat yet prevent them from diverting too much effort away from the groves. While the piece rate encouraged careful tending, the provision of cheap land for self-provisioning kept labor costs down (as it did under slavery), achieving a profitable balance between labor discipline and wage compression.

Nevertheless, planters still sought whatever advantage they could. Thus, even as contracts obligated workers to weed their groves monthly, replant ailing trees, and prepare for the harvest, planters employed local supervisors to watch for any shirking. Fines were levied for absenteeism, malformed trees, and weed infestations. Laws were passed by the planter-dominated state government to outlaw unions and strikes. Finally, planters underweighed coffee bags and prevented the appearance of cheaper alternatives to company stores.

As in the peasant economies of early modern Europe, the compression of earnings pushed family heads to find gainful outlets for underemployed household labor. Planters took advantage of this behavior, preferring to recruit married men who would deploy the work of their wives and children to raise food while they tended the coffee trees. At harvest time, the promise of the piece rate pushed all family members into the groves, where they maximized the returns on their employer's investment in capital and their investment in labor.

When still more labor was needed, the planters hired workers by the day, week, or month from neighboring communities of impoverished smallholders. Accounting for the profitability of coffee growing, São Paulo assembly deputy Bento Sampaio Vidal thus explained in 1940: "Coffee was autarkic; it demanded for its cultivation the simultaneous production of the most varied crops, even cattle raising. These were subsidiary crops, no doubt, but their total production was voluminous. It was *cheap production, because it was an accessory that offered the people abundant and healthy food.*"[14]

Colonato sharecropping dominated the coffee estates until the 1960s, when changes in the labor and land laws pushed planters to switch to wage labor. Under new legislation, the *colonos* secured legal protection against termination, big planters were pressed to shed property in an effort to solve rural landlessness, and public lands were made available for homesteading. Together, these reforms strengthened the bargaining position of the *colonos*, leaving planters flummoxed: "One can no longer do anyone a good turn," reported a São Paulo landowner in 1968. "On one occasion I hired an unemployed and starving family on my estate. I gave a light job to the *cabolo* who was incapacitated. A few months later he and his wife took me to court demanding payment of the minimum wage, vacation and the annual bonus. . . . from now on I will only keep indispensable workers. Otherwise I'll have to sell my land."[15] Ever adaptable, however, the planters responded by replacing tenants with casual wage labor, which was more abundant than at any time before thanks to decades of immigration.

Under the new labor laws, the planters had to offer the minimum wage and provide some compensation upon dismissal, but could fire at will. No longer obliged to provide workers with land to support wives and children, planters added to their bottom line by converting land formerly used by the *colonato* for the growing of subsistence crops to coffee, cash crops, or pasture for cattle. Drawing upon the experience with slavery, planters contracted overseers who in turn organized hired hands into gangs for tasking, badgering them to work harder, reporting poor performers, and docking pay. Now that wages were paid by the week, planters had every incentive to make field hands work long hours, even on the rainiest days. In short, planters responded to laws intending to improve the workers' lot by finding new avenues to exploit. Reflecting on the change, an old *colono* reported:

> Before it was better; in those days I had enough to eat; my capital were the animals I raised and there was more than enough; thus I did not have to buy anything. . . . Nowadays it is much worse . . . those laws demanding that time worked be indemnified, that vacations be paid. In order not to pay, the landlord began to dismiss the workers. In those days the estates were full of people, now they work with people from outside. . . . First of all, they began to take away the food plots; people then thought that without them they could not manage. With the laws they [the landlords] had to pay compensation for dismissal; therefore they began to do this [forbid food crops]. The people had no

strength to react; it is the landlord who is in command. The people thought they could not manage and left of their own accord.[16]

Up to this point, there had been little improvement in technique and no additions of machinery. Increases in productivity had come from rising prices, wage suppression, greater work discipline, and the addition of new land. Reflecting on the expansion by additions of land, José Monteiro Lobato, the famed Brazilian author of the "Woodpecker Farm" children's books, imagined coffee estates as octopuses. "The production of the red pulp is exuberant, but insatiable of humus," he wrote. "An octopus with millions of tentacles, coffee rolls over the forest and makes it vanish bleeding the landscape and deforesting hillsides."[17] The broad availability of unfarmed land, coupled with successes in luring European migrants, encouraged and permitted this approach to farming, though, like the cotton plantations of the US South, it caused great environmental and human damage.

As long as growth by assart produced profits, Brazil's planter-merchant class (like that of the US South) adhered to laissez-faire trade policies, vehemently rejecting increases in excise taxes that would raise their prices and their expenses. By the 1880s, however, commodity earnings were tested by growing global economic turbulence as prices were no longer determined by local or even regional movements in supply and demand, but by production and product cycles halfway around the world. And, as bust and boom cycles intensified, national governments took measures to protect domestic farmers. In the face of the prolonged global depression of the 1870s and 1880s, Brazil's planter-merchant class secured state programs that supported exports and prices through government purchases and stockpiling. Nationally the federal government cheapened the currency to boost exports. These efforts only exacerbated the cycles as each expansion in global demand encouraged more tree planting, while guaranteed prices during the downturns gave relief to inefficient producers and kept markets glutted. As overproduction continued, and prices remained depressed, state governments vainly asked planters to take land out of production.

By the end of World War I, it was apparent that commodity production did not provide a clear path to development and modernization. In orthodox terms, Brazil's "comparative advantage" lay with cheap land and relatively inexpensive labor, embodied in its highly commercialized yet undercapitalized agriculture. Whereas the planter-merchant class and regional states were happy to exploit these advantages, by the 1910s it was clear that this course left Brazil under-industrialized and geopolitically weak. In response the federal government took steps to foster modern development through investments in transportation and industry, while putting up tariff barriers to promote and protect fledgling manufacturers. These early forays into economic policy produced only modest outcomes. By 1950 industrial manufacturing accounted for only one-fifth of the economy, employed less than 10 percent of workers, and remained heavily concentrated in low-technique textiles and food processing.

The arrival of the Cold War and the development of new economic techniques combined to offer new pathways to development. We have already seen how the governments of Taiwan and France took advantage of these means to transform their backward agricultural sectors and unleash manufacturing. With the backing of US advisers and institutions like the World Bank, the Brazilian government intervened more intensely than before. It increased the number and levels of tariffs, it deployed multiple exchange rates to cheapen strategic imports and protect precious manufacturers, and it established state-owned enterprises in key capital and intermediary goods such as steel (Cosipa, Usiminas), plastics, electric power (FUNRAS), and fuel (Petrobrás). The National Development Bank was strengthened and directed to forward discounted loans to private manufacturers as well as agriculture and foreign firms were encouraged to invest and transfer technology.

The 1964 military coup hardened economic policies, especially the very loose money regime, and moved the government rightward on social ones. The junta attacked leftists, the peasant leagues, labor unions, and student associations in a self-declared war against Communism. It restricted money supply to rein in inflation and created the Government Economic Action Program (PAEG) to discipline labor and businesses. The PAEG cut government budgets (both national and state), kept interest rates high, made borrowing more difficult, and supported the economic elite in their effort to suppress wages. Finally, as in Taiwan, the junta moved to subordinate the agricultural sector to the needs of manufacturing.

The military government recognized the inefficiency of the prevailing property system. It was disconcerted by the vast quantities of uncultivated and poorly tended land held by the wealthiest proprietors and the scale of landless among the rural poor. It responded by reconfirming public ownership of millions of hectares in public land and passing the 1964 Land Law (*Estatuto da Terra*). The new law discouraged speculation (holding land without farming it) and encoded the right of the landless to farm. Yet the junta lacked the courage of its own convictions and did little to break up large and inefficient holdings or deal with rural poverty.

Ultimately, agricultural policy under the military departed little from the previous postwar governments. They all took their cue from organizations such as the Joint Brazil-US Economic and Technical Commission, which concluded that "market inefficiency," not the labor or land regimes, was the chief obstacle to improvement. Distorting monopsony powers, policy gurus argued, inhibited improvements by artificially suppressing smallholder earnings to levels that prohibited savings. With insufficient savings at hand, they argued, smallholders could not rationalize and enlarge their farms in an effort to introduce machines. Brazil was advised to invest in transportation and storage, to foster competition among buyers, and to raise the prices paid to farmers.

Outcomes were mixed. Commodity exports briefly benefited from a boom in world demand and especially a jump in the price of coffee. Yet the problem of overproduction in the coffee sector quickly returned. More startling for politicians were the periodic food shortages. Basic food production remained the purview of the small-holding sector, which did not respond to the stimuli as expected. Though food output on the whole exceeded growth of real incomes in the 1950s and 1960s, thus slowing wage inflation, periodic food shortages still hit cities. These came to a head in the early 1970s. The problem lay with the junta. Unwilling to undo the power of Brazil's latifundistas, and opposed to any signs of peasant political organization, it left the marginalized smallholders and sharecroppers too weak to affect policy. Peasants received little to no rural credit, while technical assistance, which was located near state-built infrastructure, went overwhelmingly to the latifundistas in the export sector. So long as food production remained the domain of millions of minifundist smallholders, who were left to expand production largely by way of colonizing the frontiers, there was little hope for the incessant introduction of cost-cutting measures that would yield ongoing increases in the food surplus.

Meanwhile, vast amounts of production on the frontiers remained oriented to self-provisioning, where the typical peasant mode of behavior prevailed among homesteaders. In Rio Grande do Sul's Alto Uruguai, originally homesteaded by Germans and Italians, one-fifth of cultivated acreage was held in units of ten hectares or less, and the majority of farms were under the fifteen hectares needed to be viable. Under the combined pressures of rising land prices, shrinking farm size, and weakening soil, even once commercially viable *minifundia* (small farms) were progressively undermined. They first leaned on excess and cheap family labor to compete in the grain and coffee markets. But advances in the productive technique of neighboring larger farms not only undercut off-farm employment opportunities for the poor, and diminished demand for their increasingly lower-quality product, but also diminished any cost-cutting advantage that had accrued through self-exploitation. By the 1970s, the descendants of the original homesteaders greeted each new year without savings. Having exhausted the once-rich soils, they either reverted to the most rudimentary farming methods or migrated to Amazonia where they hoped to re-establish their independence.

This extensive pattern of growth reached its limits by the end of the 1970s, with millions of *minifundia* trapped in low-technique and low-productivity farming. As food supplies failed to keep up with demand, the cost of basic calories doubled after a slight decline in the 1960s. Imports of US wheat grew, before a spate of grain purchases by the USSR, coupled with the 1973 oil shock, drove up world wheat prices. As Brazil's grain import bill swelled and urban wages shrank, the military government resorted to subsidizing food while pushing more credit to agriculture. Yet even as rural loans as a percentage of net agricultural product rose from 15 to 50 to 100 percent, the main recipients were once again the tiny minority of large-scale growers. The military junta remained captured by landholding interests that were inimical to providing the smallholders a way forward at their expense.

The junta also proved unable to discipline business. Through the 1970s the military leveraged cheap petro-dollars to support an indiscriminate investment boom. By 1980 the nation's debt reached one-fifth and interest payments one-half of GDP. The debt bubble burst in 1983 and the ensuing balance of payment crisis compelled major economic restructuring. In exchange for foreign emergency loans, the government was required to tighten the money supply and reduce public spending, as it had in 1964, but this time it was also required to liberalize the economy. Credit subsidies were slashed, tariffs were lowered, trade licensing was ended, and export limitations were eliminated. The transition to democracy in 1985 consolidated the new economic order, under which farmers lost price and export supports, government procurements, and subsidized credit. Market-based solutions to the problem of maldistribution of land were normalized.

The upshot of a half century of ignoring the land problem has left deep marks. Of Brazil's 4.6 million farmers in 1996, 3.8 million (82.6 percent) worked fewer than fifty hectares and managed 12 percent of all farmland, whereas 460,000 farmers controlled 45 percent of the land and managed operations that averaged one thousand hectares plus. A decade later, 70 percent of farmers worked on average twenty-two hectares, a mere 146,000 farmers managed in excess of one thousand hectares, and 41,000 managed farms of an astounding ten thousand hectares plus. A further breakdown shows that eight of ten farms were family run, of which two-thirds were subsistence growers and only one-third produced enough to cover expenses and sell a regular surplus. The redistributive efforts of the military years did little to improve the lot of most farmers, benefiting speculators as much as peasants, while recent market approaches have ended up favoring the formation of a new export sector that rests of mega farms.

An analysis of the expansion of soybean cultivation—first promoted among smallholders in the 1960s as a cash crop, but monopolized in recent years by vast commercial and exporting operations—illustrates the dilemma facing the majority of farmers, and the ways policies have disfavored them.

The soybean plant was introduced to southern Brazil in the late nineteenth century by Japanese migrants, who found the climate there suitable to their cultivars. By the 1960s southern households relied on soybeans to reduce market purchases of feed and fertilizer, while they focused efforts on food staples such as rice, manioc, potatoes, and maize for the family. These growers—such as the Germans and Italians of Alto Uruguai—typically worked small holdings, which they acquired cheaply at a time when land was still plentiful. Some had migrated from Brazil's north and east, where their farms had grown too small to support them and land too expensive to make additions. Those settlers who took on debt found the soil rich enough that they could repay the capital and interest after only a couple of years of growing and selling soybeans. The land's productiveness also reduced the farmers' bills by eliminating any need to buy fertilizer, while the government kept the tax burden low to encourage settlement.

Benefiting from the abundance of their land, these growers did remarkably well, as evidenced in the long-term stability of their land tenure. While some farms shrank, and a few households fell into landlessness, most remained in the twenty to fifty hectare range, and very few had recourse to leaseholds to supplement their income. Unburdened by debt, rent, or taxes, and supplied with rich soils and sufficient land, they were free to pursue immediate needs, and few chose to subordinate their decisions to the force of prices. When the surge in global demand for soy oil and meal began to affect prices positively in the 1970s, southern smallholders seemed perfectly placed to benefit.

The military government had already singled out soybeans as a potential export crop and was willing to provide more seed, fertilizer, pesticides, and loans to growers. It secured plants from the local subsidiaries of Cargill, Anderson Clayton, and Bunge and Born to process soy meal pellets and oil for both export and domestic consumption. Under these propitious conditions, a small number of capital-intensive growers, backed with discounted loans, converted southern cattle ranches and forestry operations to soybean cultivation and, in the process, greatly improved market infrastructure for their neighboring smallholders. Leveraging their larger scale, these producers negotiated directly with processors for favorable prices and so undercut the monopolistic powers of the petty merchants that had previously suppressed rural earnings. As farm gate prices for soybeans rose, profits were more or less guaranteed to big and small growers.

Although this happy coincidence set off a brief boom in southwest Paraná, only a third of households were able to acquire farms large enough to accommodate the machinery required to continue. Whereas forty hectares were needed to support the use of a tractor, necessary in hauling, plowing, and clearing, a farmer without a mechanical soybean harvester could only hope to manage two hectares. Growers that had inherited their patrimony intact, and had access to family savings, rationalized and enlarged their farms to accommodate machinery. They purchased land from their neighbors, tore down walls, filled in ditches, leveled buildings, uprooted orchards, and eliminated gardens. They built up one-hundred-hectare-plus farms suitable to mechanized monocropping and then took on more debt to upgrade their machinery. They also increased their outlays on fertilizers and pesticides to repair the taxed soils and manage the white beetles that thrived in the increasingly undifferentiated soybean fields. Some tried to cut corners by sharing or renting equipment. Despite the success of a few, most smallholders found themselves unable to compete in this cutthroat world and had no choice but to return to growing the traditional food crops that fed their families.

A few large operations took advantage of the crisis among smallholders and added to their farms, hoping to make up for falling profit margins by increasing the scale of their operations. But ultimately what determined the future of soybean monoculture in southwest Paraná was the development of corporate agriculture to the north, on the Cerrado. Today, this tropical savanna is home to vast farms that dump on the world's markets bewildering quantities of soybeans, cotton, and maize. Its development lifted Brazil's share of soybean output from 4 to 40 percent between 1970 and 2005. In 2010, the zone accounted for 28 percent of world soybean exports and 70 percent of Brazil's total soybean harvest. In the process, it wiped out the Southern growers.

In less than thirty years, thanks to the conversion of tropical savanna to industrial-scale monoculture, complete with chemical fertilizers, irrigation, and massive machines, Brazil has moved from a net food importer to a net exporter. The speed of the Cerrado's transformation is astonishing especially given the ecological barriers to cultivation of its chief crop. Asian and North American soybean cultivars were entirely unsuited to the region when first introduced. The prevalent high humidity produces a deadly rust and the short days and constant diurnal temperatures cause premature flowering and stunt growth. The soils are moreover too acidic and lack necessary micronutrients such as zinc and phosphate. They are deficient too in humus and retain so little water that constant irrigation is needed. In short, massive efforts at reengineering were required to make the land grow soybeans.

That work began in 1952, when the state-funded agricultural research organization EMBRAPA, with assistance from US agronomists, developed the soybean hybrid IAC2. Researchers at the University of Wisconsin and Rio Grande do Sul then developed a recipe for restructuring the Cerrado soil that included an application to each hectare of three metric tons of lime, five hundred kilograms of phosphates, and four hundred kilograms of potassium with micronutrients (mostly zinc). The initial application was followed by a cover crop of oats or rice, which was plowed back to build humus, as well as additions of lime and phosphorus every two to five years as required. The scale of these interventions was remarkable. In 2004, twenty-five million tons of additional lime was spread, or roughly five tons per hectare.

But, if the ecological hurdles to commercial exploitation were significant, so too were the social barriers. Like much of Brazil's frontier, the Cerrado was rife with land-title fraud. The state and private organizations enforced regularity. They allotted land in large contiguous tracts of one hundred to four hundred hectares, financed infrastructure (roads, clinics, schools), provisioned loans, and procured deeds. While early settlement fostered relatively small operations, with the state's backing the scale of farms only grew. A single farm on the eastern edge of the Cerrado in Bahia today is an astonishing twenty-four thousand hectares. It requires five thousand 30-ton trucks just to haul and dump lime. At two hundred times the size of the average Iowa farm, it is one thousand times the typical southern soybean Brazilian farm of the 1980s. In short, capitalist farming and accompanying property relations were introduced to the Cerrado sui generis.

While such unprecedented scales of operation are responses to global demands on efficiency, they are supported and made possible in the first instance with state approval and the assistance of multinational firms. As the Brazilian state retreated from the economy in general and agriculture in particular, multinational suppliers and buyers have stepped in to provide technical services. Leading-edge farmers are eager to link up with agricultural corporations or agribusinesses to acquire the necessary industrial inputs and secure access to markets, while these same businesses hope to steer large-scale farmers toward more profitable lines whenever they appear.

Today, multinationals are the chief provisioners of fertilizer, pesticides, herbicides, farm machinery, and new technologies. Monsanto, for example, sells both genetically modified "Roundup Ready" soybeans (at $115 per hectare) and a paired biocide, which is needed to destroy the pests that are now endemic to the vast monocropping operations. Multinational fiber and grain buyers such as Anderson Clayton, Cargill, and Bunge, as well as food processors such as Sara Lee and Nestlé, shape farming innovation and field practices to conform to their specific quality, health, and industrial demands. Combining economies of scale in processing, purchasing, and financing, as well as the advantages of lowered transaction costs through vertical integration (linking up with large suppliers and buyers), these agro-corporations simultaneously afford commercial farms cost-cutting avenues while subordinating production decisions to the disciplining effects of international markets and consumer demands.

The effect on farming cannot be understated. According to *The Economist* magazine,

> Three years ago the Cremaq farm was a failed experiment in growing cashews. Its barns were falling down and the scrub was reasserting its grip. Now the farm—which . . . is owned by BrasilAgro, a company that buys and modernises neglected fields—uses radio transmitters to keep track of the weather; runs SAP software; employs 300 people under a *gaúcho* from southern Brazil; has 200km (124 miles) of new roads criss-crossing the fields; and, at harvest time, resounds to the thunder of lorries which, day and night, carry maize and soya to distant ports.[18]

Speaking to this transformation of the regional ecology, the same magazine reports that the vast soybean farms "could hardly have existed until recently because soya would not grow on this hottest, most acidic of Brazilian backlands. The variety of soya [soybean] now being planted there did not exist five years ago."

At first glance, these vast enterprises might seem the direct descendants of nineteenth-century *latifundia*. But, while they share similarities of scale and commercial intent, they differ in two key areas. In the first instance, wage labor and commercial tenancy have replaced the coercive labor regimes (slaves, indentured coolies, sharecroppers). In the second, production is subordinated to the cost-cutting requirements of the market by virtue of reliance upon financing and purchased inputs.

These qualitative shifts in the condition of production explain the quantitative leap in dynamism. The *latifundia* were profitable, but innovatively sluggish. When squeezed by rising costs and falling prices, they leveraged political influence to lower labor costs, put up protections, and receive price subsidies. Modern agribusinesses are of course not adverse to these instruments, but they cannot depend upon them entirely, given the innovative environments of their global competitors and the constraints of new trade deals. They must economize. This entails the introduction of the latest cost-cutting and yield-boosting biotechnologies, fertilizers, field management methods, and machines. They use GPS and satellite technology to plant, irrigate, spray, and harvest at the optimal moment. The appearance and character of the new mode is summed up by the "Sem Terra" (landless peasant) activist and critic of agribusiness João Pedro Stédile:

> In agriculture, the entry of international capital was put on the fast-track, together with what they call the application of the North American model to Brazilian farming, and the internationalization of our food production. The concentration of land and agro-industry in the hands of large-scale capital was speeded up. All agricultural trade is now under the control of the multinationals.[19]

The triumph of modern farming should not be overstated, however, for these large operations continue to swim in a sea of poor smallholders. *The Economist*, in its idiosyncratic style, also writes that "Brazil is divided between productive giant operations and inefficient hobby farms. According to Mauro and Ignez Lopes of the Fundacão Getulio Vargas, a university in Rio de Janeiro, half the country's 5m [5 million] farms earn less than 10,000 *reais* a year and produce just 7% of total farm output; 1.6m are large commercial operations which produce 76% of output."[20]

The "hobby farms" are of course nothing of the sort. These are not the weekend distractions of bankers, doctors, and movies stars, but the primary sources of income for millions of land-poor peasants who eke out a subsistence with crude tools and family labor while earning some wages on nearby ranches and corporate farms. They are the bottom third of farmers, who control less than 1.6 percent of the land. The repercussions for Brazil's national income structure are staggering. While the top 10 percent of Brazilians hold 45 percent of income, the poorest 20 percent receives less than 3 percent, and with six million landless rural households one out of seven people suffer from hunger. One only needs to compare this with postwar Taiwan to notice how Brazil has historically avoided an honest reckoning of the land problem and suffers the social consequences to this day.

Recent efforts have done little to reduce social inequity. In line with market liberalization, the government introduced in the 1990s what advocates in the World Bank and elsewhere term "market-led agrarian reform" (MLAR) to address both inequity and the supposed inefficiencies of land-to-the-tiller programs. The MLAR approach posits that the initial burst of growth produced by state-led green revolutions vanished when peasants failed to continue seeking efficiencies. That failure, it is argued, stemmed in large part from policies that provided households with land at a cost too low to require its rational use, prevented more efficient farmers from acquiring land, and slowed the exit of inefficient producers. Traditional land reform, in other words, supposedly shielded peasants from the full disciplining force of the market. (As we saw in chapter 9, Taiwanese policymakers found means to both distribute land equitably and levy pressure sufficient to elicit specialization and cost-cutting, while embarking on spectacular industrialization).

The MLAR approach relies on debt to capture peasant production at the moment of land acquisition. In the words of the World Bank official managing MLAR in Brazil, recipients "choose the land and negotiate for its purchase. They decide how to use the land, and what investment is required to make it productive, and what technical assistance they will need."[21] Though the operating mechanisms are left unspoken, the intention is clear. Land purchases at the market price will shape subsequent production decisions: it is understood, but unstated, that in order to meet debt obligations, peasants must bring to market those crops (or livestock) that obtain the best returns on their investment.

In practice, however, asymmetries in power allow landlords to fix prices while many peasants are denied financial assistance. Not without reason, the MLAR is controversial and the Landless Workers Movement (Movimento dos Trabalhadores Rurais Sem Terra, or MST) organizes against it. Founded in 1984, the MST claims to have led more than 2,500 land occupations, with about 370,000 families, on 7.5 million hectares. Its manifesto calls for an end to the corporate model of farming that "prioritizes output in the form of extensive, large scale monocultures, affecting the environment and requiring large amounts of poisons that harm the health and quality of food." It criticizes a mode of farming that in "Brazil consumes more than a billion gallons of poison per year, becoming the world's largest consumer!" The manifesto proposes, instead, policies that

> prevent the concentration of private ownership of land, forests and water. Make a wide distribution of the largest farms, establishing a maximum size limit of ownership of natural resources; ensure that Brazilian agriculture is controlled by Brazilians and that it is based on healthy food production, the organization of agricultural industries in the form [of] cooperatives in all municipalities in the country; and adopt production techniques that seek to increase the productivity of labor and land, respecting the environment and agroecology. Struggle for the phase out [of] the use of pesticides, which contaminate food and nature.[22]

The efforts of MST have spurred politicians and elites to try to criminalize the organization. Its leader Stédile has received death threats. Brazil's long tradition of rural violence, land expropriation, labor exploitation, and environmental degradation for the purpose of profit-making extraction and export will no doubt persist so long as profits are possible and the state remains captive to business and rural elite interests.

THE UNITED STATES

The farmers of the United States have worked extraordinarily productively since about the 1850s. They have earned foreign exchange, generated savings, grown to be a consumer market, and released workers to other sectors of the economy. Farmers have made food available to the point of glut. Within this success story, two regions stand out: the South for its relatively low productivity and standard of living, and California for its astonishing record of unfettered capitalist triumph in domestic and world markets.

In the decades following the Civil War, the South formed the sole region of the United States in which farmers did not systematically make their labor more productive in order to enhance their competitiveness. Southern cultivators did not accumulate surpluses, adopt the latest techniques, or specialize their products and skills ever more precisely to the market. When slavery ended, the planters laid hold of large estates and, with the support of federal officials, sought to reestablish production on the basis of the free labor of the formerly captive workers. Just as the planters of the seventeenth and eighteenth centuries, studied in chapter 5, knew that free workers or indentured servants recruited from Africa or elsewhere for their sugarcane farms in the Caribbean would set up subsistence plots and withdraw from the labor market at the end of their contracts, so too textile industrialists, bankers, and merchants of the northern United States knew that distributing land to the ex-slaves would spread subsistence agriculture and deprive manufacturing of the cotton supply. They had already observed the way in which food plants for household use crowded out cash crops in Haiti after emancipation at the beginning of the nineteenth century. But the effort to establish commercial plantations in the southern United States on the basis of free labor faced opposition from the former slaves. Prior to the 1860s, the masters had utilized the labor of the entire slave family. After emancipation, the former slaves withdrew the labor of women and children. The freed slaves sometimes refused to work, especially when most in demand at harvest time, with the aim of bargaining employers against one another and obtaining better wages. They organized proto-trade unions to negotiate over conditions, wages, and hours.

The former slaves, in this way, made capitalist plantations economically unfeasible and led the planters to settle instead on sharecropping. By 1900, many white, and most black, farmers had become sharecroppers. From the landlords' standpoint, sharecropping prevented the workforce from enhancing its market value by threatening desertion at inopportune moments. From the farmers' standpoint, sharecropping assured employment and allowed them to control the labor of their households.

Cotton farming became even more prevalent after the Civil War. The price of fertilizer fell, facilitating the expansion of the area suitable for cultivation onto formerly marginal lands. Prior to the 1860s, independent whites and slaves produced their own consumption goods on small holdings and plantations. In times of shortage, they deprived themselves or moved in with kinfolk. But by the end of the century, in a process similar to the one that took hold in West Africa, Brazilian rubber forests, and India, merchants began to offer essential goods for a lien on the cotton, which never amounted to enough to cover interest and principal payments, and left the farmers poor, indebted, and often hungry. Sharecroppers specialized in cotton to meet these financial obligations and purchase the low-cost grain and meat that poured into the South from capitalist farms in the Midwest.

The farmers evidently would have preferred to continue working for their subsistence. They often blamed the merchants for requiring that cotton or tobacco be grown as a condition for credit. The landlords did not want the sharecroppers to grow household crops or move into other lines, because they obtained sure profits from cotton without incurring the expenses of technology, marketing, or storage. Many sharecroppers joined the Southern People's Party and Farmers' Alliances to fight for homestead tax exemptions, government-owned banks, paper money for inexpensive credit, and lower freight rates for farmers. The prospect of an alliance of these political organizations, white and black farmers, and Northern workers prompted the planters to counterattack, with the support of Northern business interests, in the 1890s and the beginning of the twentieth century. The landlords exploited divisions between black sharecropper and white cash-tenants to legally segregate public facilities, disenfranchise African Americans and many poor whites through poll taxes and literacy tests, and maintain order through Klan terror and lynching in the plantation districts. The planters and their business allies headed off calls for high taxes and effective schools. Their overall aim was to suppress opposition politics and social movements.

In this way, cotton expanded on tenancies and sharecropping units farmed by poor blacks and whites for the benefit of Southern landlords. Similar to vines, maize, potatoes, and animal husbandry in nineteenth-century France, cotton represented an intensification of land use, yielding more value per acre than did corn, though profit margins diminished in outlays for fertilizer, implements, and marketing. Cotton required year-round intensive labor done in much the same way it had been before the Civil War. Sharecroppers plowed in the late winter and planted in spring. In the summer they saw to weeding, and tilled the fields a number of times with a mule before enduring raw hands in the course of several back-breaking harvests while the cotton ripened at different dates. Growers in the North, in competition with one another, had to get as much monetary value from their labor as possible by augmenting the arable acreage of their farms and purchasing more machines to work it all. In Virginia, North Carolina, Georgia, and the rest of the South, by contrast, sharecroppers focused on household subsistence by maintaining labor on the farm as a form of social security. In this context, farm sizes persistently diminished between 1880 and 1930, as the landed classes divided their holdings so that the growing number of sharecropping households could till smaller farms more intensively.

The timing of Southern economic spurts and relapses closely adhered to cotton demand, not productivity. Demand picked up after 1900 but then turbulence in international trade after 1920 led the market to contract over the following decade. Per capita income grew from 1880 to 1930 but only amounted to about half of the national average.

California, by contrast, was one of the few places on earth, along with the Brazilian Cerrado examined above, where capitalism did not develop out of feudalism, household production, sharecropping, slave plantations, or other agrarian relations in which the tillers of the soil saw to subsistence on the farm. At the time of the Gold Rush, the rapid economic expansion of the 1850s, and the Victorian boom in Europe, California's growers focused straightaway on the world market. Wheat and cattle lands were bought up and developed with fortunes made in mining and commerce in the 1860s and 1870s. When A. P. Giannini, founder of the Bank of Italy (later the Bank of America), offered loans, he favored business-minded growers intent on commercial pursuits rather than self-sufficient households. The Southern Pacific Railroad declared in its promotion of the Imperial Valley that its irrigated lands were for innovative farmers with capital, not poor homesteaders. Family farms never spread across California the way they did in the Northern states. Instead, urban investors monopolized the countryside for the profit available in commodity production and precluded the development of the rural towns of family farmers who thrived in other parts of the country.

From the very beginning, California has been characterized by the capitalist drive to launch products and beget new sources of value. New crops represented extra measures of profit when novel and scarce. The high rate of profit called forth investment until market glut drove down earnings. In this way, the profusion of crops resembles any other industrial business that diversifies into new, more profitable commodities as older lines become too crowded. Yet amid such diversification, California growers have continually practiced monoculture on their farms. They have always relied on hired labor even when little of it was available during the first Mexican cattle boom of the 1850s. Large expanses of grain were sown and harvested with modest land preparation. Cattle wandered free with slight supervision. This period saw a wheat glut during the recession of the 1850s and then a livestock bubble in 1863. Growers turned to intensive sheep ranching until its peak around 1875. Wheat saw a renewed expansion until the general crisis of the 1870s. Wheat hit a new peak in 1888 only to collapse dramatically in 1893.

After the 1870s, growers began an era of specialized horticulture, farming grapes, tree crops, and vegetables. Farm sizes decreased by more than a half, as these intensive lines came to dominate the state's agricultural output. By 1920, most US oranges, prunes, plums, grapes, and figs were grown in California. The state became a world leader in grapes, citrus, and many deciduous fruits.

The farmers outcompeted Mediterranean growers, despite higher labor and shipping costs, thanks to biological and organizational innovations. In 1890, the San Jose scale insect (SJS) attacked the orchards of Southern California and threatened to wipe out all of the deciduous fruit interests of the Pacific coast. Farmers began to strip the rough bark off the trees and scrub them with a caustic solution of lye. They drenched the foliage using a handheld syringe sprayer or home-rigged force pumps. Newly formed pesticide companies perfected formulas of lime-sulfur sprays, which farmers purchased and learned to apply in the dormant season when the sprays did less damage to the trees. By 1908, however, the SJS developed resistance, the first instance of pesticide tolerance in the US, and new chemical treatments had to be introduced. The fight against the SJS helped develop the chemical and spray equipment industries, which then proved invaluable in fighting other agricultural pests.

In addition, agriculturalists competed successfully on national and international markets thanks to the development of water pumps to irrigate the land. The deep-well turbine pump, launched by the Layne and Bowler Company of Chicago in 1907, helped growers irrigate half of California's farmland by 1950. Electrification facilitated the spread of irrigation pumps in the

San Joaquin Valley, the Los Angeles plain, the Salinas Valley, the Delta, and southern Sacramento Valley, California's prime agricultural lands. The Central Valley became the largest stretch of irrigated farmland in the world in the 1920s. Prominent businessmen and growers lobbied for the irrigation districts. These were established through state law and ended up firmly in the hands of the landowners and urban developers.

The horticultural era demanded much labor and precise timing: picking at harvest time, packing, canning, and shipping to ensure delicate crops arrived at market. The post–Civil War workforce consisted of US-born whites, immigrant Irish, Germans, Chinese, and Portuguese, many of them ex-miners. About twenty thousand Chinese played a leading part, amounting to anywhere from 5 to 50 percent of the workers in the farm counties of Northern California. This labor dwindled as a result of the racially motivated Exclusion Acts of 1882, 1892, and 1902 opposed by many growers. But the Chinese continued to labor in the fields during the 1920s in Delta towns like Walnut Grove and in Santa Clara Valley settlements like Alviso. They could not own land, on account of the racial laws, but still managed to become tenant farmers in the Sierra foothills and the Delta. Chinese farmers, like those from other parts of the world, enriched California with their knowledge of new crops and techniques.

So Yung Ng, an immigrant from southern China, explained in 1984 that he came as a laborer, first to pick cotton in Mexicali and then clandestinely to San Francisco in 1921. He worked at a market in Locke, California, south of Sacramento, during the Great Depression and then had the chance to join other growers as tenants of three hundred acres belonging to Mr. Paul Emmet in the Sacramento-San Joaquin River Delta northeast of San Francisco. Emmet provided all the equipment and materials. The elder tenant, Mr. Lee Jok Nam, made the decisions, even though So Yung Ng "discovered that the farm was not run properly." When Lee Jok Nam died, So Yung Ng agreed to stay on provided that he could make changes in the orchard. "When Mr. Lee was operating the farm he wouldn't release water during April and July. At that time the orchard only yielded about 100 tons of pears. Much of the fruit was the size of a candle because it was not fully developed." So Yung Ng then applied some of his observations.

> I realized that the climate of [southern] China and the United States was very different. In China the weather is hot and wet during the summer. From day to night the temperature does not change that much. On the other hand, [in the Sacramento-San Joaquin River Delta] it is hot and dry during the summer. The temperature in the day is quite different from the temperature at night. The methods of farming should not be the same in both places. Also, in Courtland, the orchards usually cover a large piece of land but in China the orchards are divided into small sections and built on different levels. Many water ditches must be built to control the water flow from one section to another. Due to

weather and poor knowledge of farming, fruit farming in China didn't produce good yields compared to here. I was pleased I worked here. Can you believe what happened? The first year after I began managing the farm, the crop yields increased from 100 tons to 160 tons. During the following years it even reached 180 tons and the price was 100$ per ton. This was my opportunity. My boss and I made some money during those years.[23]

So Yung Ng worked for Paul Emmet for almost twenty years and retired at age sixty. He had three children, all of whom attended college.

Italian, Greek, and Portuguese immigrants took over most of the packing jobs in Northern California, as did Mexican workers in Southern California, when the Chinese labor supply dwindled after the Exclusion Acts. White males held supervisory positions, women the bulk of ordinary jobs. Alfred Jung, as a Chinese American packer on a farm in Locke since the age of twelve in 1913, represented something of an anomaly to this exclusion of Chinese immigrants from packing jobs. His parents had come from Zhong-shan in 1901. "There were six to eight workers in the packing department," Jung stated, "with the same Chinese workers being hired back every year to pack the fruit. These workers were very experienced in the process so they worked very fast. Although there were machines to help, most of the work was still done by hand." After the harvest, once the fruit had been taken to the shed,

> workers put the fruit into a machine which had a long conveyor belt in it. The machine washed the fruit and moved it to the belt then transported it to a disc for sorting. Several workers stood beside the belt and picked out the bad ones, leaving the good fruit to the sorting process. The fruit then went through a separating disc and was sorted into large, medium and small sizes. Then it was ready for packing in the boxes. We worked from 6 a.m. to 6 p.m. Sometimes we worked overtime.[24]

Wong Yow, an immigrant from China, stated in 1984 that his father followed in the footsteps of his great-grandfather and grandfather who both came to the United States. "My father was about forty years old when he emigrated. He first went to Mexico, but while he was working there some friends told him that work was more plentiful in the United States, and wages were higher. So he found a company in San Francisco that would sponsor his entrance into the country."[25]

Wong Yow himself arrived on Angel Island in San Francisco Bay from Hong Kong in 1921. He did not get steady work straightaway. "I sometimes went to Lodi to harvest grapes. There I was recruited for the job of harvesting hops. The contractor transported the workers to camp by car. There were forty to fifty of us. . . . Our employers provided the food and hired a cook to feed us. The maximum amount of hops I could harvest in a day was 600 pounds." Wong Yow then began to travel between Sutter Island and Lodi, both south of Sacramento, for about ten years. "On Sutter Island I picked fruit, pruned trees, and irrigated. During August and September I went to Lodi to harvest grapes, returning to Sutter Island in October." His wages came to ten cents an hour during the Great Depression. "But I didn't care how little they were as long as I had a job. If I made $1 a day, I could still save some of it because the cost of living was so low at that time."[26] Wong Yow worked in Courtland and Locke after World War II and then on a ranch in Walnut Grove in Sacramento County from 1952 until his retirement in 1968.

> Once I remember the workers wanted a raise. The boss, however, did not want to give us one so he pulled a trick on us. He raised our wages by fifty cents a day and at the same time increased our food expenses by fifty cents. We thought we would get better food to justify the increased prices. (A food service took over the food service for him on his ranch.) Yet on Saturdays when we did not work we also did not get paid but still had to pay the additional fifty cents for the food, so we were actually losing money. Despite this, our employer treated us well. He was humorous even though we did not understand his language.[27]

By the 1920s, California growers increasingly relied on Mexican laborers, in part because they seemed less likely to unionize. Growers complained about a labor shortage, and in 1942, the governor lobbied the US secretary of agriculture, stating that it would prove disastrous for the food-production part of the war effort. The federal government negotiated with the Mexican authorities to import farm workers, known as *braceros*, for five years, guaranteeing them transportation, living expenses, repatriation, and exemption from military service. From 1942 to 1947, 219,000 Mexicans worked in US agriculture, half in California. The program was supposed to end with the war, but the growers had become so dependent on it that they succeeded in getting an extension. About 445,000 *braceros* entered the USA in 1956, and most of them went to California and Texas. The farmers housed the *braceros* in closed camps, bused them to the fields, and sent them home to Mexico once the season was over. The growers used the *braceros* to break strikes. Their wages only crept up from seventy-five cents to a dollar twenty-five an hour over twenty years of the greatest economic prosperity ever known to the United States. Wherever *braceros* were employed in large numbers, farm wages stagnated or fell. The abusive program did not come to an end until the civil rights movement in 1964.

In the meantime the farmers continued to employ Mexican immigrants. The efforts of the workers to organize in the Imperial Valley in the 1920s provoked fierce resistance among the growers, who mobilized the police, media, tribunals and the Immigration and Naturalization Service (INS), and even the Mexican consulate in Calexico. Decades later, Cesar Chavez formed the United Farm Workers of America (UFW) within the American Federation of Labor after many years of organizing agricultural laborers. He had success organizing boycotts of grocery chains in cities around the country to discourage the purchase of non-union produce. The union brought fifty thousand workers under contract by 1970.

But even at this high point of Chavez's success, the growers organized a counteroffensive. They stalled the signing of contracts, harassed organizers, and changed production routines to reduce labor demand. Alfredo Figueroa, a participant in the formation of the UFW in Southern California, recalled in 2005 that back in 1971, "the UFW had been plagued with strikebreakers coming from Mexico. . . . We spent a lot of time meeting with Mexican Union Officials . . . in Mexicali and reaching out to the . . . immigrants at the border cities. . . . After the first three years of the [UFW] Strike in Coachella and Delano [east of Los Angeles and San Diego] we found that educating the new immigrant approach was not working out." At this time, a state senator put forward the Dixon Arnett Bill granting employers the power to scrutinize the workers' immigration status. "The Mexicans were labeled as parasites and a burden to the Anglo way of life." The UFW supported the law. After 1971, the UFW "wanted all of [its] officers to report any undocumented workers in the farms and to report them to the INS and they wanted monthly tabulations of the numbers reported."[28]

The growers mustered the International Brotherhood of Teamsters to compete against, and weaken, the UFW. In 1973, the UFW filed suit against the Teamsters for its efforts, in collusion with the growers and packers, to prevent union organizing. One of the UFW's legal documents listed over thirty-five violent incidents perpetrated by Teamsters. "Richard Lopez," for instance, "was beaten to near unconsciousness, given a bloody nose and his mouth was busted and had three teeth broken."[29] Two years later, Ramon Perez Mejia, a rank-and-file UFW worker in the Coachella Valley, stated in a deposition that the Teamsters appealed to, and threatened, workers to switch their allegiance. "We were told that they wanted us to come to Sacramento— that we were to go there to support Teamsters and not the strike. I told the organizers, 'I can't go.' The foreman told me, 'If you don't go or sign our petition, you will have no more work.'"[30]

By this time, the UFW lost decertification elections right and left, and shrank until only a few thousand workers remained under contract in 1980. The union did not promote internal democracy and neglected basic organizing. One difficulty for organizers has been the American dream of becoming a farmer and capitalist. Some European immigrants became farm operators, though many Chinese had to content themselves with tenancy on account of racial restrictions. But in either case, many of the rural workers aspired to the role of directing farm operations rather than of uniting with their peers in a union. Overall, more than a century of labor militancy has accomplished very little. Today, conditions are hardly better than they were at any time in the past. The gap between profits and wages is very high, and for over 150 years has permitted California to become the most lucrative agricultural region of the advanced industrial nations, accounting for about 12 percent of agricultural output and one-third of the table food consumed in the USA. California has led the nation in food processing for half a century, shipping over fifty billion dollars in food products in 1997, while Illinois, ranked second, shipped only ten billion.

Farmers in the rest of the country, obliged since before the 1850s to sell their crops and animal products in order to cover the costs of taxes, mortgages, and inputs, faced the same cost-cutting pressures as did the growers of California. The difference, we saw in chapter 6, was that the farms of the East and Midwest were operated by capitalist households reliant on the unpaid labor of family members. They depended on the mechanical reapers, threshers, and harvesters sold by McCormick, John Deere, and other companies to cultivate additional acreage. The resultant gains in output offset the price competition caused by the simultaneous gains realized on the farms of their peers.

From the late 1880s into the 1920s, such gains in productivity included the conversion of virtually every dairy cow into the more productive and profitable purebred. Specialized breeding made the sheep, hogs, and steers of 1940 bear slight resemblance to their antecedents of the 1800s. The new breeds offered more wool and weight, and reached an age at which they offered marketable products in half the time they had in 1800. Farmers the world over had perpetually struggled to preserve animal feed through the winter. In 1873, Fred L. Hatch of McHenry County, Illinois, designed the tower silo to preserve cut green fodder and thereby extend the milking season by up to ten weeks. Silos quickly spread across the northern states and Canada. Cultivators developed plant varieties resistant to diseases and easy to harvest. By 1920, wheat had become a separate genetic class from what it had been in the first decades of the nineteenth century. In 1926, Henry A. Wallace, later secretary of agriculture and vice-president under Franklin Roosevelt, became the first commercial producer of hybrid corn, raising yields from 40 to 120 bushels per acre. It could not be bred, however, because it degenerated on planting. Farmers had to return to the seed company every year.

These innovations, while increasing output about 30 percent, lagged behind the consumer demand of the rapidly growing US population. Agricultural prices rose faster than did prices for other goods in the first two decades of the twentieth century. Farmers enjoyed unprecedented prosperity producing for national and international markets during World War I. Farm income more than doubled in the second decade of the twentieth century. Land prices rose rapidly, and by 1920 farmers had used the equity to take on nearly three times as much debt as they had in 1910, for the purchase of land, tractors, and threshing machines. US farmers were among the first purchasers of automobiles in the world. All farms, outside of the South, had a car by the 1930s. In an article in *Harper's* in 1933, Remley J. Glass, a lawyer from Mason City, Iowa, wrote about the boom years of 1919–1920.

> Bankers and lawyers, doctors and ministers left their offices and clients and drove pell mell over the country to procure options and contracts upon this farm and that, paying a few hundred dollars down and expecting to sell the rights before the following March brought settlement day. Not to be in the game marked one as an old fogy, while paper profits were pyramided and Cadillac cars and pleasure trips to the cities took the place of Fords and Sunday afternoon picnics.[31]

But during the 1920s, commodity prices, and the purchasing power of farmers, declined, and about two million of them left for the towns. The stock market crash of October 1929, and the ensuing economic contraction, drove prices and profits down further still. Per capita farm income fell more than two-thirds, as global demand withered, and wheat and meat exports plummeted. Farmers did not reduce production, despite President Hoover's pleas, because they needed income to cover debts on land and equipment (much of it taken on during the boom years) and because they did not want to lose out to other farmers who did not cut output. Yet for many there was no one to buy their produce. Oscar Ameringer of Oklahoma City described the tragic results before a congressional committee in February 1932. "In Oregon I saw thousands of bushels of apples rotting in the orchards. Only absolute flawless apples were still saleable, at from 40 to 50 cents a box containing 200 apples. At the time, there are millions of children who, on account of the poverty of their parents, will not eat one apple this winter."[32]

Great efforts were made to reduce production and resuscitate prices. The Agricultural Adjustment Administration (AAA), established as part of the New Deal in 1932, paid farmers for output reductions. The US Department of Agriculture (USDA) under Wallace destroyed crops and killed livestock. The program targeted cotton fields of the South, where a third of US farmers, five million whites and three million blacks, lived. Roosevelt and his advisers hoped to raise prices, enhance the purchasing power in rural areas, and stimulate manufacturing. But their programs limited acreage, not overall output, and did not compensate for scientific and technological developments, which increased efficiency and production. The farmers raised yields on the acres under cultivation and expanded total output faster than the growth of the population from 1930 to 1940. The farmers' margins, after outlays required to keep up with competitors, diminished.

What these farm programs accomplished, as they were amended over subsequent decades, was to help large-scale growers withstand the low prices resulting from output in excess of aggregate demand. The federal government maintained trade barriers in agriculture and made price-supporting loans from the Commodity Credit Corporation, created by executive order in 1933, to limit the acreage of wheat and cotton. It has made "deficiency payments" to offset the difference for sales below "target prices." The government purchased surplus commodities and subsidized exports to diminish the glut and reduce storage costs. These policies have made it difficult for the small-scale farmers unable to withdraw acres from production and obtain the subsidies. Growers able to purchase land and equipment, and cultivate more efficiently thanks to government help, have held their own against the competitive prices of low-cost farms benefiting from unpaid family labor. The large-scale growers of cotton and rice, rather than the more modest farmers of corn and wheat, receive a disproportionate share of the subsidies relative to their numbers. By the turn of the twentieth century, operations with one hundred thousand dollars or more in annual sales received 62 percent of the subsidies even though they amounted to only 16.7 percent of the farms. Subsidies based on volume rather than need permitted multimillion-dollar corporations, government agencies, and wealthy landowners, such as billionaire Ted Turner, professional athletes, and an heir to the Rockefeller fortune, to receive payments.

In this way, the years 1933–1934 proved decisive in eliminating low-income farms so that the profit margins of the largest producers were protected, investment persisted, and capital and labor could be allocated to more profitable sectors of the economy. It was in the mid-1930s that the yields of corn, wheat, rye, oats, hay, barley, and cotton had their fastest rates of growth. The farm programs of the New Deal, coming on the heels of the dust bowl, took marginal lands out of production and dramatically raised average yields. Petroleum-propelled combines became available prior to World War I yet harvested only 30 percent of Kansas wheat in 1926. Thanks to state subsidies, Kansas farmers were able to cut seasonable labor costs, harvesting 82 percent of the wheat with the combines by 1938. The combines then spread, albeit less rapidly, across much of the rest of the country.

The New Deal thus served to lay the groundwork for farmers to invest, improve labor productivity, and join the wider consumer market. In 1930, only 10 percent of rural homes had electricity, because the utility companies determined that the returns did not compensate for the costs of providing the service to sparsely populated rural communities. The Rural Electrification Administration (REA), created by executive order in 1935, financed the production of electricity, the stringing of power lines, and the wiring of homes through loans to rural cooperatives. By 1945, 75 percent of households in the Tennessee Valley had electricity compared to 2 percent in 1933. Pulsating suction milking machines had been available since the early 1900s but hardly caught on. Dairying still required one and a half times more labor than did producing cotton. It was only in the 1940s, thanks to rural electrification, improved sanitary practices, and increased incomes, that mechanical milking machines spread. Every US cow, to all intents and purposes, was milked mechanically by the mid-1960s. The REA also permitted farm families to purchase sewing machines, vacuum cleaners, indoor plumbing, hot water heaters, refrigerators, electric irons, stoves, and other apparatuses. Most farmers had telephones, running water, and electric lighting by 1955. Government programs had in a very short time made consumers of millions of farmers.

They also permitted farmers to enhance output and cut labor costs. Federal subsidies allowed farmers to replace horses with tractors. As horses disappeared from agriculture, the farmers, by 1960, converted about a quarter of fields from feed crops to marketable produce. Tractors do not need rest time, like horses and mules do, and thus permitted farmers to till more land. As growers gave up their animals, they ceased using manure and became a large market for the synthetic fertilizer industry. The perfection of corn head attachments in the early 1950s permitted farmers to dispense with hired pickers and led to greater dependence on the petroleum and farm-implement industries.

The AAA and other supply management policies saved Southern planters from the depression prices of the 1930s and, over subsequent decades, prompted them to abandon the unproductive crop-lien tenancy that had bound millions of families to the land since the 1870s. Motorized implements for the preharvest operations of cotton had been available to Southern farmers since the 1920s but were not adopted until the generous credits of the New Deal made mechanization profitable and reduced the need for the intensive work of poor tenants. The landowners no longer had an incentive to retain labor through debt peonage. At the same time, war precipitated massive spending on military bases, industrial plants, and infrastructure, as the federal government used the conflict to develop the South. The federal government, in these ways, undermined plantation tenancy and loosened the social glue tying young Southerners to the land. A flood of people migrated out of the South, two-thirds of them African Americans. Labor shortages then struck during the harvests. But long-serving Democratic legislators from the South at the head of committees, and thus enjoying disproportionate influence over the federal government, assured preferential deliveries of rationed fuel to farmers. In these circumstances, the mechanical pickers, launched by International Harvester at the end of the 1940s, met with great success.

Southern agriculture aligned itself more closely with the rest of the country as a result of the federal subsidies. Tenant farming began a steady decline in the 1930s, as the same system prevalent in most of the country, of owner-operators, took hold. Farm owners invested heavily in tractors. Subsidized acreage limitations on wheat and cotton prompted them to diversify to soybeans. Southern landowners, who previously had clamored for these subsidies, came to oppose limitations on the new crops. Soy feed-grains brought Southern growers into the growing national and international livestock industry. The growers then began to follow agriculturalists elsewhere in the US in opposing federal supply management policies.

Southern farmers, in this manner, have become part of the system common to most of the country whereby they depend on industrial inputs to enhance yields and farm more land. One grower farms ever more land without any labor expenses and thus offsets the steady decline of prices. What the federal subsidies, begun in the 1930s, accomplished was to furnish Monsanto, DuPont, Syngenta, and other corporations with more leverage. The federal government helps farmers all over the country to take out loans for the purchase of the inputs promoted by land grant colleges, corporate research, and state experiment stations. Indebted growers often suffer from overproduction by anticipating a large market, financing land and inputs, and then seeing lower returns at the time of sale. Each cycle of expansion and contraction represents a new round of purchases of machinery, fertilizer, and land. Investment in machinery increased more than 800 percent from 1945 to 1979.

This industrial farming, then, has resulted from an economic context in which farmers do not control aggregate output or prices. Declining real prices diminished per capita farm income to less than half the national average in the 1950s. This trend led economists to predict that the 32.1 million farmers of the 1950s would decline to 580,000 by 2000. Yet in 2000, the US still had two million farmers, and the reason is that off-farm earnings in manufacturing and services enable them to remain in business. In 1995, growers obtained an average of over three times as much from nonfarm activities as they did from agriculture.

A USDA study released in 2013 found that 96.4 percent of crop farms are "ones in which the principal operator, and people related to the principal operator by blood or marriage, own more than half."[33] The farms that raise the calves, until they are ready to be fattened in corporate-run confined finishing operations, belong to over seven hundred thousand families. Farming generally does not bring in much money. Big business gets higher returns from processing and packaging, and selling fuel, equipment, seeds, fertilizer, and feed. Corporations will never take over the farms since they cannot exploit their employees as well as the farmers exploit themselves.

The results of capitalist agriculture—in which families deprive themselves, work off the farm, and rely on state aid and credit to finance scientific technologies and meet competitive prices —have been impressive. Farmers increased yields rapidly by spreading nitrogen to nearly all corn acreage and increasing the rate of application nearly tenfold from 1947 to 1980. Patent and copyright laws spur investment by giving researchers temporary monopolies and allowing them to capture the benefits of their creativity. Hybrid corn has thicker stalks and stronger roots, withstands mechanical harvesting, stands tall enough to get sunlight in a crowd, and allows farmers to plant it closer together. Farms in Iowa yielded seventy to eighty bushels per acre in the 1950s, twice that after 2000, and as much as two hundred bushels of corn per acre some years. The labor required to grow one hundred bushels of corn fell from 135 to 3 hours from 1910 to 1990.

Farmers have adopted cotton varieties, developed by scientists to grow at a uniform height and ripen at a uniform date, for a once-over drive-through with the mechanical picker. A large spray rig, a four-hundred-gallon tank filled with Monsanto's Roundup Ready, and fuel to drive it through the fields once or twice a season saves tremendous outlays on hoeing crews for weeding. The spray kills everything but the cotton grown from seeds that have been genetically engineered by Monsanto to resist it. Farmers grow tomatoes scientifically developed to withstand the rough handling of picking machines, though the tomatoes are only suitable for sauces and pastes.

Patented genetically engineered seeds currently beget the lion's share of soybean and corn. Farmers sell these commodities as cattle feed, rather than for human consumption, because livestock products fetch higher prices, making it more cost-effective to burn usable nutrition in the metabolism of animals. The industries rearing the livestock face inexorable pressure to increase levels of labor productivity and enhance the rates at which the feed is converted into saleable flesh, eggs, and milk. As a result, animal densities increase within highly automated spaces to reduce infrastructure and labor costs. Bovine growth hormones, antibiotics, breeding through artificial insemination, and other biomedical innovations have spurred livestock to reach the age of sexual maturity and lactation very quickly. Whereas wild cattle, boars, and jungle fowl can live for twenty years or more, and whereas, cattle, pigs, and chickens often live for many years on mixed farms, cattle started on grasses and finished on feedlots can now be brought to commercial slaughter weight in eighteen months, industrial pigs in as little as six months, and broiler chickens in a mere six weeks. Farm animals grow to a uniform size amenable to machinery. The valuable body parts grow relatively large.

As a result of these innovations, cows yielded nearly four times more milk in 2000 than they did in 1940. An hour of dairy farming in 1910 yielded the same amount as three minutes in 1990. Poultry farmers turn out tens of thousands of chickens a day. A fully automated assembly line carries the seed, droppings, and eggs. Artificial lighting overcomes the natural daily cycle and permits the continuous laying of as many as half a million eggs on some farms every twenty-four-hour cycle.

At the end of the 1990s, Americans spent less than 12 percent of their disposable income on food, the lowest rate in the industrialized world. Even from an environmental standpoint, forest mass began to expand after World War II thanks to new growth thicker than the original trees cut down in prior centuries. Lumber companies find it more profitable to replant forests than to continually transport their expensive equipment and infrastructure to new areas. Forests also spread thanks to the drastic decline in market demand for wood, as manufacturers turned to steel, aluminum, and plastics.

But capitalist farming, as it has developed in the US, only looks impressive if one ignores the deleterious effects of price competition. Farmers replaced two million acres of native grasses with corn and soy in North Dakota, Minnesota, Iowa, and Nebraska from 2006 to 2011 on account of the market opportunities for feed grains generated by growing meat consumption worldwide. Farmers earn the largest margins by repeatedly tilling the fields of corn and soy and leaving them bare over the winter. This practice causes the soil to erode and wash away. To offset the losses of nutrients and crop productivity caused by erosion, farmers spread more ammonium nitrate on their fields than necessary for fear of not getting optimum yields. Ammonia makes its way into the air, from the fertilizer, as well as from manure on livestock farms, and reacts with other air pollutants to create tiny particles that can lodge deep in the lungs, causing asthma attacks, bronchitis, and heart attacks.

The chemical also washes into waters such as the Des Moines River, and in the spring, when runoff is heaviest, parents are warned not to give their children tap water, because the nitrates bind to hemoglobin and hinder blood from carrying oxygen to the brain. The fertilizers washed away, from soil left bare in the winter, have caused annual dead zones in the Gulf of Mexico. When researchers of the US Geological Survey examined the fossil record in 2006, they found that dead zones were relatively rare until around 1950 and then became increasingly common. This chronology coincides with the large-scale use of synthetic fertilizers. The US Geological Survey has determined that "in total, agricultural sources contribute more than 70 percent of the nitrogen and phosphorus delivered to the Gulf, versus only 9 to 12 percent from urban sources."[34] Much of the eastern edge of the Midwest drains into the Great Lakes, and there too, specialized corn and soy growing causes fertilizer-fed algae blooms. A record-setting, oxygen-depleting bloom smothered living things over two thousand square miles of Lake Erie, an area about the size of Delaware, in 2011. "That's more than three times larger than any previously observed Lake Erie algae bloom," a University of Michigan report found. The cause was severe storms in the spring, plus "agricultural practices that provide the key nutrients that fuel large-scale blooms."[35] Recognizing the problem, Minnesota is contemplating the creation of an "agricultural water quality certification" program to reduce the effect of farm runoff on rivers.

Fall plantings of cover crops, to blanket the ground in the winter and rot in place in the spring, would keep the ground moist beneath the muddy surface. They would absorb water and prevent it from cutting ruts in the earth as it carries away the chemical inputs. Vetch, one of a number of legume cover crops grown in the fall and spring, fixes nitrogen, aerates soil compacted by machinery, creates a variable plant rotation, and thus prevents the carryover of insect pests and diseases. Soil scientist Rattan Lal of Ohio State University has shown that if all US farms adopted this practice they could absorb as much as twenty-five times more carbon than they currently do— equivalent to removing nearly 10 percent of US cars from the roads. A study conducted in 2012 at Iowa State University found that adding one or two crops to the Midwest's typical corn-soy rotations would reduce synthetic fertilizer needs by 80 percent, enhance output, conserve water, cut irrigation costs, and mitigate the flow of pollution into watercourses.

Although sunflower, buckwheat, and other cover crops are becoming more common in Illinois, Indiana, and Ohio, only a minority of farmers plant them, because federal payouts and subsidized insurance compensate the costs of fertilizer and water, and give the farmers little short-term incentive to change. What is more, using diverse cover crops to control weeds and maintain fertility requires more labor than does using chemicals. In a context of competitive pricing, such rotations would therefore require a reorientation of federal regulations and subsidies to make the additional outlays on labor viable. But a reorientation of this sort would diminish the farmers' dependence on the vendors of agricultural inputs and diminish the profits of these corporations.

Like cover crops, pastures for mobile herds of grazing animals contribute to healthy soil that traps nutrients. The grasses on rangelands grow more rapidly than do trees and other plants and take more carbon dioxide underground, thanks to their proportionally greater subterranean biomass of roots. A research team from the University of Tennessee and Bard College calculated that if Midwestern farmers switched a portion of their corn land to cow pastures, they would absorb enough carbon into the soil to reduce annual greenhouse gas emissions from agriculture by 36 percent. Competitive pressure, however, has forced Midwestern farmers to specialize in corn and soy feed for livestock. This livestock spends its last days fattening in a handful of confined animal feeding operations (CAFOs) operated by corporations. World Bank scientists estimated in 2009 that animal rearing worldwide emits at least 51 percent of the atmosphere's greenhouse gases every year, more than does the entire global transportation industry. The air at some of these CAFOs is dirtier than in the most polluted US cities.

Corporate leverage over farmers appears most glaringly in the patents for living organisms. The patents permit agricultural corporations to monopolize the global seed and, hence, food markets. The corporations file suit against farmers alleged to have violated the patent agreements. Humans need seeds to survive, and if competition forces all farmers to abandon the diverse seeds they have bred to adapt to local climates and soil conditions, and instead rely on GMOs for soy and corn, then biodiversity will decline and more and more of our food will consist of these cheap ingredients. The massive spending by Monsanto on lobbying and advertising to prevent states from passing laws requiring labels on food containing GMOs speaks volumes about their un-popularity. Companies like Kellogg's, General Mills, and Smucker's will not label in just one or two states. They would have to label in all of them and then perhaps have to go GMO-free to avoid slumping sales. The agricultural corporations therefore broadcast over and over that labeling food makes no sense, allows special-interest exemptions, triggers lawsuits, and costs consu-mers money at the checkout counter. Empirical studies, however, demon-strate that offering consumers the right to know what is in their food does not raise prices. Since the European Union started labeling GMOs in the 1990s, there has been "no resulting increase in grocery costs."[36] China, Brazil, Ja-pan, Australia, and India also have enacted labeling laws without any addi-tional costs to consumers.

What is disconcerting about our age is that whereas the industrial inputs sold since the 1850s dramatically increased output and decreased prices, the ones sold most recently have not. The addition of nitrogen fertilizer to the fields has ceased to increase yields very much since the 1960s. The latest research out of the University of Wisconsin has determined that GMO crops do not increase yields. The most one can say about them is that they may make yields more stable from year to year and help farmers cope with the challenges of global warming. Then again, farmers who use cover crops conserve water and nutrients, stifle weed growth by a factor of six to ten, achieve better than average crop yields, and attain nearly the normal season average during droughts, whereas other farmers see theirs drop 50 percent or lose their crop entirely.

This technological impasse also appears in the failure of GMO crops to cut the use of chemical inputs. While GMO crops have allowed farmers to spray lower levels of insecticides, this benefit has been more than offset by the increased usage of herbicides. The USDA has found that farmers use as much as 26 percent more chemicals per acre on herbicide-resistant crops than on non-GMO ones. As weeds grow resistant to the herbicide, researchers develop new chemicals to kill them and new crops able to survive the chemi-cals, a cycle promising ever more vicious weeds and potent herbicides. Re-sistant weeds drive up the volume of herbicide needed each year by about 25 percent, a percentage slated to increase rapidly in years to come. According to an entry by a weed-control expert in the trade magazine *Corn and Soybean Digest*,

For those with a known resistance problem, it's not uncommon to see them use a fall burndown plus a residual herbicide, and two or more in-season herbicide applications. If you can catch the resistant weeds early enough, paraquat does a good job of controlling them. But once Palmer amaranth [a common resistant weed] gets 6 ft. tall, you can't put on enough paraquat to kill it. [37]

"Burndown" refers to the flattening of all vegetation in a field through liberal doses of paraquat. This chemical preparation has entered US streams, killed off frogs, and polluted drinking water. It has been banned in thirty-two countries. Monsanto's most popular herbicide, used with corn and soy genetically engineered to survive it, has been found, in a peer-reviewed study written by a scientist and senior researcher at MIT, to potentially cause inflammatory bowel disease, obesity, depression, Alzheimer's disease, Parkinson's disease, multiple sclerosis, cancer, cachexia, infertility, and developmental malformations.

Neonicotinoids are used to treat many seeds and virtually all genetically engineered Bt corn grown in the US. Companies introduced these pesticides in the 1990s, when resistance rendered many older ones useless. Today, there are nearly three hundred registered neonicotinoid products available in California alone. They are water-soluble and break down slowly in the environment. The disappearance of bee colonies, needed to grow many food crops, has accelerated in the US in proportion to the growing sales of these new pesticides in the mid-2000s.

A further impasse has emerged in the meat industry. On the one hand, the ratios of feed conversion into animal products ultimately butts up against biophysical limits, because no matter how intensely animals are immobilized and transfigured, much of the feed will still be burned off as energy, excreted and channeled into non-edible body parts. Even in industrial broiler production, where feed-to-flesh ratios are the lowest, about half to two-thirds of the feed is lost in metabolic processes.

On the other hand, the meat industry has created enormous problems for human health. A report, issued by the US Food and Drug Administration (FDA) on several egg-producing facilities in Iowa in 2010, exposed fecal pits spilling over, chicken dung oozing through building foundations, and eight-foot piles of droppings on which escaped hens climbed to peck feed from overcrowded cages. Within the CAFOs, where corporations have crammed livestock together to fatten on corn and soy, the animals ingest growing volumes of antibiotics to prevent the inevitable diseases. The antibiotics also spur animal growth. Whereas human consumption of antibiotics has leveled off at about eight billion pounds annually, livestock consumption grew to 29.9 billion in 2011, and the amount continues to rise. The bacteria that live in animals develop resistance, making the meat rife with antibiotic-resistant pathogens. These superbugs in a warming climate have led to twenty-one to thirty-five billion dollars in additional medical costs, eight million hospital days, and a drag of 0.4 to 1.6 annually on US GDP. In response, the FDA, in 2013, restricted the use of antibiotics to treat diseases. But businesses can still put them in feed preventatively with the intent of spurring growth. Without restricting the use of antibiotics to specific illnesses detected by a veterinarian, the quantity of antibiotics fed to livestock will undoubtedly continue to grow.

American farm policy in the twentieth century encouraged the maximizing of yields. Since price supports were guaranteed so long as farmers met restrictions on acres planted, but not on yields, farmers took the subsidies, controlled their acreage, and sought profits by raising output on the land they did plant. The agro-industrial complex met this desire by providing fertilizers, pesticides, and machinery. Between 1945 and 1970 yields of corn, wheat, and cotton grew rapidly. Food surpluses were vented overseas as aid to Europe and Asia. Once agriculture recovered in these regions, however, US exports became a burden on global farm incomes. The Eisenhower administration signed into law the Agricultural Trade and Assistance law, or PL 480, "the basis for a permanent expansion of our exports of agricultural products with lasting benefits to ourselves and peoples of other lands." In promoting exports, PL 480 allowed foreign governments to purchase food in local currencies, thus saving valuable dollar reserves. Most agricultural exports soon came under the law's provisions.

Postwar global agreements under the GATT (General Agreement on Tariffs and Trade) moved to lower trade barriers in financial services and manufacturing, yet allowed barriers and subsidies in agriculture to continue. World governments responded predictably. They raised farm incomes through price adjustments, import barriers, and subsidies. The resultant flood of exports was a boon for grain traders. Six commodity companies—Andre & Co., Bunge, Cargill, Continental, Dreyfus, and Mitsui-Cook—accounted for upward of 90 percent of US wheat and corn exports, as well as the vast majority of farm exports from Argentina, Australia, and Europe. These companies invested worldwide in supply chains, building up storage facilities, feedlots, poultry farms, and fast food. A combination of government support, lower export costs, and cuts to government spending in Asia, Africa, and Latin America rendered farmers in Europe, Canada, Australia, Brazil, and Argentina globally competitive. Producing in much the same way as in the US, these growers increased their global market share in the 1980s. In 1986, facing massive budget deficits, and demand for assistance from growers in political constituencies, President Reagan pushed to have agriculture subject to GATT trade norms, a move that effectively called on countries worldwide to phase out subsidies and dumping.

The new trade norms have not ended subsidies in the US or western Europe. The effect has been worldwide expansion of farm output on the basis, not of peasant production, but of corporate farms of the sort found in the US Midwest and California, and in Brazil's Cerrado. Measured worldwide, peasants still far outnumber corporate farmers. But probably for the first time in history, they account for a minority of global food and fiber production. Prices paid for food in the market are certainly at an all-time low, especially when measured as a share of family income. Manufacturers in developing countries have benefited from the anti-inflationary effect on wages.

The trend, however, has diminished peasant incomes and access to land. According to the United Nations, 805 million people receive insufficient food and 45 percent of early childhood deaths are due to hunger. One-quarter of the world's children are "stunted" and one-sixth underweight. Women are more likely to go hungry than men.[38] Corporate farms, moreover, have caused tremendous environmental damage, including carbon dioxide emissions from carbon-heavy technologies. It is for good reason that a growing chorus of protests, from nongovernmental organizations such as the Minneapolis-based Institute for Agriculture and Trade Policy and the worldwide Via Campesina social movements, is calling for "sustainability" and "food justice." We will look at this alternative vision of a stable future in the subsequent concluding chapter.

NOTES

1. José Monteiro Lobato, 1920, quoted in Christian Brannstrom, "Coffee Labor Regimes and Deforestation on a Brazilian Frontier, 1915–1965," *Economic Geography* 76.4 (October 2000), 326.

2. Platform of Via Campesina for Agriculture, May 2010, http://www.mstbrazil.org/about-mst/platform-campesina-agriculture.

3. Quoted in Warren Dean, *Brazil and the Struggle for Rubber: A Study in Environmental History* (Cambridge: Cambridge University Press, 1987), 38.

4. Quoted in Warren Dean, "Latifundia and Land Policy in Nineteenth-Century Brazil," *Hispanic American Historical Review* 51.4 (1971), 612.

5. Dean, *Brazil and the Struggle for Rubber*, 41.

6. Verena Stolke, *Coffee Planters, Workers and Wives: Class Conflict and Gender Relations on Sao Paulo Plantations, 1850–1980* (New York: St. Martin's Press, 1988), 5.

7. Dean, "Latifundia and Land Policy," 618–19.

8. Robert Conrad, "The Planter Class and the Debate over Chinese Immigration to Brazil, 1850–1893," *International Migration Review* 9.1 (Spring 1975), 50.

9. Ibid.

10. Stolke, *Coffee Planters, Workers and Wives*, 15.

11. Ibid., 28.

12. Barbara Weinstein, "The Persistence of Precapitalist Relations of Production in a Tropical Export Economy: The Amazon Rubber Trade, 1850–1920," in *Proletarians and Protest: The Roots of Class Formation in an Industrializing World*, ed. M. Hanagan and C. Stephenson (New York: Greenwood Press, 1986), 66.

13. Stolke, *Coffee Planters, Workers and Wives*, 7.

14. Ibid., 23. Emphasis added.

15. Ibid., 66.

16. Ibid., 123–24.

17. José Monteiro Lobato, 1920, quoted in Christian Brannstrom, "Coffee Labor Regimes and Deforestation on a Brazilian Frontier, 1915–1965," *Economic Geography* 76.4 (October 2000), 326.

18. "The Miracle of the Cerrado," *The Economist*, August 26, 2010, accessed March 19, 2015, http://www.economist.com/node/16886442.

19. João Pedro Stédile, "Landless Battalions," *New Left Review* 15 (May–June 2002), 95.

20. "The Miracle of the Cerrado."

21. World Bank, *Community-Based Development in Northeast Brazil: Rural Poverty Alleviation Projects* (available at www.worldbank.org/), cited in S. M. Borras Jr., "Questioning Market-Led Agrarian Reform: Experiences from Brazil, Colombia and South Africa," *Journal of Agrarian Change* 3.3 (July 2003), 375.

22. Platform of Via Campesina for Agriculture, available at http://www.mstbrazil.org/about-mst/platform-campesina-agriculture.

23. Peter C. Y. Leung and L. Eve Armentrout Ma, *One Day, One Dollar: Locke, California, and the Chinese Farming Experience in the Sacramento Delta* (El Cerrito, Calif.: Chinese American History Project, 1984), 57–58.

24. Ibid., 61–62.

25. Ibid., 48.

26. Ibid., 49–50.

27. Ibid., 50.

28. Alfredo Figueroa, "The U.F.W. Anti-immigration Campaign and Falling Out with Bert Corona, M.A.P.A., and Other Chicano Groups (2005)," in *Speaking Out: Activism and Protest in the 1960s and 1970s*, ed. Heather Ann Thompson (Upper Saddle River, N.J.: Prentice Hall, 2010), 99.

29. "UFW, United Farm Workers Union, AFL-CIO, et al. Plaintiffs, International Brotherhood of Teamsters, et al. Defendants (1973)," court filing, in *Speaking Out*, 101–2.

30. Ramon Perez Mejia, "Declaration (1975)," in *Speaking Out*, 100.

31. Remley Glass, "Gentlemen, the Corn Belt!" *Harper's* 167 (July 1933), 200–206.

32. Oscar Ameringer, "Unemployment in the United States," in *Hearings before a Subcommittee of the Committee on Labor, House of Representatives, 72nd Cong., 1 Sess., on H.R. 206, H.R. 6011, H.R. 8088* (Washington: Government Printing Office, 1932), 98–99.

33. James MacDonald, "Family Farming in the United States," *United States Department of Agriculture Economic Research Service*, March 4, 2014, accessed April 29, 2016, http://www.ers.usda.gov/amber-waves/2014-march/family-farming-in-the-united-states.aspx#.VyPbJ_krKUk.

34. US Geological Survey, "Differences in Phosphorus and Nitrogen Delivery to the Gulf of Mexico from the Mississippi River Basin," March 4, 2014, accessed April 29, 2016, https://water.usgs.gov/nawqa/sparrow/gulf_findings/.

35. Fish Information and Services, "Harmful Algal Blooms Getting Worse," April 2, 2013, accessed April 29, 2016, http://fis.com/fis/worldnews/worldnews.asp?l=e&id=59838&ndb=1.

36. American Sustainable Business Council, "The Business Case for Labeling GMOs," accessed April 29, 2016, http://asbcouncil.org/label%20gmos.

37. Iowa Soybean Association On-Farm Network, "Managing Herbicide-Resistant Weeds," *Corn and Soybean Digest*, January 28, 2013, accessed April 29, 2016, http://cornandsoybeandigest.com/crop-chemicals/managing-herbicide-resistant-weeds.

38. Food and Agriculture Organization of the United Nations, "The State of Food Insecurity in the World" (2014), accessed April 29, 2016, http://www.fao.org/publications/sofi/en/.

Conclusion

[handwritten annotations: "indicated"; "is this true a song? lek mrz a:?"]

It has been documented in this book that sustained advances in agriculture have resulted from market dependency, namely the compulsion to match the prices of rivals by reducing the manual effort of bringing commodities to market. Rising labor productivity, needless to say, has benefited the possessing classes. Employers pay for work to the extent that it generates value above its cost. But still, enhanced productivity of the time spent farming enlarges the economic pie and creates the margins for the people actually working the land to see some of the benefits. Increasingly productive labor, first in agriculture and then in industry, has generated the wealth of modern society. We conclude that market dependency, and the consequent rural development, cannot be assumed. To account for it, one must study history: specifically the bygone relations between the tillers of the soil and the landed classes interested in taking the fruits of their labor.

The dominant view, which we have countered in this book, is that urbanization and population growth beget economic demand for agricultural supplies, allow the rural population to eye the opportunity for gain and the enjoyment of new commodities manufactured in the towns, and thereby induce the farmers to specialize in those crops and livestock fetching the highest prices on the city markets. According to this scenario, when transportation infrastructure and credit institutions, offering capital for investment, become available, the agriculturalists improve crop production. The cultivators enhance yields by selecting seeds, weeding intensively, and adopting better implements. They carry out drainage projects and clear new lands, or alternatively they reduce farm sizes, depending on the crop in question, in order to cut costs and augment gains from sales. *[handwritten: demolition of fairy-tale narrative]*

This market- or trade-based view of growth, widely accepted by scholars, *[handwritten: rvtr ?]* takes its cue from Adam Smith, who famously wrote that wealth grows from *[handwritten: economic history]*

323

the human "propensity to truck, barter, and exchange."[1] Our criticism, detailed in this book, is on two levels. First, the dominant classes of precapitalist times, when presented with opportunities, through sales to urban markets, have not invested in turning out agricultural commodities more productively. They have instead funded the buildup of their political power in order to take additional output from the farmers.

Thus in England, amid the rising prices of the thirteenth century, the feudal lords did not invest with the aim of enhancing output. To realize gains from sales, these pre-capitalist elites consolidated their legal status by having the law courts of the monarchy consign the peasants to their legal jurisdictions. They thus enhanced their feudal capacity to take farm output from the serf population. Similarly, the market demand for cotton generated by the industrial revolution in England did not lead planters of the US South down a path of development toward technologically advanced farming reliant on diminishing inputs of labor. To the contrary, the plantation owners built up their power by augmenting the number of slaves and the acreage worked by them. The slaveholders built up a formidable military force in a bid to retain ownership of the labor force and clear the way for its expansion.

Second, when peasants have perceived potential gains from selling their output to urban consumers, they have taken advantage of the opportunity not by putting all of their eggs in the basket of the most lucrative agricultural commodity and then competing with rival producers for market share. Rather, rural households have taken the gains from trade and put them back into the security of subsistence farming by acquiring untilled land for future generations, cultivating a diversity of fibers and food crops, and adding livestock to their holdings. Market sales, even in the vicinity of large towns such as Philadelphia, allowed the farmers of colonial North America to extend their holdings in their prime so they could later sell land or divide acreage among offspring, and thus assure their livelihood when old and no longer able to till the fields. Rather than develop productive farm implements, or more valuable strains of crops and livestock, with the aim of building up cash reserves, the households acquired extra farm animals and acreage of untilled land, and grew more cattle feed. French peasants too were presented with opportunities for gain as a result of the industrial and urban growth of the nineteenth and early twentieth centuries. Yet at the time of World War II, about half of the population still lived in rural areas off of the products of local farms. The point is not that the farmers avoided the market. To the contrary, they found the market useful in making their households more secure. Proceeds from trade permitted the farmers to avoid relying on sales of crops and livestock, and on purchases of needed supplies, to survive.

A second variant of the urban demand-driven view holds that within rural communities entrepreneurial and better-off households seized on opportunities for gain in the market by taking on longer leases, purchasing land from

[handwritten margin notes: "to some extent forge a European mould on the rest of the world", "t for"]

households on the decline, hiring poorer villagers as field hands, and adopting new crops and methods. Thus on the basis of this peasant differentiation the entrepreneurial farmers forged a sustained course of development.

What we have shown, however, is that this sort of differentiation—the division of the rural population into richer and poorer peasants—led to both non-development and capitalist growth. What determined these outcomes was the historical context. In France in the eighteenth and nineteenth centuries, as well as in Russia after the liberation of the serfs in the second half of the nineteenth century, cases studied in chapters 4 and 8, the better-off acquisitive peasants adopted the same economic practices as the seigneurs and former lords. Well-to-do peasants loaned funds to other villagers at exorbitant rates of interest and imposed meagerly remunerated labor services on them. The richer peasants were able to compensate fellow villagers so negligibly because the villagers obtained some of their subsistence, though not enough to avoid working for rural elites, from cottage industry and their own patches of land. Peasant differentiation, in this context, led to labor-intensive farming by poor villagers. It militated against investment in productive inputs and rural development.

Likewise, the peasantry of medieval England, analyzed in chapter 2, had undergone differentiation since at least the eleventh century yet had also shared common rights in rural communities. Better-off peasants, farming about thirty acres, ones who nevertheless worked as serfs, accumulated bits of their poorer neighbors' lands. They profited from the wage labor of villagers experiencing hardship due to plot fragmentation and indebtedness amid the rise of population and prices of the 1200s. Some of the well-to-do peasants administered the lords' rights for profit. Yet they also often rallied villagers to protect common rights and fend off the imposition of heavier seigneurial dues. Rather than form capitalist dynasties, the better-off peasants sought by and large to limit participation in the market and reproduce themselves as they were. They even downgraded their farms in typical peasant fashion by dividing up their holdings on inheritance.

By the 1500s, England had few towns relative to other parts of Europe. According to the dominant view, positing the towns as the catalyst for rural development, one would not expect the agricultural revolution of the following centuries. Yet during the fourteenth-century crisis, as towns and market opportunities declined, some of the wealthier peasants took up the leases of the demesnes as prices dropped and made direct farming by the lords unprofitable. These leases created a mutually beneficial relationship between the lords who held the land and the farmers who paid to manage it. Although the population downturn of the fourteenth century facilitated the development of middling peasants, their property titles were undermined, as the wealthier farmers, over subsequent centuries, exploited the lords' capacity to raise payments for the use of the land and thus compel the peasants to augment saleable output. This capacity, we hold, constituted the distinctive variable behind the revolutionary development of English agriculture. It was the outcome of conflict between lords and peasants rather than market forces. In this unprecedented historical context, tenants had to raise income from their output relative to the money spent in farming. They had little choice but to improve their operations. They then accumulated leasehold land, which, unlike in the thirteenth century, did not get divided at death.

Differentiation of the rural population accelerated in the sixteenth and seventeenth centuries as a result of this novel context of property relations in England. Differentiation in this new capitalist context required new modes of behavior, which precluded the trends common to France, China, and Russia. These trends included usurious lending, labor services, rack renting, peasant self-exploitation, and state and seigneurial levies. Such practices redistributed wealth from the tillers of the soil to the landholders and to the well-to-do stewards managing these exploitative practices. In the new capitalist context in England, by contrast, tenant farmers invested in implements, draft animals, and a multitude of improvements required to match the competitive prices of their peers and to meet the terms of the leases contracted with the landowners.

A global variant of the trade-based view explains the various forms of farming that took shape across the world since the 1500s as outcomes of the market for new commodities in Europe. Operating with what is known as World Systems theory, scholars have argued that nobles elected on the basis of pricing to specialize in serfdom for grain exports in eastern Europe while merchants specialized in slavery for sugar and cotton exports in Brazil, the Caribbean, and the southern United States. The benefits of the global division of labor based on long-distance trade accrued among the countries of western Europe, whose ruling elites elected to industrialize, at the same time as they underdeveloped the rest of the world.

While we accept that colonialism often trapped peasants in poverty, our problem with this argument is that serfdom and slavery presuppose the historical conflicts necessary for one group of people to dominate others and compel work from them. Elites did not have the ability to choose labor regimes upon weighing relative input costs against commodity prices. The forms of labor and the division of the land arose out of the actions taken by social classes vis-à-vis one another. As we saw in the discussion of early agriculture in chapters 1 and 2, the outcome of the struggles was far from certain and actually varied in different parts of Europe, Asia, Africa, and the Americas. In sum, the context resulting from these conflicts over land and labor, rather than the markets in Europe or elsewhere, shaped the course of development.

As an illustration, the demand for sugar in Europe did not vow Africans to slavery in the Americas. Historical struggles first had to play themselves out.

Handwritten annotation at top: Economic historians have not yet come to terms with non being direct or simple to apply to China: several differences were severe but not probing the way we tend to think they have to be. pity

In the first instance, planters had to carve out and protect estates against Native Americans. Their success depended on ships, weaponry, and political organization. In the second instance, failing to lure European peasants to the New World in sufficient numbers, and defeated in their efforts to harness the labor of natives to their plantations, planters turned to the already existing market in African slaves. However, the slave trade depended too on the outcomes of conflicts in Africa, where numerous competitive states (European and African) struck deals, developed their means of war, and greatly augmented the flow of slaves from the African hinterland to the coast. _slaves from Af. left to (continue?)_

Just as slavery, in a word, was not called into being by the markets for tobacco, cotton, indigo, or sugarcane, but by the foregoing actions taken by people vis-à-vis one another, so the English ruling class was not induced by the emerging world system to introduce commercial farming and industrial capitalism at home. Capitalist property relations had already come into being in England by the early 1500s. While the accumulation of planter profits certainly added to English growth, this growth was not dependent upon them. In the context of absolute monarchy in France, by contrast, the massive fortunes made from the sugar plantations of Saint-Domingue (Haiti) came to nothing, spent on offices, titles, luxuries, and manors.

Lastly, we have written against the view that endowments of natural resources—cattle in Europe, coal in England, and the lack thereof in South America and China—determined the developmental path of these regions. In early modern England, for instance, the chronology shows that coal in the Midlands and Lancashire did not favor industrialization in these regions more than any other part of the world. The Midlands had been the main grain-producing region in the early sixteenth century. But by this time, the social conflicts of the feudal period—by which the peasants threw off feudal constraints but could not make the lords accept the inheritability of their plots—had played out and obliged the farmers to sell their output at competitive market prices. Farmers determined, over the following century, that the light soils of southern England sustained nitrogen-restoring fodder crops at lower labor costs. The farmers of the regions north of London could not match the cereal prices of the south and had to find other cash-generating activities. Had they been able to farm for their subsistence, as had been the case in the feudal period, the profit-generating capacity of their lands would not have mattered much to them. But since the inhabitants of the Midlands had to farm for the market to fulfill the terms of leases, they ended up having to reorient production toward cattle rearing and eventually toward manufacturing. From 1750 to 1830 the Lancashire textile mills at the forefront of the industrial revolution were powered almost entirely by water, which remained cheap, accessible, and far more reliable than coal-powered steam.

Just as the coal of the Midlands and Lancashire did not propel England toward industrialization, California's land and mild climate did not destine it to become a world leader in agribusiness. The fact is that European settlers, lured to the region during the boom in mining and commerce of the 1850s and 1860s, monopolized the land and oriented it toward speculative farming. From the earliest years of European settlement, California agriculture has been characterized by surges of investment, market glut, and falling revenue but then the development of new profitable economic lines. For 150 years, California has thus seen a profusion of cash crops, all produced on specialized farms. To beat out competitors, California's growers invested in biological inputs to enhance yields and combat pests. They have put money into clearing and leveling fields, controlling areas of natural inundations, moving surface water through canal and ditch systems, and pioneering the use of pumps.

In the comparable natural environment around the Mediterranean, peasants controlled much of the land and continued to farm diverse grains for local use until after World War II. California, by contrast, never knew the hindrance of feudalism, family farms, and sharecropping, existent in other parts of the world. Investors were free to create monocultures of wheat, hay, hops, almonds, Thai chilies, Champagne grapes, garlic, flowers, landscape plants, or whatever other commodity offered the highest return.

Around the Mediterranean, conversely, as in most of the rest of the world, we have shown that over the last ten thousand years, the historical context has generally permitted peasants to plan their survival by using land, labor, and tools under their direct control. This farming for local use was achieved by dint of great effort to defend possession of the land. In the cases examined in this book, when the peasants successfully fended for themselves in China, West Africa, continental Europe in the fifteenth century, colonial North America, and Russia in the 1920s, they experienced variable weather, harvest failures, and dearth. They had no control over the prices of their output or of the goods they had to purchase to survive. Logic therefore dictated caution, subsistence farming, and diversifying their crops and animals to assure the availability of harvests at different times of the year. Diversity allowed the peasants to do useful work all year long and avoid idleness during the downtimes of the production cycles of the various crops and animals. They made their own clothing, and found too that they could market extra garments, raw fiber, and other simple manufactures. These sideline occupations allowed them to buy land to better set up their offspring on farms and assure their basic needs when sick or old and no longer able to work.

Because of this interest in security, the peasants preferred hardy crops regardless of the prices they fetched. Such crops offered reliable sources of nourishment, naturally resisted diseases and pests, and took to various soils and climates. They planted emmer, rye, barley, sorghum, maize, millet, sweet potatoes, and potatoes even though these crops often required more labor and yielded less income than other economic lines. Meeting their basic needs on their own, peasants consequently did not constitute much of a market for the wider economy. They tended to shun labor-saving methods and tools when they could avoid the purchase and maintenance costs by doing the same work with the members of their households. French, Chinese, and Andean peasants of the late nineteenth century still used tools that would have been recognizable to their fourteenth-century forebearers. For these reasons, gains in productivity have been episodic rather than rapid and sustained, and development has been the exception rather than the rule, in most societies across global history.

The peasant pattern, of labor-intensive farming for local use, was only supplanted as a result of coercive ruptures. These took an unintended form in the earliest cases in England and Japan analyzed in chapter 3. In seventeenth- and eighteenth-century Japan, the *oyakata* and ex-samurai used the power delegated from the Tokugawa state to carve out estates but did not have the wherewithal to force villagers to work for them. They then began to lease out their holdings or manage them directly with hired hands. In this way, they inadvertently emerged as a class of commercial landowners in a society increasingly freed from feudal constraints. Growers found they had to sell on competitive markets for the money needed to acquire and retain the rental property, and in so doing they perceived the profits to be obtained from the careful management of costs. The agriculturalists then made innovations, such as new fertilizers from fish and oil cakes, and new tools that enhanced the labor productivity of rice farming. Farmers located in areas less conducive to the adoption of new methods could not compete and eventually reallocated capital. Some directed time to working up cloth or other manufactured items along watercourses and roadways, and soon out-competed established urban manufacturers.

These coercive ruptures took the deliberate form of state policies in post-war France, Taiwan, and Brazil examined in chapters 9 and 10. Social conflicts, between investors and officials on the one hand and farmers for local use on the other, forced the latter to reduce labor expenditures relative to output. This logic has since come to prevail across much of the planet and has led to an extraordinary growth of production. Farmers now deliver food for a global population that has grown sixfold since 1800 at stable or even slightly declining real prices. Less than one-sixth of the world's population is considered undernourished today compared to one-quarter in 1970, while the average calories eaten a day has risen about 17 percent since 1970.

To take a case in point, the federal government of the United States intervened to resolve the rural poverty caused by price competition and glut in the 1920s and 1930s. Subsidies afforded the wealthier farmers the margins to invest in the latest technologies. The rate of productivity growth took off after the 1930s, as agriculture became less sustainable for households with smaller farms, often on less productive lands. The removal of these farms raised the average productivity of the remaining growers. In the 1950s and 1960s capital-intensive farms yielded more food per hectare and per worker than ever before thanks to agriculture based on industrial principles. Today, US consumers pay lower real prices for their food as a result.

Yet the success of capitalist agriculture comes at a cost. The world faces an ecological crisis. The farmers of North Dakota, Minnesota, Iowa, Nebraska, and a number of other states, where the land lends itself to animal grazing, have replaced two million acres of native grasses with corn and soy since the price of these crops doubled in real terms from 2006 to 2011. Grasslands have been converted to farming at rates comparable to deforestation in Brazil, Malaysia, and Indonesia.

This trend owes much to the crop insurance provided by the governments. Thanks to subsidies, growers purchase package deals of seeds, fertilizers, and pesticides sold by Monsanto, DuPont, BASF, Bayer, and other corporations. They then grow corn, soybeans, wheat, cotton, canola, rice, alfalfa, and sugar beets. This industrial farming deprives the land of its natural capacity to stimulate plant growth and sequester carbon, while the nitrous oxide emitted in the production and use of the fertilizers and pesticides contributes to climate disruption.

Moreover, the corn and soy are not even farmed for human consumption but rather for sale to confined animal feeding operations (CAFOs). The use of land to support cattle has had a negative effect on the environment. Not only do we get back far fewer calories in meat and dairy than we had in the edible crops, but we also waste several times more water. CAFOs, furthermore, discharge up to 51 percent of the world's greenhouse gases, or more than the entire global transportation industry. Some scientists have labeled these factory farms "mini Chernobyls" for the way they pollute the air, soil, ground, and surface water. Despite these facts, the efforts to mitigate climate change have not focused on reversing or reforming this unsustainable, climate-disrupting mode of farming, which is ignored and thus unregulated.

Climate change from carbon emissions, in turn, causes water loss through evapotranspiration and the depletion of soil moisture, poor vernalization for some temperate cereal crops, and, in some climate-change scenarios, decreases in precipitation. Heat accelerates the growing process and leaves less time for grains to develop. According to the most reliable estimates, which account for the offsetting fertilization of plants caused by the carbon in the atmosphere, climate change will diminish global farm output 3 percent over the course of this century. In industrial countries, on aggregate, output will rise 7.7 percent, as regions such as Alaska and Scandinavia become better suited to farming. But output will fall 7 percent in Asia, 9 percent in the Middle East, and 13 percent in Latin America. India stands to lose 30 percent of its farm output. Excluding Egypt, a country with an abnormal capacity for irrigation, agricultural output will fall 18.9 percent in Africa. These regions, moreover, have less capacity to adapt to the consequences of temperature increases and proportionately more of their GDP in farming.

If farmers switched some of their cornland to pasture, they would no longer contribute to a cycle of carbon emission. Herds of grazing animals deposit dung and urine on grasses. The herds trample them so that they degrade biologically, develop vegetation, and restore soil. Vegetation and soil absorb and hold seasonal rains. The land would then store carbon and break down methane sufficient to reduce much of the annual greenhouse gas emissions from agriculture. This reform would also make available higher-quality, grass-fed beef.

To make changes of this sort, governments must alter their policies. Labeling foods containing genetically modified organisms (GMOs) would be a good place to start. The rapidly growing use of herbicides in the cultivation of GMO crops leads to problems for public health. Scientific peer-reviewed studies conducted on animals fed with GMO corn sprayed with Monsanto's Roundup herbicide found organ damage, tumors, endocrine and immune system dysfunction, and premature death. A growing body of peer-reviewed studies of GMO crops and the animals to whom they are fed has revealed a high incidence of allergies, organ toxicity, diabetes, cancer, autoimmune disorders, birth defects, high infant mortality rates, fertility problems, and sterility. Foods containing GMOs should be labeled so consumers can avoid these foods if they so desire. Labeling would thus create a disincentive for all that follows from GMOs, starting with the monocrops of cattle feed sprayed with pesticides destructive of the soil's natural capacity to support plant growth.

States must promote the rescue, reproduction, and distribution of native varieties of seeds that farmers have bred over millennia. If seeds become the intellectual property of a handful of corporations, as is currently the trend, not only do the variety and quality of food diminish, but humans also run the risk of seeing the seeds reach their biological limits, no longer able to resist the weeds and pests that mutate and evolve against them. The monopolization of the seed market leaves farmers no choice but to compound the present course toward monocultures, increased energy and chemical inputs, soil sterilization, carbon emissions, and global warming.

Governments must implement regulations and incentives to reverse the growing ratio of energy inputs to calorie outputs. Agriculture in the United States uses eighty times more energy per kilo of rice than do traditional farms in the Philippines. US farmers use thirty-three times more energy per kilo of corn than do traditional farms in Mexico. Organic approaches to producing corn and beans in the United States use 30 percent less fossil fuel, conserve more water in the soil, induce less erosion, and conserve more biological resources than does industrial farming. To change in this way, states must develop regulations so that the highest returns on labor, under the law, do not emit so much carbon, waste so much water, and erode so much soil.

Just as the world faces ecological crisis from climate change and land destruction, so too does it face an economic challenge on a scale not seen since the depression of the 1930s. Overcapacity has plagued the global economy since the 1970s. Performance indicators, such as the growth of GDP, debt, capital stock, labor productivity, and real wages, demonstrate the deterioration of the economies of the US, Germany, Japan, and other industrialized countries since the 1970s. The capacity of the domestic markets of these countries to drive growth has waned further since 2007, and the once fast-growing economies of China, Brazil, and India are unwinding as a result.

Though most manifest in the manufacturing and financial sectors of the economy, the long downturn has an agricultural component that affects hundreds of millions of peasant and small-scale growers the world over. Since the 1940s, the European Union (as well as the European Economic Community and its other predecessors), Australia, Canada, the US, and other agricultural powers have protected their home markets, subsidized growers, and promoted food exports to relieve the oversupply. The US 2002 farm bill, for instance, guaranteed an additional 180 billion dollars in subsidies over ten years, upping them to record levels; maintained supports beneficial to large-scale corporate growers; and added a ten-billion-dollar export credit program. The US gave more than three billion dollars in cotton subsidies to twenty-five thousand large-scale farmers, augmenting their productivity and thus depressing prices from the mid-1990s by 25–50 percent, with devastating consequences for eleven million farmers in West Africa for whom cotton is the main source of income. At the same time, executives of transnational corporations such as Cargill, who form part of US negotiating teams at trade summits, pursue international accords not only to lower foreign tariffs on exports but also to override US legal regulations on hormones and pharmaceuticals in the domestic meat industry and labeling requirements for GMOs.

The economic problem lies in the peasants abroad, such as the cotton farmers of West Africa, who grow poorer in competition with productive growers in North America and Europe. The danger for contemporary societies is that the continued loss of rural employment, consequent on falling prices, will exceed job creation. As poor rural inhabitants join the ranks of the urban unemployed, they reduce the cost of labor to the threshold of survival for poor peasants in agriculture. Insufficient economic demand, on a global scale, results from the insolvency of much of the world population prey to the poor remuneration of farming. Industrial centers are stifled by the lack of outlets not only because of rural poverty but also because of the low incomes and purchasing power in the cities. Urban residents face wage repression from all of the migrants fleeing destitution in the countryside.

For this reason, free markets, intensified global competition, declining costs of production, and falling world food prices do not offer a way out of the long downturn. They will only exacerbate rural poverty in the developing world. Conversely, if developing countries pursued policies to raise rural incomes, and to induce cultivators to stay on the land and farm for domestic markets, the effects would ripple positively across these national economies. It has been documented in this book that revolutionary increases in labor productivity in agriculture preceded and sustained the industrialization of England, Japan, the US, and France. In this way, policies to promote rural development in emergent nations offer a means to counteract the long downturn of the world economy. Otherwise, under the current free-trade model, industrial overcapacity worsens on account of the disproportionate growth of productivity in the US, France, Australia, and other agricultural giants. Farmers in these countries drive down agricultural prices, oblige peasants in the developing world to leave rural areas, reduce wages in the wider economy, and diminish aggregate demand on a world scale.

The policies pursued by the French government examined in chapter 9 on late development offer an example as to how countries might augment the rural standard of living. In the late 1950s, the administrators under de Gaulle set out to attain US levels of productivity. They offered low-interest loans for the settlement of relatively young farmers but excluded the smaller ones from this advantage. The policy made land available for productive households but encumbered large farmers apt to hire laborers and depress wages in agriculture. The state created inter-professional offices by product to make markets transparent and facilitate sales. It guaranteed prices and erected tariffs on imports. The growers benefited from subsidized inputs and research institutes. Thanks to these policies, the number of tractors, combine harvesters, moto-mowers, balers, and mechanical seed drills, as well as the application of industrial fertilizers, grew by leaps and bounds over the course of the 1960s. Gains in agricultural productivity exceeded those in the rest of the economy, stimulated the farm-implement and food-processing industries, and propelled France into the forefront of the world economy.

Policies of this sort, rather than trade liberalization and international price competition, ought to form the agenda of developing countries so that the world's peasants can increase their standard of living at the same time as they produce affordable food for fellow citizens in an ecologically sustainable manner. Yet as things stand, peasants of the developing world suffer from the same problems as those documented for prerevolutionary China, eighteenth- and nineteenth-century France, Russia after the 1860s, and northern Nigeria and India under British rule. Peasants are prey to agrarian elites and moneylenders backed by the power of the state. In these conditions, the lowest-income farmers apply insufficient soil amendments to fully replenish the nutrients removed at harvest or through exposure of the earth to wind and water runoff.

Typical of recent trends was the decision of the Mexican government to dismantle the national seed-producing and fertilizer companies in the 1980s and 1990s so that investors could profit from these markets. The government drastically reduced the budget of the Ministry of Agriculture and Water Resources, and radically curtailed the provision of irrigation to small farmers. After the signing of the North American Free Trade Agreement in 1994, when US farmers improved their access to the market south of the border, the Mexican agricultural trade surplus turned into a deficit of $2.7 billion by 2003. Today the country imports 40 percent of its food. Many Mexican farmers cannot make ends meet amid falling prices. A full-blown economic depression, with unemployment and industrial bankruptcies, extended across the country in 1994. Mass migration northward and the violent drug trade result from the economic and social devastation of thirty years of government cutbacks, free trade, and the insolvency of millions of farmers.

Commentators partial to the foregoing path of trade liberalization point out that the world's population will grow from about 7.2 billion today to about 9.6 billion in 2050 and that if the population is to be fed, agriculture must rely even more heavily on GMOs and accompanying inputs sold by corporations. Nevertheless, in actual fact, smaller-scale farmers are capable of meeting the growing food needs if given the support to make a living selling to domestic consumers. Despite all the difficulties they face, the number of peasants and smallholders in the Global South has remained remarkably stable over the last forty years. In Latin America, rural households have over a third of the cultivated land in small farms, yet produce over half of the maize, most of the potatoes, and the lion's share of beans in their respective countries. They produce as much as 90 percent of the food in African countries.

These peasants have grown poorer as a result of competition with the subsidized growers of North America and Europe but have not been squeezed out of existence by them. Despite this difficulty, and the consequent migration of rural residents to urban slums, family farmers continue to eke out a living thanks to the particularities of agricultural markets. The seasonal nature of farming limits capitalist rationalization. The advantages of mechanization have biological limits. Small farms have a greater capacity to react to microclimatic variation and changing biological processes. Rural inhabitants seek to reproduce the family enterprise rather than maximize profit. They therefore socialize children through periodic reductions in productivity and profit in order to teach skills and work ethics. Farms with paid employees, management bills, and profit goals cannot sustain a fall in income during a period of training for a new line. In times of low prices, family farms increase off-farm employment to gain supplemental income, and stay in existence through reduced consumption, additional inputs of unpaid household labor, and expanded output. Industrial farms, by contrast, must continue to meet payroll or lose skilled labor. In these ways, self-exploitation, so to speak, permits the survival of household farms, even in the US. But to have these small farmers work toward the development of their national economies and counteract the long downturn in the world economy, governments must facilitate their work and help them to raise their standard of living.

Small cultivators of grains, fruits, vegetables, fodder, and animal products not only outproduce large single-crop farms but also, with proper support, could do so without all the ecological damage of industrial agriculture. In the US the typical item journeys over a thousand miles prior to consumption and undergoes refrigeration, waxing, coloring, irradiation, fumigation, and packaging. It has been genetically modified against rotting and consequently is not so nutritious, if not downright toxic. The path to a sustainable future would be for governments to support farmers engaged in ecologically sensitive husbandry for the people of their areas by erecting tariffs and by providing cheap credit and access to agronomic research. The governments must strive to make their countries self-sufficient in agriculture, and cease to rely on the food from farms using the latest inputs of agribusiness.

Of course, such policies are resisted tooth and nail by corporations and governments in the US, western Europe, Brazil, and elsewhere. To face down these powers would require a massive movement of consumers, environmentalists, and farmers worldwide. Even if such a movement succeeded in making the countries of Asia, Africa, and Latin America self-sufficient in food, they would still run into problems if rural development resulted from cost-cutting production methods of growers obliged to reduce outlays relative to income and amass cash reserves in order to compete with other national farmers. Rural development, in this context, would eventually lead to environmental degradation and overproduction just as it did for José Bové and François Dufour after the agricultural revolution in France in the 1960s analyzed in chapter 9.

For this reason, a mass movement of global proportions should seek an expansive structural transformation to take agriculture out of the profit-making business cycle. What is necessary is democratic planning on a world scale with the aim of assuring a decent standard of living, safe food, and protection of the natural environment. This objective, of course, challenges the current hegemony of the possessing classes of the world. Yet it is an eminently rational objective and the only one offering a sustainable future for humanity.

NOTE

1. Adam Smith, "The Wealth of Nations," in *The Essential Adam Smith*, ed. Robert Heilbroner (New York: W. W. Norton, 1986), 168.

Selected Bibliography

Articles and book chapters are indicated by inverted commas and monographs by italics, followed by date of publication.

INTRODUCTION

For our analytical approach, and in addition to our own works listed below, see Robert Brenner's "Property and Progress: Where Adam Smith Went Wrong," "The Low Countries in the Transition to Capitalism," "Property Relations and the Growth of Agricultural Productivity in Late Medieval and Early Modern Europe," both his keynote essay and longer response to his critics in *The Brenner Debate: Agrarian Class Structure and Economic Development in Pre-industrial Europe*, and "The Origins of Capitalist Development: A Critique of Neo-Smithian Marxism." Also see Ellen Meiksins Wood, *The Origin of Capitalism*.

CHAPTER 1: SETTLED AGRICULTURE

For the rarity of warfare among hunter-gatherers see Douglas Fry, *The Human Potential for Peace: An Anthropological Challenge to Assumptions about War and Violence*. Alan Simmons, *The Neolithic Revolution in the Near East: Transforming the Human Landscape*, presents the standard, generally held view that population growth put pressure on resources and led people to begin to rely on farming. Charles A. Reed, *Origins of Agriculture: Discussion and Some Conclusions*, points out, however, that social and cultural changes must also have been necessary for people to come to rely on farming. Jacques Cauvin, *The Birth of the Gods and the Origins of Agriculture*, develops a radical and compelling case for cultural changes—in humans' relationships to one another and animals, and in their view of the world and cosmos—as the ultimate explanation for human reliance on agriculture. Brian Fagan wrote a good wide-ranging description of agriculture among prehistoric civilizations: *World Prehistory: A Brief Introduction*.

Marvin Harris, *Cannibals and Kings: The Origins of Cultures*, offers a classic anthropological interpretation for the origins of patriarchy in prehistory. It is still worthwhile to read Simone de Beauvoir, *The Second Sex*, to get an interpretation of the motivations that led men to seek dominance over female members of the species.

One obtains useful insights into the relationship between the farming populations and the urban areas in ancient civilizations from Karl Marx, *Precapitalist Economic Formations*. Charles Keith Maisels, *Early Civilizations of the Old World: The Formative Histories of Egypt, the Levant, Mesopotamia, India, and China*, is the latest, most detailed description of Mesopotamian agriculture. Chris Harman, *A People's History of the World*, provides a good account of the class relations governing the farming of ancient Mesopotamia. Harriet Crawford, *Sumer and the Sumerians*, provides detailed information on Sumerian farming. Daniel Potts, *Mesopotamian Civilization: The Material Foundations*, offers a compelling interpretation of ancient Mesopotamian farming.

Ancient Rome and Greece

For general surveys of work and the economy, see P. A. Blunt, *Italian Manpower: 225 BC–AD 14*; A. H. M. Jones, *The Roman Economy: Studies in Ancient Economic and Administrative History*; G. E. M. de Ste. Croix, *The Class Struggle in the Ancient Greek World: From the Archaic Age to the Arab Conquest*; and Dennis Kehoe, "The Early Roman Empire: Production." On property systems in the Roman Empire, see Dennis Kehoe, *Law and Rural Economy in the Roman Empire*. On Roman farming, see K. D. White, *Roman Farming*; Joan Frayn, *Subsistence Farming in Roman Italy*, and M. S. Spurr, *Arable Cultivation in Roman Italy, 200 BC–AD 100*. Also see John Evans' "Wheat Production and Its Social Consequences in the Roman World," Paul Erdkamp's "Agriculture, Underemployment, and the Cost of Rural Labour in the Roman World," and Paul Halstead's "Traditional and Ancient Rural Economy in Mediterranean Europe: Plus ça Change?" On trade, see Keith Hopkins, "Taxes and Trade in the Roman Empire (200 B.C.–A.D. 400)." On food supply, see Peter Garnsey, *Famine and Food Supply in the Greco-Roman World: Responses to Risk and Crisis*. Also see Richard Duncan-Jones, *The Economy of the Roman Empire: Quantitative Studies*. Perry Anderson's *Passages from Antiquity to Feudalism* and Chris Wickham's *The Inheritance of Rome* are essential readings for the transition from the ancient to the medieval world. Also see Aldo Schiavone, *The End of the Past: Ancient Rome and the Modern West*.

Ancient China

For a general survey of political and social developments, see Mark Lewis' *The Early Chinese Empires: Qin and Han*. Francesca Bray's comprehensive study of Chinese agriculture and its technology (volume 6.2) in Joseph Needham's Science and Civilisation in China series is essential reading. The most thorough English-language study of ancient agriculture remains Cho-yun Hsu's *Han Agriculture: The Formation of the Early Chinese Agrarian Economy (206 B.C.–A.D. 220)*. Cho-yun Hsu's *Ancient China in Transition: An Analysis of Social Mobility, 722–222 B.C.* provides useful background on the social change before the Han dynasty.

CHAPTER 2: FROM ANTIQUITY TO THE EVE OF AGRARIAN CAPITALISM

Feudal Europe

Max Weber, *General Economic History*, remains an insightful work for its description of the distinctive logic of peasant agriculture in feudal Europe. French historians carried on in this sociological tradition capturing the distinguishing rationality of the feudal economy: Marc Bloch, *Feudal Society*; Georges Duby, *Rural Economy and Country Life in the Medieval West*; Duby, *Le moyen âge 987–1460*; Duby, *William Marshal: The Flower of Chivalry*; and Guy Fourquin, "Le Temps de la croissance" and "Au seuil du XIVe siècle." Among English scholars, R. H. Hilton, *Class Conflict and the Crisis of Feudalism: Essays in Medieval Social History*, is similarly a well-researched collection of provocative essays on the social and economic relationships of English feudalism. Robert Brenner's work has brought all of this research, and then some, together in a compelling explanation of the logic and evolution of the feudal economy; see "The Rises and Declines of Serfdom in Medieval and Early Modern Europe" and "Property and Progress: Where Adam Smith Went Wrong." Spencer Dimmock, *The Origins of Capitalism in England 1400–1600*, provides the latest empirically based study of the distinctive manner in which English feudalism came to an end. Terence Byres, "Differentiation of the Peasantry under Feudalism and the Transition to Capitalism: In Defence of Rodney Hilton," offers a provocative criticism of Brenner's work.

Historians have recently revised the tradition stemming from Weber, Bloch, and Duby and now analyze the medieval period in the same way they would capitalist economies. See B. M. S. Campbell, *English Seigniorial Agriculture, 1250–1450*, and Steven Epstein, *An Economic and Social History of Later Medieval Europe, 1000–1500*.

The Inca

A general survey of Inca society, polity, and economy can be found in Terence N. D'Altroy's *The Incas*. John V. Murra's *The Economic Organization of the Inka State* and his article "El Archipielago Revisited" in *Andean Ecology and Civilization* are essential reading. Also see D. Browman, R. Burger, and M. Rivera, *Social and Economic Organization in the Prehispanic Andes*. On Inca state formation and society, also see Brian Bauer and R. Alan Covey, "Processes of State Formation in the Inca Heartland (Cuzco, Peru)," and especially Covey's *How the Inca Built Their Heartland: State Formation and the Innovation of Imperial Strategies in the Sacred Valley, Peru*. For a study of regional administration under the Inca, see Covey's "Inka Administration of the Far South Coast of Peru." On the "gift" economy, see Lido Valdez's "Maize Beer Production in Middle Horizon Peru."

On Andean civilization generally, see the following three articles by Charles Stanish: "The Hydraulic Hypothesis Revisited: Lake Titicaca Basin Raised Fields in Theoretical Perspective," "Nonmarket Imperialism in the Prehispanic Americas: The Inka Occupation of the Titicaca Basin," and "The Origins of State Societies in South America." Also see Arthur Morris, "The Agricultural Base of the Pre-Incan Andean Civilizations."

On Andean ecosystems and Inca farming, see Karl Zimmerer, "Agricultural Biodiversity and Peasant Rights to Subsistence in the Central Andes during Inca Rule" and "Wetland Production and Smallholder Persistence: Agricultural Change in a Highland Peruvian Region"; P. Baker and M. Little, *Man in the Andes: A Multidisciplinary Study of High-Altitude Quechua*; S. Masuda, I. Shimada, and C. Morris, *Andean Ecology and Civilization: An Interdisciplinary Perspective on Andean Ecological Complementarity*; Stephen Brush, *Mountain, Field and Family: The Economy and Human Ecology of an Andean Valley*; and Daniel Gade, *Plants, Man and the Land in the Vilcanota Valley of Peru*. On the importance and adaptability of the potato, see Stephen Brush, H. Carney, and Z. Huamán, "Dynamics of Andean Potato Agriculture." Clark Erikson's "Prehistoric Landscape Management in the Andean Highlands: Raised Field Agriculture and Its Environmental Impact" provides useful technical details regarding Andean field systems. Kenneth Kelly discusses cropping regimes and ecology in "Land-Use Regions in the Central and Northern Portions of the Inca Empire."

West Africa

A general survey of the West African economy is found in A. G. Hopkins, *An Economic History of West Africa*; Philip Curtin, *Economic Change in Precolonial Africa: Senegambia in the Era of Slave Trade*; Walter Rodney, *A History of the Upper Guinea Coast, 1545–1800*; Ray Kea, *Settlements, Trade, and Polities in the Seventeenth-Century Gold Coast*; and Patrick Manning, *Slavery and African Life: Occidental, Oriental, and African Slave Trades*. J. D. Fage's "Upper and Lower Guinea" in *The Cambridge History of Africa, 1050–1600* provides a general survey of social and political change. A useful analysis is Richard Roberts' *Linkages and Multiplier Effects in the Ecologically Specialized Trade of Precolonial West Africa*. George E. Brooks, *Landlords and Strangers: Ecology, Society, and Trade in Western Africa, 1000–1630*, provides an examination of social change and landholding systems, as does Stephen Hymer's article "Economic Forms in Pre-colonial Ghana." West African rice farming is detailed in Judith Carney, *Black Rice: The African Origins of Rice of Cultivation in the Americas*, and Walter Hawthorne, *Planting Rice and Harvesting Slaves: Transformations along the Guinea-Bissau Coast, 1400–1900*. M. Widgren and J. Sutton, *Islands of Intensive Agriculture in Eastern Africa*, provides accounts of some of pre-colonial Africa's most productive agrarian systems. William Allen, *The African Husbandman*, gives a general survey of both eco- and farming systems throughout Africa. J. Harlan, J. De Wet, and A. Stemlar's *The Origins of African Plant Domestication* is a comprehensive study of earliest farming in Africa.

CHAPTER 3: AGRARIAN CAPITALISM IN THE EARLY MODERN WORLD

England

Robert Allen, *Enclosure and the Yeoman*, shows distinctively large farms of England compared to western Europe during the early modern period. Mark Overton, *Agricultural Revolution in England: The Transformation of the Agrarian Economy, 1500–1850*, amounts to a good overview of the agricultural revolution. Bruce M. S. Campbell and Mark Overton, "A New Perspective on Medieval and Early Modern Agriculture: Six Centuries of Norfolk Farming c. 1250–c.1850," demonstrates the very early and exceptional accumulation of farm animals in regions of England best suited to animal husbandry. Joan Thirsk, *Economic Policy and Projects: The Development of a Consumer Society in Early Modern England*, likewise demonstrates the early advance of the English economy with exceptionally developed manufacturing arising out of productive capitalist farming. E. L. Jones, "Agricultural Origins of Industry," shows that industry developed out of the agricultural revolution rather than vice versa. Anthony Wrigley, "Urban Growth and Agricultural Change: England and the Continent in the Early Modern Period," shows the distinctively rapid urbanization of England and the development of new towns out of agricultural settlements rather than the expansion of older commercial centers of the feudal era.

Robert Allen, "Agricultural Productivity and Rural Incomes in England and the Yangtze Delta, c. 1620–c. 1820," demonstrates the great advance in the labor productivity of English agriculture relative to the Chinese. Gregory Clark, "Too Much Revolution: Agriculture in the Industrial Revolution, 1700–1860," provides statistical evidence of the exceptional advances in labor productivity in English farming. E. L. Jones' "Editor's Introduction" to *Agriculture and Economic Growth in England, 1650–1815* amounts to an informative brief synthesis of the research showing the capitalist development of English agriculture. E. A. Wrigley, "The Transition to an Advanced Organic Economy: Half a Millennium of English Agriculture," demonstrates the early transition to an advanced economy long before the diffusion of the steam engine. Robert Allen, "Agriculture during the Industrial Revolution," provides a useful description and analysis of the tremendous growth in agriculture in eighteenth-century England. Robert Brenner lastly explains the agricultural revolution in England, and why England diverged from western Europe in terms of economic development and urbanization, in "Property and Progress: Where Adam Smith Went Wrong."

Japan

On Tokugawa Japan, see Grace Kwon, *State Formation, Property Relations, and the Development of the Tokugawa Economy*; Thomas Smith, *The Agrarian Origins of Modern Japan*; and Susan Hanley and Kozo Yamamura, *Economic and Demographic Change in Preindustrial Japan, 1600–1868*. Also see Thomas Smith's *Native Sources of Japanese Industrialization, 1750–1920*, and on family size see his *Nakahara: Family Farming and Population in a Japanese Village, 1717–1830* and Fabian Drixler's *Mabiki: Infanticide and Population Growth in Eastern Japan, 1660–1950*. Conrad Totman's *Politics in Tokugawa Bakufu, 1600–1843* provides an excellent overview of the Tokugawa state. Frederick Notehelfer's "Meiji through the Rearview Mirror: Top-Down vs Bottom-Up History" is an original reconceptualization of the links between Meiji modernization and developments in the Tokugawa. On the Tokugawa Village, see Herman Ooms' *Tokugawa Village Practice: Class, Status, Power, Law*. Osamu Saito, "Land, Labour and Market Forces in Tokugawa Japan," examines tenancy and labor markets. On trade and commerce, see Ronald Toby, "Both a Borrower and a Lender Be:

From Village Moneylender to Rural Banker in the Tempo Era," and E. S. Crawcour, "Changes in Japanese Commerce in the Tokugawa Period."

CHAPTER 4: MALTHUSIAN LIMITS IN THE EARLY MODERN WORLD

France

Very good overviews of French agriculture in the eighteenth and nineteenth centuries include Maurice Aymard, "Autoconsommation et marchés: Chayanov, Labrousse ou Le Roy Ladurie?"; Gérard Béaur, *Histoire agraire de la France au XVIIIe siècle: Inerties et changements dans les campagnes françaises entre 1715 et 1815*; Edward Berenson's first chapter in *Populist Religion and Left-Wing Politics in France, 1830–1852*; Serge Bianchi et al., *La terre et les paysans en France et en Grande-Bretagne du début du XVIIe à la fin du XVIIIe siècle*; George Grantham, "Scale and Organization in French Farming, 1840 to 1880"; and Jean Meuvret, *Le problème des subsistances à l'époque Louis XIV*. For the long-term evolution of French agriculture stretching back to the feudal period, Marc Bloch's *French Rural History: An Essay on Its Basic Characteristics* remains informative.

For the debate as to whether agriculture underwent a capitalist process of economic growth or continued along a path of stagnation, Philip Hoffman, *Growth in a Traditional Society: The French Countryside, 1450–1815*, represents the first position. For the second, more critical view of French growth see Thomas Brennan, "Peasants and Debt in Eighteenth-Century Champagne"; Robert Brenner, "Property and Progress: Where Adam Smith Went Wrong"; Jean Jacquart, "Le rente foncière, indice conjoncturel?"; Ernest Labrousse, *La crise de l'économie française à la fin de l'Ancien Régime et au début de la Révolution*; and Stephen Miller, "French Absolutism and Agricultural Capitalism: A Comment on Henry Heller's Essays." For this debate as it applies to the Paris Basin, Jean-Marc Moriceau, *Les Fermiers de l'île de France: L'ascension d'un patronat agricole (XVe–XVIIIe siècle)*, and Jean-Marc Moriceau and Gilles Postel-Vinay, *Ferme, entreprise, famille: Grande exploitation et changements agricoles: Les Chartier, XVIIe–XIXe siècles*, represent the former position in favor of capitalist development. One can read the skeptical position in Jean-Michel Chevet, "Production et productivité: Un modèle de développement économique des campagnes de la région parisienne aux xviiie et xixe siècles"; George Grantham, "The Diffusion of the New Husbandry in Northern France, 1815–1840"; and two articles by Gérard Béaur, "Investissement foncier, epargne et cycle de vie dans le pays chartrain au XVIIIe siècle" and "Les Chartier et le mystère de la révolution agricole."

For the land market in the Paris Basin see Gérard Béaur, *Le marché foncier à la veille de la Révolution: Les mouvements de Propriété beaucerons dans les régions de Maintenon et de Janville de 1761 à 1790*. For the agrarian structure of the Île-de-France see Pierre Brunet, *Structure agraire et économie rurale des plateaux tertiaires entre la Seine et l'Oise*; Omer Tulippe, *L'habitat rural en Seine-et-Oise: Essai de géographie du peuplement*, and I. Loutchisky, "Régime Agraire et populations agricoles dans les environs de Paris à la veille de la Révolution." A convincing work on the agriculture of the Paris Basin remains Jean Jacquart, *La crise rurale en île-de-France 1550–1670*. Other sound empirical works showing slow growth, even stagnation, in the Paris Basin are Emile Mireaux, *Une province française au temps du grand roi: La Brie*, and Marc Venard, *Bourgeois et paysans au XVIIe siècle: Recherché sur le role des bourgeois parisiens dans la vie agricole au Sud de Paris au XVIIe siècle*.

For the agrarian structure in other parts of France see Louis Merle, *La métairie et l'évolution agraire de la Gâtine poitevine de la fin du Moyen Age à la Révolution*. Works documenting the labor-intensive peasant-led economic growth in the provinces include Annie Antoine, "Systèmes agraires de la France de l'Ouest: Une rationalité méconnue?"; André Benoist, "Vie paysanne et protestantisme en 'Moyen-Poitou' du XVIe siècle à La Révolution"; Philippe Bossis, "Le milieu paysan aux confins de l'Anjou, du Poitou et de la Bretagne 1771–1789"; Georges Durand, *Vin vigne et vignerons en lyonnais et Beaujolais*; François-P. Gay, *La champagne du Berry: Essai sur la formation d'un paysage agraire et l'évolution d'une société rurale*; Alain Gérard, *Pourquoi la Vendée?*; Sébastian Jahan, "La route des motives: Les travailleurs saisonniers des confins marchois en Loudunais (XVIIe–XVIIIe siècles)"; Stephen Miller, "The Economy of France in the Eighteenth and Nineteenth Centuries: Market Opportunity and Labor Productivity in Languedoc"; Jacques Peret, *Les paysans de Gâtine poitevine au XVIIIe siècle*; and Charles Tilly, *The Vendée*.

China

For a general overview of the period, see the relevant chapters in F. W. Mote's *Imperial China, 900–1800*. Two key works on the Qing rural economy are Philip Huang's *The Peasant Economy and Social Change in North China* and *The Peasant Family and Rural Development in the Yangzi Delta, 1350–1988*. Sucheta Mazumdar's *Sugar and Society in China: Peasants, Technology, and the World Market* provides a lucid account of agrarian developments in south China, with emphasis too on land tenure systems and proto-industry. Robert Mark's *Tigers, Rice, and Silt: Environment and Economy in Late Imperial South China* and Peter Perdue's *Exhausting the Earth: State and Peasant in Hunan* describe in detail peasant settlement, environmental degradation, and state intervention in south and central China respectively. An excellent study of China's environmental history, and the labor-intensive quality of late imperial Chinese farming, is Mark Elvin's *The Retreat of the Elephants: An Environmental History of China*. E. C. Ellis and S. M. Wang's "Sustainable Traditional Agriculture in the Lake Tai Region of China" provides a very instructive account of late imperial farming—with emphasis on the lengths to which peasants fertilized their fields—in the low Yangzi region. Christopher Isett's *State, Peasant and Merchant in Qing Manchuria* and John Shepherd's *Statecraft and Political Economy on the Taiwan Frontier, 1600–1800* describe agrarian developments (farming, land tenure, merchant activity) on the frontiers of the Qing empire. A general survey of the Qing economy is found in Ramon Myers and Yejian Wang's "Economic Developments, 1644–1800." The key overview of farming methods and technology in Chinese history remains Francesca Bray's agriculture volume in Joseph Needham's series Science and Civilisation in China, volume 6, part 2. Her study *Rice Economies: Technology and Development in Asian Societies* is a significant contribution to our understanding of the labor-intensive nature of Asian riziculture. In addition, an excellent firsthand description of intensive farming in China is available in H. H. King's *Farmers of Forty Centuries: Organic Farming in China, Korea, and Japan*. What might be called the neo-Malthusian account of Chinese development can be found in Mark Elvin's *The Pattern of the Chinese Past*.

On China's population history (estimates, regional differences, migration, and the importance of New World crops) one must begin with Ping-t'i Ho's *Studies on the Population of China, 1368–1953*. Estimates of population, acreage, and yield data can be found in Dwight Perkins' *Agricultural Development in China, 1368–1968* as well. James Lee and Wang Feng's *One Quarter of Humanity: Malthusian Mythology and Chinese Realities, 1700–2000* argues against the neo-Malthusian account from the demographic perspective. For a very convincing restatement of the Malthusian position, however, see Arthur Wolf and Theo Engelen's "Fertility and Fertility Control in Pre-Revolutionary China." Pierre-Etienne Will's *Bureaucracy and Famine in Eighteenth-Century China* and Lillian Li's *Fighting Famine in North China: State, Market, and Environmental Decline 1690s–1900s* provide clear evidence of the increasingly desperate environmental and social conditions in north China associated with heightened population pressures.

The English-language historiography of China's cities, manufacturing, and trade is less well developed. See G. William Skinner's "Regional Urbanization in Nineteenth-Century China" for estimates of China's urban population and Chao Kang's *The Development of Cotton Textile Production in China* for a full description of late imperial cotton manufacturing. On grain prices, see Yejian Wang's "Food Supply and Grain Prices in the Yangzi Delta in the Eighteenth Century."

On the subject of legal rights to land and the legal and social standing of labor see the following: Philip Huang's *Civil Justice in China: Representation and Practice in the Qing* and *Code, Custom, and Legal Practice in China*; Jing Junjian's "Legislation Related to the Civil Economy in the Qing Dynasty"; H. Franz Schurmann's "Traditional Property Concepts in China"; and Sucheta Mazumdar's "Rights in People, Rights in Land: Concepts of Customary Property in Late Imperial China."

On the subject of women and women's work in sidelines, see Hill Gates' "Footloose in Fujian: Economic Correlates of Footbinding"; Melissa J. Brown et al.'s "Marriage Mobility and Footbinding in Pre-1949 Rural China: A Reconsideration of Gender, Economics, and Meaning in Social Causation"; Susan Mann's *Precious Records: Women in China's Long Eighteenth Century*; and Francesca Bray's *Technology and Gender: Fabrics of Power in Late Imperial China*. On the value of rural wives to their farmer husbands as fungible assets see Matthew Sommer's "Making Sex Work: Polyandry as a Survival Strategy in Qing Dynasty China."

Finally, Robert Brenner and Christopher Isett's "England's Divergence from China's Yangzi Delta: Property Relations, Microeconomics, and Patterns of Economic Development" provides a comparative accounting of China and England's economic divergence.

CHAPTER 5: THE NEW WORLD

On the institution and practices of Caribbean slavery associated with sugar see Russell Menard, *Sweet Negotiations: Sugar, Slavery, and Plantation Agriculture in Early Barbados*; and Stuart Schwartz, *Sugar Plantations in the Formation of Brazilian Society: Bahia, 1550–1835, Tropical Babylon: Sugar and the Making of the Atlantic World, 1450–1680*, "Indian Labor and New World Plantations: European Demands and Indian Responses in Northeastern Brazil," "Resistance and Accommodation in Eighteenth-Century Brazil: The Slaves' View of Slavery," and "Patterns of Slaveholding in the Americas: New Evidence from Brazil." Other significant work includes Robin Blackburn, *The Making of New World Slavery: From Baroque to the Modern*; Richard Sheridan, *Sugar and Slavery: An Economic History of the British West Indies, 1623–1775*; Richard Dunn, *Sugar and Slaves: The Rise of the Planter Class in the English West Indies, 1624–1713*; and Eric Williams, *Capitalism and Slavery*. On technology and slavery see R. K. Aufhauser, "Slavery and Technological Change."

CHAPTER 6: AMERICAN FARMING

Charles Post, *The American Road to Capitalism: Studies in Class-Structure, Economic Development and Political Conflict, 1620–1877*, is an impressive book taking up all the crucial debates on the history of US agriculture, including the self-sufficient communities of colonial New England, the transition to capitalism as settlement spread westward across the Appalachians, the relationship between agriculture and industry, the distinctive logic of the Southern slave economy, and the causes of the Civil War.

Several excellent works demonstrate the persistence and stubbornness of self-sufficient farming on the East Coast of the United States all the way until the 1850s: Michael Merrill, "Cash Is Good to Eat: Self-Sufficiency and Exchange in the Rural Economy of the United States"; James Henretta, "Families and Farms: Mentalité in Pre-industrial America"; Daniel Vickers, *Farmers and Fishermen: Two Centuries of Work in Essex County, Massachusetts, 1630–1850*; Christopher Clark, *The Roots of Rural Capitalism: Western Massachusetts, 1780–1860*; Richard Lyman Bushman, "Markets and Composite Farms in Early America"; and Allan Kulikoff, *From British Peasants to Colonial American Farmers*. William Cronon, *Changes in the Land: Indians, Colonists, and the Ecology of New England*, shows the ecological consequences of this household/community farming. John McCusker and Russell Menard, *The Economy of British America, 1607–1789*, is an overview of the North American economy in the colonial era.

Winifred Rothenberg has written two excellent articles on the efforts of the political and economic elite of Massachusetts to extricate the land and labor markets from the self-sufficient households: "The Emergence of a Capital Market in Rural Massachusetts, 1730–1838" and "The Emergence of Farm Labor Markets and the Transformation of the Rural Economy: Massachusetts, 1750–1855." David Szatmary, *Shays' Rebellion: The Making of an Agrarian Insurrection*, analyzes the social and political conflict arising out of the imposition of market-oriented farming on the inhabitants of New England.

John Mack Faragher, *Sugar Creek: Life on the Illinois Prairie*, shows that the first settlers of the Midwest sought the security of self-sufficient farming even when they became prosperous and increased the size of their landholdings. Several works show the efforts of investors, land speculators, and federal and state governments to raise land values, prevent squatting and self-sufficient farming, and encourage capitalist agriculture on the frontiers: Andrew Cayton, *The Frontier Republic: Ideology and Politics in the Ohio Country, 1780–1825*; Robert P. Swierenga, *Pioneers and Profits: Land Speculation on the Iowa Frontier*; Alan Taylor, "Land and Liberty on the Post-Revolutionary Frontier"; Thomas Slaughter, *The Whiskey Rebellion: Frontier Epilogue to the American Revolution*; Clarence Danhof, "Farm-Making Costs and the 'Safety Valve': 1850–1860"; and Paul Wallace Gates, "The Homestead Act in an Incongruous Land System." Harriet Friedman, "World Market, State, and Family Farm: Social Bases of Household Production in the Era of Wage Labor," describes the capitalist family farming in the Midwest. For the contrary position—that settlers already had commercial farming in mind in relocating across the Appalachians and that land speculators and the government had little to do with the emergence of capitalist agriculture—see two essays by Jeremy Atack, Fred Bateman, and William Parker, "The Farm, the Farmer, and the Market" and "Northern Agriculture and the Westward Movement."

Brian Page and Richard Walker, "From Settlement to Fordism: The Agro-industrial Revolution in the American Midwest," is an excellent work showing that capitalist agriculture laid the basis for the industrialization of the US economy.

Allan Kulikoff, *Tobacco and Slaves: The Development of Southern Cultures in the Chesapeake, 1680–1800*, is an excellent work on slave agriculture in the Atlantic states during the colonial period.

Two outstanding books show the distinctive non-capitalist logic of slave agriculture in the cotton South: Eugene D. Genovese, *The Political Economy of Slavery: Studies in the Economy and Society of the Slave South*, and Gavin Wright, *The Political Economy of the Cotton South: Households, Markets, and Wealth in the Nineteenth Century*. John Ashworth, *Slavery, Capitalism, and Politics in the Antebellum Republic: Commerce and Compromise, 1820–1850*, offers a brilliant analysis of the ways in which Southern politics grew out of the constraints of slave agriculture. Alan Olmstead and Paul Rhode, "Biological Innovation and Productivity Growth in the Antebellum Cotton Economy," shows the techniques used to make slaves as productive as possible. Marc Egnal, *Clash of Extremes: The Economic Origins of the Civil War*, contains useful insights on the divergent politics and culture of the North and South prior to the Civil War.

CHAPTER 7: NEW IMPERIALISM

Africa

Mike Davis, *Late Victorian Holocausts: El Niño Famines and the Making of the Third World*, amounts to the most comprehensive narrative of the violence visited upon rural populations worldwide during the new imperialism at the end of the nineteenth and beginning of the twentieth centuries.

A good narrative of this story in the Belgian Congo is Adam Hochschild, *King Leopold's Ghost: A Story of Greed, Terror, and Heroism in Colonial Africa*. Other good studies of the holocaust in the Belgian Congo include Robert Harms, "The World Abir Made: The Maringa-Lopori Basin, 1885–1903"; Isidore Ndaywel è Nziem, *Histoire générale du Congo: De l'héritage ancien à la République Démocratique*; and Aldwin Roes, "Towards a History of Mass Violence in the Etat Indépendant du Congo,

1885–1908." Osumaka Likaka, *Rural Society and Cotton in Colonial Zaire*, constitutes a very good book on the period after the Belgian state shifted its focus from rubber to cotton. Allen Isaacman, *Cotton Is the Mother of Poverty: Peasants, Work, and Rural Struggle in Colonial Mozambique, 1938–1961*, is an excellent work presenting much the same story of the use of force to oblige peasants to farm cash crops.

For the region of Western Africa, where independent peasant agriculture continued to prevail, see James McCann, *Green Land, Brown Land, Black Land: An Environmental History of Africa 1800–1990*; Gareth Austin, *Labour, Land and Capital in Ghana: From Slavery to Free Labour in Asante, 1807–1956*; Sven Beckert, *Empire of Cotton: A Global History*; and Steven Pierce, *Farmers and the State in Colonial Kano: Land Tenure and the Legal Imagination*. A great book on this subject is Michael Watts, *Silent Violence: Food, Famine, and Peasantry in Northern Nigeria*.

For the expropriation of farmers in northern Africa see David Prochaska, *Making Algeria French: Colonialism in Bône, 1870–1920.* An excellent book on the European colonial plantations of North Africa is Diana Davis, *Resurrecting the Granary of Rome: Environmental History and French Colonial Expansion in North Africa*.

For the expropriations of African farmers by European settlers in southern Africa see James McCann, *Maize and Grace: Africa's Encounter with a New World Crop, 1500–2000*; Maud Muntemba, "Thwarted Development: A Case Study of Economic Change in the Kabwe District of Zambia, 1902–70"; and Leonard Monteath Thompson and Monica Wilson, *The Oxford History of South Africa*, volume 2, *South Africa 1870–1966*.

Many peasants in southern Africa were heavily taxed and forced onto the market. This process is analyzed and described by Colin Bundy, "The Transkei Peasantry, c. 1890–1914: 'Passing through a Period of Stress'"; Ian Phimister, "Peasant Production and Underdevelopment in Southern Rhodesia, 1890–1914, with Particular Reference to the Victoria District"; and Martin Murray and Charles Post, "The 'Agrarian Question,' Class Struggle and the Capitalist State in the United States and South Africa."

India

Several outstanding works show the peasants' growing poverty, as they sought to grow cash crops for the market to supplement their subsistence plots: Sugata Bose, *Peasant Labour and Colonial Capital: Rural Bengal since 1770*; Vasant Kaiwar, "Property Structures, Demography and the Crisis of the Agrarian Economy of Colonial Bombay Presidency"; T. C. A. Raghavan, "Malguzars and Peasants: The Narmada Valley, 1860–1920"; Imran Ali, *The Punjab under Imperialism, 1885–1947*; and Sven Beckert, "Emancipation and Empire: Reconstructing the Worldwide Web of Cotton Production in the Age of the American Civil War."

Colonial Taiwan

For general conditions, see R. Myers and M. Peattie, *The Japanese Colonial Empire, 1895–1945*; Peter Duus and Ramon Myers, *The Japanese Informal Empire in China, 1895–1937*; George Barclay, *Development and Population in Taiwan*; and Samuel Ho, *Economic Development of Taiwan, 1860–1970*. Chih-ming Ka, *Japanese Colonialism in Taiwan: Land Tenure, Development, and Dependency, 1895–1945*, provides the best English-language study on Taiwan agriculture under Japan. Also see Samuel Ho, *Agricultural Transformation under Colonialism: The Case of Taiwan*, and Teng-hui Lee, *Intersectional Capital Flows in the Economic Development of Taiwan, 1895–1960*.

CHAPTER 8: SOCIALIST AGRICULTURE

Soviet Collectivization

The great debate on the Russian peasantry prior to collectivization is represented by the divergent positions of V. I. Lenin, "The Development of Capitalism in Russia," who saw peasant differentiation and an evolution toward capitalism, and A. V. Chayanov, *The Theory of the Peasant Economy*, written in the Soviet Union in the 1920s amid the New Economic Policy, a book that, for us, captures the logic of peasant farming not only in the period prior to collectivization but also for much of history more generally.

Perry Anderson wrote a good comparative study of social development in Soviet Russia and Communist China, "Two Revolutions." Robert Brenner's intervention at the "Eastern Bloc Symposium: Which Class Rules in the USSR?" offers the suitable theoretical model for understanding the Soviet economy. Teodor Shanin, *The Awkward Class: Political Sociology of Peasantry in a Developing Society—Russia 1910–1925*, is a good book influenced by Chayanov. Ronald Suny, *The Soviet Experiment: Russia, the USSR, and the Successor States*, though a textbook, offers insightful analyses of the problems of peasant agriculture during the 1920s and of the process of collectivization. R. W. Davies, Mark Harrison, and S. G. Wheatcroft, *The Economic Transformation of the Soviet Union, 1913–1945*, offers useful empirical data on collectivization and the economy of the period. Maurice Dobb, *Soviet Economic Development since 1917*, is a useful work on collectivization, especially the problems it was intended to overcome, though one must have patience for Dobb's sympathy with Soviet policy. Dobb, like many scholars of the Left at that time, did not know, or chose to overlook, the horrors of Stalinism. Robert Allen, *Farm to Factory: A Reinterpretation of the Soviet Industrial Revolution*, provides useful information about labor productivity in Soviet agriculture, though the comparisons with the Midwest of the USA are sometimes taken too far out of context.

Isaac Deutscher, *The Prophet Outcast: Trotsky, 1929–1940*, still provides a good analysis of the tragic failures of collectivization. Moshe Lewin, *The Making of the Soviet System: Essays in the Social History of Interwar Russia*, offers an informative analysis of the problems facing the Soviet leaders at the end of the 1920s and their subsequent policy failures. Stephen Cohen, *Rethinking the Soviet Experience: Politics and History since 1917*, makes crucial points about the radical departure in state policy with the advent of Stalin's collectivization.

One gains only a partial picture of the life of the Soviet peasantry after collectivization without an evaluation of gender; Gail Warshofky Lapidus, *Women in Soviet Society*, supplies the facts needed to fill out one's understanding and Sheila Fitzpatrick, *Stalin's Peasants: Resistance and Survival in the Russian Village after Collectivization*, offers useful descriptions of life on collective farms. Alec Nove, *The Soviet Economy: An Introduction*, offers a detailed description of the organization of agriculture on the collective farms.

People's Republic of China

The best overview of Maoist China is Maurice Meisner's *Mao's China and After: A History of the People's Republic*. A general survey of the economy under Mao can be found in Chris Bramall, *Chinese Economic Development*. On land policy in the Maoist era, see John Wong, *Land Reform in the People's Republic of China: Institutional Transformation in Agriculture*, and Vivienne Shue, *Peasant China in Transition: The Dynamics of Development toward Socialism, 1949–1956*.

For agricultural production (including methods and techniques) see Robert Ash, *Agricultural Development in China, 1949–1989: The Collected Papers of Kenneth R. Walker*; Chao Kang, *Agricultural Production in Communist China, 1949–1965*; Benedict Stavis, *The Politics of Agricultural Mechanization in China*; Robert Hsu, *Food for One Billion: China's Agriculture since 1949*; and Philip Huang, *The Peasant Family and Rural Development in the Yangzi Delta, 1350–1988*. On food output and distribution, see Kenneth Walker, *Food Grain Procurement and Consumption in China*, and Alan Lee Piazza, *Food and Consumption and Nutritional Status in the People's Republic of China*.

Life in the countryside under Mao is detailed in Potter and Potter, *China's Peasants: The Anthropology of a Revolution*; Anita Chan, Richard Madsen, and Jonathan Unger, *Chen Village under Mao and Deng*; and C. K. Yang, *Chinese Communist Society: The Family and the Village*. Agricultural modernization, especially vertical integration, in the 2000s is described in Qian Forrest Zhang and John A. Donaldson, "The Rise of Agrarian Capitalism with Chinese Characteristics: Agricultural Modernization, Agribusiness and Collective Land Rights," and Philip Huang, "China's New-Age Small Farms and Their Vertical Integration: Agribusiness or Co-ops?"

Cuba

Lawry Nelson, *Rural Cuba*, amounts to one of the most detailed descriptions of Cuban agriculture prior to the revolution. Terence Cannon, *Revolutionary Cuba*, offers an informative history of Cuba with much information about farming, highlighting especially the successes of the revolution, much more apparent in the 1970s than today. Juan M. del Aguila, *Cuba: Dilemmas of a Revolution*, is a critical study of revolutionary Cuba with much evidence on the difficulties Cuba has had in growing sufficient food. Louis A. Pérez Jr., *Cuba: Between Reform and Revolution*, and especially Marifeli Pérez-Stable, *The Cuban Revolution: Origins, Course, and Legacy*, provide useful narratives, particularly on the century prior to the revolution. Louis Pérez examines the Cuban economy's dependence on the United States. Robin Blackburn, "Prologue to the Cuban Revolution," though published a half century ago, is still an excellent analysis of the society and politics, with much information about agriculture in the prerevolutionary and revolutionary periods. Samuel Farber, *The Origins of the Cuban Revolution Reconsidered*, constitutes a thoroughly researched and convincing examination of the impressive, though uneven, growth of the Cuban economy prior to 1959 and the ways in which this growth led to the revolution.

Juan Martinez-Alier, *Haciendas, Plantations and Collective Farms: Agrarian Class Societies—Cuba and Peru*, explains the background to the establishment of collective farms in the 1960s. Laura J. Enríquez, *Small Farmers in the Economic Reshaping of Nicaragua, Cuba, Russia, and China*, offers a well-researched exposition of the ways in which the Cuban government and farmers have sought to cope with the depression of the late 1980s and early 1990s, showing the changes in Cuban society over the last two decades. Julia Wright, *Sustainable Agriculture and Food Security in an Era of Oil Scarcity: Lessons from Cuba*, and Mavis Alvarez et al., "Surviving Crisis in Cuba: The Second Agrarian Reform and Sustainable Agriculture," amount to glowing portraits of the responses to the depression of the late 1980s and early 1990s, highlighting the new sustainable techniques developed by the government and farmers. Samuel Farber, *Cuba since the Revolution of 1959: A Critical Assessment*, by contrast, is much more pessimistic about the recent changes in Cuban agriculture. Henry Veltmeyer and Mark

Rushton, *The Cuban Revolution as Socialist Human Development*, amounts to a good recent analysis of agriculture since the revolution, including a balanced assessment of the changes of the last two decades.

CHAPTER 9: LATE DEVELOPMENT

France

The most comprehensive book on French farming since the Revolution is Annie Moulin, *Peasantry and Society in France since 1789*. Jean-Pierre Jessenne, *Les Campagnes françaises: Entre mythe et histoire (XVIIIe–XXIe siècle)*, is also a good overview of the last two centuries of French agriculture. Pierre Barral, "Le Secteur agricole dans la France industrialisée, 1950–1974," offers an adequate overview of agriculture since 1945. Gordon Wright, *Rural Revolution in France: The Peasantry in the Twentieth Century*, describes the changes in the politics of French farmers' associations after World War II. Henri Mendras and Laurence Duboys Fresney, *La Seconde Révolution française: 1965–1984*, demonstrates the tremendous transformation of rural life in the 1960s. Michael Bess, *The Light-Green Society: Ecology and Technological Modernity in France, 1960–2000*, provides fascinating reflections on the rapid changes in farming after the 1950s. Peter Amann, *The Corncribs of Buzet: Modernizing Agriculture in the French Southwest*, is an outstanding book about the persistence of traditional agriculture until just several decades ago. Geneviève Gavignaud-Fontaine, *La Révolution rurale dans la France contemporaine XVIIIe–XXe siècle*, focuses especially on the difficulties farmers have faced since the revolution in economic relationships in the countryside in the 1960s.

Taiwan

The best survey of postwar economic change is Thomas Gold, *State and Society in the Taiwan Miracle*. A general survey of agriculture is provided by Erik Thorbecke, "Agricultural Development," and for a general survey of the economy see Samuel Ho, *Economic Development of Taiwan, 1860–1970*. Land reform is covered extensively in Martin Yang, *Socio-economic Results of Land Reform in Taiwan*. The link between industry and agricultural development is discussed in Yu-Kang Mao and Chi Schive, "Agricultural and Industrial Development in Taiwan"; Sen-chung Hsieh and Teng-hui Lee, *Agricultural Development and Its Contributions to Economic Growth in Taiwan*; and Teng-hui Lee, *Intersectional Capital Flows in the Economic Development of Taiwan, 1895–1960*. On changes to the farming economy, see Sophie Huang, "Structural Change in Taiwan's Agricultural Economy," and

Jack Williams, "Vulnerability and Change in Taiwan's Agriculture." An excellent local study of the path and effects of agrarian change is Irene Bain, *Agricultural Reform in Taiwan: From Here to Modernity?* Also see Gallin and Gallin, "Socioeconomic Life in Rural Taiwan: Twenty Years of Development and Change." On the link between technology, farming, and the current impasse, see Kuei-Mei Lo and Hsin-Hsing Chen, "Technological Momentum and the Hegemony of the Green Revolution: A Case Study of an Organic Rice Cooperative in Taiwan."

CHAPTER 10: CORPORATE AGRICULTURE

On the development of capitalism in the nineteenth and twentieth century, especially its global character, see Eric Hobsbawm's *The Age of Capital* and *The Age of Empire*, still the best studies of this period.

Brazil

Celso Furtado, *The Economic Growth of Brazil: A Survey from Colonial to Modern Times*, is the best historical survey of Brazil's economy. Also see Werner Baer, *The Brazilian Economy: Growth and Development*. Excellent examinations of the postwar agrarian economy are David Goodman's "Rural Economy and Society"; Gordon Smith's "Brazilian Agricultural Policy, 1950–1967"; and Julian Chacel's "The Principal Characteristics of the Agrarian Structure and Agricultural Production in Brazil."

Agrarian property relations are analyzed in Joe Foweraker, *The Struggle for Land: A Political Economy of the Frontier in Brazil from 1930 to the Present Day*, which provides an overview of twentieth-century developments in property relations; Martin Katzman, "Colonization as an Approach to Regional Development: Northern Parana, Brazil"; and Warren Dean, "Latifundia and Land Policy in Nineteenth-Century Brazil." For a comprehensive examination of rubber, see Warren Dean, *Brazil and the Struggle for Rubber: A Study in Environmental History*. For the expansion of soybeans, see Philip Warnken, *The Development and Growth of the Soybean Industry in Brazil*, and Holger Matthey et al., *Brazil: The Future of Modern Agriculture?* Brazilian agribusiness is discussed in Maros Sawaya Jank et al., "Concentration and Internationalization of Brazilian Agribusiness Exporters." Frans Papma, *Contesting the Household Estate: Southern Brazilian Peasants and Modern Agriculture*, examines the place of the small farm in commercial farming. For the effect on the environment and climate of clearing the Cerrado for soybean cultivation see Autumn Spanne, "Hunger for Meat Plows Up Brazil's Cerrado Plains."

On the problem of land reform, see Cristóbal Kay, "Why East Asia Overtook Latin America: Agrarian Reform, Industrialisation and Development."

On experiments in "market led agrarian reform" see Wendy Jepson, "Private Agricultural Colonization on a Brazilian Frontier, 1970–1980," and Leonilde Servolo de Medeiros, "Social Movements and the Experience of Market-Led Agrarian Reform in Brazil." The Landless Movement is discussed in Miguel Carter, "The Landless Rural Workers Movement and Democracy in Brazil." On agrarian elites, see France Hagopian, "Traditional Politics against State Transformation in Brazil."

David Goodman and Michael Redclift, *From Peasant to Proletarian: Capitalist Development and Agrarian Transitions*, provides an excellent analysis of postwar labor systems and agrarian change. Robert Conrad, "The Planter Class and the Debate over Chinese Immigration to Brazil, 1850–1893," discusses the problem of labor supply and failed experiments with coolie labor.

Excellent studies of crops and agrarian labor regimes are Verena Stolke, *Coffee Planters, Workers and Wives: Class Conflict and Gender Relations on Sao Paulo Plantations, 1850–1980*; Barbara Weinstein, "The Persistence of Precapitalist Relations of Production in a Tropical Export Economy: The Amazon Rubber Trade, 1850–1920"; and B. Barham and O. Coomes, *Prosperity's Promise: The Amazon Rubber Boom and Distorted Economic Development*. Also see Christian Brannstrom, "Coffee Labor Regimes and Deforestation on a Brazilian Frontier, 1915–1965."

The United States

R. Douglas Hurt, *Problems of Plenty: The American Farmer in the Twentieth Century*, is the most comprehensive informative narrative on this subject. Bruce Gardner, *American Agriculture in the Twentieth Century: How It Flourished and What It Cost*, and Alan Olmstead and Paul Rhode, "The Transformation of Northern Agriculture, 1910–1990," are both adequate histories of twentieth-century farming in the US. They highlight the great successes of farmers and predict further ones in the coming decades. Olmstead and Rhode, *Creating Abundance: Biological Innovation and American Agricultural Development*, touts the scientific prowess of US farmers. Michael Williams, "The Death and the Rebirth of the American Forest: Clearing and Reversion in the United States, 1900–1980," reveals the positive environmental consequences of rising labor productivity in agriculture.

Richard Walker, "Crisis and Change in U.S. Agriculture: An Overview," provides a more sobering picture of what capitalist competition has done to American farming. Michael Pollan, *The Omnivore's Dilemma: A Natural History of Four Meals*, is similarly a sobering portrait of what current farming practices have done to food. Tom Philpott and Ronnie Cummins have written excellent essays, too numerous to list, over the last several years, Philpott in *Mother Jones* and Cummins in *Organic Consumers Association*.

These articles demonstrate the environmental problems and poor food quality generated by the latest farm practices. Another good book on the subject is Tony Weis, *The Ecological Hoofprint: The Global Burden of Industrial Livestock.*

Gavin Wright, *Old South New South: Revolutions in the Southern Economy since the Civil War*, offers an adequate explanation for the rise of sharecropping across the cotton South in the decades following the Civil War. Bill Winders, *The Politics of Food Supply: U.S. Agricultural Policy in the World Economy*, is an excellent study of the ways in which New Deal subsidies served to wean Southern planters away from sharecropping and, through the Southern senators' disproportionate influence over the federal government, change federal subsidies from production controls to crop insurance. For our analysis of agriculture in California, we have relied mainly on Richard Walker, *The Conquest of Bread: 150 Years of Agribusiness in California.*

CONCLUSION

In writing the conclusion we relied on Robert Brenner, "The Origins of Capitalist Development: A Critique of Neo-Smithian Marxism." Most of the information in the conclusion is drawn from the content of the rest of our book. But several works contributed to our views on the current agricultural and economic trends. For an optimistic view of the last century of agricultural development and what it promises for the future see Giovanni Federico, *Feeding the World: An Economic History of Agriculture, 1800–2000.* For facts about GMO crops, and especially all of the pesticides used in their cultivation, see Earth Open Source, "*GMO Myths and Truths* (3rd Edition): *GMO Myths and Truths* Updated, Condensed, and Now Available as a Book." For the most thorough study of climate change's likely consequences for world agriculture see William Cline, *Global Warming and Agriculture: Impact Estimates by Country.* Excellent works on the place of agriculture in the current economic and ecological crisis are Tony Weis, *The Global Food Economy: The Battle for the Future of Farming*; Vandana Shiva, *Soil Not Oil: Environmental Justice in an Age of Climate Crisis*; Marcel Mazoyer and Laurence Roudart, *A History of World Agriculture: From the Neolithic Age to the Current Crisis*; and Walden Bello, *The Food Wars.*

References

Ado, Anatoli. *Paysans en Révolution: Terre, pouvoir et jacquerie 1789–1794.* Paris: Société des Études Robespierristes, 1996.

Aguila, Juan M. del. *Cuba: Dilemmas of a Revolution.* Boulder, Colo.: Westview Press, 1984.

Ali, Imran. *The Punjab under Imperialism, 1885–1947.* Princeton, N.J.: Princeton University Press, 1988.

Allen, Robert. *Enclosure and the Yeoman.* Oxford: Clarendon Press, 1992.

———. "Agriculture during the Industrial Revolution." In *The Economic History of Britain since 1700.* Vol. 1: *1700–1860*, edited by R. Floud and D. McCloskey. Cambridge: Cambridge University Press, 1994.

———. "Agricultural Productivity and Rural Incomes in England and the Yangtze Delta, c. 1620–c. 1820." *Economic History Review* 62 (2009): 525–50.

———. *Farm to Factory: A Reinterpretation of the Soviet Industrial Revolution.* Princeton, N.J.: Princeton University Press, 2009.

Allen, Will, and Ronnie Cummins. "Climate Chaos: Boycott Genetically Engineered and Factory-Farmed Foods." *Organic Consumers Association*, May 2, 2013. https://www.organicconsumers.org/essays/climate-chaos-boycott-genetically-engineered-and-factory-farmed-foods, accessed May 9, 2016.

Allen, William. *The African Husbandman.* New York: Barnes and Noble, 1967.

Alvarez, Mavis, et al. "Surviving Crisis in Cuba: The Second Agrarian Reform and Sustainable Agriculture." In *Promised Land: Competing Visions of Agrarian Reform*, edited by Peter Rosset, Raj Patel, and Michael Courville. Oakland, Calif.: Food First Books, 2006.

Amann, Peter. *The Corncribs of Buzet: Modernizing Agriculture in the French Southwest.* Princeton, N.J.: Princeton University Press, 1990.

American Sustainable Business Council. "The Business Case for Labeling GMOs." http://asbcouncil.org/label%20gmos, accessed April 29, 2016.

Ameringer, Oscar. "Unemployment in the United States." In *Hearings before a Subcommittee of the Committee on Labor, House of Representatives, 72nd Cong., 1 Sess., on H.R. 206, H.R. 6011, H.R. 8088.* Washington: Government Printing Office, 1932.

Anderson, Perry. *Passages from Antiquity to Feudalism.* London: Verso, 1974.

———. *Lineages of the Absolutist State.* London: Verso, 1979.

———. *La pensée tiède: Un regard critique sur la culture française.* Paris: Seuil, 2005.

———. "Two Revolutions." *New Left Review* 61 (2010): 59–96.

Antoine, Annie. "Systèmes agraires de la France de l'Ouest: Une rationalité méconnue?" *Histoire, économie et société* 18 (1999): 107–32.

Ash, Robert, ed. *Agricultural Development in China, 1949–1989: The Collected Papers of Kenneth R. Walker.* Oxford: Oxford University Press, 1998.

Ashworth, John. *Slavery, Capitalism, and Politics in the Antebellum Republic: Commerce and Compromise, 1820–1850*. Cambridge: Cambridge University Press, 1995.

Atack, Jeremy, Fred Bateman, and William N. Parker. "The Farm, the Farmer, and the Market." In *The Cambridge Economic History of the United States*. Vol. 2: *The Long Nineteenth Century*, edited by Stanley L. Engerman and Robert E. Gallman. Cambridge: Cambridge University Press, 2000.

———. "Northern Agriculture and the Westward Movement." In *The Cambridge Economic History of the United States*. Vol. 2: *The Long Nineteenth Century*, edited by Stanley L. Engerman and Robert E. Gallman. Cambridge: Cambridge University Press, 2000.

Aufhauser, R. K. "Slavery and Technological Change." *Journal of Economic History* 34.1 (1974): 36–50.

Austin, Gareth. *Labour, Land and Capital in Ghana: From Slavery to Free Labour in Asante, 1807–1956*. Rochester, N.Y.: University of Rochester Press, 2005.

Aymard, Maurice. "Autoconsommation et marchés: Chayanov, Labrousse ou Le Roy Ladurie?" *Annales. Économies, sociétés, civilisations* 38 (1983): 1392–410.

Baer, Werner. *The Brazilian Economy: Growth and Development*. Westport, Conn.: Praeger, 2001.

Bain, Irene. *Agricultural Reform in Taiwan: From Here to Modernity?* Hong Kong: The Chinese University Press, 1993.

Baker, P., and M. Little. *Man in the Andes: A Multidisciplinary Study of High-Altitude Quechua*. Stroudsburg, Pa.: Hutchinson and Ross, 1976.

Barclay, George. *Development and Population in Taiwan*. Princeton: Princeton University Press, 1954.

Barham, B., and O. Coomes. *Prosperity's Promise: The Amazon Rubber Boom and Distorted Economic Development*. Boulder: Westview Press, 1996.

Barral, Pierre. "Le secteur agricole dans la France industrialisée, 1950–1974." In *Histoire économique et sociale de la France*. Tome 4 : *L'ère industrielle et la société d'aujourd'hui (siècle 1880–1980)*. Tome 3: *Années 1950–1980, le second XXe siècle. Vers quells horizons?* edited by Fernand Braudel and Ernest Labrousse. Paris: Presses Universitaires de France, 1982.

Bauer, Brian, and R. Alan Covey. "Processes of State Formation in the Inca Heartland (Cuzco, Peru)." *American Anthropologist* 104.3 (2002): 846–64.

Béaur, Gérard. *Le marché foncier à la veille de la Révolution: Les mouvements de Propriété beaucerons dans les régions de Maintenon et de Janville de 1761 à 1790*. Paris: Editions de l'École des Hautes Études en Sciences Sociales, 1984.

———. "Investissement foncier, epargne et cycle de vie dans le pays chartrain au XVIIIe siècle." *Histoire et mesure* 6 (1991): 275–88.

———. "Les Chartier et le mystère de la révolution agricole." *Histoire et Mesure* 11 (1996): 367–88.

———. *Histoire agraire de la France au XVIIIe siècle: Inerties et changements dans les campagnes françaises entre 1715 et 1815*. Paris: SEDES, 2000.

Beauvoir, Simone de. *The Second Sex*. 1952. Reprint, translated by H. M. Parshley, New York: Vintage Books, 1989.

Beckert, Sven. "Emancipation and Empire: Reconstructing the Worldwide Web of Cotton Production in the Age of the American Civil War." *American Historical Review* 109 (2004): 1405–38.

———. *Empire of Cotton: A Global History*. New York: Alfred A. Knopf, 2014.

Bello, Walden. *The Food Wars*. London: Verso, 2009.

Benoist, André. "Vie paysanne et protestantisme en 'Moyen-Poitou' du XVIe siècle à La Révolution." *Annales de Bretagne et des pays de l'Ouest* 92 (1985): 161–82.

Berenson, Edward. *Populist Religion and Left-Wing Politics in France, 1830–1852*. Princeton: Princeton University Press, 1984.

Bess, Michael. *The Light-Green Society: Ecology and Technological Modernity in France, 1960–2000*. Chicago: University of Chicago Press, 2003.

Bianchi, Serge, et al. *La terre et les paysans en France et en Grande-Bretagne du début du XVIIe à la fin du XVIIIe siècle*. Paris: Armand Colin, 1999.

Blackburn, Robin. "Prologue to the Cuban Revolution." *New Left Review* 21 (1963): 52–91.

———. *The Making of New World Slavery: From the Baroque to the Modern.* London: Verso Press, 2010.

Blackstone, William. *Commentaries on the Laws of England.* Oxford: Clarendon Press, 1765.

Bloch, Marc. *French Rural History: An Essay on Its Basic Characteristics.* 1931. Reprint, translated by Janet Sondheimer, Berkeley: University of California Press, 1966.

———. *Feudal Society.* 1961. Reprint, Chicago: University of Chicago Press, 1968.

Blunt, P. A. *Italian Manpower: 225 BC–AD 14.* Oxford: Clarendon Press, 1987.

Boelaert, E., H. Vinck, and Ch. Lonkama. "Témoignages africains de l'arrivée des Premiers blancs aux bords des rivières de l'equateur (rd congo)." *Annales Æquatoria* 16 (1995): 36–117.

Borras, S. M., Jr. "Questioning Market-Led Agrarian Reform: Experiences from Brazil, Colombia and South Africa." *Journal of Agrarian Change* 3 (2003): 367–94.

Bose, Sugata. *Peasant Labour and Colonial Capital: Rural Bengal since 1770.* Cambridge: Cambridge University Press, 1993.

Bossis, Philippe. "Le milieu paysan aux confins de l'Anjou, du Poitou et de la Bretagne 1771–1789." *Etudes rurales* 47 (1972): 122–47.

Bové, José, François Dufour, and Gilles Luneau. *The World Is Not for Sale: Farmers against Junk Food.* London: Verso, 2002.

Bowman, Isaiah. *The Andes of Southern Peru.* New York: Henry Holt, 1916.

Bramall, Chris. *Chinese Economic Development.* New York: Routledge, 2009.

Brannstrom, Christian. "Coffee Labor Regimes and Deforestation on a Brazilian Frontier, 1915–1965." *Economic Geography* 76.4 (2000): 326–46.

Bray, Francesca. *Science and Civilisation in China: Agriculture.* Vol. 6, part 2: *Biology and Technology,* edited by Joseph Needham. Cambridge: Cambridge University Press, 1984.

———. *Rice Economies: Technology and Development in Asian Societies.* Berkeley: University of California Press, 1994.

———. *Technology and Gender: Fabrics of Power in Late Imperial China.* Berkeley: University of California Press, 1997.

Brennan, Thomas. "Peasants and Debt in Eighteenth-Century Champagne." *Journal of Interdisciplinary History* 38 (2006): 175–200.

Brenner, Robert. "The Origins of Capitalist Development: A Critique of Neo-Smithian Marxism." *New Left Review* 1.104 (1977): 25–92.

———. "The Agrarian Roots of European Capitalism." In *The Brenner Debate: Agrarian Class Structure and Economic Development in Pre-industrial Europe,* edited by T. H. Ashton and C. H. E. Philpin. Cambridge: Cambridge University Press, 1985.

———. "The Social Basis of Economic Development." In *Analytical Marxism,* edited by John Roemer. Cambridge: Cambridge University Press, 1986.

———. "Eastern Bloc Symposium: Which Class Rules in the USSR?" 1989. http://www.workersliberty.org/system/files/USSR1989debate.pdf, accessed May 5, 2016.

———. "The Rises and Declines of Serfdom in Medieval and Early Modern Europe." In *Serfdom and Slavery: Studies in Legal Bondage,* edited by M. L. Bush. London: Longman, 1996.

———. "Property Relations and the Growth of Agricultural Productivity in Late Medieval and Early Modern Europe." In *Economic Development and Agricultural Productivity,* edited by Amit Bhaduri and Rune Skarstein. Cheltenham: Edward Elgar, 1997.

———. "The Low Countries in the Transition to Capitalism." *Journal of Agrarian Change* 1.2 (2001): 169–241.

———. "The Low Countries in the Transition to Capitalism." In *Peasants into Farmers? The Transformation of Rural Economy and Society in the Low Countries (Middle Ages–Nineteenth Century) in Light of the Brenner Debate,* edited by Peter Hoppenbrouwers and Jan Luiten van Zanden. Turnhout, Belgium: Brepols, 2001.

———. "Property and Progress: Where Adam Smith Went Wrong." In *Marxist History-Writing for the Twenty-First Century,* edited by Chris Wickham, 49–111. Oxford: Oxford University Press, 2007.

Brenner, Robert, and Christopher Isett. "England's Divergence from China's Yangzi Delta: Property Relations, Microeconomics, and Patterns of Development." *Journal of Asian Studies* 61.2 (2002): 609–62.

British South Africa Company. *Reports on the Administration of Rhodesia.* 1889/1892, 1900/1902.

Brooks, George E. *Landlords and Strangers: Ecology, Society, and Trade in Western Africa, 1000–1630.* Boulder: Westview Press, 1993.

Browman, D., R. Burger, and M. Rivera. *Social and Economic Organization in the Prehispanic Andes.* Oxford: BAR, 1984.

Brown, Melissa J., et al. "Marriage Mobility and Footbinding in Pre-1949 Rural China: A Reconsideration of Gender, Economics, and Meaning in Social Causation." *Journal of Asian Studies* 71 (2012): 1035–67.

Brunet, Pierre. *Structure agraire et économie rurale des plateaux tertiaires entre la Seine et l'Oise.* Caen: Société d'Impressions Caron, 1960.

Brush, Stephen. *Mountain, Field and Family: The Economy and Human Ecology of an Andean Valley.* Philadelphia: University of Pennsylvania Press, 1977.

Brush, Stephen, H. Carney, and Z. Huamán. "Dynamics of Andean Potato Agriculture." *Economic Botany* 35.1 (1981): 70–88.

Buck, John Lossing. *Chinese Farm Economy: A Study of 2866 Farms in Seventeen Localities and Seven Provinces in China.* Taipei: Southern Materials Center, 1978.

Bundy, Colin. "The Transkei Peasantry, c. 1890–1914: 'Passing through a Period of Stress.'" In *The Roots of Rural Poverty in Central and Southern Africa*, edited by R. Palmer and N. Parsons. Berkeley: University of California Press, 1977.

Bushman, Richard Lyman. "Markets and Composite Farms in Early America." *William and Mary Quarterly* 55 (1998): 351–74.

Byres, Terence. "Differentiation of the Peasantry under Feudalism and the Transition to Capitalism: In Defence of Rodney Hilton." *Journal of Agrarian Change* 6 (2006): 17–68.

Caines, John E. *The Slave Power: Its Character, Career, and Design.* London: Parker, Son, and Bourn, 1862.

Campbell, B. M. S. *English Seigniorial Agriculture, 1250–1450.* Cambridge: Cambridge University Press, 2000.

Campbell, Bruce M. S., and Mark Overton. "A New Perspective on Medieval and Early Modern Agriculture: Six Centuries of Norfolk Farming c. 1250–c.1850." *Past and Present* 141 (1993): 38–105.

Cannon, Terence. *Revolutionary Cuba.* New York: Thomas Y. Crowell, 1981.

Carney, Judith. *Black Rice: The African Origins of Rice of Cultivation in the Americas.* Cambridge, Mass.: Harvard University Press, 2001.

Carter, Miguel. "The Landless Rural Workers Movement and Democracy in Brazil." *Latin American Research Review* 45, Special Issue: Living in Actually Existing Democracies (2010): 186–217.

Cauvin, Jacques. *The Birth of the Gods and the Origins of Agriculture.* Translated by Trevor Watkins. Cambridge: Cambridge University Press, 2000.

Cayton, Andrew. *The Frontier Republic: Ideology and Politics in the Ohio Country, 1780–1825.* Kent, Ohio: Kent State University Press, 1986.

Chacel, Julian. "The Principal Characteristics of the Agrarian Structure and Agricultural Production in Brazil." In *The Economy of Brazil*, edited by Howard Ellis. Berkeley: University of California Press, 1969.

Chan, Anita, Richard Madsen, and Jonathan Unger. *Chen Village under Mao and Deng.* Berkeley: University of California Press, 1992.

Chayanov, A. V. *The Theory of the Peasant Economy.* Homewood, Ill.: Published for the American Economic Association by R. D. Irwin, 1966.

Chevet, Jean-Michel. "Production et productivité: Un modèle de développement économique des campagnes de la région parisienne aux xviiie et xixe siècles." *Histoire et mesure* 9 (1994): 101–45.

Cieza de Leon, Pedro de. *The Travels of Pedro de Cieza de Leon, A.D. 1532–50, Contained in the First Part of His Chronicle of Peru.* Translated and edited, with notes and introduction, by Clements B. Markham. London: Hakluyt Society, 1864.

Clark, Christopher. *The Roots of Rural Capitalism: Western Massachusetts, 1780–1860.* Ithaca, N.Y.: Cornell University Press, 1990.

Clark, Gregory. "Too Much Revolution: Agriculture in the Industrial Revolution, 1700–1860." In *The British Industrial Revolution: An Economic Perspective*, edited by Joel Mokyr. 2nd ed. Boulder: Westview Press, 1999.

Cline, William. *Global Warming and Agriculture: Impact Estimates by Country.* Washington, D.C.: Center for Global Development and Peterson Institute for International Economics, 2007.

Cobo, Bernabé. *History of the Inca Empire: An Account of the Indians' Customs and Their Origin, Together with a Treatise on Inca Legends, History, and Social Institutions.* Austin: University of Texas Press, 1979.

Cohen, Stephen. *Rethinking the Soviet Experience: Politics and History since 1917.* New York: Oxford University Press, 1985.

Columella. *De Re Rustica.* Translated by Harrison Boyd Ash. Loeb Classical Library, vol. 1. Cambridge, Mass.: Harvard University Press, 1941.

Conrad, Robert. "The Planter Class and the Debate over Chinese Immigration to Brazil, 1850–1893." *International Migration Review* 9.1 (Spring 1975): 41–55.

Cooper, Michael. *They Came to Japan: An Anthology of Reports on Japan, 1543–1640.* Berkeley: University of California Press, 1965.

Covey, Alan. "Inka Administration of the Far South Coast of Peru." *Latin American Antiquity* 11.2 (2000): 119–38.

———. *How the Inca Built Their Heartland: State Formation and the Innovation of Imperial Strategies in the Sacred Valley, Peru.* Ann Arbor: University of Michigan Press, 2006.

Crawcour, E. S. "Changes in Japanese Commerce in the Tokugawa Period." *Journal of Asian Studies* 22 (1963): 387–400.

Crawford, Harriet. *Sumer and the Sumerians.* Cambridge: Cambridge University Press, 2004.

Crèvecoeur, J. Hector St. John de. *Letters from an American Farmer.* 1792. Reprint, Carlisle, Mass.: Applewood, 2007.

Cronon, William. *Nature's Metropolis: Chicago and the Great West.* New York: W. W. Norton, 1991.

———. *Changes in the Land: Indians, Colonists, and the Ecology of New England.* New York: Hill & Wang, 2003.

Cummins, Ronnie, and Zack Kaldveer. "Food, Farms, Forests and Fracking: Connecting the Dots." *Organic Consumers Association*, May 9, 2013. https://www.organicconsumers.org/news/food-farms-forests-and-fracking-connecting-dots, accessed May 9, 2016.

Cummins, Ronnie, and Katherine Paul. "GMOs Are Killing the Bees, Butterflies, Birds and . . . ?" *Organic Consumers Association*, February 14, 2014. https://www.organicconsumers.org/essays/gmos-are-killing-bees-butterflies-birds-and, accessed May 9, 2016.

———. "Five New Reasons Monsanto's 'Science' Doesn't Add Up." *Organic Consumers Association*, February 27, 2014. https://www.organicconsumers.org/essays/five-new-reasons-monsanto%E2%80%99s-%E2%80%98science%E2%80%99-doesn%E2%80%99t-add, accessed May 9, 2016.

Curtin, Philip. *Economic Change in Precolonial Africa: Senegambia in the Era of Slave Trade.* Madison: University of Wisconsin Press, 1975.

D'Altroy, Terence N. *The Incas.* Wiley-Blackwell, 2002.

Danhof, Clarence. "Farm-Making Costs and the 'Safety Valve': 1850–1860." *Journal of Political Economy* 49 (1941): 317–59.

Davidson, James. *The Island of Formosa: Historical View from 1430 to 1900.* London: MacMillan, 1903.

Davies, R. W., Mark Harrison, and S. G. Wheatcroft. *The Economic Transformation of the Soviet Union, 1913–1945.* Cambridge; New York: Cambridge University Press, 1994.

Davis, Diana. *Resurrecting the Granary of Rome: Environmental History and French Colonial Expansion in North Africa.* Athens: Ohio University Press, 2007.

Davis, Mike. *Late Victorian Holocausts: El Niño Famines and the Making of the Third World.* London: Verso, 2001.

Dean, Warren. "Latifundia and Land Policy in Nineteenth-Century Brazil." *Hispanic American Historical Review* 51.4 (1971): 606–25.

———. *Brazil and the Struggle for Rubber: A Study in Environmental History.* Cambridge: Cambridge University Press, 1987.

Decennial Reports on the Trade Navigation Industries, etc., of the Ports Open to Foreign Commerce and on the Condition and Development of the Treaty Port Provinces, 1902–1911. Statistical Series no. 6, vol. 3. Moukden, China: Maritime Customs, 1913.

Defoe, Daniel. *The Life and Adventures of Robinson Crusoe.* New York: Penguin, 2001.

Deutscher, Isaac. *The Prophet Outcast: Trotsky, 1929–1940.* London: Oxford University Press, 1963.

Dimmock, Spencer. *The Origins of Capitalism in England 1400–1600.* Chicago: Haymarket Books, 2015.

Dobb, Maurice. *Soviet Economic Development since 1917.* New York: International Publishers, 1948.

Dontenwill, Serge. "Rapports ville-campagne et espace economique microrégional: Charlieu et son plat-pays au XVIIIe siècle." In *Villes et campagnes, XVe–XXe siècle,* edited by Françoise Bayard. Lyon: Presses Universitaires de Lyon, 1977.

Drixler, Fabian. *Mabiki: Infanticide and Population Growth in Eastern Japan, 1660–1950.* Berkeley: University of California Press, 2013.

Duby, Georges. *Rural Economy and Country Life in the Medieval West.* Columbia: University of South Carolina Press, 1968.

———. *William Marshal: The Flower of Chivalry.* 1984. Translated by Richard Howard. 1st American paperback ed., New York: Pantheon Books, 1986.

———. *Le moyen âge 987–1460.* Paris: Hachette, 1987.

Duncan-Jones, Richard. *The Economy of the Roman Empire: Quantitative Studies.* Cambridge: Cambridge University Press, 1974.

Dunn, Richard. *Sugar and Slaves: The Rise of the Planter Class in the English West Indies, 1624–1713.* Chapel Hill: University of North Carolina Press, 2000.

Durand, Georges. *Vin vigne et vignerons en lyonnais et Beaujolais.* Paris: École des Hautes Études en Sciences Sociales, 1979.

Duus, Peter, and Ramon Myers. *The Japanese Informal Empire in China, 1895–1937.* Princeton: Princeton University Press, 1989.

Eagleton, Terry. *The Idea of Culture.* Oxford: Blackwell, 2000.

Earth Open Source. "*GMO Myths and Truths* (3rd Edition): *GMO Myths and Truths* Updated, Condensed, and Now Available as a Book." 2015. http://earthopensource.org/earth-open-source-reports/gmo-myths-truths-3rd-edition/, accessed May 9, 2016.

Edwards, Bryan. *The History, Civil and Commercial, of the British Colonies in the West Indies.* London: John Stockdale, 1793.

Egnal, Marc. *Clash of Extremes: The Economic Origins of the Civil War.* New York: Hill & Wang, 2009.

Ellis, E. C., and S. M. Wang. "Sustainable Traditional Agriculture in the Lake Tai Region of China." *Agriculture, Ecosystems, and Environment* 61 (1997): 177–93.

Elvin, Mark. *The Pattern of the Chinese Past.* Palo Alto: Stanford University Press, 1977.

———. *The Retreat of the Elephants: An Environmental History of China.* New Haven: Yale University Press, 2004.

Enríquez, Laura J. *Small Farmers in the Economic Reshaping of Nicaragua, Cuba, Russia, and China.* University Park: Pennsylvania State University Press, 2010.

Epstein, Steven. *An Economic and Social History of Later Medieval Europe, 1000–1500.* Cambridge: Cambridge University Press, 2009.

Erdkamp, Paul. "Agriculture, Underemployment, and the Cost of Rural Labour in the Roman World." *Classical Quarterly, New Series* 49.2 (1999): 556–72.

Erikson, Clark. "Prehistoric Landscape Management in the Andean Highlands: Raised Field Agriculture and Its Environmental Impact." *Population and Environment* 13.4 (1992): 285–300.

Evans, J. K. "Wheat Production and Its Social Consequences in the Roman World." *Classical Quarterly, New Series* 31.2 (1981): 428–42.

Fagan, Brian. *World Prehistory: A Brief Introduction*. New York: Longman, 1999.

Fage, J. D. "Upper and Lower Guinea." In *The Cambridge History of Africa, 1050–1600*, edited by Roland Oliver, 463–518. Cambridge: Cambridge University Press, 1975.

Faragher, John Mack. *Sugar Creek: Life on the Illinois Prairie*. New Haven: Yale University Press, 1986.

Farber, Samuel. *The Origins of the Cuban Revolution Reconsidered*. Chapel Hill: University of North Carolina Press, 2006.

———. *Cuba since the Revolution of 1959: A Critical Assessment*. Chicago: Haymarket Books, 2011.

Federico, Giovanni. *Feeding the World: An Economic History of Agriculture, 1800–2000*. Princeton: Princeton University Press, 2005.

Figueroa, Alfredo. "The U.F.W. Anti-immigration Campaign and Falling Out with Bert Corona, M.A.P.A., and Other Chicano Groups (2005)." In *Speaking Out: Activism and Protest in the 1960s and 1970s*, edited by Heather Ann Thompson. Upper Saddle River, N.J.: Prentice Hall, 2010.

Fish Information and Services. "Harmful Algal Blooms Getting Worse." April 2, 2013. http://fis.com/fis/worldnews/worldnews.asp?l=e&id=59838&ndb=1, accessed April 29, 2016.

Fitzpatrick, Sheila. *Stalin's Peasants: Resistance and Survival in the Russian Village after Collectivization*. New York: Oxford University Press, 1994.

Food and Agriculture Organization of the United Nations. "The State of Food Insecurity in the World." 2014. http://www.fao.org/publications/sofi/en/, accessed April 29, 2016.

Fourquin, Guy. "Au seuil du XIVe siècle." In *Histoire de la France rurale*. Vol. 1: *La formation des campagnes françaises des origines à 1340*, edited by Georges Duby and Armand Wallon. Paris: Edition de Seuil, 1975–1977.

———. "Le Temps de la croissance." In *Histoire de la France rurale*. Vol. 1: *La formation des campagnes françaises des origines à 1340*, edited by Georges Duby and Armand Wallon. Paris: Edition de Seuil, 1975–1977.

Foweraker, Joe. *The Struggle for Land: A Political Economy of the Frontier in Brazil from 1930 to the Present Day*. Cambridge: Cambridge University Press, 1981.

Frayn, Joan. *Subsistence Farming in Roman Italy*. Fontwell: Centaur Press, 1979.

Friedman, Harriet. "World Market, State, and Family Farm: Social Bases of Household Production in the Era of Wage Labor." *Comparative Studies in Society and History* 20 (1978): 545–86.

Fry, Douglas. *The Human Potential for Peace: An Anthropological Challenge to Assumptions about War and Violence*. New York: Oxford University Press, 2006.

Furtado, Celso. *The Economic Growth of Brazil: A Survey from Colonial to Modern Times*. Berkeley: University of California Press, 1971.

Gade, Daniel. *Plants, Man and the Land in the Vilcanota Valley of Peru*. The Hague: Dr. W. Junk B.V., Publishers, 1975.

Gallin, Bernard, and Rita Gallin. "Socioeconomic Life in Rural Taiwan: Twenty Years of Development and Change." *Modern China* 8 (1982): 205–46.

Gardner, Bruce. *American Agriculture in the Twentieth Century: How It Flourished and What It Cost*. Cambridge, Mass.: Harvard University Press, 2002.

Garnier, Josette. *Bourgeoisie et propriété immobilière en Forez aux XVIIe et XVIIIe siècles*. Saint-Etienne: Centre d'Études Foréziennes, 1982.

Garnsey, Peter. *Famine and Food Supply in the Greco-Roman World: Responses to Risk and Crisis*. Cambridge: Cambridge University Press, 1989.

Gates, Hill. "Footloose in Fujian: Economic Correlates of Footbinding." *Comparative Studies in Society and History* 43.1 (2001): 130–48.

Gates, Paul Wallace. "The Homestead Act in an Incongruous Land System." In *The Public Lands: Studies in the History of the Public Domain*, edited by Vernon Rosco Carstensen. Madison: University of Wisconsin Press, 1963.

Gavignaud-Fontaine, Geneviève. *La Révolution rurale dans la France contemporaine XVIIIe–XXe siècle*. Paris: Editions L'Harmattan, 1996.

Gay, François-P. *La champagne du Berry: Essai sur la formation d'un paysage agraire et l'évolution d'une société rurale*. Bourges: Tardy, 1967.

Genovese, Eugene D. *The Political Economy of Slavery: Studies in the Economy and Society of the Slave South*. Middletown, Conn.: Wesleyan University Press, 1989.

Gérard, Alain. *Pourquoi la Vendée?* Paris: Armand Colin, 1990.

Glass, Remley. "Gentlemen, the Corn Belt!" *Harper's* 167 (July 1933): 199–209.

Gold, Thomas. *State and Society in the Taiwan Miracle*. Boulder: Westview Press, 1986.

Goodman, David. "Rural Economy and Society." In *Social Change in Brazil, 1945–85: The Incomplete Transition*, edited by Edmar L. Bacha and Herbert S. Klein. Albuquerque: University of New Mexico Press, 1989.

Goodman, David, and Michael Redclift. *From Peasant to Proletarian: Capitalist Development and Agrarian Transitions*. New York: St. Martin's Press, 1982.

Grantham, George. "Scale and Organization in French Farming, 1840 to 1880." In *European Peasants and Their Markets*, edited by W. N. Parker and E. L. Jones. Princeton, N.J.: Princeton University Press, 1975.

———. "The Diffusion of the New Husbandry in Northern France, 1815–1840." *Journal of Economic History* 38 (1978): 311–37.

Hagopian, France. "Traditional Politics against State Transformation in Brazil." In *State Power and Social Forces*, edited by Joel S. Migdal et al. Cambridge: Cambridge University Press, 1994.

Halstead, Paul. "Traditional and Ancient Rural Economy in Mediterranean Europe: Plus ça Change?" *Journal of Hellenic Studies* 107 (1987): 77–87.

Hanley, Susan, and Kozo Yamamura. *Economic and Demographic Change in Preindustrial Japan, 1600–1868*. Princeton: Princeton University Press, 1977.

Harlan, J., J. De Wet, and A. Stemlar. *The Origins of African Plant Domestication*. The Hague: Mouton, 1976.

Harman, Chris. *A People's History of the World*. London: Verso, 2008.

Harms, Robert. "The World Abir Made: The Maringa-Lopori Basin, 1885–1903." *African Economic History* 12 (1983): 122–39.

———. *The Diligent: A Voyage through the Worlds of the Slave Trade*. New York: Basic Books, 2002.

Harris, Marvin. *Cannibals and Kings: The Origins of Cultures*. New York: Random House, 1978.

Hawthorne, Walter. *Planting Rice and Harvesting Slaves: Transformations along the Guinea-Bissau Coast, 1400–1900*. Portsmouth, N.H.: Heinemann, 2003.

Henretta, James. "Families and Farms: Mentalité in Pre-industrial America." *William and Mary Quarterly* 35 (1978): 3–32.

Henry, Patrick. *Economic, Political, and Domestic Life in Late Eighteenth-Century Virginia*. Washington, D.C.: National Park Service, 1989.

Hilton, R. H. *Class Conflict and the Crisis of Feudalism: Essays in Medieval Social History*. 1985. Reprint, London: Verso, 1990.

Hindus, Maurice Gerschon. *Red Bread: Collectivization in a Russian Village*. Bloomington: Indiana University Press, 1988.

Ho, Ping-t'i. *Studies on the Population of China, 1368–1953*. Cambridge, Mass.: Harvard University Press, 1959.

Ho, Samuel. *Agricultural Transformation under Colonialism: The Case of Taiwan*. New Haven: Yale University Press, 1968.

———. *Economic Development of Taiwan, 1860–1970*. New Haven: Yale University Press, 1978.

Hobsbawm, Eric. *The Age of Capital*. New York: Vintage, 1975.

———. *The Age of Empire*. New York: Vintage, 1987.

Hochschild, Adam. *King Leopold's Ghost: A Story of Greed, Terror, and Heroism in Colonial Africa*. Boston: Houghton Mifflin, 1998.

Hoffman, Philip. *Growth in a Traditional Society: The French Countryside, 1450–1815*. Princeton: Princeton University Press, 1996.

Hopkins, A. G. *An Economic History of West Africa*. New York: Columbia University Press, 1973.

Hopkins, Keith. "Taxes and Trade in the Roman Empire (200 B.C.–A.D. 400)." *Journal of Roman Studies* 70 (1980): 101–25.

Hsieh, Sen-chung, and Teng-hui Lee. *Agricultural Development and Its Contributions to Economic Growth in Taiwan*. Taipei: Chinese-American Joint Commission on Rural Reconstruction, 1966.

Hsu, Cho-yun. *Ancient China in Transition: An Analysis of Social Mobility, 722–222 B.C.* Palo Alto: Stanford University Press, 1965.

———. *Han Agriculture: The Formation of the Early Chinese Agrarian Economy (206 B.C.–A.D. 220)*. Seattle: University of Washington Press, 1980.

Hsu, Robert. *Food for One Billion: China's Agriculture since 1949*. Boulder: Westview, 1982.

Huang, Philip. *The Peasant Economy and Social Change in North China*. Palo Alto: Stanford University Press, 1985.

———. *The Peasant Family and Rural Development in the Yangzi Delta, 1350–1988*. Palo Alto: Stanford University Press, 1990.

———. *Civil Justice in China: Representation and Practice in the Qing*. Palo Alto: Stanford University Press, 1996.

———. *Code, Custom, and Legal Practice in China*. Palo Alto: Stanford University Press, 2001.

———. "China's New-Age Small Farms and Their Vertical Integration: Agribusiness or Co-ops?" *Modern China* 37.2 (2011): 107–34.

Huang, Sophie. "Structural Change in Taiwan's Agricultural Economy." *Economic Development and Cultural Change* 42.1 (1993): 43–65.

Hurt, R. Douglas. *Problems of Plenty: The American Farmer in the Twentieth Century*. Chicago: Ivan R. Dee, 2002.

Hymer, Stephen. "Economic Forms in Pre-colonial Ghana." *Journal of Economic History* 30.1 (1970): 33–50.

Iowa Soybean Association On-Farm Network. "Managing Herbicide-Resistant Weeds." *Corn and Soybean Digest*, January 28, 2013. http://cornandsoybeandigest.com/crop-chemicals/managing-herbicide-resistant-weeds, accessed April 29, 2016.

Isaacman, Allen. *Cotton Is the Mother of Poverty: Peasants, Work, and Rural Struggle in Colonial Mozambique, 1938–1961*. Portsmouth, N.H.: Heinemann, 1996.

Isett, Christopher. *State, Peasant and Merchant in Qing Manchuria*. Palo Alto: Stanford University Press, 2007.

Jacquart, Jean. *La crise rurale en île-de-France 1550–1670*. Paris: Armand Colin, 1974.

———. "Le rente foncière, indice conjoncturel?" *Revue historique* 514 (1975): 355–76.

Jahan, Sébastian. "La route des motives: Les travailleurs saisonniers des confins marchois en Loudunais (XVIIe–XVIIIe siècles)." *Bulletin du groupe de recherches historiques et archéologiques de l'Isle-Jourdain* 11 (2001): 29–42.

Jank, Maros Sawaya, et al. "Concentration and Internationalization of Brazilian Agribusiness Exporters." *International Food and Agribusiness Management Review* 2.3/4 (2001): 359–74.

Jepson, Wendy. "Private Agricultural Colonization on a Brazilian Frontier, 1970–1980." *Journal of Historical Geography* 32 (2006): 839–63.

Jessenne, Jean-Pierre. *Les Campagnes françaises: Entre mythe et histoire (XVIIIe–XXIe siècle)*. Paris: A. Colin, 2006.

Jing, Junjian. "Legislation Related to the Civil Economy in the Qing Dynasty." In *Civil Law in Qing and Republican China*, edited by Philip Huang and Kathryn Bernhardt. Palo Alto: Stanford University Press, 1994.

Johnstone, Frederick. *Class, Race, and Gold: A Study of Class Relations and Racial Discrimination in South Africa*. London: Routledge & K. Paul, 1976.

Jones, A. H. M. *The Roman Economy: Studies in Ancient Economic and Administrative History.* Oxford: Blackwell, 1974.

Jones, E. L. "Editor's Introduction." In *Agriculture and Economic Growth in England, 1650–1815,* edited by E. Jones. London: Methuen, 1967.

———. "Agricultural Origins of Industry." *Past and Present* 40 (1968): 58–71.

Ka, Chih-ming. *Japanese Colonialism in Taiwan: Land Tenure, Development, and Dependency, 1895–1945.* Boulder: Westview Press, 1998.

Kaiwar, Vasant. "Property Structures, Demography and the Crisis of the Agrarian Economy of Colonial Bombay Presidency." In *Agricultural Production and Indian History,* edited by David Ludden. Oxford: Oxford University Press, 1994.

Kang, Chao. *Agricultural Production in Communist China, 1949–1965.* Madison: University of Wisconsin Press, 1970.

———. *The Development of Cotton Textile Production in China.* Cambridge, Mass.: Harvard University Press, 1977.

Katzman, Martin. "Colonization as an Approach to Regional Development: Northern Parana, Brazil." *Economic Development and Cultural Change* 26.4 (1978): 709–24.

Kay, Cristóbal. "Why East Asia Overtook Latin America: Agrarian Reform, Industrialisation and Development." *Third World Quarterly* 23.6 (2002): 1073–102.

Kea, Ray. *Settlements, Trade, and Polities in the Seventeenth-Century Gold Coast.* Baltimore: Johns Hopkins University Press, 1982.

Kehoe, Dennis. "The Early Roman Empire: Production." In *The Cambridge Economic History of the Greco-Roman World,* edited by Ian Morris, Walter Scheidel, and Richard P. Saller. Cambridge: Cambridge University Press, 2007.

———. *Law and Rural Economy in the Roman Empire.* Ann Arbor: University of Michigan Press, 2007.

Kelly, Kenneth. "Land-Use Regions in the Central and Northern Portions of the Inca Empire." *Annals of the Association of American Geographers* 55.2 (1965): 327–38.

King, H. H. *Farmers of Forty Centuries: Organic Farming in China, Korea, and Japan.* Madison, Wis.: Mrs. F. H. King, 1911.

Kolendo, Jerzy. "The Peasant." In *The Romans,* edited by Andrea Giardina. Chicago: Chicago University Press, 1993.

Kulikoff, Allan. *Tobacco and Slaves: The Development of Southern Cultures in the Chesapeake, 1680–1800.* Chapel Hill: University of North Carolina Press, 1986.

———. *From British Peasants to Colonial American Farmers.* Chapel Hill: University of North Carolina Press, 2000.

Kwon, Grace. *State Formation, Property Relations, and the Development of the Tokugawa Economy.* New York: Routledge, 2002.

Labrousse, Ernest. *La crise de l'économie française à la fin de l'Ancien Régime et au début de la Révolution.* 1944. Reprint, Paris: Presse Universitaire de France, 1990.

Lapidus, Gail Warshofky. *Women in Soviet Society.* Berkeley: University of California Press, 1979.

Lee, James, and Wang Feng. *One Quarter of Humanity: Malthusian Mythology and Chinese Realities, 1700–2000.* Cambridge, Mass.: Harvard University Press, 2001.

Lee, Mabel Ping-hua. *The Economic History of China with Special Reference to Agriculture.* New York: Columbia University Press, 1921.

Lee, Teng-hui. *Intersectional Capital Flows in the Economic Development of Taiwan, 1895–1960.* Ithaca, N.Y.: Cornell University Press, 1971.

Lenin, V. I. "The Development of Capitalism in Russia." 1899. Reprint in *Collected Works,* vol. 3. Moscow: Progress Publishers, 1960; third printing, 1972.

Lester, Julius. *To Be a Slave.* New York: Puffin Books, 2000.

Leung, Peter C. Y., and L. Eve Armentrout Ma. *One Day, One Dollar: Locke, California, and the Chinese Farming Experience in the Sacramento Delta.* El Cerrito, Calif.: Chinese American History Project, 1984.

Lewin, Moshe. *The Making of the Soviet System: Essays in the Social History of Interwar Russia.* New York: Pantheon Books, 1985.

Lewis, Mark. *The Early Chinese Empires: Qin and Han.* Cambridge, Mass.: Harvard University Press, 2007.

Lewis, Oscar, Ruth Lewis, and Susan Rigdon. *Four Women: Living the Revolution—An Oral History of Contemporary Cuba.* Vol. 2. Urbana: University of Illinois Press, 1977.

Li, Lillian. *Fighting Famine in North China: State, Market, and Environmental Decline 1690s–1900s.* Palo Alto: Stanford University Press, 2007.

Ligon, Richard. *A True and Exact History of the Island of Barbados.* London: Peter Parker, 1673.

Likaka, Osumaka. *Rural Society and Cotton in Colonial Zaire.* Madison: University of Wisconsin Press, 1997.

Linares, Olga F. "African Rice (Oryza Glaberrima): History and Future Potential." *Proceedings of the National Academy of Sciences of the United States of America* 99 (2002): 16361.

Lo, Kuei-Mei, and Hsin-Hsing Chen. "Technological Momentum and the Hegemony of the Green Revolution: A Case Study of an Organic Rice Cooperative in Taiwan." *East Asian Science, Technology and Society: An International Journal* 5 (2011): 135–72.

Locke, John. *Two Treatises of Government.* London: Whitmore and Fen, 1901.

Loutchisky, I. "Régime Agraire et populations agricoles dans les environs de Paris à la veille de la Révolution." *Revue d'histoire moderne* 7 (1933): 97–142.

MacDonald, James. "Family Farming in the United States." *United States Department of Agriculture Economic Research Service,* March 4, 2014. http://www.ers.usda.gov/amber-waves/2014-march/family-farming-in-the-united-states.aspx#.V2nV6a5q6lx, accessed April 29, 2016.

MacFarquhar, Roderick. *The Origins of the Cultural Revolution.* Volume 2: *The Great Leap Forward, 1958–1960.* New York: Columbia University Press, 1983.

MacKay, George Leslie. *From Far Formosa: The Island, Its People, and Missions.* Edinburgh: Oliphant Anderson and Ferrier, 1896.

Maisels, Charles Keith. *Early Civilizations of the Old World: The Formative Histories of Egypt, the Levant, Mesopotamia, India, and China.* London: Routledge, 1999.

Mann, Susan. *Precious Records: Women in China's Long Eighteenth Century.* Palo Alto: Stanford University Press, 1997.

Manning, Patrick. *Slavery and African Life: Occidental, Oriental, and African Slave Trades.* Cambridge: Cambridge University Press, 1990.

Mao, Yu-Kang, and Chi Schive. "Agricultural and Industrial Development in Taiwan." In *Rural Development in Taiwan and Mainland China,* edited by Peter Calkins, Wen Chern, and Francis Tuan. Boulder: Westview Press, 1995.

Mark, Robert. *Tigers, Rice, and Silt: Environment and Economy in Late Imperial South China.* Cambridge: Cambridge University Press, 2006.

Martinez-Alier, Juan. *Haciendas, Plantations and Collective Farms: Agrarian Class Societies—Cuba and Peru.* London: Frank Cass, 1977.

Marx, Karl. *The Eighteenth Brumaire of Napoleon Bonaparte.* 1852.

———. *Pre-capitalist Economic Formations.* 1857–1858. Reprint, translated by Jack Cohen, New York: International Publishers, 1964.

———. *The Grundisse.* London: Penguin Books, 1993.

———. *Capital.* Volume 1.

Masuda, S., I. Shimada, and C. Morris. *Andean Ecology and Civilization: An Interdisciplinary Perspective on Andean Ecological Complementarity.* Tokyo: Tokyo University Press, 1985.

Matthey, Holger, et al. *Brazil: The Future of Modern Agriculture?* Ames: Midwest Agribusiness Trade Research and Information Center, Iowa State University, 2004. http://www.card.iastate.edu/publications/dbs/pdffiles/04mbp6.pdf.

Mazoyer, Marcel, and Laurence Roudart. *A History of World Agriculture: From the Neolithic Age to the Current Crisis.* London: Earthscan, 2006.

Mazumdar, Sucheta. *Sugar and Society in China: Peasants, Technology, and the World Market.* Cambridge: Cambridge University Press, 1998.

———. "Rights in People, Rights in Land: Concepts of Customary Property in Late Imperial China." *Extrême-Orient, Extrême-Occident* 23 (2001): 89–107.

McCann, James. *Green Land, Brown Land, Black Land: An Environmental History of Africa 1800–1990*. Portsmouth, N.H.: Heinemann, 1999.

———. *Maize and Grace: Africa's Encounter with a New World Crop, 1500–2000*. Cambridge, Mass.: Harvard University Press, 2005.

McCusker, John, and Russell Menard. *The Economy of British America, 1607–1789*. Chapel Hill: University of North Carolina Press, 1985.

Medeiros, Leonilde Servolo de. "Social Movements and the Experience of Market-Led Agrarian Reform in Brazil." *Third World Quarterly* 28.8 (2007): 1501–18.

Meisner, Maurice. *Mao's China and After: A History of the People's Republic*. New York: Simon & Schuster, 1999.

Mejia, Ramon Perez. "Declaration (1975)." In *Speaking Out: Activism and Protest in the 1960s and 1970s*, edited by Heather Ann Thompson. Upper Saddle River, N.J.: Prentice Hall, 2010.

Menard, Russell. *Sweet Negotiations: Sugar, Slavery, and Plantation Agriculture in Early Barbados*. Charlottesville: University of Virginia Press, 2006.

Mendras, Henri, and Laurence Duboys Fresney. *La Seconde Révolution française: 1965–1984*. Paris: Gallimard, 1988.

Merle, Louis. *La métairie et l'évolution agraire de la Gâtine poitevine de la fin du Moyen Age à la Révolution*. Paris: S.E.V.P.E.N., 1958.

Merrill, Michael. "Cash Is Good to Eat: Self-Sufficiency and Exchange in the Rural Economy of the United States." *Radical History Review* 13 (1977): 42–71.

Meuvret, Jean. *Le problème des subsistances à l'époque Louis XIV*. Paris: École des Hautes Études en Sciences Sociales, 1987.

Miller, Stephen. "The Economy of France in the Eighteenth and Nineteenth Centuries: Market Opportunity and Labor Productivity in Languedoc." *Rural History* 20 (2009): 1–30.

———. "French Absolutism and Agricultural Capitalism: A Comment on Henry Heller's Essays." *Historical Materialism* 20 (2012): 141–61.

"The Miracle of the Cerrado." *The Economist*, August 26, 2010. http://www.economist.com/node/16886442, accessed March 19, 2015.

Mireaux, Emile. *Une province française au temps du grand roi: La Brie*. Paris: Hachette, 1958.

Montesquieu, Charles-Louis. *The Spirit of Laws*, ed. Ann Cohler et al. Cambridge: Cambridge University Press, 1989.

Moriceau, Jean-Marc. *Les Fermiers de l'île de France: L'ascension d'un patronat agricole (XVe–XVIIIe siècle)*. Paris: Fayard, 1994.

Moriceau, Jean-Marc, and Gilles Postel-Vinay. *Ferme, entreprise, famille: Grande exploitation et changements agricoles: Les Chartier, XVIIe–XIXe siècles*. Paris: École des Hautes Études en Sciences Sociales, 1992.

Morris, Arthur. "The Agricultural Base of the Pre-Incan Andean Civilizations." *Geographical Journal* 165 (1999): 286–95.

Mote, Frederick. *Imperial China, 900–1800*. Cambridge, Mass.: Harvard University Press, 1999.

Moulin, Annie. *Peasantry and Society in France since 1789*. Translated by Mark C. Cleary and M. F. Cleary. Cambridge: Cambridge University Press, 1991.

Muntemba, Maud. "Thwarted Development: A Case Study of Economic Change in the Kabwe District of Zambia, 1902–70." In *The Roots of Rural Poverty in Central and Southern Africa*, edited by R. Palmer and N. Parsons. Berkeley: University of California Press, 1977.

Murra, John V. *The Economic Organization of the Inka State*. Greenwich, Conn.: JAI Press, 1980.

———. "El Archipielago Revisited." In *Andean Ecology and Civilization: An Interdisciplinary Perspective on Andean Ecological Complementarity*, edited by Shodo Masuda, Izumi Shimada, and Craig Morris. Tokyo: Tokyo University Press, 1985.

Murray, Martin, and Charles Post. "The 'Agrarian Question,' Class Struggle and the Capitalist State in the United States and South Africa." *Critical Sociology* 11 (1983): 37–56.

Myers, R., and M. Peattie. *The Japanese Colonial Empire, 1895–1945*. Princeton: Princeton University Press, 1987.

Myers, Ramon, and Yejian Wang. "Economic Developments, 1644–1800." In *The Cambridge History of China*. Vol. 9, part 1: *The Qing*, edited by Willard J. Peterson. Cambridge: Cambridge University Press, 2002.

Myths from Mesopotamia: Creation, the Flood, Gilgamesh and Others. Translated, with introduction and notes, by Stephanie Dalley. Oxford: Oxford University Press, 1989.

Needham, Joseph, ed. *Science and Civilisation in China: Introductory Orientations*. 7 vols. Cambridge University Press, 1954–2004.

Neeve, P. W. de. *Peasants in Peril: Location and Economy in Italy in the Second Century B.C.* Amsterdam: J.C. Gieben, 1984.

Nelson, Lawry. *Rural Cuba*. Minneapolis: University of Minnesota Press, 1950.

Nicolas, Jean. *Le rébellion française: Mouvements populaires et conscience sociale (1661–1789)* . Paris: Seuil, 2002.

Notehelfer, Frederick. "Meiji through the Rearview Mirror: Top-Down vs Bottom-Up History." *Monumenta Nipponica* 42.2 (1990): 207–28.

Nove, Alec. *The Soviet Economy: An Introduction*. New York: F.A. Praeger, 1969.

Nziem, Isidore Ndaywel è. *Histoire générale du Congo: De l'héritage ancien à la République Démocratique*. Bruxelles: Duculot, 1998.

Olmstead, Alan, and Paul Rhode. "The Transformation of Northern Agriculture, 1910–1990." In *The Cambridge Economic History of the United States*. Vol. 3: *The Twentieth Century*, edited by Stanley L. Engerman and Robert E. Gallman. Cambridge: Cambridge University Press, 2000.

———. "Biological Innovation and Productivity Growth in the Antebellum Cotton Economy." *Journal of Economic History* 68 (2008) 1123–71.

———. *Creating Abundance: Biological Innovation and American Agricultural Development*. New York: Cambridge University Press, 2008.

Ooms, Herman. *Tokugawa Village Practice: Class, Status, Power, Law*. Berkeley: University of California Press, 1996.

Overton, Mark. *Agricultural Revolution in England: The Transformation of the Agrarian Economy, 1500–1850*. Cambridge: Cambridge University Press, 1996.

Page, Brian, and Richard Walker. "From Settlement to Fordism: The Agro-industrial Revolution in the American Midwest." *Economic Geography* 67 (1991): 281–315.

Papma, Frans. *Contesting the Household Estate: Southern Brazilian Peasants and Modern Agriculture*. Amsterdam: CEDLA, 1992.

Pasternak, Boris. *Doctor Zhivago*. New York: Pantheon, 1958.

Perdue, Peter. *Exhausting the Earth: State and Peasant in Hunan*. Cambridge, Mass.: Harvard University Press, 1987.

Peret, Jacques. *Les paysans de Gâtine poitevine au XVIIIe siècle*. La Crèche: Geste éd., 1998.

Pérez, Louis A., Jr. *Cuba: Between Reform and Revolution*. New York: Oxford University Press, 1988.

Pérez-Stable, Marifeli. *The Cuban Revolution: Origins, Course, and Legacy*. New York: Oxford University Press, 1994.

Perkins, Dwight. *Agricultural Development in China, 1368–1968*. Chicago: Aldine Publishing Company, 1969.

Philpott, Tom. "Monsanto Claims to Ditch Herbicide while Actually Selling More of It." *Mother Jones*, April 10, 2013. http://www.motherjones.com/tom-philpott/2013/04/roundup-usual-suspect-herbicide-sales-drive-monsanto-profit, accessed May 9, 2016.

———. "Why This Year's Gulf Dead Zone Is Twice as Big as Last Year's." *Mother Jones*, August 14, 2013. http://www.globalpossibilities.org/why-this-years-gulf-dead-zone-is-twice-as-big-as-last-years/, accessed May 9, 2016.

———. "One Weird Trick to Fix Farms Forever." *Mother Jones*, September 9, 2013. http://www.motherjones.com/environment/2013/09/cover-crops-no-till-david-brandt-farms, accessed May 9, 2016.

———. "Does 'Corporate Farming' Exist? Barely." *Mother Jones*, September 25, 2013. http://www.motherjones.com/tom-philpott/2013/09/does-corporate-farming-exist-barely, accessed May 9, 2016.

———. "Are Agriculture Exports Killing Us?" *Mother Jones*, January 22, 2014. http://www. motherjones.com/tom-philpott/2014/01/are-agriculture-exports-killing-us, accessed May 9, 2016.

Phimister, Ian. "Peasant Production and Underdevelopment in Southern Rhodesia, 1890–1914, with Particular Reference to the Victoria District." In *The Roots of Rural Poverty in Central and Southern Africa*, edited by R. Palmer and N. Parsons. Berkeley: University of California Press, 1977.

Piazza, Alan Lee. *Food and Consumption and Nutritional Status in the People's Republic of China*. Boulder: Westview Press, 1986.

Pierce, Steven. *Farmers and the State in Colonial Kano: Land Tenure and the Legal Imagination*. Bloomington: Indiana University Press, 2005.

Platform of Via Campesina for Agriculture, May 2010. http://www.mstbrazil.org/about-mst/platform-campesina-agriculture.

Plutarch. *Caius Gracchus*. Translated by John Dryden. http://classics.mit.edu/Plutarch/gracchus.html, accessed April 23, 2014.

———. *Parallel Lives*. Translated by Bernadotte Perrin. Loeb Classical Library, vol. 10. Cambridge, Mass.: Harvard University Press, 1921.

Pollan, Michael. *The Omnivore's Dilemma: A Natural History of Four Meals*. New York: Penguin Press, 2006.

Post, Charles. *The American Road to Capitalism: Studies in Class-Structure, Economic Development and Political Conflict, 1620–1877*. Chicago: Haymarket Books, 2012.

Potter, Jack, and Sulamith Potter. *China's Peasants: The Anthropology of a Revolution*. Cambridge: Cambridge University Press, 1990.

Potts, D. T. *Mesopotamian Civilization: The Material Foundations*. London: Athlone Press, 1997.

Prochaska, David. *Making Algeria French: Colonialism in Bône, 1870–1920*. Cambridge: Cambridge University Press, 1990.

Raghavan, T. C. A. "Malguzars and Peasants: The Narmada Valley, 1860–1920." In *Agricultural Production and Indian History*, edited by David Ludden. Oxford: Oxford University Press, 1994.

Reed, Charles A. *Origins of Agriculture: Discussion and Some Conclusions*. The Hague: Mouton, 1977.

Roberts, Richard. "Linkages and Multiplier Effects in the Ecologically Specialized Trade of Precolonial West Africa." *Cahiers d'études Africaines* 20.77 (1980): 135–48.

Rodney, Walter. *A History of the Upper Guinea Coast, 1545–1800*. Oxford: Clarendon Press, 1970.

Roes, Aldwin. "Towards a History of Mass Violence in the Etat Indépendant du Congo, 1885–1908." *South African Historical Journal* 62 (2010): 634–70.

Rothenberg, Winifred. "The Emergence of a Capital Market in Rural Massachusetts, 1730–1838." *Journal of Economic History* 45 (1985): 781–808.

———. "The Emergence of Farm Labor Markets and the Transformation of the Rural Economy: Massachusetts, 1750–1855." *Journal of Economic History* 48 (1988): 537–66.

Saito, Osamu. "Land, Labour and Market Forces in Tokugawa Japan." *Continuity and Change* 24.1 (2009): 169–96.

Schiavone, Aldo. *The End of the Past: Ancient Rome and the Modern West*. Cambridge, Mass.: Harvard University Press, 2000.

Schurmann, H. Franz. "Traditional Property Concepts in China." *Far Eastern Quarterly* 15.4 (1956): 507–16.

Schwartz, Stuart. "Resistance and Accommodation in Eighteenth-Century Brazil: The Slaves' View of Slavery." *Hispanic American Historical Review* 57.1 (1977): 69–81.

———. "Indian Labor and New World Plantations: European Demands and Indian Responses in Northeastern Brazil." *American Historical Review* 83.1 (1978): 43–79.

———. "Patterns of Slaveholding in the Americas: New Evidence from Brazil." *American Historical Review* 87.1 (1982): 55–86.

———. *Sugar Plantations in the Formation of Brazilian Society: Bahia, 1550–1835*. Cambridge: Cambridge University Press, 1985.

————. *Tropical Babylon: Sugar and the Making of the Atlantic World, 1450–1680.* Chapel Hill: University of North Carolina Press, 2004.

Shanin, Teodor. *The Awkward Class: Political Sociology of Peasantry in a Developing Society—Russia 1910–1925.* Oxford: Clarendon Press, 1972.

Shepherd, John. *Statecraft and Political Economy on the Taiwan Frontier, 1600–1800.* Palo Alto: Stanford University Press, 1993.

Sheridan, Richard. *Sugar and Slavery: An Economic History of the British West Indies, 1623–1775.* Baltimore: Johns Hopkins University Press, 1974.

Shiva, Vandana. *Soil Not Oil: Environmental Justice in an Age of Climate Crisis.* Berkeley: North Atlantic Books, 2015.

Shue, Vivienne. *Peasant China in Transition: The Dynamics of Development toward Socialism, 1949–1956.* Berkeley: University of California Press, 1980.

Simmons, Alan. *The Neolithic Revolution in the Near East: Transforming the Human Landscape.* Tucson: University of Arizona Press, 2007.

Skinner, G. William. "Regional Urbanization in Nineteenth-Century China." In *The City in Late Imperial China*, edited by G. William Skinner. Stanford: Stanford University Press, 1977.

Slaughter, Thomas. *The Whiskey Rebellion: Frontier Epilogue to the American Revolution.* New York: Oxford University Press, 1986.

Smith, Adam. *An Inquiry into the Nature and Causes of the Wealth of Nations.* N.p.: Alex Murray & Co., 1872.

Smith, Gordon. "Brazilian Agricultural Policy, 1950–1967." In *The Economy of Brazil*, edited by Howard Ellis. Berkeley: University of California Press, 1969.

Smith, Thomas. *The Agrarian Origins of Modern Japan.* Palo Alto: Stanford University Press, 1959.

————. *Nakahara: Family Farming and Population in a Japanese Village, 1717–1830.* Palo Alto: Stanford University Press, 1977.

————. *Native Sources of Japanese Industrialization, 1750–1920.* Berkeley: University of California Press, 1989.

Sneller, Anne Gertrude. *A Vanished World.* Syracuse, N.Y.: Syracuse University Press, 1964.

Sommer, Matthew. "Making Sex Work: Polyandry as a Survival Strategy in Qing Dynasty China." In *Gender in Motion: Divisions of Labor and Cultural Change in Late Imperial and Modern China*, edited by Bryna Goodman and Wendy Larson, 29–54. New York: Rowman & Littlefield, 2005.

Spanne, Autumn. "Hunger for Meat Plows Up Brazil's Cerrado Plains." *Scientific American.* http://www.scientificamerican.com/article/hunger-for-meat-plows-up-brazils-cerrado-plains/, accessed May 10, 2016.

Spurr, M. S. *Arable Cultivation in Roman Italy, 200 BC–AD 100.* London: Society for the Promotion of Roman Studies, 1986.

Stanish, Charles. "The Hydraulic Hypothesis Revisited: Lake Titicaca Basin Raised Fields in Theoretical Perspective." *Latin American Antiquity* 5.4 (1994): 312–32.

————. "Nonmarket Imperialism in the Prehispanic Americas: The Inka Occupation of the Titicaca Basin." *Latin American Antiquity* 8 (1997): 195–216.

————. "The Origins of State Societies in South America." *Annual Review of Anthropology* 30 (2001): 41–64.

Statutes at Large of South Carolina, edited by Thomas Cooper. Columbia, S.C.: A. S. Johnston, 1838.

Stavis, Benedict. *The Politics of Agricultural Mechanization in China.* Ithaca, N.Y.: Cornell University Press, 1978.

Ste. Croix, G. E. M. de. *The Class Struggle in the Ancient Greek World: From the Archaic Age to the Arab Conquest.* Ithaca, N.Y.: Cornell University Press, 1981.

Stédile, João Pedro. "Landless Battalions." *New Left Review* 15 (May–June 2002): 77–104.

Stolke, Verena. *Coffee Planters, Workers and Wives: Class Conflict and Gender Relations on Sao Paulo Plantations, 1850–1980.* New York: St. Martin's Press, 1988.

Suny, Ronald. *The Soviet Experiment: Russia, the USSR, and the Successor States.* New York: Oxford University Press, 1998.

Swierenga, Robert P. *Pioneers and Profits: Land Speculation on the Iowa Frontier*. Ames: Iowa State University Press, 1968.

Szatmary, David. *Shays' Rebellion: The Making of an Agrarian Insurrection*. Amherst: University of Massachusetts Press, 1980.

Takekoshi, Yosaburo. *Japanese Rule in Formosa*. London: Longmans, Green, 1907.

Taylor, Alan. "Land and Liberty on the Post-Revolutionary Frontier." In *Devising Liberty: Preserving and Creating Freedom in the New American Republic*, edited by David Thomas Konig. Palo Alto: Stanford University Press, 1995.

Thirsk, Joan. *Economic Policy and Projects: The Development of a Consumer Society in Early Modern England*. Oxford: Oxford University Press, 1978.

Thompson, Peter. "Henry Drax's Instructions on the Management of a Seventeenth-Century Barbadian Sugar Plantation." *William and Mary Quarterly*, 3rd series, 66.3 (July 2009): 566–604.

Thompson, Leonard Monteath, and Monica Wilson. *The Oxford History of South Africa*. Vol. 2: *South Africa 1870–1966*. New York: Oxford University Press, 1969–1971.

Thorbecke, Erik. "Agricultural Development." In *Economic Growth and Structural Change in Taiwan*, edited by E. L. Galenson. Ithaca, N.Y.: Cornell University Press, 1979.

Tilly, Charles. *The Vendée*. Cambridge, Mass.: Harvard University Press, 1964.

Toby, Ronald. "Both a Borrower and a Lender Be: From Village Moneylender to Rural Banker in the Tempo Era." *Monumenta Nipponica* 46 (1991): 483–512.

Totman, Conrad. *Politics in Tokugawa Bakufu, 1600–1843*. Cambridge, Mass.: Harvard University Press, 1967.

Tucker, Robert. *Stalin in Power: The Revolution from Above, 1928–1941*. New York: W. W. Norton, 1992.

Tulippe, Omer. *L'habitat rural en Seine-et-Oise: Essai de géographie du peuplement*. Paris: Sirey, 1934.

"UFW, United Farm Workers Union, AFL-CIO, et al. Plaintiffs, International Brotherhood of Teamsters, et al. Defendants (1973)." Court filing. In *Speaking Out: Activism and Protest in the 1960s and 1970s*, edited by Heather Ann Thompson. Upper Saddle River, N.J.: Prentice Hall, 2010.

United Nations General Assembly. Resolution 96(I), The Crime of Genocide. December 11, 1946.

United States Department of Agriculture, Natural Resources Conservation Service New York. "Cover Crops: Keeping Soil in Place while Providing Other Benefits." http://www.nrcs.usda.gov/wps/portal/nrcs/detail/ny/technical/?cid=nrcs144p2_027252, accessed April 29, 2016.

US Geological Survey. "Differences in Phosphorus and Nitrogen Delivery to the Gulf of Mexico from the Mississippi River Basin." March 4, 2014. https://water.usgs.gov/nawqa/sparrow/gulf_findings/, accessed April 29, 2016.

Valdez, Lido. "Maize Beer Production in Middle Horizon Peru." *Journal of Anthropological Research* 62.1 (2006): 53–80.

Vega, Garcilaso de la. *Royal Commentaries on the Incas and General History of Peru*. 9 vols. Austin: University of Texas Press, 1989.

Veltmeyer, Henry, and Mark Rushton. *The Cuban Revolution as Socialist Human Development*. Leiden: Brill, 2012.

Venard, Marc. *Bourgeois et paysans au XVIIe siècle: Recherché sur le role des bourgeois parisiens dans la vie agricole au Sud de Paris au XVIIe siècle*. Paris: S.E.V.P.E.N., 1957.

Vickers, Daniel. *Farmers and Fishermen: Two Centuries of Work in Essex County, Massachusetts, 1630–1850*. Chapel Hill: University of North Carolina Press, 1994.

Viola, Lynne. *The War against the Peasantry, 1927–1930: The Tragedy of the Soviet Countryside*. New Haven: Yale University Press, 2005.

Walker, Kenneth. *Food Grain Procurement and Consumption in China*. Cambridge: Cambridge University Press, 1984.

Walker, Richard. "Crisis and Change in U.S. Agriculture: An Overview." In *Agribusiness in the Americas*, edited by Roger Burbach and Patricia Flynn. New York: Monthly Review Press, 1980.

————. *The Conquest of Bread; 150 Years of Agribusiness in California.* New York: The New Press, 2004.

Walter, Rodney. *A History of the Upper Guinea Coast, 1545–1800.* Oxford: Clarendon Press, 1970.

Wang, Yejian. "Food Supply and Grain Prices in the Yangzi Delta in the Eighteenth Century." In *The Second Conference on Modern Chinese History.* Taipei: Academia Sinica, 1989.

Warnken, Philip. *The Development and Growth of the Soybean Industry in Brazil.* Ames: Iowa State University Press, 1999.

Watts, Michael. *Silent Violence: Food, Famine, and Peasantry in Northern Nigeria.* Athens: University of Georgia Press, 2013.

Weber, Max. *General Economic History.* Translated by Frank H. Knight. London: George Allen and Unwin, 1927.

Weinstein, Barbara. "The Persistence of Precapitalist Relations of Production in a Tropical Export Economy: The Amazon Rubber Trade, 1850–1920." In *Proletarians and Protest: The Roots of Class Formation in an Industrializing World,* edited by M. Hanagan and C. Stephenson. New York: Greenwood Press, 1986.

Weis, Tony. *The Global Food Economy: The Battle for the Future of Farming.* London: Zed Books, 2007.

————. *The Ecological Hoofprint: The Global Burden of Industrial Livestock.* London: Zed Books, 2013.

Whistler, Henry. "Extracts from Henry Whistler's Journal of the West Indies Expedition." In *The Narrative of General Venables,* edited by C. H. Firth. New York: Longmans, Green, 1900.

White, K. D. *Roman Farming.* Ithaca, N.Y.: Cornell University Press, 1970.

Wickham, Chris. *The Inheritance of Rome.* New York: Penguin Books, 2009.

Widgren, M., and J. Sutton. *Islands of Intensive Agriculture in Eastern Africa.* Oxford and Athens: James Currey and Ohio University Press, 2004.

Wiedemann, Thomas E. *Greek and Roman Slavery.* New York: Routledge Press, 1981.

Will, Pierre-Etienne. *Bureaucracy and Famine in Eighteenth-Century China.* Palo Alto: Stanford University Press, 1990.

Williams, Eric. *Capitalism and Slavery.* Chapel Hill: University of North Carolina Press, 1994.

Williams, Jack. "Vulnerability and Change in Taiwan's Agriculture." In *The Other Taiwan: 1945 to the Present,* edited by Murray Rubenstein. Armonk, N.Y.: M. E. Sharpe, 1994.

Williams, Michael. "The Death and the Rebirth of the American Forest: Clearing and Reversion in the United States, 1900–1980." In *World Deforestation in the Twentieth Century,* edited by John Richards and Richard Tucker. Durham: Duke University Press, 1988.

Wilson, Monica, and Leonard Monteath Thompson. *The Oxford History of South Africa.* Vol. 2: *South Africa 1870–1966.* Oxford: Clarendon Press, 1971.

Winders, Bill. *The Politics of Food Supply: U.S. Agricultural Policy in the World Economy.* New Haven: Yale University Press, 2009.

Wolf, Arthur, and Theo Engelen. "Fertility and Fertility Control in Pre-Revolutionary China." *Journal of Interdisciplinary History* 38.3 (2008): 345–75.

Wong, John. *Land Reform in the People's Republic of China: Institutional Transformation in Agriculture.* New York: Praeger, 1973.

Wood, Ellen Meiksins. *The Origin of Capitalism.* London: Verso, 1999.

Worlidge, John. *A Compleat System of Husbandry and Gardening; or, The Gentleman's Companion, in the Business and Pleasures of a Country Life . . . The Whole Collected from, and Containing What Is Most Valuable in All the Books Hitherto Written upon this Subject; . . .* N.p.: J. Pickard, A. Bettesworth, and E. Curll, 1716.

Wright, Gavin. *The Political Economy of the Cotton South: Households, Markets, and Wealth in the Nineteenth Century.* New York: W. W. Norton, 1984.

————. *Old South New South: Revolutions in the Southern Economy since the Civil War.* New York: Basic Books, 1986.

Wright, Gordon. *Rural Revolution in France: The Peasantry in the Twentieth Century.* Palo Alto: Stanford University Press, 1964.

Wright, Julia. *Sustainable Agriculture and Food Security in an Era of Oil Scarcity: Lessons from Cuba.* London: Earthscan, 2009.

Wrigley, Anthony. "Urban Growth and Agricultural Change: England and the Continent in the Early Modern Period." *Journal of Interdisciplinary History* 15 (1985): 683–728.

———. "The Transition to an Advanced Organic Economy: Half a Millennium of English Agriculture." *Economic History Review* 59 (2006): 435–80.

Xenophon. *The Economist.* http://www.gutenberg.org/files/1173/1173-h/1173-h.htm, accessed May 5, 2014.

Yang, C. K. *Chinese Communist Society: The Family and the Village.* Cambridge: MIT Press, 1959.

Yang, Martin. *Socio-economic Results of Land Reform in Taiwan.* Honolulu: East-West Center Press, 1970.

Young, Arthur. *Travels in France during the Years 1787, 1788 and 1789.* 1792. Reprint, abridgement of the 2nd ed., edited with an introduction by Jeffry Kaplow, Garden City, N.Y.: Doubleday, 1969.

Zhang, Qian Forrest, and John A. Donaldson. "The Rise of Agrarian Capitalism with Chinese Characteristics: Agricultural Modernization, Agribusiness and Collective Land Rights." *China Journal* 60 (2008): 25–47.

Zimmerer, Karl. "Wetland Production and Smallholder Persistence: Agricultural Change in a Highland Peruvian Region." *Annals of the Association of American Geographers* 81.3 (1991): 443–63.

———. "Agricultural Biodiversity and Peasant Rights to Subsistence in the Central Andes during Inca Rule." *Journal of Historical Geography* 19 (1993): 15–32.

Index

About the Authors

Christopher Isett is associate professor of history at the University of Minnesota.

Stephen Miller is associate professor of history at the University of Alabama at Birmingham.